Microsoft
Office 2016
Step by Step

Joan Lambert
Curtis Frye

PUBLISHED BY
Microsoft Press
A division of Microsoft Corporation
One Microsoft Way
Redmond, Washington 98052-6399

Library of Congress Control Number: 2015934879
ISBN: 978-0-7356-9923-6

Printed and bound in the United States of America.

4   17

Microsoft Press books are available through booksellers and distributors worldwide. If you need support related to this book, email Microsoft Press Support at mspinput@microsoft.com. Please tell us what you think of this book at http://aka.ms/tellpress.

This book is provided "as-is" and expresses the authors' views and opinions. The views, opinions, and information expressed in this book, including URL and other Internet website references, may change without notice.

Some examples depicted herein are provided for illustration only and are fictitious. No real association or connection is intended or should be inferred.

Microsoft and the trademarks listed at www.microsoft.com on the "Trademarks" webpage are trademarks of the Microsoft group of companies. All other marks are property of their respective owners.

Acquisitions and Developmental Editor: Rosemary Caperton
Editorial Production: Online Training Solutions, Inc. (OTSI)
Technical Reviewers: Steve Lambert and Rozanne Whalen (OTSI)
Copyeditors: Kathy Krause, Jaime Odell, and Val Serdy (OTSI)
Indexers: Susie Carr, Angela Martin, and Ginny Munroe (OTSI)
Cover: Twist Creative • Seattle

Contents

Part 1: Microsoft Office 2016

Give us feedback
Tell us what you think of this book and help Microsoft
improve our products for you. Thank you!
http://aka.ms/tellpress

2   Create and manage files

Part 2: Microsoft Word 2016

3   Modify the structure and appearance of text

4 Collaborate on documents 115

5 Merge data with documents and labels 159

Part 3: Microsoft Excel 2016

Part 4: Microsoft PowerPoint 2016

Part 5: Microsoft Outlook 2016

Give us feedback
Tell us what you think of this book and help Microsoft
improve our products for you. Thank you!
http://aka.ms/tellpress

Introduction

Welcome! This *Step by Step* book has been designed to make it easy for you to learn about key aspects of four of the Microsoft Office 2016 apps—Word, Excel, PowerPoint, and Outlook. In each part, you can start from the beginning and build your skills as you learn to perform specialized procedures. Or, if you prefer, you can jump in wherever you need ready guidance for performing tasks. The how-to steps are delivered crisply and concisely—just the facts. You'll also find informative, colorful graphics that support the instructional content.

Who this book is for

Microsoft Office 2016 Step by Step is designed for use as a learning and reference resource by home and business users of Microsoft Office apps who want to use Word, Excel, and PowerPoint to create and edit files, and Outlook to organize email, contacts, and appointments. The content of the book is designed to be useful for people who have previously used earlier versions of the apps, and for people who are discovering the apps for the first time. Although the chapters in this book thoroughly cover key skill sets for each of the four apps, *Microsoft Office 2016 Step by Step* is best used as an introduction. For a full discussion of each app, including in-depth coverage of advanced topics, refer to the *Step by Step* book for each app: *Microsoft Word 2016 Step by Step*, *Microsoft PowerPoint 2016 Step by Step*, and *Microsoft Outlook 2016 Step by Step*, all by Joan Lambert (Microsoft Press, 2015), and *Microsoft Excel 2016 Step by Step* by Curtis Frye (Microsoft Press, 2015). A listing of the contents of each book is provided at the end of this book.

The *Step by Step* approach

The book's coverage is divided into parts, each of which provides a thorough introduction to one of the four apps covered. Each part is divided into chapters representing some of the app's key skill set areas, and each chapter is divided into topics that group related skills. Each topic includes expository information followed by generic procedures. At the end of the chapter, you'll find a series of practice tasks you can complete on your own by using the skills taught in the chapter. You can use the practice files that are available from this book's website to work through the practice tasks, or you can use your own files.

Download the practice files

Before you can complete the practice tasks in this book, you need to download the book's practice files to your computer from *http://aka.ms/Office2016sbs/downloads*. Follow the instructions on the webpage.

 IMPORTANT The Office 2016 apps are not available from the book's website. You should install the apps before working through the procedures and practice tasks in this book.

If you later want to repeat practice tasks, you can download the original practice files again.

 SEE ALSO For information about opening and saving files, see Chapter 2, "Create and manage files."

The following table lists the practice files for this book.

Chapter	Folder	File
Part 1: Microsoft Office 2016		
1: Explore Office 2016	Ch01	None
2: Create and manage files	Ch02	DisplayProperties.xlsx
		DisplayViews.pptx
		NavigateFiles.docx

Chapter	Folder	File
Part 2: Microsoft Word 2016		
3: Modify the structure and appearance of text	Ch03	ApplyStyles.docx ChangeTheme.docx CreateLists.docx FormatCharacters.docx FormatParagraphs.docx StructureContent.docx
4: Collaborate on documents	Ch04	ControlChanges.docx MergeDocs1.docx MergeDocs2.docx ReviewComments.docx TrackChanges.docx
5: Merge data with documents and labels	Ch05	CreateEnvelopes.docx CustomerList.xlsx InsertFields.docx PolicyholdersList.xlsx RefineData.docx StartMerge.docx
Part 3: Microsoft Excel 2016		
6: Perform calculations on data	Ch06	AuditFormulas.xlsx BuildFormulas.xlsx CreateArrayFormulas.xlsx CreateConditionalFormulas.xlsx CreateExcelTables.xlsx CreateNames.xlsx SetIterativeOptions.xlsx
7: Manage worksheet data	Ch07	LimitData.xlsx SummarizeValues.xlsx ValidateData.xlsx
8: Reorder and summarize data	Ch08	LookupData.xlsx OrganizeData.xlsx SortCustomData.xlsx SortData.xlsx

Chapter	Folder	File
9: Analyze alternative data sets	Ch09	BuildSolverModel.xlsx
		CreateScenarios.xlsx
		DefineDataTables.xlsx
		ManageMultipleScenarios.xlsx
		PerformGoalSeekAnalysis.xlsx
		PerformQuickAnalysis.xlsx
		UseDescriptiveStatistics.xlsx
Part 4: Microsoft PowerPoint 2016		
10: Create and manage slides	Ch10	AddRemoveSlides.pptx
		ApplyThemes.pptx
		ChangeBackgrounds.pptx
		CreateSections.pptx
		ImportOutline.docx
		RearrangeSlides.pptx
		ReuseSlides.pptx
11: Insert and manage simple graphics	Ch11	Chickens.jpg
		DrawShapes.pptx
		EditPictures.pptx
		Fish.jpg
		Flamingos.jpg
		Flowers01.jpg
		InsertPictures.pptx
		InsertScreens.pptx
		Penguins01.jpg
		Penguins02.jpg
		Tiger01.jpg
		Tiger02.jpg
		YellowBird.jpg
12: Add sound and movement to slides	Ch12	AddAudio.pptx
		AddVideo.pptx
		AnimateSlides.pptx
		Butterfly.wmv
		CustomizeAnimation.pptx
		SoundTrack.wma
		Wildlife.wmv

Chapter	Folder	File
Part 5: Microsoft Outlook 2016		
13: Send and receive email messages	Ch13	AttachFiles.docx
14: Organize your Inbox	Ch14	None
15: Manage scheduling	Ch15	None

Ebook edition

If you're reading the ebook edition of this book, you can do the following:

- Search the full text
- Print
- Copy and paste

You can purchase and download the ebook edition from the Microsoft Press Store at *http://aka.ms/Office2016sbs/details*.

Get support and give feedback

This topic provides information about getting help with this book and contacting us to provide feedback or report errors.

Errata and support

We've made every effort to ensure the accuracy of this book and its companion content. If you discover an error, please submit it to us at *http://aka.ms /Office2016sbs/errata*.

If you need to contact the Microsoft Press Support team, please send an email message to *mspinput@microsoft.com*.

For help with Microsoft software and hardware, go to *http://support.microsoft.com*.

We want to hear from you

At Microsoft Press, your satisfaction is our top priority, and your feedback our most valuable asset. Please tell us what you think of this book at *http://aka.ms/tellpress*.

The survey is short, and we read every one of your comments and ideas. Thanks in advance for your input!

Stay in touch

Let's keep the conversation going! We're on Twitter at *http://twitter.com/MicrosoftPress*.

Part 1

Microsoft Office 2016

Explore Office 2016

The Microsoft Office 2016 suite of apps includes many apps that serve different purposes but are designed to work together to maximize efficiency.

The elements that control the appearance of an app and the way you interact with it are collectively referred to as the *user interface*. Some user interface elements, such as the color scheme, are cosmetic. Others, such as toolbars, menus, and buttons, are functional. Each app has standard settings based on the way that most people work with the app. You can modify cosmetic and functional user interface elements in each app to suit your preferences and working style.

The Office apps share many common user interface elements and functions. The ways in which you perform tasks such as opening, saving, searching, printing, and sharing files are standardized across the apps so that you can concentrate your learning efforts on the skills and features that are specific to the app or to the document, workbook, or presentation you're creating.

This chapter guides you through procedures that are common to Word 2016, Excel 2016, PowerPoint 2016, and some aspects of Outlook 2016. It includes procedures related to working in the Office user interface, changing options for Office and for specific apps, and customizing the Quick Access Toolbar and ribbon.

In this chapter

- Work in the Office user interface
- Change Office and app options
- Customize the Quick Access Toolbar
- Customize the ribbon

Practice files

No practice files are necessary to complete the practice tasks in this chapter.

Work in the Office user interface

The goal of the Office working environment is to make working with Office files, including Word documents, Excel workbooks, PowerPoint presentations, and Outlook email messages, as intuitive as possible.

The way that you start an Office 2016 app is dependent on the operating system you're running on your computer. For example:

- In Windows 7, you can start an app from the Start menu, All Programs menu, or Start menu search results.

- In Windows 8.1, you can start an app from the Apps screen or Start screen search results.

- In Windows 10, you can start an app from the Start menu, the All Apps menu, the Start screen, or the taskbar search box.

You might also have shortcuts to apps on your desktop or on the Windows taskbar.

When you start Word, Excel, or PowerPoint without opening a specific file, the app Start screen appears. The Start screen is a hybrid of the Open and New pages of the Backstage view. It displays links to recent files in the left pane, and new file templates in the right pane.

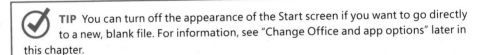

TIP You can turn off the appearance of the Start screen if you want to go directly to a new, blank file. For information, see "Change Office and app options" later in this chapter.

When you're working with a file, it is displayed in an app window that contains all the tools you need to add and format content.

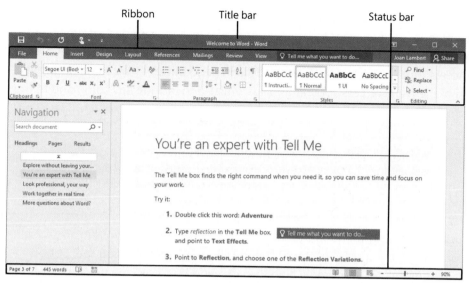

Ribbon   Title bar   Status bar

A typical app window

Identify app window elements

A typical Office 2016 app window contains the elements described in this section. Commands for tasks you perform often are readily available, and even those you might use infrequently are easy to find.

Title bar

At the top of the app window, this bar displays the name of the active file, identifies the app, and provides tools for managing the app window, ribbon, and content.

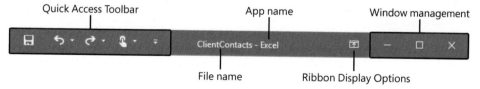

Quick Access Toolbar   App name   Window management

File name   Ribbon Display Options

The title bar elements are always on the left end, in the center, and on the right end of the title bar

The Quick Access Toolbar at the left end of the title bar can be customized to include any commands that you want to have easily available. Each app has a default set of Quick Access Toolbar buttons that you can build on; most commonly, the default Quick Access Toolbar displays the Save, Undo, and Redo buttons. You can change the location of the Quick Access Toolbar and customize it to include any command to which you want to have easy access.

> **TIP** You might find that you work more efficiently if you organize the commands you use frequently on the Quick Access Toolbar and then display it below the ribbon, directly above the workspace. For information, see "Customize the Quick Access Toolbar" later in this chapter.

Four buttons at the right end of the title bar serve the same functions in all Office apps. You control the display of the ribbon by clicking commands on the Ribbon Display Options menu, temporarily hide the app window by clicking the Minimize button, adjust the size of the window by clicking the Restore Down/Maximize button, and close the active document or exit the app by clicking the Close button.

Ribbon

Below the title bar, all the commands for working with an Office file are gathered together in this central location so that you can work efficiently with the app.

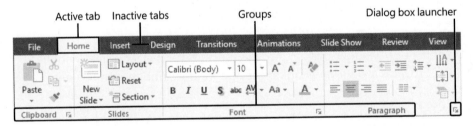

The File tab leads to the Backstage view

> **TIP** Don't be alarmed if your ribbon looks different from those shown in our screens. You might have installed programs that add their own tabs to the ribbon, or your screen settings might be different. For more information, see "Customize the ribbon" later in this chapter.

Across the top of the ribbon is a set of tabs. Clicking a tab displays an associated set of commands arranged in groups.

Commands related to managing the app and files (rather than file content) are gathered together in the Backstage view, which you display by clicking the File tab located at the left end of the ribbon. Commands available in the Backstage view are organized on named pages, which you display by clicking the page tabs in the colored left pane. You redisplay the document and the ribbon by clicking the Back arrow located above the page tabs.

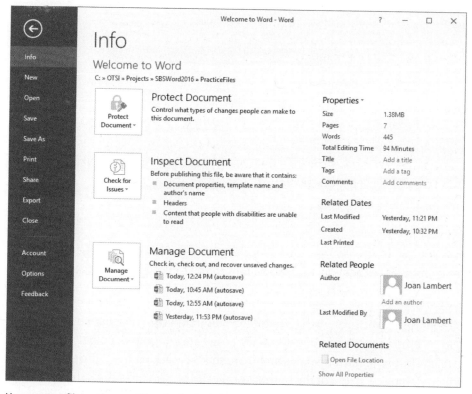

You manage files and app settings in the Backstage view

Commands related to working with document content are represented as buttons on the remaining tabs of the ribbon. The Home tab, which is active by default, contains the most frequently used commands. When a graphic element such as a picture, table, or chart is selected in a document, one or more *tool tabs* might appear at the right end of the ribbon to make commands related to that specific object easily accessible. Tool tabs are available only when the relevant object is selected.

> **TIP** Some older commands no longer appear as buttons on the ribbon but are still available in the app. You can make these commands available by adding them to the Quick Access Toolbar or the ribbon. For more information, see "Customize the Quick Access Toolbar" and "Customize the ribbon" later in this chapter.

On each tab, buttons representing commands are organized into named groups. You can point to any button to display a ScreenTip with the command name, a description of its function, and its keyboard shortcut (if it has one).

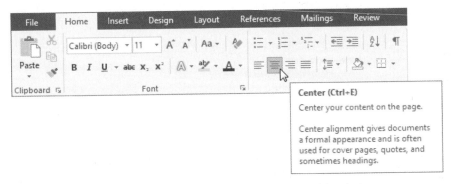

ScreenTips can include the command name, keyboard shortcut, and description

> **TIP** You can control the display of ScreenTips and of feature descriptions in ScreenTips. For more information, see "Change Office and app options" later in this chapter.

Some buttons include an arrow, which might be integrated with or separate from the button. To determine whether a button and its arrow are integrated, point to the button to activate it. If both the button and its arrow are shaded, clicking the button displays options for refining the action of the button. If only the button or arrow is shaded when you point to it, clicking the button carries out its default action or applies the current default formatting. Clicking the arrow and then clicking an action carries out the action. Clicking the arrow and then clicking a formatting option applies the formatting and sets it as the default for the button.

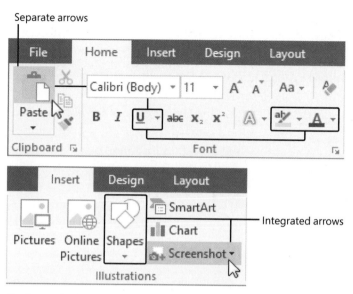

The Font Color button is an example of one that changes its default formatting

When a formatting option has several choices available, they are often displayed in a gallery of images, called *thumbnails*, that provide a visual representation of each choice. When you point to a thumbnail in a gallery, the Live Preview feature shows you what the active content will look like if you click the thumbnail to apply the associated formatting. When a gallery contains more thumbnails than can be shown in the available ribbon space, you can display more content by clicking the scroll arrow or More button located on the right edge of the gallery.

Related but less common commands are not represented as buttons in a group. Instead, they're available in a dialog box or pane, which you display by clicking the dialog box launcher located in the lower-right corner of the group.

> **TIP** To the right of the groups on the ribbon is the Collapse The Ribbon button, which is shaped like a chevron. For more information, see "Work with the ribbon and status bar," later in this topic.

Tell me what you want to do

Entering a term in the Tell Me What You Want To Do box located to the right of the ribbon tabs displays a list of related commands and links to additional resources online. Or you can press F1 to open the Help window for the current app.

The easy path to help in any Office app

Status bar

Across the bottom of the app window, the status bar displays information about the current file and provides access to certain app functions. You can choose the statistics and tools that appear on the status bar. Some items, such as Document Updates Available, appear on the status bar only when that condition is true.

You can specify which items you want to display on the status bar

At the right end of the status bar in the Word, Excel, and PowerPoint app windows are the View Shortcuts toolbar, the Zoom slider, and the Zoom button. These tools provide you with convenient methods for adjusting the display of file content.

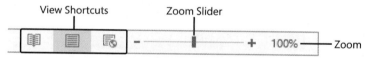

You can change the file content view from the View Shortcuts toolbar and change the magnification by using the Zoom tools

 SEE ALSO For information about changing the file content view, see "Display different views of files" in Chapter 2, "Create and manage files."

Work with the ribbon and status bar

The goal of the ribbon is to make working with file content as intuitive as possible. The ribbon is dynamic, meaning that as its width changes, its buttons adapt to the available space. As a result, a button might be large or small, it might or might not have a label, or it might even change to an entry in a list.

For example, when sufficient horizontal space is available, the buttons on the References tab of the Word app window are spread out, and you can review the commands available in each group.

At 1024 pixels wide, most button labels are visible

If you decrease the horizontal space available to the ribbon, small button labels disappear and entire groups of buttons might hide under one button that represents the entire group. Clicking the group button displays a list of the commands available in that group.

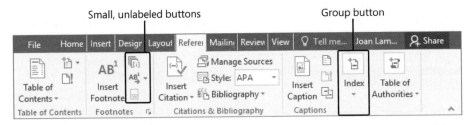

Labels disappear, and groups collapse under buttons

When the ribbon becomes too narrow to display all the groups, a scroll arrow appears at its right end. Clicking the scroll arrow displays the hidden groups.

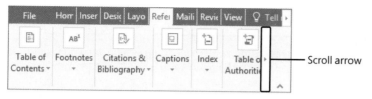

Scroll arrow

Scroll to display additional group buttons

The width of the ribbon depends on these three factors:

- **App window width** Maximizing the app window provides the most space for the ribbon.

- **Screen resolution** Screen resolution is the size of your screen display expressed as pixels wide × pixels high. The greater the screen resolution, the greater the amount of information that will fit on one screen. Your screen resolution options are dependent on the display adapter installed in your computer, and on your monitor. Common screen resolutions range from 800 × 600 to 2560 × 1440 (and some are larger). The greater the number of pixels wide (the first number), the greater the number of buttons that can be shown on the ribbon.

- **The magnification of your screen display** If you change the screen magnification setting in Windows, text and user interface elements are larger and therefore more legible, but fewer elements fit on the screen.

You can hide the ribbon completely if you don't need access to any of its buttons, or hide it so that only its tabs are visible. (This is a good way to gain vertical space when working on a smaller screen.) Then you can temporarily redisplay the ribbon to click a button, or permanently redisplay it if you need to click several buttons.

To maximize the app window

1. Do any of the following:

   - Click the **Maximize** button.

   - Double-click the title bar.

   - Drag the borders of a non-maximized window.

   - Drag the window to the top of the screen. (When the pointer touches the top of the screen, the dragged window maximizes.)

To change the screen resolution

 TIP Methods of changing screen resolution vary by operating system, but you should be able to access the settings in Windows 7, Windows 8.1, and Windows 10 by using these methods.

1. Do any of the following:

   - Right-click the Windows 7 or Windows 8.1 desktop, and then click **Screen resolution**.

   - Right-click the Windows 10 desktop, and then click **Display settings**. At the bottom of the **Display** pane of the **Settings** window, click the **Advanced display settings** link.

   - Enter screen resolution in Windows Search, and then click **Change the screen resolution** in the search results.

   - Open the **Display** Control Panel item, and then click **Adjust resolution**.

2. Click or drag to select the screen resolution you want, and then click **Apply** or **OK**. Windows displays a preview of the selected screen resolution.

3. If you like the change, click **Keep changes** in the message box that appears. If you don't, the screen resolution reverts to the previous setting.

To completely hide the ribbon

1. Near the right end of the title bar, click the **Ribbon Display Options** button.

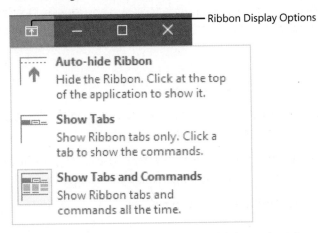

The Ribbon Display Options button is on the title bar so that it is available when the ribbon is hidden

2. On the **Ribbon Display Options** menu, click **Auto-hide Ribbon**.

 TIP To redisplay the ribbon, click the Ribbon Display Options button and then click Show Tabs or Show Tabs And Commands.

To display only the ribbon tabs

1. Do any of the following:

   - Double-click any tab name.

   - Near the upper-right corner of the app window, click the **Ribbon Display Options** button, and then click **Show Tabs**.

   - In the lower-right corner of the ribbon, click the **Collapse the Ribbon** button.

   - Press **Ctrl+F1**.

To temporarily redisplay the ribbon

1. Click any tab name to display the tab until you click a command or click away from the ribbon.

To permanently redisplay the ribbon

1. Do any of the following:

   - Double-click any tab name.

   - Near the upper-right corner of the app window, click the **Ribbon Display Options** button, and then click **Show Tabs and Commands**.

   - Press **Ctrl+F1**.

To specify the items that appear on the status bar

1. Right-click the status bar to display the Customize Status Bar menu. A check mark indicates each item that is currently enabled.

2. Click to enable or disable a status bar indicator or tool. The change is effected immediately. The menu remains open to permit multiple selections.

3. When you finish, click away from the menu to close it.

Adapt exercise steps

This book contains many images of user interface elements (such as the ribbons and the app windows) that you'll work with while performing tasks in Word, Excel, PowerPoint, or Outlook on a Windows-based computer. Depending on your screen resolution or app window width, the app window ribbons on your screen might look different from those shown in this book. As a result, exercise instructions that involve the ribbon might require a little adaptation.

Simple procedural instructions use this format:

1. On the **Insert** tab, in the **Illustrations** group, click the **Chart** button.

If the command is in a list, our instructions use this format:

1. On the **Home** tab, in the **Editing** group, click the **Find** arrow and then, in the **Find** list, click **Go To**.

If differences between your display settings and ours cause a button to appear differently on your screen than it does in this book, you can easily adapt the steps to locate the command. First click the specified tab, and then locate the specified group. If a group has been collapsed into a group list or under a group button, click the list or button to display the group's commands. If you can't immediately identify the button you want, point to likely candidates to display their names in ScreenTips.

Multistep procedural instructions use this format:

1. To select the paragraph that you want to format in columns, triple-click the paragraph.

2. On the **Layout** tab, in the **Page Setup** group, click the **Columns** button to display a menu of column layout options.

3. On the **Columns** menu, click **Three**.

On subsequent instances of instructions that require you to follow the same process, the instructions might be simplified in this format because the working location has already been established:

1. Select the paragraph that you want to format in columns.

2. On the **Columns** menu, click **Three**.

The instructions in this book assume that you're interacting with on-screen elements on your computer by clicking (with a mouse, touchpad, or other hardware device). If you're using a different method—for example, if your computer has a touchscreen interface and you're tapping the screen (with your finger or a stylus)—substitute the applicable tapping action when you interact with a user interface element.

Instructions in this book refer to user interface elements that you click or tap on the screen as *buttons*, and to physical buttons that you press on a keyboard as *keys*, to conform to the standard terminology used in documentation for these products.

When the instructions tell you to enter information, you can do so by typing on a connected external keyboard, tapping an on-screen keyboard, or even speaking aloud, depending on your computer setup and your personal preferences.

Change Office and app options

You access app settings from the Backstage view; specifically, from the Account page and the Options dialog box.

Manage account information

The Account page of the Backstage view in each Office app displays information that is specific to your installation of the app. This information includes:

- Your Microsoft account and links to manage it.

- The current app window background and theme.

- Storage locations and services (such as Facebook and LinkedIn) that you've connected Office to.

- Your subscription information and links to manage the subscription, if you have Office through an Office 365 subscription.

- The app version number and update options.

Account information in Excel

The two ways you can personalize the appearance of your app window are by choosing an Office background and an Office theme. (These are specific to Office and aren't in any way associated with the Windows theme or desktop background.) The background is a subtle design that appears in the title bar of the app window. There are 14 different backgrounds to choose from, or you can choose to not have a background.

Backgrounds depict a variety of subjects

At the time of this writing, there are three Office themes:

- **Colorful** Displays the title bar and ribbon tabs in the color specific to the app, and the ribbon commands, status bar, and Backstage view in light gray
- **Dark Gray** Displays the title bar and ribbon tabs in dark gray, and the ribbon commands, status bar, and Backstage view in light gray
- **White** Displays the title bar, ribbon tabs, and ribbon commands in white, and the status bar in the app-specific color

There are rumors that another theme will be released in the near future, but it hasn't yet made an appearance.

> **TIP** The images in this book depict the No Background option to avoid interfering with the display of any user interface elements, and the Colorful theme so that it's easy to differentiate between the Office apps.

From the Connected Services area of the page, you can connect Office to Facebook, Flickr, and YouTube accounts to access pictures and videos; to Microsoft SharePoint sites and OneDrive storage locations; and to LinkedIn and Twitter accounts to share documents. You must already have an account with one of these services to connect Office to it.

The changes that you make on the Account page apply to all the Office apps installed on all the computers associated with your account. For example, changing the Office background in Word on one computer also changes it in Outlook on any other computer on which you've associated Office with the same account.

To display your Office account settings

1. Start Word, Excel, PowerPoint, or Outlook.

2. Click the **File** tab to display the Backstage view of the app, and then do either of the following:

   - In Word, Excel, or PowerPoint, click **Account**.

   - In Outlook, click **Office Account**.

To manage your Microsoft account connection

1. Display the **Account** page of the Backstage view.

2. In the **User Information** area, click any of the links to begin the selected process.

To change the app window background for all Office apps

1. Display the **Account** page of the Backstage view.

2. In the **Office Background** list, point to any background to display a live preview in the app window, and then click the background you want.

To change the app window color scheme for all Office apps

1. Display the **Account** page of the Backstage view.

2. In the **Office Theme** list, click **Colorful**, **Dark Gray**, or **White**.

To connect to a cloud storage location or social media service

1. Display the **Account** page of the Backstage view.

2. At the bottom of the **Connected Services** area, click **Add a service**, click the type of service you want to add, and then click the specific service.

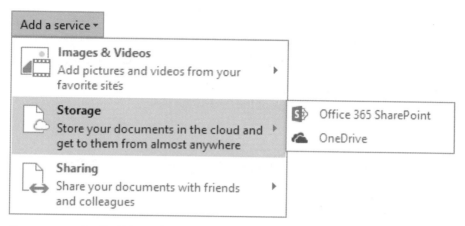

You can connect to OneDrive and OneDrive For Business sites by clicking the OneDrive link

To manage your Office 365 subscription

1. Display the **Account** page of the Backstage view.

2. In the **Product Information** area, click the **Manage Account** button to display the sign-in page for your Office 365 management interface.

3. Provide your account credentials and sign in to access your options.

To manage Office updates

1. Display the **Account** page of the Backstage view.

2. Click the **Update Options** button, and then click the action you want to take.

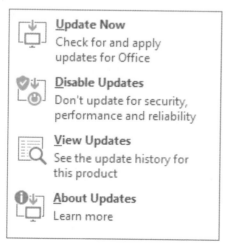

You can install available updates from the Backstage view before the automatic installation occurs

Manage app options

Clicking Options in the left pane of the Backstage view opens the app-specific Options dialog box. Every Options dialog box has a General tab that contains user-specific information that is shared among the Office apps. Some of this is the same information you can configure on the Account page of the Backstage view.

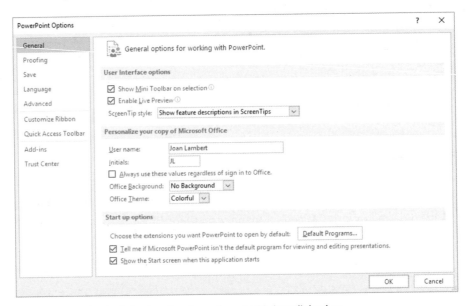

You can customize the behavior of each app from its Options dialog box

Each app's Options dialog box contains hundreds of settings that are specific to that app. For example, you can make the following useful changes:

- In Word, you can change the default behavior when pasting content, or automatically download local copies of remote files, and update the remote files when you save the local versions.

- In Excel, you can change the direction that the cell selection moves when you press the Enter key, or hide comment indicators in cells.

- In PowerPoint, you can hide the toolbar that appears by default in full-screen slide shows, or choose to not automatically display a black slide at the end of slide shows.

- In Outlook, you can customize your calendar so that the working days reflect your schedule, or add the holidays of any country or region to your calendar.

There are also settings that are specific to the file you're working in. For example, you can hide spelling or grammar errors in a specific document, or specify the image compression level for a document or presentation to increase image quality or decrease file size.

> **TIP** Although detailed coverage of each app's Options dialog box is beyond the scope of this book, extensive information is available in the *Step by Step* book for each app: *Microsoft Word 2016 Step by Step*, *Microsoft PowerPoint 2016 Step by Step*, and *Microsoft Outlook 2016 Step by Step*, all by Joan Lambert (Microsoft Press, 2015), and *Microsoft Excel 2016 Step by Step* by Curtis Frye (Microsoft Press, 2015).

Some settings are available in all the app Options dialog boxes, including the following:

- You can turn off the Mini Toolbar, which hosts common formatting commands and appears by default when you select content.

- You can turn off the Live Preview feature if you find it distracting to have document formatting change when the pointer passes over a formatting command.

- You can minimize or turn off the display of ScreenTips when you point to buttons.

- You can specify the user name and initials you want to accompany your comments and tracked changes, and override the display of information from the account associated with your installation of Office.

- You can turn off the Start screens for Word, Excel, and PowerPoint individually. When the Start screen is turned off, starting the app without opening a specific file automatically creates a new, blank file.

After you work with an app for a while, you might want to refine more settings to tailor the app to the way you work. Knowing what options are available in the Options dialog box is helpful in determining the changes that you can make to the app so that you can work most efficiently.

> **TIP** Two app elements you can customize from the Options dialog box are the Quick Access Toolbar and the ribbon. For information, see "Customize the Quick Access Toolbar" and "Customize the ribbon" later in this chapter.

To open an app-specific Options dialog box

1. Click the **File** tab to display the Backstage view.

2. In the left pane, click **Options**.

To enable or disable the Mini Toolbar

1. Open the app-specific **Options** dialog box.

2. On the **General** page, in the **User Interface options** area, select or clear the **Show Mini Toolbar on selection** check box. Then click **OK**.

To enable or disable the Live Preview feature

1. Open the app-specific **Options** dialog box.

2. On the **General** page, in the **User Interface options** area, select or clear the **Enable Live Preview** check box. Then click **OK**.

To control the display of ScreenTips

1. Open the app-specific **Options** dialog box.

2. On the **General** page, in the **User Interface options** area, display the **ScreenTip style** list, and then click any of the following:

    *   Show feature descriptions in ScreenTips

    *   Don't show feature descriptions in ScreenTips

    *   Don't show ScreenTips

To change the user identification that appears in comments and tracked changes

 IMPORTANT The User Name and Initials settings are shared by all the Office apps, so changing them in any one app changes them in all the apps.

1. Open the app-specific **Options** dialog box.

2. On the **General** page, in the **Personalize your copy of Microsoft Office** area, do the following:

    *   In the **User name** and **Initials** boxes, enter the information you want to use.

    *   Select the **Always use these values regardless of sign in to Office** check box.

3. In the **Options** dialog box, click **OK**.

To enable or disable the Start screen for the app

1. Open the app-specific **Options** dialog box.

2. On the **General** page, in the **Start up options** area, select or clear the **Show the Start screen when this application starts** check box.

Customize the Quick Access Toolbar

By default, buttons representing the Save, Undo, and Redo commands appear on the Quick Access Toolbar. If you regularly use a few commands that are scattered on various tabs of the ribbon and you don't want to switch between tabs to access the commands, you might want to add them to the Quick Access Toolbar so that they're always available to you.

You can add commands to the Quick Access Toolbar directly from the ribbon, or from the Quick Access Toolbar page of the app-specific Options dialog box.

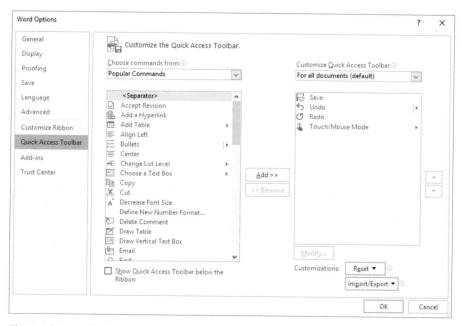

The Quick Access Toolbar is the most convenient command organization option

> **✓ TIP** You can display a list of commands that do not appear on the ribbon by clicking Commands Not In The Ribbon in the Choose Commands From list on the Quick Access Toolbar or Customize Ribbon page of the app-specific Options dialog box.

You can customize the Quick Access Toolbar in the following ways:

- You can define a custom Quick Access Toolbar for all documents, or you can define a custom Quick Access Toolbar for a specific document.

- You can add any command from any group of any tab, including tool tabs, to the toolbar.

- You can display a separator between different types of buttons.

- You can move commands around on the toolbar until they are in the order you want.

- You can reset everything back to the default Quick Access Toolbar configuration.

After you add commands to the Quick Access Toolbar, you can reorganize them and divide them into groups to simplify the process of locating the command you want.

As you add commands to the Quick Access Toolbar, it expands to accommodate them. If you add a lot of commands, it might become difficult to view the text in the title bar, or all the commands on the Quick Access Toolbar might not be visible, defeating the purpose of adding them. To resolve this problem and also position the Quick Access Toolbar closer to the file content, you can move the Quick Access Toolbar below the ribbon.

To add a command to the Quick Access Toolbar from the ribbon

1. Do either of the following:

   - Right-click a command on the ribbon, and then click **Add to Quick Access Toolbar**. You can add any type of command this way; you can even add a drop-down list of options or gallery of thumbnails.

   - At the right end of the Quick Access Toolbar, click the **Customize Quick Access Toolbar** button. On the menu of commonly used commands, click a command you want to add.

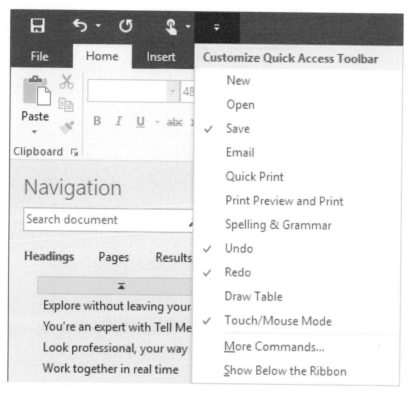

Commonly used commands are available from the menu

To display the Quick Access Toolbar page of the Options dialog box

1. Do any of the following:

   • At the right end of the Quick Access Toolbar, click the **Customize Quick Access Toolbar** button, and then click **More Commands**.

   • Click the **File** tab and then, in the left pane of the Backstage view, click **Options**. In the left pane of the **Options** dialog box, click **Quick Access Toolbar**.

   • Right-click any ribbon tab or empty area of the ribbon, and then click **Customize Quick Access Toolbar**.

To add a command to the Quick Access Toolbar from the Options dialog box

1. Display the **Quick Access Toolbar** page of the **Options** dialog box.

2. In the **Choose commands from** list, click the tab the command appears on, or click **Popular Commands**, **Commands Not in the Ribbon**, **All Commands**, or **Macros**.

3. In the left list, locate and click the command you want to add to the Quick Access Toolbar. Then click the **Add** button.

4. Make any other changes, and then click **OK** in the **Options** dialog box.

To move the Quick Access Toolbar

1. Do either of the following:

   - At the right end of the Quick Access Toolbar, click the **Customize Quick Access Toolbar** button, and then click **Show Below the Ribbon** or **Show Above the Ribbon**.

   - Display the **Quick Access Toolbar** page of the **Options** dialog box. Below the Choose Commands From pane, select or clear the **Show Quick Access Toolbar below the Ribbon** check box.

To define a custom Quick Access Toolbar for a specific file

1. Display the **Quick Access Toolbar** page of the **Options** dialog box.

2. In the **Customize Quick Access Toolbar** list (above the right pane) click **For** *file name*.

3. Add the commands to the toolbar that you want to make available to anyone who edits the file, and then click **OK**. The app displays the file-specific Quick Access Toolbar to the right of the user's own Quick Access Toolbar.

 TIP If a command is on a user's Quick Access Toolbar and also on a file-specific Quick Access Toolbar, it will be shown in both toolbars.

To display a separator on the Quick Access Toolbar

1. Display the **Quick Access Toolbar** page of the **Options** dialog box.

2. In the right pane, click the command after which you want to insert the separator.

1

3. Do either of the following:

   • In the left pane, double-click **<Separator>**.

   • Click **<Separator>** in the left pane, and then click the **Add** button.

4. Make any other changes you want, and then click **OK**.

To move buttons on the Quick Access Toolbar

1. Display the **Quick Access Toolbar** page of the **Options** dialog box.

2. In the right pane, click the button you want to move. Then click the **Move Up** or **Move Down** arrow until it reaches the position you want.

To reset the Quick Access Toolbar to its default configuration

1. Display the **Quick Access Toolbar** page of the **Options** dialog box.

2. In the lower-right corner, click **Reset**, and then click either of the following:

   • Reset only Quick Access Toolbar

   • Reset all customizations

3. In the **Microsoft Office** message box verifying the change, click **Yes**.

> ⚠️ **IMPORTANT** Resetting the Quick Access Toolbar does not change its location. You must manually move the Quick Access Toolbar by using either of the procedures described earlier.

Customize the ribbon

The ribbon was designed to make all the commonly used commands visible so that people can more easily discover the full potential of an Office 2016 app. But many people use the same app to perform the same set of tasks all the time, and for them, seeing buttons (or even entire groups of buttons) that they never use is just another form of clutter.

Would you prefer to display fewer commands, not more? Or would you prefer to display more specialized groups of commands? Well, you can. From the Customize Ribbon page of an an app's Options dialog box, you can control the tabs that appear on the ribbon, and the groups that appear on the tabs.

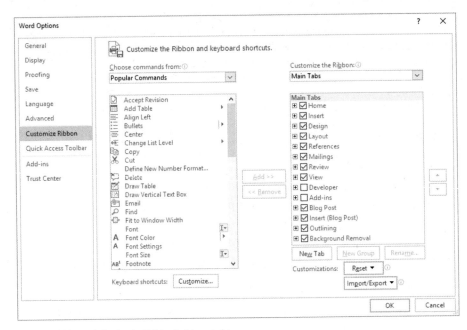

You can hide and display individual ribbon tabs

On this page, you can customize the ribbon in the following ways:

- You can hide an entire tab.

- You can remove a group of commands from a tab. (The group is not removed from the app, only from the tab.)

- You can move or copy a group of commands to another tab.

- You can create a custom group on any tab and then add commands to it. (You cannot add commands to a predefined group.)

- You can create a custom tab. For example, you might want to do this if you use only a few commands from each tab and you find it inefficient to flip between them.

Don't be afraid to experiment with the ribbon to come up with the configuration that best suits the way you work. If at any point you find that your new ribbon is harder to work with rather than easier, you can easily reset everything back to the default configuration.

⚠ **IMPORTANT** Although customizing the default ribbon content might seem like a great way of making the app yours, we don't recommend doing so. A great deal of research has been done about the way that people use the commands in each app, and the ribbon has been organized to reflect the results of that research. If you modify the default ribbon settings, you might end up inadvertently hiding or moving commands that you need. Instead, consider the Quick Access Toolbar to be the command area that you customize and make your own. If you add all the commands you use frequently to the Quick Access Toolbar, you can hide the ribbon and have extra vertical space for document display (this is very convenient when working on a smaller device). Or, if you really want to customize the ribbon, do so by gathering your most frequently used commands on a custom tab, and leave the others alone.

To display the Customize Ribbon page of the Options dialog box

1. Do either of the following:

   - Display the **Options** dialog box, and in the left pane, click **Customize Ribbon**.

   - Right-click any ribbon tab or empty area of the ribbon, and then click **Customize the Ribbon**.

To permit or prevent the display of a tab

1. Display the **Customize Ribbon** page of the **Options** dialog box.

2. In the **Customize the Ribbon** list, click the tab set you want to manage:

   - All Tabs

   - Tool Tabs

   - Main Tabs

3. In the right pane, select or clear the check box of any tab other than the File tab. (You can't hide the File tab.)

To remove a group of commands from a tab

1. Display the **Customize Ribbon** page of the **Options** dialog box.

2. In the **Customize the Ribbon** list, click the tab set you want to manage.

3. In the right pane, click the **Expand** button (+) to the left of the tab you want to modify.

4. Click the group you want to remove, and then in the center pane, click the **Remove** button.

To create a custom tab

1. Display the **Customize Ribbon** page of the **Options** dialog box.

2. On the **Customize Ribbon** page, click the **New Tab** button to insert a new custom tab below the active tab in the right pane. The new tab includes an empty custom group.

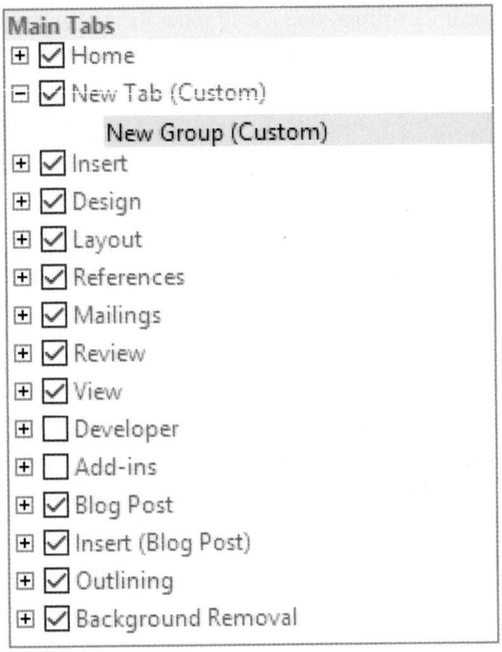

```
Main Tabs
⊞ ☑ Home
⊟ ☑ New Tab (Custom)
        New Group (Custom)
⊞ ☑ Insert
⊞ ☑ Design
⊞ ☑ Layout
⊞ ☑ References
⊞ ☑ Mailings
⊞ ☑ Review
⊞ ☑ View
⊞ ☐ Developer
⊞ ☐ Add-ins
⊞ ☑ Blog Post
⊞ ☑ Insert (Blog Post)
⊞ ☑ Outlining
⊞ ☑ Background Removal
```

Creating a new tab and group

To rename a custom tab

1. Click the custom tab, and then click the **Rename** button.

2. In the **Rename** dialog box, replace the existing tab name with the tab name you want, and then click **OK**.

To rename a custom group

1. Click the custom group, and then click the **Rename** button to open a **Rename** dialog box that includes icons.

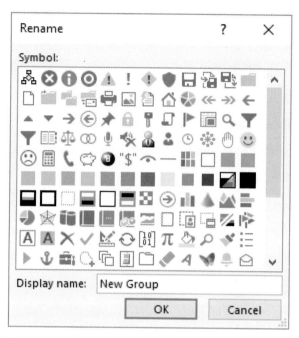

You can assign an icon to appear when the group is narrow

2. In the **Rename** dialog box, change the display name, click the symbol you want to display when the ribbon is too narrow to display the group's commands, and then click **OK**.

To create a custom group

1. Display the **Customize Ribbon** page of the **Options** dialog box.

2. On the **Customize Ribbon** page, in the right pane, click the tab you want to add the group to. Then click the **New Group** button to add an empty custom group.

To add commands to a custom group

1. Display the **Customize Ribbon** page of the **Options** dialog box.

2. In the **Customize the Ribbon** list, expand the tab set you want to manage, and then click the group you want to add the commands to.

3. In the **Choose commands from** list, click the tab the command appears on, or click **Popular Commands**, **Commands Not in the Ribbon**, **All Commands**, or **Macros**.

4. In the left list, locate and click the command you want to add to the group. Then click the **Add** button.

5. Make any other changes, and then click **OK**.

To reset the ribbon to its default configuration

1. Display the **Customize Ribbon** page of the **Options** dialog box.

2. In the lower-right corner, click **Reset**, and then click either of the following:

   - Reset only selected Ribbon Tab

   - Reset all customizations

Skills review

In this chapter, you learned how to:

- Work in the Office user interface

- Change Office and app options

- Customize the Quick Access Toolbar

- Customize the ribbon

Practice tasks

No practice files are necessary to complete the practice tasks in this chapter.

Work in the Office user interface

Start Word, create a new blank document, maximize the app window, and then perform the following tasks:

1. On each tab of the ribbon, do the following:

    *   Review the available groups and commands.

    *   Display the ScreenTip of any command you're not familiar with. Notice the different levels of detail in the ScreenTips.

    *   If a group has a dialog box launcher in its lower-right corner, click the dialog box launcher to display the associated dialog box or pane.

2. Change the width of the app window and notice the effect it has on the ribbon. When the window is narrow, locate a group button and click it to display the commands.

3. Maximize the app window. Hide the ribbon entirely, and notice the change in the app window. Redisplay the ribbon tabs (but not the commands). Temporarily display the ribbon commands, and then click away from the ribbon to close it.

4. Use any of the procedures described in this chapter to permanently redisplay the ribbon tabs and commands.

5. Display the status bar shortcut menu, and identify the tools and statistics that are currently displayed on the status bar. Add any indicators to the status bar that will be useful to you.

6. Keep Word open for use in a later set of practice tasks.

Change Office and app options

Start Excel, create a new blank workbook, and then perform the following tasks:

1. Display the **Account** page of the Backstage view and review the information that is available there.

2. Expand the **Office Background** list. Point to each theme to display a live preview of it. Then click the theme you want to apply.

3. Apply each of the Office themes, and consider its merits. Then apply the theme you like best.

> 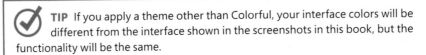 **TIP** If you apply a theme other than Colorful, your interface colors will be different from the interface shown in the screenshots in this book, but the functionality will be the same.

4. Review the services that Office is currently connected to. Expand the **Add a service** menu and point to each of the menu items to display the available services. Connect to any of these that you want to use.

5. Click the **Update Options** button and note whether updates are currently available to install.

> 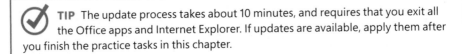 **TIP** The update process takes about 10 minutes, and requires that you exit all the Office apps and Internet Explorer. If updates are available, apply them after you finish the practice tasks in this chapter.

6. On the **Update Options** menu, click **View Updates** to display the *What's New and Improved in Office 2016* webpage in your default browser. Review the information on this page to learn about any new features that interest you.

7. Return to Excel and open the **Excel Options** dialog box.

8. Explore each page of the dialog box. Notice the sections and the settings in each section. Note the settings that apply only to the current file.

9. Review the settings on the **General** page, and modify them as necessary to fit the way you work. Then close the dialog box.

10. Keep Excel open for use in the next set of practice tasks.

Customize the Quick Access Toolbar

Display the Excel app window, and then perform the following tasks:

1. Move the Quick Access Toolbar below the ribbon. Consider the merits of this location versus the original location.

2. From the **Customize Quick Access Toolbar** menu, add the **Sort Ascending** command to the Quick Access Toolbar.

3. From the **Home** tab of the ribbon, add the following commands to the Quick Access Toolbar:

   • From the **Number** group, add the **Number Format** list.

   • From the **Styles** group, add the **Format as Table** command.

Notice that each of the commands is represented on the Quick Access Toolbar exactly as it is on the ribbon. Clicking Number Format displays a list, and clicking Format As Table displays a gallery.

4. From the **Sheet Options** group on the **Page Layout** tab, add the **View Gridlines** command and the **View Headings** commands to the Quick Access Toolbar. Notice that the commands are represented on the Quick Access Toolbar as identically labeled check boxes.

5. Point to each of the **View** commands on the Quick Access Toolbar and then on the ribbon to display its ScreenTip. Notice that ScreenTips for commands on the Quick Access Toolbar are identical to those for commands on the ribbon.

6. Display the **Quick Access Toolbar** page of the **Excel Options** dialog box, and then do the following:

   • In the left pane, display the commands that appear on the **View** tab.

   • Add the **Page Break Preview** button from the **View** tab to the Quick Access Toolbar.

   • In the right pane, move the **Sort Ascending** button to the bottom of the list so that it will be the rightmost button on the Quick Access Toolbar (immediately to the left of the Customize Quick Access Toolbar button).

   • Insert a separator between the original commands and the commands you added in this task set.

   • Insert two separators between the **Number Format** and **Format As Table** commands.

7. Close the **Excel Options** dialog box and observe your customized Quick Access Toolbar. Note the way that a single separator sets off commands, and the way that a double separator sets off commands.

8. Redisplay the **Quick Access Toolbar** page of the **Excel Options** dialog box.

9. Reset the Quick Access Toolbar to its default configuration, and then close the dialog box. Notice that resetting the Quick Access Toolbar does not change its location.

10. Close the workbook without saving it.

Customize the ribbon

Display the Word app window, and then perform the following tasks:

1. Display the **Customize Ribbon** page of the **Word Options** dialog box.

2. Remove the **Mailings** tab from the ribbon, and add the **Developer** tab (if it isn't already shown).

3. Create a custom tab and name it MyShapes.

4. Move the **MyShapes** tab to the top of the right pane so that it will be the leftmost optional ribbon tab (immediately to the right of the File tab).

5. Change the name of the custom group on the **MyShapes** tab to Curved Shapes, and select a curved or circular icon to represent the group.

6. Create another custom group on the **MyShapes** tab. Name the group Angular Shapes, and select a square or triangular icon to represent the group.

7. In the **Choose commands from** list, click **Commands Not in the Ribbon**. From the list, add the **Arc** and **Oval** commands to the **Curved Shapes** group. Then add the **Isosceles Triangle** and **Rectangle** commands to the **Angular Shapes** group.

8. Close the **Word Options** dialog box and display your custom tab. Click the **Arc** command, and then drag on the page to draw an arc.

9. Change the width of the app window to collapse at least one custom group, and verify that the group button displays the icon you selected.

10. Restore the app window to its original width and redisplay the **Customize Ribbon** page of the **Word Options** dialog box.

11. Reset the ribbon to its default configuration, and then close the dialog box.

12. Close the document without saving it.

Create and manage files

When working in Microsoft Word, Excel, or PowerPoint, you save content in individual files. In each app, you can save files as different types depending on each file's purpose. The standard files are Word documents, Excel workbooks, and PowerPoint presentations. Regardless of the app or file type, you use similar techniques for creating and working in files, for changing the display of content, and for displaying and modifying the information that is stored with each file (its properties).

You don't often create files when working with Outlook items (although you can create template files and save items as files). The component of this chapter that relates to Outlook is the discussion of views. In Outlook, you choose views not of a file but of an entire module—such as the Calendar module. Displaying different views of modules can help you to locate specific items or information more easily. Similarly, displaying different views of files or different file elements can make it easier to work in a document, on a worksheet, or on a slide. Each app offers a variety of content views.

This chapter guides you through procedures related to creating files, opening and moving around in files, displaying different views of files, displaying file properties, and saving and closing files, using techniques that are common to working in files created in Word, Excel, or PowerPoint.

In this chapter

- Create files
- Open and move around in files
- Display different views of files
- Display and edit file properties
- Save and close files

Practice files

For this chapter, use the practice files from the Office2016SBS\Ch02 folder. For practice file download instructions, see the introduction.

Create files

When creating a new document, workbook, or presentation, you can start by using a blank file or by using a file that is based on a design template or content template.

- Word and Excel offer content templates that provide purpose-specific place-holder content for documents or workbooks.

- PowerPoint has some content templates, but most are design templates that control thematic elements (colors, fonts, and graphic effects) and slide layouts. Each template has a corresponding theme, so you can create a presentation based on one template, but then entirely change its appearance by applying a different theme.

When you start Word, Excel, or PowerPoint, the app displays a Start screen that gives you options for opening an existing file or creating a new one.

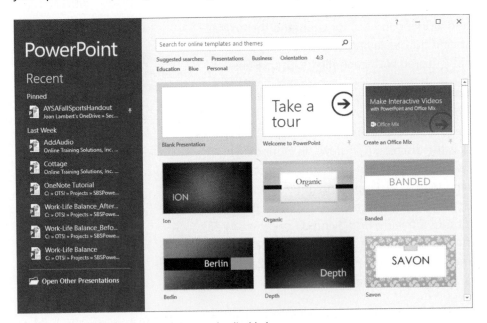

The Start screen appears by default but can be disabled

> **⚠ IMPORTANT** The templates that appear by default in your installation of Word, Excel, or PowerPoint might be different from those shown in images in this book. The templates can change depending on your use of the app and the installation of app updates.

There are different ways to start new files:

- You can start from a blank document, workbook, or presentation that contains one page, worksheet, or slide. You can then add content, apply structure and design elements, and make any necessary configuration changes.

- You can save time by basing your file on one of the many content and design templates that come with the Office apps. You can also preview and download many prepopulated templates from the Office website. These templates provide not only the design elements but also suggestions for content that is appropriate for different types of presentations, such as reports or product launches. After you download a template, you simply customize the content provided in the template to meet your needs.

To create a new blank document, workbook, or presentation

1. Start the app.
2. When the Start screen appears, press the **Esc** key.

Or

1. If the app is already running, click the **File** tab to display the Backstage view.
2. In the left pane of the Backstage view, click **New** to display the New page.
3. On the **New** page of the Backstage view, click the **Blank** *file* thumbnail.

To preview design templates

1. Display the **New** page of the Backstage view.
2. On the **New** page, scroll the pane to view the design templates that were installed with the app.
3. Click any thumbnail to open a preview window that displays a sample document page, worksheet, or title slide.
4. Do any of the following:

   - Click the **Create** button to create a document, workbook, or presentation based on the template that is active in the preview window.

   - Click the arrow to the right of the preview window to view the next template, or the arrow to the left to view the previous template.

   - In the upper-right corner of the preview window, click the **Close** button to close the preview window without creating a document, workbook, or presentation.

To create a document, workbook, or presentation based on an installed template

1. Display the **New** page of the Backstage view.

2. Scroll the pane to locate the design you want to use.

3. Double-click the thumbnail to create the file.

To create a document, workbook, or presentation based on an online template

1. Display the **New** page of the Backstage view.

2. In the search box at the top of the page, enter a term related to the template content or design you're looking for, and then click the **Search** button.

   Or

   Below the search box, click one of the suggested searches.

Enter a search term to display related templates

3. In the **Category** list, click any category or categories to further filter the templates.

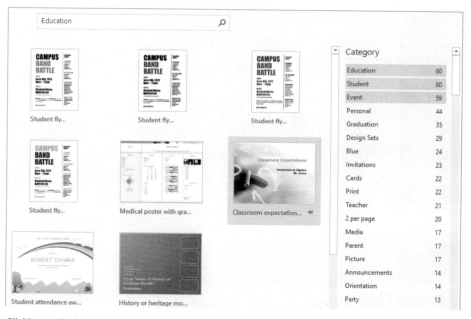

Clicking multiple categories applies multiple filters

> **TIP** Applied category filters are indicated by colored bars at the top of the Category list. To remove a filter, point to it and then click the X that appears to the right of the category name, or double-click the category name.

4. Scroll the pane to locate a design that fits your needs.

5. Double-click any thumbnail to create a file based on the template.

> **TIP** If the app supports template preview, click any thumbnail to preview the design template, and click the More Images arrows to see the content defined as part of the template. Then click the Create button in the preview window to create the file.

Open and move around in files

The Start screen that appears by default when you start Word, Excel, or PowerPoint displays a list of files you worked on recently in that app, and a link to open other existing files. If the file you want to open appears on the Start screen, you can open it directly from there. Otherwise, you open files from the Open page of the Backstage view.

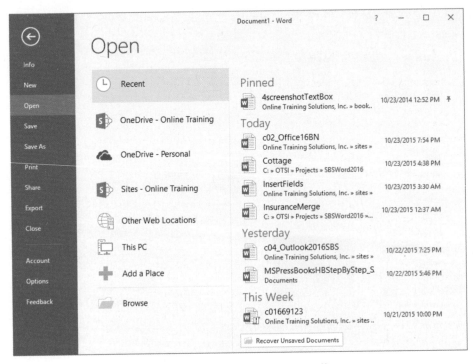

The Open page includes all the locations you've linked to from an Office app

If you open a document that is too long to fit entirely on the screen, you can bring off-screen content into view without changing the location of the cursor by using the vertical scroll bar in the following ways:

- Click the scroll arrows to move up or down by one line.

- Click above or below the scroll box to move up or down by the height of one screen.

- Drag the scroll box on the scroll bar to display the part of the document corresponding to the location of the scroll box. For example, dragging the scroll box to the middle of the scroll bar displays the middle of the document.

If the document is too wide to fit on the screen, Word displays a horizontal scroll bar that you can use in similar ways to move from side to side.

You can also move around in a document by moving the cursor. To place the cursor in a specific location, you simply click there. You can also press a keyboard key to move the cursor. For example, pressing the Home key moves the cursor to the left end of a line.

The following table lists ways to use your keyboard to move the cursor.

Cursor movement	Key or keyboard shortcut
Left one character	Left Arrow
Right one character	Right Arrow
Up one line	Up Arrow
Down one line	Down Arrow
Left one word	Ctrl+Left Arrow
Right one word	Ctrl+Right Arrow
Up one paragraph	Ctrl+Up Arrow
Down one paragraph	Ctrl+Down Arrow
To the beginning of the current line	Home
To the end of the current line	End
To the beginning of the document	Ctrl+Home
To the end of the document	Ctrl+End
To the beginning of the previous page	Ctrl+Page Up
To the beginning of the next page	Ctrl+Page Down
Up one screen	Page Up
Down one screen	Page Down

In a long document, you might want to move quickly among elements of a certain type; for example, from heading to heading, from page to page, or from graphic to graphic. You can do this from the Navigation pane.

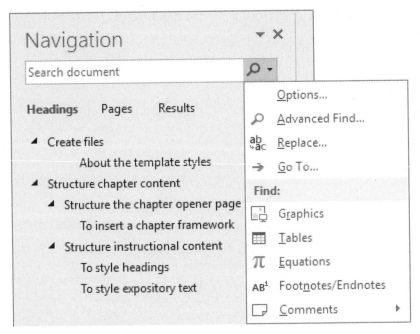

Move between objects of a specific type

To open a recent document, workbook, or presentation

1. Start Word, Excel, or PowerPoint.

2. On the **Start** screen, in the **Recent** list, click the file name of the file you want to open.

Or

1. With the app running, click the **File** tab to display the Backstage view.

2. In the left pane of the Backstage view, click **Open** to display the Open page.

3. In the right pane of the **Open** page, scroll the file list if necessary to locate the file you want to open, and then click the file name to open it.

To open any existing document, workbook, or presentation

1. Start Word, Excel, or PowerPoint.

2. On the **Start** screen, at the bottom of the left pane, click **Open Other** *Files* to display the Open page of the Backstage view.

Or

With the app running, display the Backstage view, and then click **Open** to display the Open page.

3. In the **Places** list, click the local or network storage location where the file is stored.

The Places list includes all the locations you've linked to from an Office app

4. Navigate to the file storage folder by using one of the following methods:

   • In the right pane, click a recent folder. Then click any subfolders until you reach the folder you want.

   • In the left pane, click **Browse** to open the Open dialog box. Then click folders in the **Navigation** pane, double-click folders in the file pane, or enter the folder location in the **Address** bar.

5. Double-click the file you want to open.

> **TIP** In the Open dialog box, clicking a file name and then clicking the Open arrow displays a list of alternative ways to open the selected file. To look through a file without making any inadvertent changes, you can open the file as read-only, open an independent copy of the file, or open it in Protected view. You can also open the file in a web browser. In the event of a computer crash or other similar incident, you can tell the app to open the file and try to repair any damage.

To open the Navigation pane in a document

1. On the **View** tab, in the **Show** group, select the **Navigation Pane** check box.

To browse by object in a document

1. Open the **Navigation** pane, and then do any of the following:

    - At the top of the **Navigation** pane, click **Headings**. Then click any heading to move directly to that location in the document.

    - At the top of the **Navigation** pane, click **Pages**. Then click any thumbnail to move directly to that page of the document.

    - At the right end of the search box, click the arrow. In the **Find** list, click the type of object you want to browse by. Then click the **Next** and **Previous** arrows to move among those objects.

Display different views of files

In each app, you can display the content of a file in a variety of views, each suited to a specific purpose. The views in each app are specific to that app's files.

Word 2016 includes the following views:

- **Print Layout view** This view displays a document on the screen the way it will look when printed. You can review elements such as margins, page breaks, headers and footers, and watermarks.

- **Read Mode view** This view displays as much document content as will fit on the screen at a size that is comfortable for reading. In this view, the ribbon is replaced by one toolbar at the top of the screen with buttons for searching and navigating in the document. You can view comments, but you can't edit the document in this view.

- **Web Layout view** This view displays the document the way it will look when viewed in a web browser. You can see backgrounds and other effects. You can also review how text wraps to fit the window and how graphics are positioned.

- **Outline view** This view displays the structure of a document as nested levels of headings and body text, and provides tools for viewing and changing the hierarchy.

- **Draft view** This view displays the content of a document with a simplified layout so that you can quickly enter and edit text. You cannot view layout elements such as headers and footers.

Excel 2016 includes the following views:

- **Normal view** This view displays the worksheet with column and row headers.

- **Page Layout view** This view displays the worksheet on the screen the way it will look when printed, including page layout elements.

- **Page Break Preview view** This view displays only the portion of the worksheet that contains content, and any page breaks. You can drag page breaks in this view to move them.

PowerPoint 2016 includes the following views:

- **Normal view** This view includes the Thumbnails pane on the left side of the app window, the Slide pane on the right side of the window, and an optional Notes pane at the bottom of the window. You insert, cut, copy, paste, duplicate, and delete slides in the Thumbnails pane, create slide content in the Slide pane, and record speaker notes in the Notes pane.

> **SEE ALSO** For information about working with notes, see "Prepare speaker notes and handouts" in Chapter 9, "Review presentations," of *Microsoft PowerPoint 2016 Step by Step* by Joan Lambert (Microsoft Press, 2015).

- **Notes Page view** This is the only view in which you can create speaker notes that contain elements other than text. Although you can add speaker notes in the Notes pane in Normal view, you must be in Notes Page view to add graphics, tables, diagrams, or charts to your notes.

- **Outline view** This view displays a text outline of the presentation in the Outline pane and the active slide in the Slide pane. You can enter text either directly on the slide or in the outline.

> **SEE ALSO** For information about working with outlines, see "Enter text in placeholders" in Chapter 4, "Enter and edit text on slides," of *Microsoft PowerPoint 2016 Step by Step* by Joan Lambert (Microsoft Press, 2015).

- **Reading view** In this view, which is ideal for previewing the presentation, each slide fills the screen. You can click buttons on the navigation bar to move through or jump to specific slides.

- **Slide Show view** This view displays the presentation as a full-screen slide show, beginning with the current slide. It displays only the slides and not the presenter tools.

- **Slide Sorter view** This view displays thumbnails of all the slides in the presentation. In this view, you manage the slides, rather than the slide content. You can easily reorganize the slides, group them into sections, and apply transitions to one or multiple slides. You can also apply transitions from one slide to another, and specify how long each slide should remain on the screen.

View options are available from the View Shortcuts toolbar near the right end of the status bar and from the View tab of the ribbon.

View Shortcuts toolbar

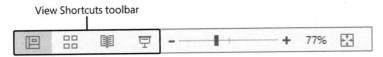

The active view is shaded

When you want to focus on the layout of a document, worksheet, or slide, you can display rulers and gridlines to help you position and align elements. You can also adjust the magnification of the content area by using the tools available in the Zoom group on the View tab, or the Zoom button or Zoom slider at the right end of the status bar.

If you want to work with different parts of a document or workbook, you can open the file in a second window and display both, or you can split a window into two panes and scroll through each pane independently. You're not limited to working with one file at a time. You can easily switch between open files, and you can display more than one app window simultaneously.

2

Not represented on the View tab is a feature that can be invaluable when you are fine-tuning the layout of a document in Word. Nonprinting characters, such as tabs and paragraph marks, control the layout of your document, and hidden characters provide the structure for behind-the-scenes processes, such as indexing. You can control the display of these characters for each window.

To switch among views of a file

1. Do either of the following:

    *   On the **View Shortcuts** toolbar, click the view button you want.

        > **TIP** Clicking the Normal button while it is active switches between Normal and Outline views.

    *   On the **View** tab, in the *File* **Views** group, click the view you want.

To change the magnification of content in the app window

1. On the **View** tab, in the **Zoom** group, click the **Zoom** button to open the Zoom dialog box.

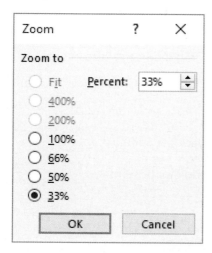

You can select a magnification or enter a specific percentage

2. In the **Zoom** dialog box, select a **Zoom to** option or enter a specific percentage in the **Percent** box, and then click **OK**.

Or

1. In the zoom controls at the right end of the status bar, do any of the following:

    - At the left end of the slider, click the **Zoom Out** button to decrease the zoom percentage.
    - At the right end of the slider, click the **Zoom In** button to increase the zoom percentage.
    - In PowerPoint, at the right end of the status bar, click the **Fit slide to current window** button.

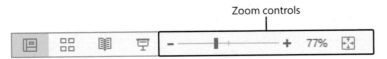

Zoom controls

Clicking the Fit Slide To Current Window button is a quick way to view a slide at the largest size that fits in the Slide pane

To display or hide rulers, gridlines, and guides in a document or presentation

1. On the **View** tab, in the **Show** group do any of the following:

    - Select or clear the **Ruler** check box.
    - Select or clear the **Gridlines** check box.
    - In PowerPoint, select or clear the **Guides** check box.

To display nonprinting characters and formatting marks in a document

1. On the **Home** tab, in the **Paragraph** group, click the **Show/Hide ¶** button.

To split a window into two panes

1. On the **View** tab, in the **Window** group, click the **Split** button.

To display a different open document, workbook, or presentation

1. Do either of the following:

    - On the **View** tab, in the **Window** group, click the **Switch Windows** button, and then click the file you want to view.
    - Point to the app button on the Windows taskbar, and then click the thumbnail of the presentation you want to display.

To display multiple open files of one type at the same time

1. On the **View** tab, in the **Window** group, click the **Arrange All** button.

Display and edit file properties

Properties are file attributes or settings, such as the file name, size, created date, author, and read-only status. Some properties exist to provide information to computer operating systems and apps. You can display properties within a document, workbook, or presentation (for example, you can display the slide number on a slide). Word, Excel, and PowerPoint automatically track some of the properties for you, and you can set others.

You can examine the properties that are attached to a file from the Info page of the Backstage view.

Properties ˅	
Size	764KB
Slides	11
Hidden slides	2
Words	164
Notes	1
Title	Company Meeting
Tags	Add a tag
Comments	Add comments
Multimedia clips	0
Presentation format	Widescreen
Template	Vapor Trail
Status	Add text
Categories	Add a category
Subject	Specify the subject
Hyperlink Base	Add text
Company	Online Training Solutio...

Related Dates

Last Modified	Today, 10:37 PM
Created	Today, 10:35 PM
Last Printed	Today, 10:37 PM

Related People

Manager	Specify the manager
Author	Joan Lambert

Some of the properties stored with a typical PowerPoint presentation

File types and compatibility with earlier versions of Office apps

The Office 2016 apps use file formats based on a programming language called Extensible Markup Language, or more commonly, XML. These file formats, called the *Microsoft Office Open XML Formats*, were introduced with Microsoft Office 2007.

Each Office 2016 app offers a selection of file formats intended to provide specific benefits. The file formats and file name extensions for Word 2016 files include the following:

- Word Document (.docx)
- Word Macro-Enabled Document (.docm)
- Word Template (.dotx)
- Word Macro-Enabled Template (.dotm)
- Word XML Document (.xml)

The file formats and file name extensions for Excel 2016 files include the following:

- Excel Workbook (.xlsx)
- Excel Macro-Enabled Workbook (.xlsm)
- Excel Binary Workbook (.xlsb)
- Excel Template (.xltx)
- Excel Macro-Enabled Template (.xltm)
- Excel Add-In (.xlam)

The file formats and file name extensions for PowerPoint 2016 files include the following:

- PowerPoint Presentation (.pptx)

- PowerPoint Macro-Enabled Presentation (.pptm)

- PowerPoint Template (.potx)

- PowerPoint Macro-Enabled Template (.potm)

- PowerPoint Show (.ppsx)

- PowerPoint Macro-Enabled Show (.ppsm)

- PowerPoint Add-In (.ppam)

- PowerPoint XML Presentation (.xml)

- PowerPoint Picture Presentation (.pptx)

Other file types that are not specific to the Office apps, such as text files, webpages, PDF files, and XPS files, are available from the Save As dialog box of each app.

You can open a file created with Office 2003, Office XP, Office 2000, or Office 97 in an Office 2016 app, but new features will not be available. The file name appears in the title bar with [Compatibility Mode] to its right. You can work in Compatibility mode, or you can convert the document to the current file format by displaying the Info page of the Backstage view and clicking the Convert button in the Compatibility Mode section. You can also click Save As in the Backstage view to save a copy of the file in the current format.

If you work with people who are using a version of Office earlier than 2007, you can save your documents in a format that they will be able to use by choosing the corresponding 97-2003 file format in the Save As Type list, or they can download the Microsoft Office Compatibility Pack for Word, Excel, and PowerPoint File Formats from the Microsoft Download Center (located at *download.microsoft.com*) so that they can open current Office files in one of those versions of Office.

You can change or remove basic properties in the default Properties pane or expand the Properties pane to make more available, or display the Properties dialog box to access even more properties.

To display file properties

1. Display the **Info** page of the Backstage view. The standard properties associated with the file are displayed in the Properties area of the right pane.

2. At the bottom of the **Properties** pane, click **Show All Properties** to expand the pane.

3. At the top of the **Properties** pane, click **Properties** and then click **Advanced Properties** to display the Properties dialog box.

To edit file properties

1. In the **Properties** pane, click the value for the property you want to edit to activate the content box.

2. Enter or replace the property value, and then press **Enter**.

Or

1. In the **Properties** dialog box, do either of the following:

   - On the **Summary** page, click the box to the right of the property you want to modify, and then enter or replace the property value.

   - On the **Custom** page, select the property you want to modify in the **Name** list, and then enter or replace the property value in the **Value** box.

Save and close files

You save a document, workbook, or presentation the first time by clicking the Save button on the Quick Access Toolbar or by displaying the Backstage view and then clicking Save As. Both actions open the Save As page, where you can select a storage location.

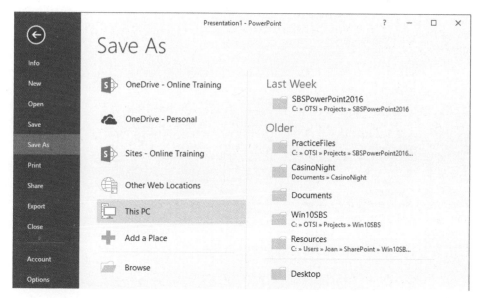

Save your presentation in an online location to access it from anywhere

You can save the file in a folder on your computer or, if you have an Internet connection, in a folder on your Microsoft OneDrive. If your company is running Microsoft SharePoint, you can add a SharePoint site so that it is available from the Places pane of the Save As page, just like any other folder.

 SEE ALSO For information about OneDrive, see the sidebar "Save files to OneDrive" later in this chapter.

Clicking Browse at the bottom of the left pane displays the Save As dialog box, in which you assign a name to the file.

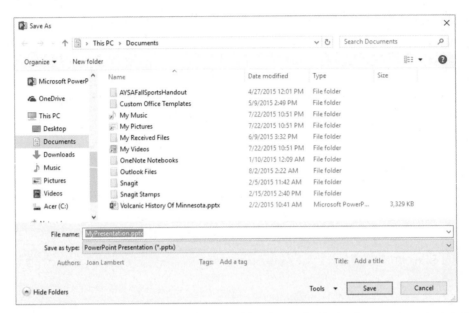

Use standard Windows techniques in either the Address bar or the Navigation pane to navigate to the folder you want

 TIP If you want to create a new folder in which to store the file, click the New Folder button on the dialog box's toolbar.

After you save a file for the first time, you can save changes simply by clicking the Save button on the Quick Access Toolbar. The new version of the file then overwrites the previous version.

 TIP By default, Word, Excel, and PowerPoint periodically save the file you are working on. To adjust the time interval between saves, display the Backstage view, and click Options. In the left pane of the Options dialog box, click Save, and then specify the period of time in the Save AutoRecover Information Every box.

Every time you open a document, workbook, or presentation, a new instance of the app starts. You can close the file and exit that instance of the app. If you have only one document, workbook, or presentation open, you can close the file and exit the app or you can close the file but leave the app running.

To save a document, workbook, or presentation for the first time

1. Click the **File** tab to display the Backstage view.

2. In the left pane of the Backstage view, click **Save As**.

3. On the **Save As** page of the Backstage view, click a storage location, and then click a recently accessed folder in the right pane, or click **Browse**.

4. In the **Save As** dialog box, browse to the folder you want to save the file in.

5. In the **File name** box, enter a name for the file.

6. If you want to save a file in a format other than the one shown in the Save As Type box, click the **Save as type** arrow and then, in the **Save as type** list, click the file format you want.

7. In the **Save As** dialog box, click **Save**.

To add a cloud storage location

1. On the **Save As** page of the Backstage view, click **Add a Place**.

2. In the **Add a Place** list, click **Office 365 SharePoint** or **OneDrive**.

3. In the **Add a service** window, enter the email address you use to sign in to the cloud storage service, and then click **Next**.

4. In the **Sign in** window, enter the password associated with the account, and then click **Sign In** to add the cloud storage location associated with that account to the Places list.

> **TIP** To save a copy of a file, display the **Save As** page of the Backstage view, and then save the file with a different name in the same location or with the same name in a different location. (You can't store two files of the same type with the same name in the same folder.)

To save a file without changing the name or location

1. Do any of the following:

   - On the Quick Access Toolbar, click the **Save** button.

   - In the left pane of the Backstage view, click **Save**.

   - Press **Ctrl+S**.

2

To close a document, workbook, or presentation

1. Do any of the following:

    - At the right end of the title bar, click the **Close** button to close the file and the app window.

    - Display the Backstage view, and then click **Close** to close the file without exiting the app.

    - On the Windows taskbar, point to the app button to display thumbnails of all open files of that type. Point to the thumbnail of the file you want to close, and then click the **Close** button that appears in its upper-right corner.

Save files to OneDrive

When you save an Office file to OneDrive, you and other people with whom you share the file can work on it by using a local installation of the Office apps or by using the Office Online apps, which are available in the OneDrive environments.

If you're new to the world of OneDrive, here's a quick tutorial to help you get started.

OneDrive is a cloud-based storage solution. The purpose of OneDrive is to provide a single place for you to store and access all your files. Although this might seem like a simple concept, it provides major value for people who use Word or other Office products on multiple devices, including Windows computers, Mac computers, iPads and other tablets, and Windows, iPhone, and Android smartphones.

For example, you can create a file on your desktop computer at work, edit it on your laptop at home, and review it on your smartphone while you're waiting for your lunch to be served at a restaurant. If you use the full suite of Office products within your organization, you can even present the file in a Skype for Business meeting from your tablet PC, all while the file is stored in the same central location.

There are currently two types of OneDrive—one for personal use and one for business use:

- **OneDrive** A *personal* OneDrive storage site is provided free with every Microsoft account. Each OneDrive is linked to a specific account.

- **OneDrive for Business** An *organizational* OneDrive storage site, formerly part of SharePoint MySites, is provided with every business-level Office 365 subscription license. These storage locations are part of an organization's Office 365 online infrastructure.

You might have both types of OneDrive available to you; if you do, you can connect to both from the Office apps.

In this book, the personal and organizational versions are referred to generically as OneDrive sites.

To make OneDrive a realistic one-stop storage solution, Microsoft has chosen to support the storage of very large files (up to 10 gigabytes [GB] each) and to provide a significant amount of free storage—from a minimum of 15 GB for every Microsoft account, to unlimited storage for Office 365 subscribers!

By default, files that you store on your OneDrive site are password-protected and available only to you. You can share specific files or folders with other people by sending a personalized invitation or a generic link that allows recipients to view or edit files. You can access files stored on your OneDrive in several ways:

- From within the Word, Excel, PowerPoint, or OneNote apps when opening or saving a file.

- Through File Explorer, when you synchronize your OneDrive site contents with the computer.

- Through a web browser. Personal OneDrive sites are available at *https://onedrive.live.com*; organizational OneDrive sites have addresses linked to your Office 365 account, such as *https://contoso-my.sharepoint.com/personal/joan_contoso_com/*.

Because OneDrive and OneDrive for Business file storage locations are easily configurable in all versions of Word, Excel, PowerPoint, and OneNote, OneDrive is a simple and useful cloud storage option. And best of all, it's completely free!

Skills review

In this chapter, you learned how to:

- Create files
- Open and move around in files
- Display different views of files
- Display and edit file properties
- Save and close files

Practice tasks

The practice files for these tasks are located in the Office2016SBS\Ch02 folder. You can save the results of the tasks in the same folder.

Create files

Complete the following tasks:

1. Start PowerPoint and create a new, blank presentation.

2. Display the available presentation design templates.

3. Preview a template that you like.

4. Without closing the preview window, preview the next or previous template.

5. From the preview window, create a presentation based on the currently displayed template. Notice that the unsaved blank presentation closes.

6. Leave the presentation open for use in a later set of practice tasks.

Open and move around in files

Start Word, and then complete the following tasks:

1. Open the **NavigateFiles** document from the practice file folder.

2. In the second line of the document title, click at the right end of the paragraph to position the cursor.

3. Use a keyboard method to move the cursor to the beginning of the line.

4. Use a keyboard method to move the cursor to the beginning of the word **Regulations**.

5. Use a keyboard method to move the cursor to the end of the document.

6. Use the scroll bar to move to the middle of the document.

 TIP If the vertical scroll bar is not visible, move the pointer and it will appear.

7. Use the scrollbar to change the view of the document by one screen.

8. Open the **Navigation** pane.

9. In the **Navigation** pane, click the **Landscaping** heading to move the cursor directly to the selected heading.

10. At the top of the **Navigation** pane, click **Pages**. On the **Pages** page, scroll through the thumbnails to review the amount of visible detail, and then click the thumbnail for page **5** to move the cursor directly to the top of the selected page.

11. At the right end of the **Navigation** pane title bar, click the **Close** button (the X) to close the pane.

12. Close the document without saving it.

Display different views of files

Open the DisplayViews presentation, and complete the following tasks:

1. In Normal view, display slide **2** of the presentation. Then switch to Slide Show view.

2. Move forward through the presentation to its end. Then switch to Slide Sorter view and select slide **1**.

3. Display the presentation in Reading view. Use any method to navigate to slide **4**, and then use the most efficient method to return to slide **1**.

4. Display the presentation in Normal view.

5. Use commands on the **View** tab to arrange the **DisplayViews** presentation and the presentation you created in the first set of practice tasks side by side on the screen.

6. In the **DisplayViews** presentation, display the gridlines. Notice that they appear in both open presentations.

7. Switch to the presentation you created in the first set of practice tasks. Display the guides. Notice the effect of these actions in the other open presentation.

8. Set the magnification of the active presentation to **60%** and notice the effect of this action in the other open presentation.

9. Leave both presentations open for use in a later set of practice tasks.

Display and edit file properties

Start Excel, and then complete the following tasks:

1. Open the **DisplayProperties** workbook.

2. Display the workbook properties.

3. Expand the **Properties** list to display all properties. Then display the advanced properties.

4. In the **Properties** dialog box, set the **Title** property to Shipping Costs. Then close the dialog box.

5. Verify that the title appears in the **Properties** list on the **Info** page of the Backstage view.

6. Close the workbook and save your changes.

Save and close files

Complete the following tasks:

1. Save a copy of the **DisplayViews** presentation in the practice file folder as MyPresentation. Close the presentation and this instance of PowerPoint.

2. Close the presentation you created in the first task without exiting PowerPoint. Then exit the app.

Part 2

Microsoft Word 2016

Modify the structure and appearance of text

Documents contain text that conveys information to readers, but the appearance of the document content also conveys a message. You can provide structure and meaning by formatting the text in various ways. Word 2016 provides a variety of simple-to-use tools that you can use to apply sophisticated formatting and create a navigational structure.

In a short document or one that doesn't require a complex navigational structure, you can easily format words and paragraphs so that key points stand out and the structure of your document is clear. You can achieve dramatic flair by applying predefined WordArt text effects. To keep the appearance of documents and other Microsoft Office files consistent, you can format document elements by applying predefined sets of formatting called *styles*. In addition, you can change the fonts, colors, and effects throughout a document with one click by applying a theme.

This chapter guides you through procedures related to applying character and paragraph formatting, structuring content manually, creating and modifying lists, applying styles to text, and changing a document's theme.

In this chapter

- Apply paragraph formatting
- Structure content manually
- Apply character formatting
- Create and modify lists
- Apply built-in styles to text
- Change the document theme

Practice files

For this chapter, use the practice files from the Office2016SBS\Ch03 folder. For practice file download instructions, see the introduction.

Apply paragraph formatting

A paragraph is created by entering text and then pressing the Enter key. A paragraph can contain one word, one sentence, or multiple sentences. Every paragraph ends with a paragraph mark, which looks like a backward P (¶). Paragraph marks and other structural characters (such as spaces, line breaks, and tabs) are usually hidden, but you can display them. Sometimes displaying these hidden characters makes it easier to accomplish a task or understand a structural problem.

 SEE ALSO For information about working with hidden structural characters, see "Structure content manually" later in this chapter.

You can change the look of a paragraph by changing its indentation, alignment, and line spacing, in addition to the space before and after it. You can also put borders around it and shade its background. Collectively, the settings you use to vary the look of a paragraph are called *paragraph formatting*.

You can modify a paragraph's left and right edge alignment and vertical spacing by using tools on the Home tab of the ribbon, and its left and right indents from the Home tab or from the ruler. The ruler is usually hidden to provide more space for the document content.

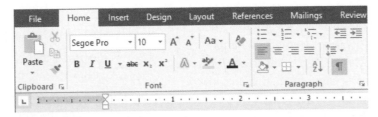

The left indent can be changed from the Home tab or the ruler

If you modify a paragraph and aren't happy with the changes, you can restore the original paragraph and character settings by clearing the formatting to reset the paragraph to its base style.

 SEE ALSO For information about styles, see "Apply built-in styles to text" later in this chapter.

When you want to make several adjustments to the alignment, indentation, and spacing of selected paragraphs, it is sometimes quicker to make changes in the Paragraph dialog box than to click buttons and drag markers.

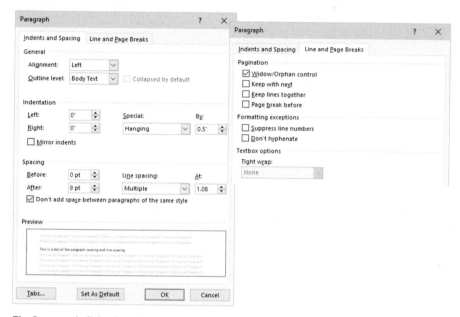

3

The Paragraph dialog box

Configure alignment

The alignment settings control the horizontal position of the paragraph text between the page margins. There are four alignment options:

- **Align Left** This is the default paragraph alignment. It sets the left end of each line of the paragraph at the left page margin or left indent. It results in a straight left edge and a ragged right edge.

- **Align Right** This sets the right end of each line of the paragraph at the right page margin or right indent. It results in a straight right edge and a ragged left edge.

- **Center** This centers each line of the paragraph between the left and right page margins or indents. It results in ragged left and right edges.

- **Justify** This alignment adjusts the spacing between words so that the left end of each line of the paragraph is at the left page margin or indent and the right end of each line of the paragraph (other than the last line) is at the right margin or indent. It results in straight left and right edges.

The icons on the alignment buttons on the ribbon depict the effect of each alignment option.

To open the Paragraph dialog box

1. Do either of the following:

    - On the **Home** tab or the **Layout** tab, in the **Paragraph** group, click the **Paragraph** dialog box launcher.

    - On the **Home** tab, in the **Paragraph** group, click the **Line and Paragraph Spacing** button, and then click **Line Spacing Options**.

To set paragraph alignment

1. Position the cursor anywhere in the paragraph, or select all the paragraphs you want to adjust.

2. Do either of the following:

    - On the **Home** tab, in the **Paragraph** group, click the **Align Left**, **Center**, **Align Right**, or **Justify** button.

    - Open the **Paragraph** dialog box. On the **Indents and Spacing** tab, in the **General** area, click **Left**, **Centered**, **Right**, or **Justified** in the **Alignment** list.

Configure vertical spacing

Paragraphs have two types of vertical spacing:

- **Paragraph spacing** The space between paragraphs, defined by setting the space before and after each paragraph. This space is usually measured in points.

- **Line spacing** The space between the lines of the paragraph, defined by setting the height of the lines either in relation to the height of the text (Single, Double, or a specific number of lines) or by specifying a minimum or exact point measurement.

The default line spacing for documents created in Word 2016 is 1.08 lines. Changing the line spacing changes the appearance and readability of the text in the paragraph and, of course, also changes the amount of space it occupies on the page.

> *The line spacing of this paragraph is set to the default, 1.08 lines.* A paragraph can contain one word, one sentence, or multiple sentences. You can change the look of a paragraph by changing its indentation, alignment, and line spacing, as well as the space before and after it. You can also put borders around it and shade its background. Collectively, the settings you use to vary the look of a paragraph are called *paragraph formatting*.
>
> *The line spacing of this paragraph is set to Double (2 lines).* A paragraph can contain one word, one sentence, or multiple sentences. You can change the look of a paragraph by changing its indentation, alignment, and line spacing, as well as the space before and after it. You can also put borders around it and shade its background. Collectively, the settings you use to vary the look of a paragraph are called *paragraph formatting*.

The effect of changing line spacing

You can set the paragraph and line spacing for individual paragraphs and for paragraph styles. You can quickly adjust the spacing of most content in a document by selecting an option from the Paragraph Spacing menu on the Design tab. (Although the menu is named Paragraph Spacing, the menu options control both paragraph spacing and line spacing.) These options, which are named by effect rather than by specific measurements, work by modifying the spacing of the Normal paragraph style and any other styles that depend on the Normal style for their spacing. (In standard templates, most other styles are based on the Normal style.) The Paragraph Spacing options modify the Normal style in only the current document, and do not affect other documents.

The following table describes the effect of each Paragraph Spacing option on the paragraph and line spacing settings.

Paragraph spacing option	Before paragraph	After paragraph	Line spacing
Default	Spacing options are controlled by the style set		
No Paragraph Space	0 points	0 points	1 line
Compact	0 points	4 points	1 line
Tight	0 points	6 points	1.15 lines
Open	0 points	10 points	1.15 lines
Relaxed	0 points	6 points	1.5 lines
Double	0 points	8 points	2 lines

To quickly adjust the vertical spacing before, after, and within all paragraphs in a document

1. On the **Design** tab, in the **Document Formatting** group, click the **Paragraph Spacing** button to display the Paragraph Spacing menu.

Each paragraph spacing option controls space around and within the paragraph

2. Click the option you want to apply to all of the paragraphs in the document.

To adjust the spacing between paragraphs

1. Select all the paragraphs you want to adjust.

2. On the **Layout** tab, in the **Paragraph** group, adjust the **Spacing Before** and **Spacing After** settings.

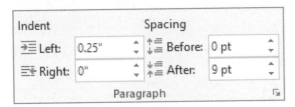

The settings in the Spacing boxes are measured in points

To adjust spacing between the lines of paragraphs

1. Position the cursor anywhere in the paragraph, or select all the paragraphs you want to adjust.

2. To make a quick adjustment to selected paragraphs, on the **Home** tab, in the **Paragraph** group, click **Line And Paragraph Spacing**, and then click any of the line spacing commands on the menu.

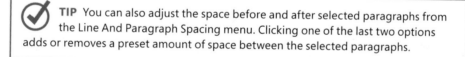

	1.0
	1.15
	1.5
	2.0
	2.5
	3.0
	Line Spacing Options...
⭷	Add Space <u>B</u>efore Paragraph
⭡	Remove Space <u>A</u>fter Paragraph

You can choose from preset internal line spacing options or adjust paragraph spacing

> ✓ **TIP** You can also adjust the space before and after selected paragraphs from the Line And Paragraph Spacing menu. Clicking one of the last two options adds or removes a preset amount of space between the selected paragraphs.

Or

1. Position the cursor anywhere in the paragraph, or select all the paragraphs you want to adjust.

2. Open the **Paragraph** dialog box. On the **Indents and Spacing** tab, in the **Spacing** area, make the adjustments you want to the paragraph spacing, and then click **OK**.

Configure indents

In Word, you don't define the width of paragraphs and the length of pages by defining the area occupied by the text; instead, you define the size of the white space—the left, right, top, and bottom margins—around the text.

> **SEE ALSO** For information about setting margins, see "Preview and adjust page layout" in Chapter 12, "Finalize and distribute documents," of *Microsoft Word 2016 Step by Step* by Joan Lambert (Microsoft Press, 2015). For information about sections, see "Control what appears on each page" in the same chapter.

Although the left and right margins are set for a whole document or for a section of a document, you can vary the position of the paragraphs between the margins by indenting the left or right edge of the paragraph.

A paragraph indent is the space from the page margin to the text. You can change the left indent by clicking buttons on the Home tab, or you can set the indents directly on the ruler. Three indent markers are always present on the ruler:

- **Left Indent** This defines the outermost left edge of each line of the paragraph.

- **Right Indent** This defines the outermost right edge of each line of the paragraph.

- **First Line Indent** This defines the starting point of the first line of the paragraph.

The ruler indicates the space between the left and right page margins in a lighter color than the space outside of the page margins.

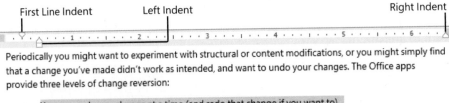

The indent markers on the ruler

The default setting for the Left Indent and First Line Indent markers is 0.0", which aligns with the left page margin. The default setting for the Right Indent marker is the distance from the left margin to the right margin. For example, if the page size is set to 8.5" wide and the left and right margins are set to 1.0", the default Right Indent marker setting is 6.5".

You can arrange the Left Indent and First Line Indent markers to create a hanging indent or a first line indent. Hanging indents are most commonly used for bulleted and numbered lists, in which the bullet or number is indented less than the main text (essentially, it is *out*dented). First line indents are frequently used to distinguish the beginning of each subsequent paragraph in documents that consist of many consecutive paragraphs of text. Both types of indents are set by using the First Line Indent marker on the ruler.

> **TIP** The First Line Indent marker is linked to the Left Indent marker. Moving the Left Indent marker also moves the First Line Indent marker, to maintain the first line indent distance. You can move the First Line Indent marker independently of the Left Indent marker to change the first line indent distance.

To display the ruler

1. On the **View** tab, in the **Show** group, select the **Ruler** check box.

> **TIP** In this book, we show measurements in inches. If you want to change the measurement units Word uses, open the Word Options dialog box. On the Advanced page, in the Display area, click the units you want in the Show Measurements In Units Of list. Then click OK.

To indent or outdent the left edge of a paragraph

1. Position the cursor anywhere in the paragraph, or select all the paragraphs you want to adjust.

2. Do any of the following:

    -   On the **Home** tab, in the **Paragraph** group, click the **Increase Indent** or **Decrease Indent** button to move the left edge of the paragraph in 0.25" increments.

> **TIP** You cannot increase or decrease the indent beyond the margins by using the Increase Indent and Decrease Indent buttons. If you do need to extend an indent beyond the margins, you can do so by setting negative indentation measurements in the Paragraph dialog box.

- Open the **Paragraph** dialog box. On the **Indents and Spacing** tab, in the **Indentation** area, set the indent in the **Left** box, and then click **OK**.

- On the ruler, drag the **Left Indent** marker to the ruler measurement at which you want to position the left edge of the body of the paragraph.

To create a hanging indent or first line indent

1. Position the cursor anywhere in the paragraph, or select all the paragraphs you want to adjust.

2. Open the **Paragraph** dialog box. On the **Indents and Spacing** tab, in the **Indents** area, click **First line** or **Hanging** in the **Special** box.

3. In the **By** box, set the amount of the indent, and then click **OK**.

Or

1. Set the left indent of the paragraph body.

2. On the ruler, drag the **First Line Indent** marker to the ruler measurement at which you want to begin the first line of the paragraph.

To indent or outdent the right edge of a paragraph

1. Position the cursor anywhere in the paragraph, or select all the paragraphs you want to adjust.

2. Do either of the following:

   - On the ruler, drag the **Right Indent** marker to the ruler measurement at which you want to set the maximum right edge of the paragraph.

   - Open the **Paragraph** dialog box. On the **Indents and Spacing** tab, in the **Indentation** area, set the right indent in the **Right** box, and then click **OK**.

> **TIP** Unless the paragraph alignment is justified, the right edge of the paragraph will be ragged, but no line will extend beyond the right indent or outdent.

Configure paragraph borders and shading

To make a paragraph really stand out, you might want to put a border around it or shade its background. (For real drama, you can do both.) You can select a predefined border from the Borders menu, or design a custom border in the Borders And Shading dialog box.

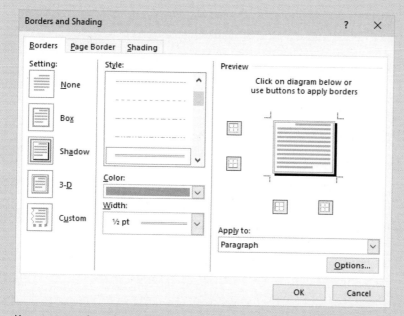

You can customize many aspects of the border

After you select the style, color, width, and location of the border, you can click the Options button to specify its distance from the text.

Structure content manually

At times it's necessary to manually position text within a paragraph. You can do this by using two different hidden characters: line breaks and tabs. These characters are visible only when the option to show paragraph marks and formatting symbols is turned on.

The hidden characters have distinctive appearances:

- A line break character looks like a bent left arrow: ↵

- A tab character looks like a right-pointing arrow: →

You can use a line break, also known as a *soft return*, to wrap a line of a paragraph in a specific location without ending the paragraph. You might use this technique to display only specific text on a line, or to break a line before a word that would otherwise be hyphenated.

> **TIP** Inserting a line break does not start a new paragraph, so when you apply paragraph formatting to a line of text that ends with a line break, the formatting is applied to the entire paragraph, not only to that line.

> **SEE ALSO** For information about page and section breaks, see "Control what appears on each page" in Chapter 12, "Finalize and distribute documents," of *Microsoft Word 2016 Step by Step* by Joan Lambert (Microsoft Press, 2015).

A tab character defines the space between two document elements. For example, you can separate numbers from list items, or columns of text, by using tabs. You can then set tab stops that define the location and alignment of the tabbed text.

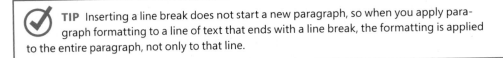

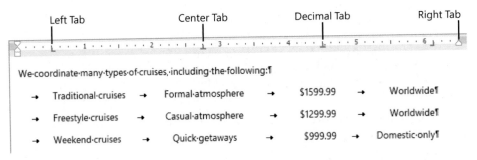

You can align text in different ways by using tabs

You can align lines of text in different locations across the page by using tab stops. The easiest way to set tab stops is directly on the horizontal ruler. By default, Word sets left-aligned tab stops every half inch (1.27 centimeters). (The default tab stops aren't shown on the ruler.) To set a custom tab stop, start by clicking the Tab button (located at the intersection of the vertical and horizontal rulers) until the type of tab stop you want appears.

The tab settings

You have the following tab options:

- **Left Tab** Aligns the left end of the text with the tab stop
- **Center Tab** Aligns the center of the text with the tab stop
- **Right Tab** Aligns the right end of the text with the tab stop
- **Decimal Tab** Aligns the decimal point in the text (usually a numeric value) with the tab stop
- **Bar Tab** Draws a vertical line at the position of the tab stop

If you find it too difficult to position tab stops on the ruler, you can set, clear, align, and format tab stops from the Tabs dialog box.

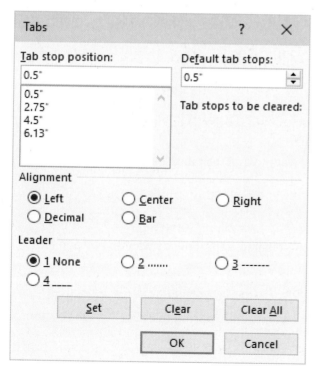

You can specify the alignment and tab leader for each tab

You might also work from this dialog box if you want to use tab leaders—visible marks such as dots or dashes connecting the text before the tab with the text after it. For example, tab leaders are useful in a table of contents to carry the eye from the text to the page number.

When you insert tab characters, the text to the right of the tab character aligns on the tab stop according to its type. For example, if you set a center tab stop, pressing the Tab key moves the text so that its center is aligned with the tab stop.

To display or hide paragraph marks and other structural characters

1. Do either of the following:

    - On the **Home** tab, in the **Paragraph** group, click the **Show/Hide ¶** button.

    - Press **Ctrl+Shift+*** (asterisk).

To insert a line break

1. Position the cursor where you want to break the line.

2. Do either of the following:

    - On the **Layout** tab, in the **Page Setup** group, click **Breaks**, and then click **Text Wrapping**.

    - Press **Shift+Enter**.

To insert a tab character

1. Position the cursor where you want to add the tab character.

2. Press the **Tab** key.

To open the Tabs dialog box

1. Select any portion of one or more paragraphs that you want to manage tab stops for.

2. Open the **Paragraph** dialog box.

3. In the lower-left corner of the **Indents and Spacing** tab, click the **Tabs** button.

To align a tab and set a tab stop

1. Select any portion of one or more paragraphs that you want to set the tab stop for.

2. Click the **Tab** button at the left end of the ruler to cycle through the tab stop alignments, in this order:

   - Left

   - Center

   - Right

   - Decimal

   - Bar

3. When the **Tab** button shows the alignment you want, click the ruler at the point where you want to set the tab.

> **TIP** When you manually align a tab and set a tab stop, Word removes any default tab stops to the left of the one you set.

Or

1. Open the **Tabs** dialog box.

2. In the **Tab stop position** box, enter the position for the new tab stop.

3. In the **Alignment** and **Leader** areas, set the options you want for this tab stop.

4. Click **Set** to set the tab, and then click **OK**.

To change the position of an existing custom tab stop

1. Do either of the following:

   - Drag the tab marker on the ruler.

   - Open the **Tabs** dialog box. In the **Tab stop position** list, select the tab stop you want to change. Click the **Clear** button to clear the existing tab stop. Enter the replacement tab stop position in the **Tab stop position** box, click **Set**, and then click **OK**.

To remove a custom tab stop

1. Do either of the following:

    - Drag the tab marker away from the ruler.

    - In the **Tabs** dialog box, select the custom tab stop in the **Tab stop position** list, click **Clear**, and then click **OK**.

Apply character formatting

The appearance of your document helps to convey not only the document's message but also information about the document's creator—you. A neatly organized document that contains consistently formatted content and appropriate graphic elements, and that doesn't contain spelling or grammatical errors, invokes greater confidence in your ability to provide any product or service.

Earlier in this chapter, you learned about methods of applying formatting to paragraphs. This topic covers methods of formatting the text of a document. Formatting that you apply to text is referred to as *character formatting*. In Word documents, you can apply three types of character formatting:

- Individual character formats including font, font size, bold, italic, underline, strikethrough, subscript, superscript, font color, and highlight color

- Artistic text effects that incorporate character outline and fill colors

- Preformatted styles associated with the document template, many of which not only affect the appearance of the text but also convey structural information (such as titles and headings)

When you enter text in a document, it is displayed in a specific font. By default, the font used for text in a new blank document is 11-point Calibri, but you can change the font of any element at any time. The available fonts vary from one computer to another, depending on the apps installed. Common fonts include Arial, Verdana, and Times New Roman.

You can vary the look of a font by changing the following attributes:

- **Size** Almost every font has a range of sizes you can select from. (Sometimes you can set additional sizes beyond those listed.) The font size is measured in points, from the top of the ascenders (letter parts that go up, as in *h*) to the bottom of the descenders (letter parts that drop down, as in *p*). A point is approximately 1/72 of an inch (about 0.04 centimeters).

- **Style** Almost every font has a range of font styles. The most common are regular (or plain), italic, bold, and bold italic.

- **Effects** Fonts can be enhanced by applying effects, such as underlining, small capital letters (small caps), or shadows.

- **Character spacing** You can alter the spacing between characters by pushing them apart or squeezing them together.

Although some attributes might cancel each other out, they are usually cumulative. For example, you might use a bold font style in various sizes and various shades of green to make words stand out in a newsletter.

You apply character formatting from one of three locations:

- **Mini Toolbar** Several common formatting buttons are available on the Mini Toolbar that appears when you select text.

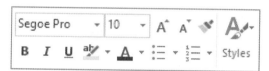

The Mini Toolbar appears temporarily when you select text, becomes transparent when you move the pointer away from the selected text, and then disappears entirely

- **Font group on the Home tab** This group includes buttons for changing the font and most of the font attributes you are likely to use.

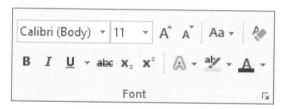

The most common font formatting commands are available on the Home tab

- **Font dialog box** Less-commonly applied attributes such as small caps and special underlining are available from the Font dialog box.

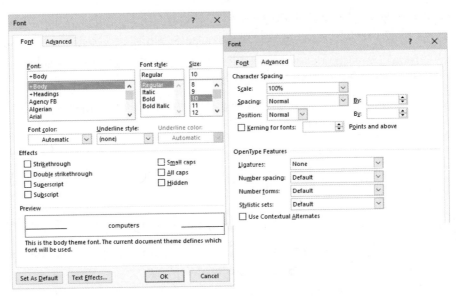

Font attributes that aren't available on the Home tab can be set here

In addition to applying character formatting to change the look of characters, you can apply predefined text effects (sometimes referred to as *WordArt*) to a selection to add more zing. The available effects match the current theme colors.

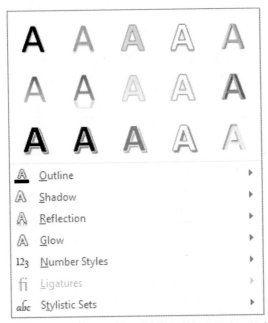

You can apply any predefined effect in the gallery or define a custom effect

These effects are somewhat dramatic, so you'll probably want to restrict their use to document titles and similar elements to which you want to draw particular attention.

To change the font of selected text

1. On the **Mini Toolbar** or in the **Font** group on the **Home** tab, in the **Font** list, click the font you want to apply.

To change the font size of selected text

1. Do any of the following on the **Mini Toolbar** or in the **Font** group on the **Home** tab:

   - In the **Font Size** list, click the font size you want to apply.

   - In the **Font Size** box, enter the font size you want to apply (even a size that doesn't appear in the list). Then press the **Enter** key.

   - To increase the font size in set increments, click the **Increase Font Size** button, or press **Ctrl+>**.

   - To decrease the font size in set increments, click the **Decrease Font Size** button, or press **Ctrl+<**.

To format selected text as bold, italic, or underlined

1. Do any of the following:

   - On the **Mini Toolbar**, click the **Bold**, **Italic**, or **Underline** button.

   - On the **Home** tab, in the **Font** group, click the **Bold**, **Italic**, or **Underline** button.

   - Press **Ctrl+B** to format the text as bold.

   - Press **Ctrl+I** to format the text as italic.

   - Press **Ctrl+U** to underline the text.

> **TIP** To quickly apply a different underline style to selected text, click the arrow next to the Underline button on the Home tab, and then in the list, click the underline style you want to apply.

To cross out selected text by drawing a line through it

1. On the **Home** tab, in the **Font** group, click the **Strikethrough** button.

To display superscript or subscript characters

1. Select the characters you want to reposition.

2. On the **Home** tab, in the **Font** group, do either of the following:

   - Click the **Subscript** button to shift the characters to the bottom of the line.

   - Click the **Superscript** button to shift the characters to the top of the line.

To apply artistic effects to selected text

1. On the **Home** tab, in the **Font** group, click the **Text Effects and Typography** button, and then do either of the following:

   - In the **Text Effects and Typography** gallery, click the preformatted effect combination that you want to apply.

   - On the **Text Effects and Typography** menu, click **Outline**, **Shadow**, **Reflection**, **Glow**, **Number Styles**, **Ligatures**, or **Stylistic Sets**. Then make selections on the submenus to apply and modify those effects.

To change the font color of selected text

1. On the **Home** tab, in the **Font** group, click the **Font Color** arrow to display the **Font Color** menu.

2. In the **Theme Colors** or **Standard Colors** palette, select a color swatch to apply that color to the selected text.

> **TIP** To apply the Font Color button's current color, you can simply click the button (not its arrow). If you want to apply a color that is not shown in the Theme Colors or Standard Colors palette, click More Colors. In the Colors dialog box, click the color you want in the honeycomb on the Standard page, or click the color gradient or enter values for a color on the Custom page.

To change the case of selected text

1. Do either of the following:

   - On the **Home** tab, in the **Font** group, click the **Change Case** button, and then click **Sentence case**, **lowercase**, **UPPERCASE**, **Capitalize Each Word**, or **tOGGLE cASE**.

   - Press **Shift+F3** repeatedly to cycle through the standard case options (Sentence case, UPPERCASE, lowercase, and Capitalize Each Word).

> ⚠️ **IMPORTANT** The case options vary based on the selected text. If the selection ends in a period, Word does not include the Capitalize Each Word option in the rotation. If the selection does not end in a period, Word does not include Sentence case in the rotation.

To highlight text

1. Select the text you want to change, and then do either of the following:

   - On the **Mini Toolbar** or in the **Font** group on the **Home** tab, click the **Text Highlight Color** button to apply the default highlight color.

   - On the **Mini Toolbar** or in the **Font** group on the **Home** tab, click the **Text Highlight Color** arrow, and then click a color swatch to apply the selected highlight color and change the default highlight color.

Or

1. Without first selecting text, do either of the following:

   - Click the **Text Highlight Color** button to select the default highlight color.

   - Click the **Text Highlight Color** arrow, and then click a color swatch to select that highlight color.

2. When the pointer changes to a highlighter, drag it across one or more sections of text to apply the highlight.

3. Click the **Text Highlight Color** button or press the **Esc** key to deactivate the highlighter.

To copy formatting to other text

1. Click anywhere in the text that has the formatting you want to copy.

2. On the **Home** tab, in the **Clipboard** group, do either of the following:

   - If you want to apply the formatting to only one target, click the **Format Painter** button once.

   - If you want to apply the formatting to multiple targets, double-click the **Format Painter** button.

3. When the pointer changes to a paintbrush, click or drag across the text you want to apply the copied formatting to.

4. If you activated the Format Painter for multiple targets, repeat step 3 until you finish applying the formatting. Then click the **Format Painter** button once, or press the **Esc** key, to deactivate the tool.

To repeat the previous formatting command

1. Select the text to which you want to apply the repeated formatting.

2. Do either of the following to repeat the previous formatting command:

   - On the **Quick Access Toolbar**, click the **Repeat** button.

   - Press **Ctrl+Y**.

To open the Font dialog box

1. Do either of the following:

   - On the **Home** tab, in the **Font** group, click the **Font** dialog box launcher.

   - Press **Ctrl+Shift+F**.

To remove character formatting

1. Select the text you want to clear the formatting from.

2. Do any of the following:

   - Press **Ctrl+Spacebar** to remove only manually applied formatting (and not styles).

   - On the **Home** tab, in the **Font** group, click the **Clear All Formatting** button to remove all styles and formatting other than highlighting from selected text.

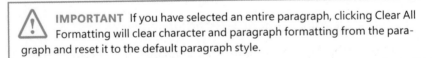

   > **IMPORTANT** If you have selected an entire paragraph, clicking Clear All Formatting will clear character and paragraph formatting from the paragraph and reset it to the default paragraph style.

   - On the **Home** tab, in the **Font** group, click the **Text Highlight Color** arrow and then, on the menu, click **No Color** to remove highlighting.

To change the character spacing

1. Select the text you want to change.

2. Open the **Font** dialog box, and then click the **Advanced** tab to display character spacing and typographic features.

3. In the **Spacing** list, click **Expanded** or **Condensed**.

4. In the adjacent **By** box, set the number of points you want to expand or condense the character spacing.

5. In the **Font** dialog box, click **OK**.

3

Character formatting and case considerations

The way you use character formatting in a document can influence its visual impact on your readers. Used judiciously, character formatting can make a plain document look attractive and professional, but excessive use can make it look amateurish and detract from the message. For example, using too many fonts in the same document is the mark of inexperience, so don't use more than two or three.

Bear in mind that lowercase letters tend to recede, so using all uppercase (capital) letters can be useful for titles and headings or for certain kinds of emphasis. However, large blocks of uppercase letters are tiring to the eye.

TIP Where do the terms *uppercase* and *lowercase* come from? Until the advent of computers, individual characters made of lead were assembled to form the words that would appear on a printed page. The characters were stored alphabetically in cases, with the capital letters in the upper case and the small letters in the lower case.

Create and modify lists

Lists are paragraphs that start with a character (usually a number or bullet) and are formatted with a hanging indent so that the characters stand out on the left end of each list item. Fortunately, Word takes care of the formatting of lists for you. You simply indicate the type of list you want to create. When the order of items is not important—for example, for a list of people or supplies—a bulleted list is the best choice. And when the order is important—for example, for the steps in a procedure—you will probably want to create a numbered list.

You can format an existing set of paragraphs as a list or create the list as you enter information into the document. After you create a list, you can modify, format, and customize the list as follows:

- You can move items around in a list, insert new items, or delete unwanted items. If the list is numbered, Word automatically updates the numbers.

- You can modify the indentation of the list. You can change both the overall indentation of the list and the relationship of the first line to the other lines.

- For a bulleted list, you can sort list items into ascending or descending order, change the bullet symbol, or define a custom bullet (even a picture bullet).

- For a numbered list, you can change the number style or define a custom style, and you can specify the starting number for a list.

To format a new bulleted or numbered list as you enter content

1. With the cursor at the position in the document where you want to start the list, do either of the following:

   - To start a new bulleted list, enter * (an asterisk) at the beginning of a paragraph, and then press the **Spacebar** or the **Tab** key before entering the list item text.

   - To start a new numbered list, enter **1.** (the number 1 followed by a period) at the beginning of a paragraph, and then press the **Spacebar** or the **Tab** key before entering the list item text.

   When you start a list in this fashion, Word automatically formats it as a bulleted or numbered list. When you press Enter to start a new item, Word continues the formatting to the new paragraph. Typing items and pressing Enter adds subsequent bulleted or numbered items. To end the list, press Enter twice; or click the Bullets arrow or Numbering arrow in the Paragraph group on the Home tab, and then in the gallery, click None.

> **TIP** If you want to start a paragraph with an asterisk or number but don't want to format the paragraph as a bulleted or numbered list, click the AutoCorrect Options button that appears after Word changes the formatting, and then in the list, click the appropriate Undo option. You can also click the Undo button on the Quick Access Toolbar or press Ctrl+Z.

To convert paragraphs to bulleted or numbered list items

1. Select the paragraphs that you want to convert to list items.

2. On the **Home** tab, in the **Paragraph** group, do either of the following:

   - Click the **Bullets** button to convert the selection to a bulleted list.

   - Click the **Numbering** button to convert the selection to a numbered list.

3

To create a list that has multiple levels

1. Start creating a bulleted or numbered list.

2. When you want the next list item to be at a different level, do either of the following:

   - To create the next item one level lower (indented more), press the **Tab** key at the beginning of that paragraph, before you enter the lower-level list item text.

   - To create the next item one level higher (indented less), press **Shift+Tab** at the beginning of the paragraph, before you enter the higher-level list item text.

   In the case of a bulleted list, Word changes the bullet character for each item level. In the case of a numbered list, Word changes the type of numbering used, based on a predefined numbering scheme.

> **TIP** For a multilevel list, you can change the numbering pattern or bullets by clicking the Multilevel List button in the Paragraph group on the Home tab and then clicking the pattern you want, or you can define a custom pattern by clicking Define New Multilevel List.

To modify the indentation of a list

1. Select the list items whose indentation you want to change, and do any of the following:

   - On the **Home** tab, in the **Paragraph** group, click the **Increase Indent** button to move the list items to the right.

   - In the **Paragraph** group, click the **Decrease Indent** button to move the list items to the left.

   - Display the horizontal ruler, and drag the indent markers to the left or right.

TIP You can adjust the space between the bullets and their text by dragging only the Hanging Indent marker.

 SEE ALSO For information about paragraph indentation, see "Apply paragraph formatting" earlier in this chapter.

To sort bulleted list items into ascending or descending order

1. Select the bulleted list items whose sort order you want to change.

2. On the **Home** tab, in the **Paragraph** group, click the **Sort** button to open the Sort Text dialog box.

3. In the **Sort by** area, click **Ascending** or **Descending**. Then click **OK**.

To change the bullet symbol

1. Select the bulleted list whose bullet symbol you want to change.

2. On the **Home** tab, in the **Paragraph** group, click the **Bullets** arrow.

3. In the **Bullets** gallery, click the new symbol you want to use to replace the bullet character that begins each item in the selected list.

To define a custom bullet

1. In the **Bullets** gallery, click **Define New Bullet**.

2. In the **Define New Bullet** dialog box, click the **Symbol**, **Picture**, or **Font** button, and make a selection from the wide range of options.

3. Click **OK** to apply the new bullet style to the list.

To change the number style

1. Select the numbered list whose number style you want to change.

2. On the **Home** tab, in the **Paragraph** group, click the **Numbering** arrow to display the Numbering gallery.

3. Make a new selection to change the style of the number that begins each item in the selected list.

To define a custom number style

1. In the **Numbering** gallery, click **Define New Number Format**.

2. In the **Define New Number Format** dialog box, do any of the following:

   - Change the selections in the **Number Style**, **Number Format**, or **Alignment** boxes.

   - Click the **Font** button, and make a selection from the wide range of options.

3. Click **OK** to apply the new numbering style to the list.

To start a list or part of a list at a predefined number

1. Place the cursor within an existing list, in the list paragraph whose number you want to set.

2. Display the **Numbering** gallery, and then click **Set Numbering Value** to open the Set Numbering Value dialog box.

3. Do either of the following to permit custom numbering:

   - Click **Start new list**.

   - Click **Continue from previous list**, and then select the **Advance value (skip numbers)** check box.

4. In the **Set value to** box, enter the number you want to assign to the list item. Then click **OK**.

You can start or restart a numbered list at any number

Format text as you type

The Word list capabilities are only one example of the app's ability to intuit how you want to format an element based on what you type. You can learn more about these and other AutoFormatting options by exploring the Auto-Correct dialog box, which you can open from the Proofing page of the Word Options dialog box.

The AutoFormat As You Type page shows the options Word implements by default, including bulleted and numbered lists.

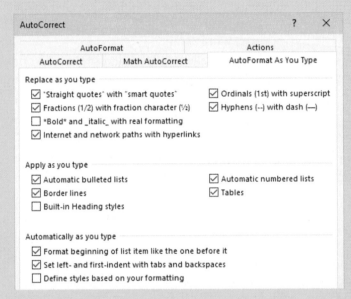

You can select and clear options to control automatic formatting behavior

One interesting option in this dialog box is Border Lines. When this check box is selected, typing three consecutive hyphens (-) or three consecutive under-scores (_) and pressing Enter draws a single line across the page. Typing three consecutive equal signs (=) draws a double line, and typing three consecutive tildes (~) draws a zigzag line.

Apply built-in styles to text

You don't have to know much about character and paragraph formatting to be able to format your documents in ways that will make them easier to read and more professional looking. With a couple of mouse clicks, you can easily change the look of words, phrases, and paragraphs by using styles. More importantly, you can build a document outline that is reflected in the Navigation pane and can be used to create a table of contents.

> **SEE ALSO** For information about tables of contents, see "Create and modify tables of contents" in Chapter 13, "Reference content and content sources," of *Microsoft Word 2016 Step by Step* by Joan Lambert (Microsoft Press, 2015).

Apply styles

Styles can include character formatting (such as font, size, and color), paragraph formatting (such as line spacing and outline level), or a combination of both. Styles are stored in the template that is attached to a document. By default, blank new documents are based on the Normal template. The Normal template includes a standard selection of styles that fit the basic needs of most documents. These styles include nine heading levels, various text styles including those for multiple levels of bulleted and numbered lists, index and table of contents entry styles, and many specialized styles such as those for hyperlinks, quotations, placeholders, captions, and other elements.

By default, most common predefined styles are available in the Styles gallery on the Home tab. You can add styles to the gallery or remove those that you don't often use.

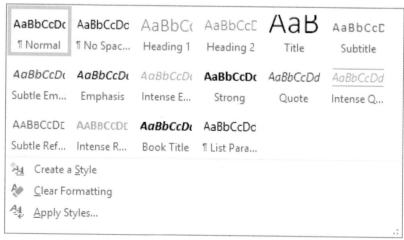

The Styles gallery in a new, blank document based on the Normal template

Styles stored in a template are usually based on the Normal style and use only the default body and heading fonts associated with the document's theme, so they all go together well. For this reason, formatting document content by using styles produces a harmonious effect. After you apply named styles, you can easily change the look of an entire document by switching to a different style set that contains styles with the same names but different formatting.

 SEE ALSO For information about document theme elements, see "Change the document theme," later in this chapter.

Style sets are available from the Document Formatting gallery on the Design tab.

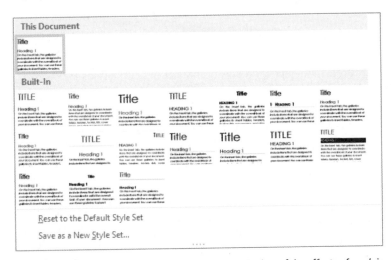

Pointing to a style set in the gallery displays a live preview of the effects of applying that style set to the entire document

✓ **TIP** Style sets provide a quick and easy way to change the look of an existing document. You can also modify style definitions by changing the template on which the document is based. For more information about styles and templates, see "Create custom styles and templates" in Chapter 15, "Work in Word more efficiently," of *Microsoft Word 2016 Step by Step* by Joan Lambert (Microsoft Press, 2015).

To open the Styles pane

1. On the **Home** tab, click the **Styles** dialog box launcher.

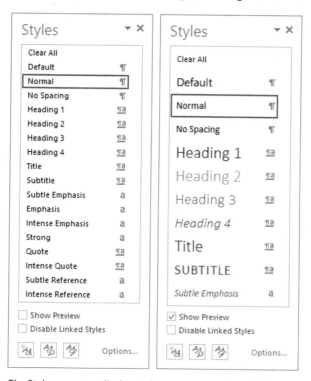

The Styles pane can display style names or previews of the styles

 TIP If the Styles pane floats above the page, you can drag it by its title bar to the right or left edge of the app window to dock it.

To change which styles are displayed in the Styles pane

1. Open the **Styles** pane, and then click **Options**.

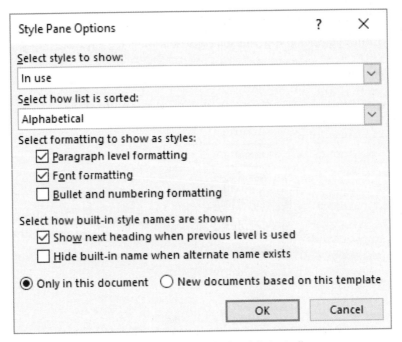

To make it easier to find specific styles, sort the list alphabetically

2. In the **Style Pane Options** dialog box, do any of the following, and then click **OK**:

    *   In the **Select styles to show** list, click one of the following:

        *   **Recommended** Displays styles that are tagged in the template as recommended for use

        *   **In use** Displays styles that are applied to content in the current document

        *   **In current document** Displays styles that are in the template that is attached to the current document

        *   **All styles** Displays built-in styles, styles that are in the attached template, and styles that were brought into the document from other templates

    *   In the **Select how list is sorted** list, click **Alphabetical**, **As Recommended**, **Font**, **Based on**, or **By type**

    *   In the **Select formatting to show as styles** area, select each check box for which you want to display variations from named styles

    *   In the **Select how built-in style names are shown** area, select the check box for each option you want to turn on

To display or hide style previews in the Styles pane

1. Open the **Styles** pane, and then select or clear the **Show Preview** check box.

To add a style to the Styles gallery

1. In the **Styles** pane, point to the style, click the arrow that appears, and then click **Add to Style Gallery**.

3

To remove a style from the Styles gallery

1. Do either of the following:

   - In the **Styles** pane, point to the style, click the arrow that appears, and then click **Remove from Style Gallery**.

   - In the **Styles** gallery, right-click the style, and then click **Remove from Style Gallery**.

To apply a built-in style

1. Select the text or paragraph to which you want to apply the style.

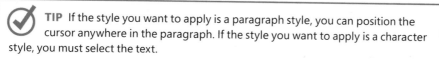

> **TIP** If the style you want to apply is a paragraph style, you can position the cursor anywhere in the paragraph. If the style you want to apply is a character style, you must select the text.

2. In the **Styles** gallery on the **Home** tab, or in the **Styles** pane, click the style you want to apply.

To change the style set

1. On the **Design** tab, in the **Document Formatting** group, click the **More** button if necessary to display all the style sets.

2. Point to any style set to preview its effect on the document.

3. Click the style set you want to apply.

Manage outline levels

Styles can be used for multiple purposes: to affect the appearance of the content, to build a document outline, and to tag content as a certain type so that you can easily locate it.

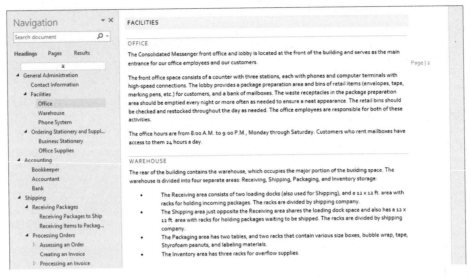

Heading styles define a document's outline

Each paragraph style has an associated Outline Level setting. Outline levels include Body Text and Level 1 through Level 9. (Most documents make use only of body text and the first three or four outline levels.)

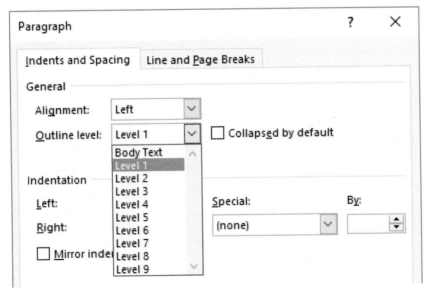

Most documents use only two to four of the outline levels

Paragraphs that have the Level 1 through Level 9 outline levels become part of the hierarchical structure of the document. They appear as headings in the Navigation pane and act as handles for the content that appears below them in the hierarchy. You can collapse and expand the content below each heading, and move entire sections of content by dragging the headings in the Navigation pane.

To display the document outline in the Navigation pane

1. In the **Navigation** pane, click **Headings** to display the document structure.

 TIP Only headings that are styled with the document heading styles appear in the Navigation pane.

To expand or collapse the outline in the Navigation pane

1. In the **Navigation** pane, do either of the following:

   - If there is a white triangle to the left of a heading, click it to expand that heading to show its subheadings.

   - If there is a downward-angled black triangle to the left of a heading, click it to collapse the subheadings under that heading.

 TIP If there is no triangle next to a heading, that heading does not have subheadings.

To expand or collapse sections in the document

1. In a document that contains styles, point to a heading to display a triangle to its left. Then do either of the following:

   - If the triangle is a downward-angled gray triangle, click the triangle to hide the content that follows the heading.

   - If the triangle is a white triangle, click the triangle to display the hidden document content.

Change the document theme

Every document you create is based on a template, and the look of the template is controlled by a theme. The theme is a combination of coordinated colors, fonts, and effects that visually convey a certain tone. To change the look of a document, you can apply a different theme from the Themes gallery.

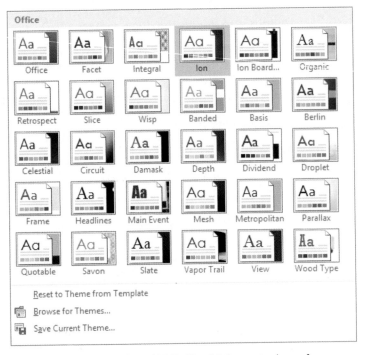

The default installation of Word 2016 offers 30 themes to choose from

Each theme has a built-in font set and color set, and an associated effect style.

- Each font set includes two fonts—the first is used for headings and the second for body text. In some font sets, the heading and body fonts are the same.

- Each color in a color set has a specific role in the formatting of styled elements. For example, the first color in each set is applied to the Title and Intense Reference styles, and different shades of the third color are applied to the Subtitle, Heading 1, and Heading 2 styles.

If you like the background elements of a theme but not the colors or fonts, you can mix and match theme elements.

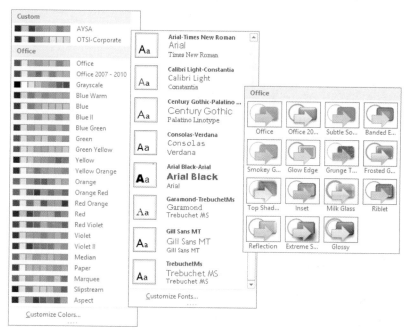

Word 2016 offers thousands of different combinations for creating a custom theme that meets your exact needs

>
> **TIP** In addition to colors and fonts, you can control the more subtle design elements, such as paragraph spacing and visual effects that are associated with a theme.

If you create a combination of theme elements that you would like to be able to use with other documents, you can save the combination as a new theme. By saving the theme in the default Document Themes folder, you make the theme available in the Themes gallery. However, you don't have to store custom themes in the Document Themes folder; you can store them anywhere on your hard disk, on removable media, or in a network location.

> ✅ **TIP** The default Document Themes folder is stored within your user profile. On a default freestanding installation, the folder is located at C:\Users\<*user name*>\AppData\Roaming\Microsoft\Templates\Document Themes. In a corporate environment with managed computer configurations, the user profile folder might be located elsewhere.

By default, Word applies the Office theme to all new, blank documents. In Word 2016, the Office theme uses a primarily blue palette, the Calibri font for body text, and Calibri Light for headings. If you plan to frequently use a theme other than the Office theme, you can make that the default theme.

> ✅ **TIP** If multiple people create corporate documents for your company, you can ensure that everyone's documents have a common look and feel by assembling a custom theme and making it available to everyone. Use theme elements that reflect your corporate colors, fonts, and visual style, and then save the theme to a central location or send the theme file by email and instruct your colleagues to save it to the default Document Themes folder.

To apply a built-in theme to a document

1. On the **Design** tab, in the **Document Formatting** group, click the **Themes** button, and then click the theme you want to apply.

> ✅ **TIP** If you have manually applied formatting to document content, the theme does not override the manual formatting. To ensure that all document elements are controlled by the theme, click Reset To The Default Style Set on the Document Formatting menu.

To change theme elements in a document

1. On the **Design** tab, in the **Document Formatting** group, do any of the following:

   - Click the **Colors** button (the ScreenTip says *Theme Colors*), and then click the color set you want to apply.

   - Click the **Fonts** button (the ScreenTip says *Theme Fonts*), and then click the font set you want to apply.

   - Click the **Effects** button (the ScreenTip says *Theme Effects*), and then click the effect style you want to apply.

To save a custom theme

1. Apply a base theme, and then modify the theme colors, fonts, and effects as you want them.

2. On the **Design** tab, in the **Document Formatting** group, click the **Themes** button.

3. At the bottom of the **Themes** menu, click **Save Current Theme** to display the contents of the Document Themes folder in the **Save Current Theme** dialog box.

4. In the **File name** box, replace the suggested name, and then click **Save**.

To apply a custom theme

1. Display the **Themes** menu. If you have created a custom theme, the Themes menu now includes a Custom area that contains your theme.

2. Click the theme to apply it to the document.

To change the default theme

1. In the document, apply the theme you want to use as the default theme.

2. On the **Design** tab, in the **Document Formatting** group, click **Set as Default**.

To apply a theme from a nonstandard location

1. On the **Design** tab, in the **Document Formatting** group, click the **Themes** button.

2. At the bottom of the **Themes** menu, click **Browse for Themes**.

3. In the **Choose Theme or Themed Document** dialog box, browse to the theme you want to apply, and then click **Open**.

To find the location of your Document Themes folder

1. On the **Design** tab, in the **Document Formatting** group, click the **Themes** button.

2. At the bottom of the **Themes** menu, click **Save Current Theme**.

3. In the **Save Current Theme** dialog box, click the icon at the left end of the address bar to display the full path to the Document Themes folder.

To delete a custom theme

1. Do either of the following:

   - Open File Explorer, browse to the **Document Themes** folder, and delete the theme file.

   - In Word, display the **Themes** menu, right-click the custom theme, and then click **Delete**.

   Note that the second method removes the theme choice from the gallery but does not remove the theme file from your Themes folder.

Skills review

In this chapter, you learned how to:

- Apply paragraph formatting

- Structure content manually

- Apply character formatting

- Create and modify lists

- Apply built-in styles to text

- Change the document theme

Practice tasks

The practice files for these tasks are located in the Office2016SBS\Ch03 folder. You can save the results of the tasks in the same folder.

Apply paragraph formatting

Open the FormatParagraphs document, display formatting marks, and then complete the following tasks:

1. Display the rulers and adjust the zoom level to display most or all of the paragraphs in the document.

2. Select the first two paragraphs (*Welcome!* and the next paragraph) and center them between the margins.

3. Select the second paragraph, and apply a first line indent.

4. Select the third paragraph and then apply the following formatting:

   - Format the paragraph so that the edges of the paragraph are flush against both the left and right margins.

   - Indent the paragraph by a half inch on the left and on the right.

5. Indent the *Be careful* paragraph by 0.25 inches.

6. Simultaneously select the *Pillows, Blankets, Towels, Limousine winery tour,* and *In-home massage* paragraphs. Change the paragraph spacing to remove the space after the paragraphs.

7. At the top of the document, apply an outside border to the *Please take a few minutes* paragraph.

8. Save and close the document.

Structure content manually

Open the StructureContent document, display formatting marks, and then complete the following tasks:

1. Display the rulers and adjust the zoom level to display most or all of the paragraphs in the document.

2. In the second paragraph (*We would like...*), insert a line break immediately after the comma and space that follow the word *cottage*.

3. Select the *Pillows*, *Blankets*, *Towels*, and *Dish towels* paragraphs. Insert a left tab stop at the **2** inch mark and clear any tab stops prior to that location.

4. In the *Pillows* paragraph, replace the space before the word *There* with a tab marker. Repeat the process to insert tabs in each of the next three paragraphs. The part of each paragraph that follows the colon is now aligned at the 2-inch mark, producing more space than you need.

5. Select the four paragraphs containing tabs, and then do the following:

    - Change the left tab stop from the **2** inch mark to the **1.25** inch mark.

    - On the ruler, drag the **Hanging Indent** marker to the tab stop at the **1.25** inch mark (the Left Indent marker moves with it) to cause the second line of the paragraphs to start in the same location as the first line. Then press the **Home** key to release the selection so you can review the results.

6. At the bottom of the document, select the three paragraphs containing dollar amounts, and then do the following:

    - Set a **Decimal Tab** stop at the **3** inch mark.

    - Replace the space to the left of each dollar sign with a tab to align the prices on the decimal points.

7. Hide the formatting marks to better display the results of your work.

8. Save and close the document.

Apply character formatting

Open the FormatCharacters document, and then complete the following tasks:

1. In the second bullet point, underline the word *natural*. Then repeat the formatting command to underline the word *all*, in the fourth bullet point.

2. In the fourth bullet point, click anywhere in the word *across*. Apply a thick underline to the word in a way that also assigns the **Thick underline** format to the **Underline** button. Then apply the thick underline to the word *departments*.

3. Select the *Employee Orientation* heading, and apply bold formatting to the heading.

4. Copy the formatting, and then paint it onto the *Guidelines* subtitle, to make the subtitle a heading.

5. Select the *Guidelines* heading, and apply the following formatting:

   - Change the font to **Impact**.

   - Set the font size to **20** points.

   - Apply the **Small caps** font effect.

   - Expand the character spacing by **10** points.

6. Change the font color of the words *Employee Orientation* to **Green, Accent 6**.

7. Select the *Community Service Committee* heading, and apply the following formatting:

   - Outline the letters in the same color you applied to *Employee Orientation*.

   - Apply an **Offset Diagonal Bottom Left** outer shadow. Change the shadow color to **Green, Accent 6, Darker 50%**.

   - Fill the letters with the **Green, Accent 6** color, and then change the text outline to **Green, Accent 6, Darker 25%**.

   You have now applied three text effects to the selected text by using three shades of the same green.

8. In the first bullet point, select the phrase *the concept of service* and apply a **Bright Green** highlight.

9. In the fifth bullet point, simultaneously select the words *brainstorming, planning,* and *leadership* and change the case of all the letters to uppercase.

10. Save and close the document.

Create and modify lists

Open the CreateLists document, display formatting marks and rulers, and then complete the following tasks:

1. Select the first four paragraphs below *The rules fall into four categories*. Format the selected paragraphs as a bulleted list. Then change the bullet character for the four list items to the one that is composed of four diamonds.

2. Select the two paragraphs below the *Definitions* heading. Format the selected paragraphs as a numbered list.

3. Select the first four paragraphs below the *General Rules* heading. Format the paragraphs as a second numbered list. Ensure that the new list starts with the number 1.

4. Format the next three paragraphs as a bulleted list. (Notice that Word uses the bullet symbol you specified earlier.) Indent the bulleted list so that it is a subset of the preceding numbered list item.

5. Format the remaining three paragraphs as a numbered list. Ensure that the list numbering continues from the previous numbered list.

6. Locate the *No large dogs* numbered list item. Create a new second-level numbered list item (a) from the text that begins with the word *Seeing*. Then create a second item (b) and enter **The Board reserves the right to make exceptions to this rule.**

7. Create a third list item (c). Promote the new list item to a first-level item, and enter **All pets must reside within their Owners' Apartments.** Notice that the *General Rules* list is now organized hierarchically.

8. Sort the three bulleted list items in ascending alphabetical order.

9. Save and close the document.

Apply built-in styles to text

Open the ApplyStyles document in Print Layout view, and then complete the following tasks:

1. Scroll through the document to gain an overview of its contents. Notice that the document begins with a centered title and subtitle, and there are several headings throughout.

2. Open the **Navigation** pane. Notice that the Headings page of the Navigation pane does not reflect the headings in the document, because the headings are formatted with local formatting instead of styles.

3. Open the **Styles** pane and dock it to the right edge of the app window.

4. Set the zoom level of the page to fit the page content between the Navigation pane and the Styles pane.

5. Apply the **Title** style to the document title, *All About Bamboo*.

6. Apply the **Subtitle** style to the *Information Sheet* paragraph.

7. Apply the **Heading 1** style to the first bold heading, *Moving to a New Home*. Notice that the heading appears in the Navigation pane.

8. Hide the content that follows the heading. Then redisplay it.

9. Apply the **Heading 1** style to *Staying Healthy*. Then repeat the formatting to apply the same style to *Keeping Bugs at Bay*.

10. Scroll the page so that both underlined headings are visible. Select the *Mites* and *Mealy Bugs* headings. Then simultaneously apply the **Heading 2** style to both selections.

11. Configure the **Styles** pane to display all styles, in alphabetical order.

12. In the **Navigation** pane, just above the headings, click the *Jump to the beginning* button to return to the document title.

13. In the first paragraph of the document, select the company name *Wide World Importers*, and apply the **Intense Reference** style.

14. In the second paragraph, near the end of the first sentence, select the word *clumping*, and apply the **Emphasis** style. Then, at the end of the sentence, apply the same style to the word *running*.

15. Close the **Navigation** pane and the **Styles** pane. Then configure the view setting to display both pages of the document in the window.

16. Apply the **Basic (Elegant)** style set to the document. Change the view to **Page Width** and notice the changes to the styled content.

17. Save and close the document.

Change the document theme

Open the ChangeTheme document, and then complete the following tasks:

1. Apply the **Facet** theme to the document.

2. Change the theme colors to the **Orange** color scheme.

3. Change the theme fonts to the **Georgia** theme set.

4. Save the modified theme in the default folder, as a custom theme named **My Theme**. Verify that the custom theme is available on the **Themes** menu.

5. Save and close the document.

Collaborate on documents

It's not unusual for several people to collaborate on the development of a document. Collaboration is simplest when contributors review electronic documents in files on a computer screen rather than paper printouts. On-screen review is very efficient; you can provide legible feedback, implement specific changes, and save trees at the same time.

One way to gather feedback from multiple reviewers is to send a file to each reviewer and then merge the reviewed versions into one file that displays all the changes for your review. If you save a file in a shared location, multiple people can review and edit the document at the same time. This highly efficient method of collaboration is called coauthoring.

Word 2016 has many tools that simplify document collaboration processes. You can make changes without deleting the original content, provide feedback in comments, and respond to comments and queries from other reviewers. To protect a document from unwanted changes, you can restrict the editing options so that Word tracks all changes, allows only certain types of changes, or doesn't allow changes at all.

This chapter guides you through procedures related to marking up and reviewing documents, comparing and merging document versions, restricting the changes that people can make to documents that you share with them, and coauthoring documents.

In this chapter

- Mark up documents
- Display and review document markup
- Compare and merge documents
- Control content changes
- Coauthor documents

Practice files

For this chapter, use the practice files from the Office2016SBS\Ch04 folder. For practice file download instructions, see the introduction.

Mark up documents

Comments and tracked changes are collectively referred to as *markup*.

Insert comments

A comment is a note that is attached to an anchor within the text. The anchor can be text or any type of object, or simply a location; wherever it is, Word displays the comment in the right margin of the document.

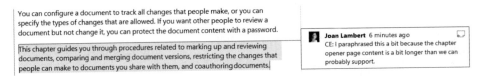

> You can configure a document to track all changes that people make, or you can specify the types of changes that are allowed. If you want other people to review a document but not change it, you can protect the document content with a password.
>
> This chapter guides you through procedures related to marking up and reviewing documents, comparing and merging document versions, restricting the changes that people can make to documents you share with them, and coauthoring documents.

Joan Lambert 6 minutes ago
CE: I paraphrased this a bit because the chapter opener page content is a bit longer than we can probably support.

Word automatically adds your name and a time stamp to the comment

Each comment is inside a container that is visible only when the comment is active (when you point to or click it). Comment containers are referred to as *balloons*. Balloons can be used for the display of various types of markup.

When comments are hidden, the hidden comments are indicated by conversation bubble icons.

This chapter guides you through procedures related to marking up and reviewing documents, comparing and merging document versions, restricting the changes that people can make to documents you share with them, and coauthoring documents.

The conversation bubble indicates a hidden comment

You can insert comments for many reasons, such as to ask questions, make suggestions, provide reference information, or explain edits. You insert and work with comments by using the commands in the Comments group on the Review tab.

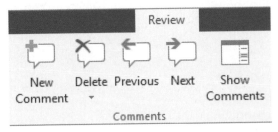

The commands in the Comments group make it easy to navigate through and remove comments

Multiple people can insert comments in a document. Word assigns a color to each person's comments and uses that color for the markup associated with comments, insertions, deletions, and formatting changes. (The color is assigned by user name, so if two people have the same user name their markup will be the same color.)

If you prefer to select specific colors and effects for comments and various types of markup, you can do so.

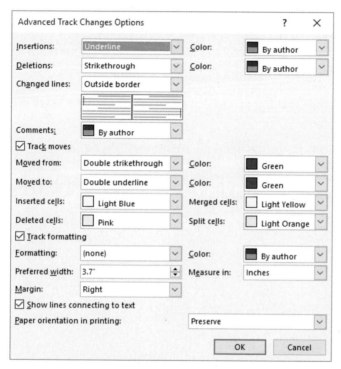

You can modify the types of changes that are tracked and the markup colors

Word uses standard colors to mark moved content and changes to table cells but doesn't track the editor, time, or date of the change. It is possible to customize these markup colors, but there really isn't any point to doing so because the custom colors won't travel with the document.

 TIP Display documents in Print Layout view so that all the collaboration commands are available.

To insert a comment

1. Select the text or object you want to anchor the comment to.

2. On the **Review** tab, in the **Comments** group, click the **New Comment** button.

3. In the comment balloon that appears in the right margin or in the **Revisions** pane, enter or paste your comment.

> **TIP** Comments are usually simple text but can include other elements and formatting such as images and active hyperlinks.

To specify the color of comments that you insert in any document

1. On the **Review** tab, click the **Tracking** dialog box launcher to open the **Track Changes Options** dialog box.

2. Click the **Advanced Options** button to open the **Advanced Track Changes Options** dialog box.

3. Click the arrow to the right of the **Comments** list to display a list of colors.

The named colors in the list are independent of the document color scheme and will not change between documents

4. In the **Comments** list, click the color you want to use for all the comments you insert in Word documents on the current computer.

5. Click **OK** in each open dialog box to close them and save your change.

Track changes

When two or more people collaborate on a document, one person usually creates and "owns" the document and the others review it, adding or revising content to make it more accurate, logical, or readable. When reviewing a document in Word, you can track your changes so they are available for review and retain the original text for comparison or reversion. You manage change tracking from the Tracking group on the Review tab.

4

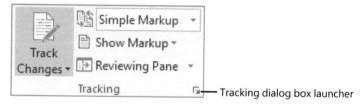

— Tracking dialog box launcher

A shaded button indicates that change tracking is active

> **TIP** Turning on the change tracking feature tracks changes in only the active document, not in any other open documents.

Word tracks insertions, deletions, movement, and formatting of content. When you display a document in All Markup view, tracked changes are indicated by different font colors and formatting. The default formatting is as follows:

- Insertions are underlined and in the color assigned to the reviewer.

- Deletions are crossed out and in the color assigned to the reviewer.

- Formatting changes appear in balloons in the markup area.

- Moves are double-underlined and green.

- All changes are marked in the left margin by a vertical line.

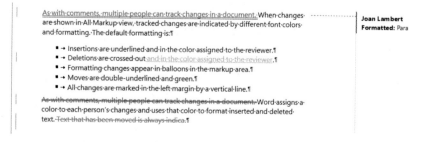

Moved text is green, and a double underline indicates its new location

As with comments, multiple people can track changes in a document. Word assigns a color to each person's changes and uses that color to format inserted and deleted text. If you prefer to select a color for your own changes, you can do so. You can also modify the formatting that indicates each type of change—for example, you could have Word indicate inserted text by formatting it as bold, italic, or with a double underline, but that change would be valid only for your profile on the computer you make the change on and would not affect the change formatting on other computers.

If you want to ensure that other reviewers track their changes to a document, you can turn on and lock the change-tracking feature and (optionally) require that reviewers enter a password to turn off change tracking.

 SEE ALSO For information about forcing change tracking by restricting editing, see "Control content changes" later in this chapter.

To turn change tracking on or off

1. Do either of the following:

   - On the **Review** tab, in the **Tracking** group, click the **Track Changes** button (not its arrow).

   - Press **Ctrl+Shift+E**.

 SEE ALSO For information about locking the change-tracking feature, see "Control content changes" later in this chapter.

To track changes without displaying them on the screen

1. On the **Review** tab, in the **Tracking** group, click the **Display for Review** arrow.

2. In the **Display for Review** list, click **Simple Markup** or **No Markup**.

 SEE ALSO For more information about the markup views, see "Display and review document markup" later in this chapter.

To specify the color of the changes you track in any document

1. On the **Review** tab, click the **Tracking** dialog box launcher to open the **Track Changes Options** dialog box.

2. Click the **Advanced Options** button to open the **Advanced Track Changes Options** dialog box.

3. In the **Color** lists adjacent to **Insertions**, **Deletions**, and **Formatting**, click the color you want to use for that type of change in Word documents on the current computer.

4. Click **OK** in each open dialog box to close them and save your changes.

To prevent reviewers from turning off change tracking

1. On the **Review** tab, in the **Tracking** group, click the **Track Changes** arrow, and then click **Lock Tracking**.

2. In the **Lock Tracking** dialog box, enter and reenter a password to prevent other people from turning off this feature.

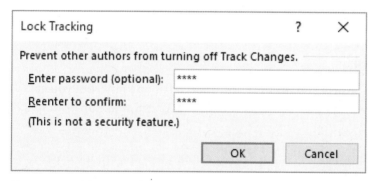

Use a password that you will remember, or make a note of it in a secure location so you can find it later

3. In the **Lock Tracking** dialog box, click **OK**.

121

To unlock change tracking

1. On the **Review** tab, in the **Tracking** group, click the **Track Changes** arrow, and then click **Lock Tracking**.

2. In the **Unlock Tracking** dialog box, enter the password you assigned when you enabled this feature, and then click **OK**.

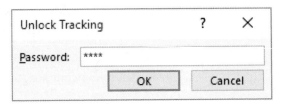

Unlocking tracking doesn't turn off change tracking; you must do that separately

Display and review document markup

After reviewers provide feedback by making changes and entering comments, you can review and process the tracked changes and comments.

Display markup

Usually you would display and review all the markup at one time, but you can also choose to display only certain types of markup, or only markup from specific reviewers.

Word 2016 has four basic Display For Review options that govern the display of tracked changes in a document. The settings are:

- **Simple Markup** This default markup view displays a red vertical line in the left margin adjacent to each tracked change. Markup is hidden.

- **All Markup** This view displays a gray vertical line in the left margin adjacent to each tracked change, and formats inserted, deleted, and moved content as configured in the Advanced Track Changes Options dialog box.

 SEE ALSO For information about controlling markup formatting, see "Mark up documents" earlier in this chapter.

- **No Markup** This view hides comments and displays the current document content as though all changes have been accepted. Changes that you make in this view are tracked (if change tracking is turned on) and visible when markup is shown.

- **Original** This view displays the original document content without any markup.

Depending on your view settings, comments are shown in the following ways:

- In balloons in the right margin

- Hidden and indicated by a comment icon in the right margin

- Hidden and indicated by highlighting in the text

You can click the comment icon or point to the highlight to display the comment text.

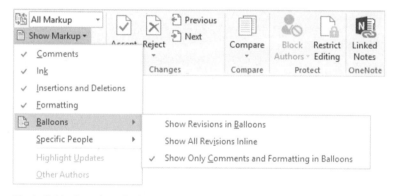

The individual markup display options

After you select a Display For Review option, you can additionally filter the display of markup in these ways:

- You can individually control the display of comments, insertions and deletions, and formatting.

- You can show all markup inline or in balloons, or keep comments in balloons and insertions, deletions, and moves inline.

- You can display or hide markup by reviewer.

If you prefer to display all the comments and tracked changes in a document at one time, you can do so in the Revisions pane. By default, this pane opens to the left of the document text (and to the right of the Navigation pane, if that is open) at the same height as the document content area. If you want to, you can dock it to the right side of the window instead.

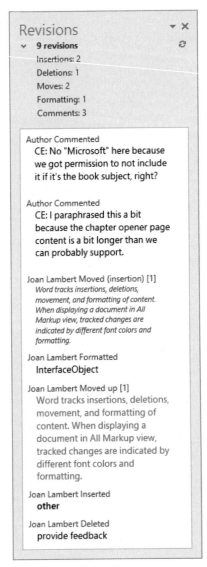

Information about the number and type of revisions is available at the top of the pane

From the ribbon, you can also display the Revisions pane horizontally. By default, the horizontal pane stretches across the bottom of the Word app window. If you want to, you can drag it to the top of the window.

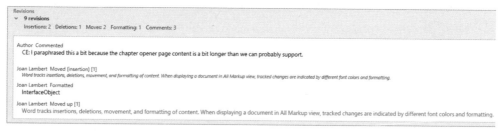

You can display the pane vertically or horizontally

When the Revisions pane is docked, the document content display area becomes narrower or shorter to make space for the pane. You can undock the pane so that it floats independently of the app window and doesn't decrease the content pane size. The floating pane has a vertical format, but you can change its height and width to fit wherever it's convenient.

The best display location depends on the amount of space you have available on your device screen.

To change the display of markup in a document

1. On the **Review** tab, in the **Tracking** group, click the **Display for Review** arrow.

2. In the **Display for Review** list, click **Simple Markup**, **All Markup**, **No Markup**, or **Original**.

Or

1. To switch between Simple Markup view and All Markup view, click the red or gray vertical line in the margin to the left of any tracked change.

To display specific types of markup in balloons

1. In the **Display for Review** list, click **All Markup**.

2. In the **Show Markup** list, click **Balloons**, and then click **Show Revisions in Balloons**, **Show All Revisions Inline**, or **Show Only Comments and Formatting in Balloons**.

To hide or display all markup of a specific type

1. On the **Review** tab, in the **Tracking** group, click the **Show Markup** button, and then click **Comments**, **Ink**, **Insertions and Deletions**, or **Formatting**.

 TIP A check mark to the left of a markup type indicates that elements of that type are visible in views of the document that display those elements.

To display only markup by a specific person

1. On the **Review** tab, in the **Tracking** group, click the **Show Markup** button.

2. In the **Show Markup** list, click **Specific People**, and then click the name of any reviewer whose comments you don't want to display.

To display individual comments in Simple Markup view

1. Do any of the following:

   - Click a comment icon to display the comments on that line in comment balloons.

   - Point to a comment icon to highlight the comments on that line in the colors associated with the comments' authors.

    TIP The reviewer name is taken from the user information stored with the user account. If you're signed in to Word with a Microsoft account, Word tracks revisions by the name associated with your Microsoft account. If the instance of Word you're working in is not linked to a Microsoft account, you can change the stored user information on the General page of the Word Options dialog box. Changing your user information affects revision tracking only when you aren't signed in with a Microsoft account.

   - Right-click highlighted, commented text, and then click **Edit Comment** to display only that comment in a comment balloon.

To display the Revisions pane

1. On the **Review** tab, in the **Tracking** group, click the **Reviewing Pane** button.

> **TIP** Clicking the button opens the Revisions pane in its most recent location. The default location in each new Word session is to the left of the page.

Or

1. In the **Tracking** group, click the **Reviewing Pane** arrow.

2. In the **Reviewing Pane** list, do either of the following:

   - Click **Reviewing Pane Vertical** to display the pane to the left or right of the document.

   - Click **Reviewing Pane Horizontal** to display the pane below the ribbon or above the status bar.

To change the location of the Revisions pane

1. Drag the pane by its header to any of the following locations:

   - Dock the pane vertically to the left or right side of the app window or against any other vertical pane,

   - Dock the pane horizontally below the ribbon or above the status bar.

   - Drag the pane inside or outside the app window to float it independently.

To change the width or height of the Revisions pane

1. Point to the right or top border of the pane.

2. When the pointer changes to a double-headed arrow, drag the border.

To display a breakdown of revision types

1. In the **Revisions** pane, to the left of the total number of revisions, click the **Expand** button (the caret symbol).

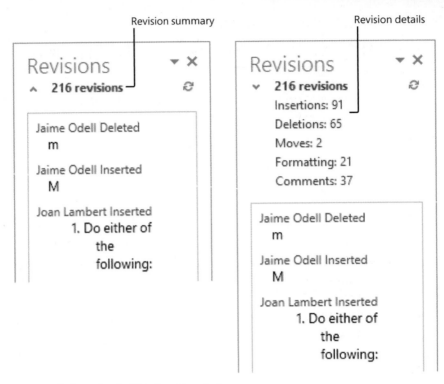

You can display a detailed list of revisions by type

To close the Revisions pane

1. Do either of the following:

   - In the upper-right corner of the pane, click the **Close** button.

   - On the **Review** tab, in the **Tracking** group, click the **Reviewing Pane** button.

Review and respond to comments

All the comments that are in a document are available for review, regardless of who created them. You can scroll through a document and review the comments as you come to them, or you can jump from comment to comment by clicking buttons on the ribbon.

> **TIP** If a document contains both comments and tracked changes, clicking the Next or Previous button in the Changes group on the Review tab moves sequentially among these elements, whereas clicking the Next or Previous button in the Comments group moves only among comments.

When reviewing comments, you can take the following actions:

- Respond to individual comments to provide further information or request clarification.

- Mark individual comments as Done to indicate that you've processed them, and retain them for later reference.

- Delete individual comments that you no longer require.

- Filter the comments by author and then delete all visible comments at the same time.

- Delete all comments in the document at the same time.

The purpose of each of these options is fairly clear. The ability to mark comments as Done was introduced in Word 2013 and is a useful feature, particularly if everyone on your review team is running Word 2013 or Word 2016. Marking a comment as Done leaves the comment intact but minimizes and recolors the comment elements so that it doesn't distract from the document content in the way that an active comment would.

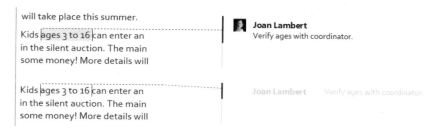

An example of a tracked comment before and after being marked as Done

To move among only comments

1. Do any of the following:

   - On the **Review** tab, in the **Comments** group, click the **Next** or **Previous** button to jump from balloon to balloon.

   - In the **Revisions** pane, click any comment to move to that comment in the document.

   - Scroll through the document to visually locate comment balloons.

To activate a comment for editing

1. Click the comment balloon.

2. Right-click the commented text, and then click **Edit Comment**.

To respond to a comment

1. In the upper-right corner of the comment balloon, click the **Reply to Comment** icon to create an indented response marked with your name and the time and date.

   Or

   Right-click the comment, and then click **Reply to Comment**.

2. Enter your additional comments, and then click away from the comment balloon to finish.

> **TIP** Word 2010 and earlier versions of Word will display your response in a separate comment balloon rather than in the original balloon.

To mark a comment as Done or reactivate a Done comment

1. Right-click the comment highlight (in the text) or balloon (in the margin), and then click **Mark Comment Done**.

To delete a comment

1. Do any of the following:

   - Click the comment balloon, and then click the **Delete** button in the **Comments** group.

   - Right-click the comment balloon, and then click **Delete Comment**.

   - Right-click the comment highlight (in the text), and then click **Delete Comment**.

Review and process tracked changes

As with comments, you can scroll through a document and review insertions, deletions, content moves, and formatting changes as you come to them, or you can jump from change to change by clicking buttons on the ribbon. You also have the option of accepting or rejecting multiple changes at the same time.

Here are the typical scenarios for reviewing and processing changes that you might consider:

- Display a document in Simple Markup view or No Markup view so you're viewing the final content. If you are happy with the document content in that view, accept all the changes at the same time.

- Display a document in All Markup view. Scan the individual changes visually. Individually reject any change that doesn't meet your requirements. As you complete the review of a section that meets your requirements, select the content of that section and approve all the changes within your selection.

- Display a document in All Markup view. Move to the first change. Accept or reject the change and move to the next. (You can perform both actions with one click.)

When reviewing tracked changes, you can take the following actions:

- Accept or reject individual changes.

- Select a section of content and accept or reject all changes therein at the same time.

- Filter the changes and then accept or reject all visible changes at the same time.

- Accept or reject all changes in the document at the same time.

To move among tracked changes and comments

1. Do either of the following:

   - On the **Review** tab, in the **Changes** group, click the **Next** or **Previous** button.

   - In the **Revisions** pane, click any comment to move to that comment in the document.

To display the time and author of a tracked change

1. Point to any revision in the text to display a ScreenTip identifying the name of the reviewer who made a specific change, and when the change was made.

To incorporate a selected change into the document and move to the next change

1. On the **Review** tab, in the **Changes** group, click the **Accept** button.

Or

1. On the **Review** tab, in the **Changes** group, click the **Accept** arrow.

2. In the **Accept** list, click **Accept and Move to Next**.

To incorporate a selected change into the document and remain in the same location

1. Do either of the following:

   - Right-click the change, and then click **Accept Deletion** or **Accept Insertion**.

   - On the **Review** tab, in the **Accept** list, click **Accept This Change**.

To remove the selected change, restore the original text, and move to the next change

1. Do either of the following:

   - On the **Review** tab, in the **Changes** group, click the **Reject** button.

   - On the **Review** tab, in the **Reject** list, click **Reject and Move to Next**.

To remove the selected change, restore the original text, and remain in the same location

1. On the **Review** tab, in the **Reject** list, click **Reject This Change**.

To accept or reject all the changes in a section of text

1. Select the text.

2. Do either of the following:

   - On the **Review** tab, in the **Changes** group, click the **Accept** button or the **Reject** button.

   - Right-click the selected text, and then click **Accept Deletion** or **Reject Deletion**.

To accept or reject all the changes in a document

1. Do either of the following:

   - On the **Review** tab, in the **Accept** list, click **Accept All Changes**.

   - On the **Review** tab, in the **Reject** list, click **Reject All Changes**.

To accept or reject all the changes of a certain type or from a certain reviewer

1. Configure the review display settings to display only the changes you want to accept or reject.

2. Do either of the following:

   - On the **Review** tab, in the **Accept** list, click **Accept All Changes Shown**.

   - On the **Review** tab, in the **Reject** list, click **Reject All Changes Shown**.

Remember to check for errors

It's a good idea to check for spelling issues in a document after you finish processing changes because it's easy to accidentally end up with a missing or extra space in the document. If the Check Spelling As You Type option is on (as it is by default), you can scroll through the document and visually scan for wavy red underlines that indicate suspected spelling errors or wavy blue underlines that indicate suspected grammar errors. Or to be entirely thorough, you can run the Spelling & Grammar tool and respond to each issue it identifies.

SEE ALSO For more information about checking spelling and grammar, see "Locate and correct text errors" in Chapter 12, "Finalize and distribute documents," of *Microsoft Word 2016 Step by Step* by Joan Lambert (Microsoft Press, 2015).

Compare and merge documents

Sometimes you might want to compare several versions of the same document. Word supports two types of document version comparison:

- Comparing a document to a separate copy of the document

- Comparing a document to a previous version of the same document

Compare and combine separate copies of a document

If you have sent a document out for soft-copy review by several colleagues, you might want to compare their edited versions with the original document. Or if you've made changes to a document and want to compare it to a previous version of the document, you can do so.

Instead of comparing multiple open documents visually, you can tell Word to compare the documents and merge the changes into one document. From within that one document, you can view all the changes from all the reviewers or view only those from a specific reviewer.

When you compare documents, Word generates a composite document in the center pane and displays the two original documents on the right. Differences between the documents, and changes that were tracked in either original document, are shown as tracked changes in the composite document and in the Revisions pane.

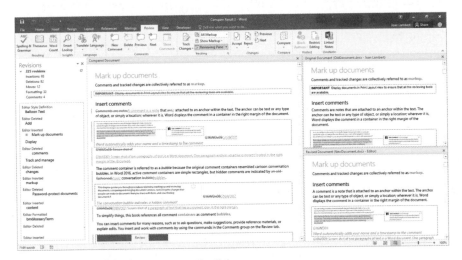

Scrolling any one of the documents scrolls all three

 TIP Word can't compare or combine documents that have Protection turned on.

You can compare any two documents. To compare multiple edited documents to one original, combine all the edited documents and then compare them with the original.

To compare or combine two documents and annotate changes

1. Start from a blank document or any existing document.

2. On the **Review** tab, in the **Compare** group, click **Compare** to track changes from only one document or **Combine** to track changes from both documents.

3. In the **Compare Documents** or **Combine Documents** dialog box, under **Original document**, click the arrow to expand the list. The list contains files you've recently worked with listed in alphabetical order.

4. If the document you want to designate as the first document appears in the list, click it. If not, click **Browse** (the first item in the list) to display the **Open** dialog box. In the dialog box, navigate to the document you want, click it, and then click **Open**.

5. Use the same technique in the **Revised document** area to select the document you want to designate as the second document.

6. In the **Label changes with** box or boxes, enter the name or names you want Word to assign as the reviewer when marking differences between the documents.

> **TIP** When comparing documents, you specify the reviewer for only the revised document; when combining documents, you specify reviewers for both documents.

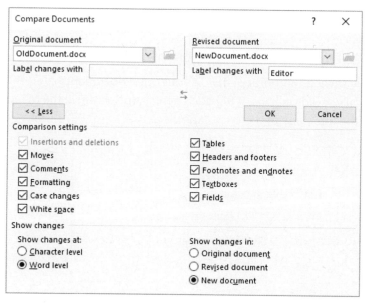

You can indicate what types of differences to identify and how to label them

7. If the dialog box doesn't include the **Comparison settings** and **Show changes** areas, click the **More** button to display them.

8. In the **Comparison settings** area of the dialog box, select the check boxes of the content differences you want to annotate.

> **TIP** By default, Word marks changes at the word level in a new document. You have the option to show changes at the character level and to show them in one of the two documents rather than in a third document. Until you're comfortable with the compare and combine operations, it's safest to retain the default settings in the Show Changes area.

9. In the **Compare Documents** or **Combine Documents** dialog box, click **OK** to create the combined document and display the combined and original documents.

> **TIP** If you compare documents that contain conflicting formatting, a message box will ask you to confirm which document's formatting should be used.

> **IMPORTANT** If the Revisions pane does not open, click the Reviewing Pane button in the Tracking group on the Review tab. If the source documents are not displayed, click the Compare button, click Show Source Documents, and then click Show Both.

Compare separate versions of a document

Word automatically saves a temporary copy of your open documents every 10 minutes. Automatically saved versions of the document are displayed in the Manage Document area of the Info page of the Backstage view.

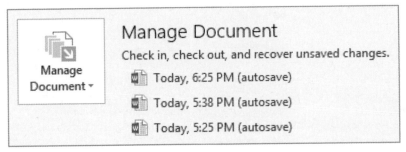

The ability to look back at an earlier version of a document you've heavily revised can come in handy

To display a previous version of a document

1. On the **Info** page of the Backstage view, in the **Manage Document** list, click the version you want to display.

To compare a document to a previous version

1. Display the previous version of the document.

2. On the information bar at the top of the previous version, click the **Compare** button.

To roll back to a previous version of a document

1. Display the previous version of the document.

2. On the information bar at the top of the previous version, click the **Revert** button.

To change how often Word automatically saves document recovery versions

1. Display the **Save** page of the **Word Options** dialog box.

2. In the **Save AutoRecover information every** box, enter the number of minutes Word should allow to pass before saving a recovery version of the document.

3. Click **OK** to close the dialog box.

Control content changes

Sometimes you'll want people to be able to display the contents of a document but not make changes to it. Other times you'll want to allow changes, but only of certain types, or only if they're tracked for your review. This section includes information about ways that you can protect the content of a document.

> **TIP** When considering content protection options, keep in mind that storing documents within a document management system that has version control can save you a lot of trouble. Word 2016 includes a built-in version tracking system that you can use to compare and restore previous versions of a document that are stored on your computer. Microsoft SharePoint document libraries provide access to previous versions of documents checked in by any team member. (At the time of this writing, SharePoint Online document libraries default to tracking 500 versions of each document.)

Restrict actions

To prevent people from introducing inconsistent formatting or unwanted changes into a document, you can restrict the types of changes that an individual document permits, in the following ways:

- **Restrict formatting** You can limit formatting changes to a specific list of styles that you select, or to the "recommended minimum" style set, which consists of all the styles needed by Word for features such as tables of contents. (The recommended minimum set doesn't necessarily include all the styles used in the document.) Restricting formatting prevents anyone from adding or applying styles that you don't want to have in your document.

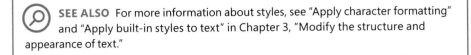

> **SEE ALSO** For more information about styles, see "Apply character formatting" and "Apply built-in styles to text" in Chapter 3, "Modify the structure and appearance of text."

- **Restrict editing** You can limit changes to comments, tracked changes, or form field content, or you can permit no changes at all.

You can implement these types of restrictions from the Restrict Editing pane.

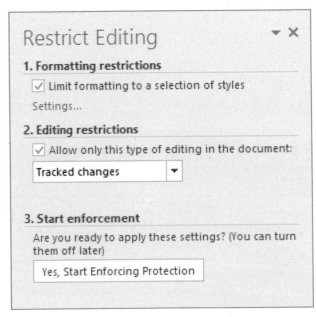

You can restrict formatting so that other people don't make unapproved content or formatting changes

SEE ALSO For information about locking change tracking without restricting editing, see "Track changes" earlier in this chapter.

When restrictions are turned on, the Restrict Editing pane provides information about the actions you can perform in the document. Ribbon buttons that apply restricted formats are unavailable (grayed out).

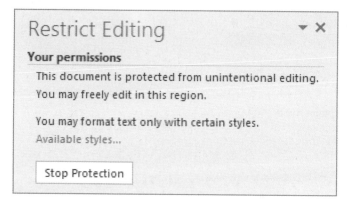

The pane reflects the specific formatting restrictions in place

To display the Restrict Editing pane

1. Do either of the following:

    *   On the **Info** page of the Backstage view, click the **Protect Document** button, and then click **Restrict Editing**.

    *   On the **Review** tab or **Developer** tab, in the **Protect** group, click the **Restrict Editing** button.

To restrict the styles permitted in a document

1. Display the **Restrict Editing** pane.

2. In the **Formatting restrictions** area of the **Restrict Editing** pane, select the **Limit formatting to a selection of styles** check box, and then click **Settings** to display the **Formatting Restrictions** dialog box.

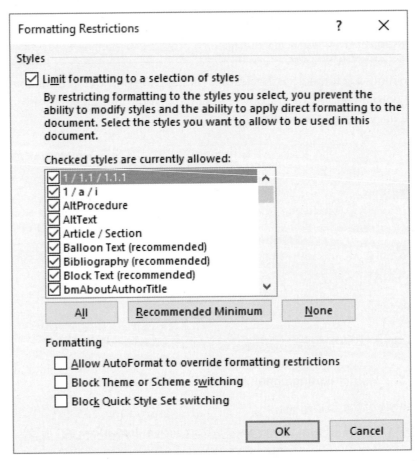

The Allow AutoFormat option permits Word to apply automatic formatting, such as list formatting

3. Select the permitted styles by doing one of the following:

   - To allow only the recommended minimum style set, click the **Recommended Minimum** button.

   - To allow only specific styles, click the **None** button and then, in the **Checked styles are currently allowed** list box, select the check boxes of the styles you want to allow.

   - To allow all styles and restrict only formatting, click the **All** button.

4. Select the permitted formatting by doing any of the following:

- To permit Word to automatically format elements such as hyperlinks, bulleted lists, and numbered lists that aren't specified by a style, select the **Allow AutoFormat to override formatting restrictions** check box.

- To permit only the current document theme, theme colors, and theme fonts, select the **Block Theme or Scheme switching** check box.

- To permit only the current style set, select the **Block Quick Style Set switching** check box.

5. Click **OK** to implement the restricted set of styles. Word displays a message warning you that restricted styles will be removed.

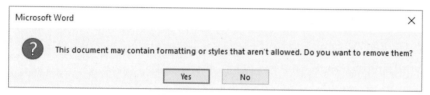

Word displays this warning regardless of whether the document contains restricted styles

6. In the message box, click **Yes** to remove any restricted formatting and revert restricted styles to Normal.

7. In the **Start enforcement** area of the **Restrict Editing** pane, click **Yes, Start Enforcing Protection** to open the **Start Enforcing Protection** dialog box.

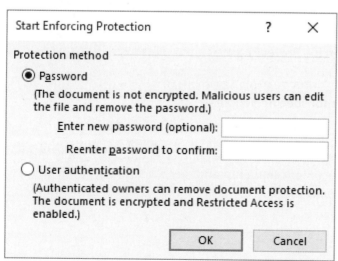

People who don't know the password can't turn off the restrictions

8. If you want to require a password to turn off the restrictions, enter the password in the **Enter new password** and **Reenter password to confirm** boxes. Otherwise, leave the boxes blank.

9. In the **Start Enforcing Protection** dialog box, click **OK** to turn on the restrictions.

To restrict the editing permitted in a document

1. Display the **Restrict Editing** pane.

2. In the **Editing restrictions** area of the pane, select the **Allow only this type of editing in the document** check box.

3. In the **Allow only this type of editing in the document** list, click one of the following:

   - Tracked changes

   - Comments

   - Filling in forms

   - No changes (Read only)

4. In the **Start enforcement** area of the **Restrict Editing** pane, click the **Yes, Start Enforcing Protection** button to open the **Start Enforcing Protection** dialog box.

5. If you want to require a password to turn off the restrictions, enter the password in the **Enter new password** and **Reenter password to confirm** boxes. Otherwise, leave the boxes blank.

6. In the **Start Enforcing Protection** dialog box, click **OK** to turn on the restrictions.

To remove restrictions for specific people

1. Display the **Restrict Editing** pane.

2. In the **Editing restrictions** area of the pane, select the **Allow only this type of editing in the document** check box and then select the type of editing you want to permit for all users.

3. In the document, select the content that you want to permit a specific person or specific people to freely edit.

4. In the **Exceptions** area, if the **Groups** or **Individuals** box does NOT list the people or person you want to permit to edit the selection, do the following:

    a. Click the **More users** link to display the **Add Users** dialog box.

    b. Enter the user credentials of the person or people you want to allow to freely edit the selection.

When granting restriction exceptions to multiple people, separate the entries by using semicolons

    c. In the **Add Users** dialog box, click **OK**.

5. In the **Exceptions** area, select the check box that precedes each group or person you want to permit to edit the selection.

6. If you want to permit the editing of additional sections of content, repeat steps 3 through 5.

7. In the **Start enforcement** area of the **Restrict Editing** pane, click the **Yes, Start Enforcing Protection** button to open the **Start Enforcing Protection** dialog box shown in the earlier procedure to restrict the styles permitted in a document.

8. In the **Start Enforcing Protection** dialog box, click **User authentication**, and then click **OK** to turn on the restrictions.

To remove editing and formatting restrictions

1. Display the **Restrict Editing** pane.

2. At the bottom of the pane, click the **Stop Protection** button.

3. The **Unprotect Document** dialog box opens regardless of whether a password is required.

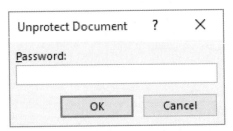

When protecting a document, always use a password you can remember, because it can't be reset

4. In the **Unprotect Document** dialog box, enter a password in the **Password** box if one is required. Otherwise, leave the **Password** box blank. Then click **OK** to remove the restrictions.

Restrict access by using a password

Sometimes, you might want only certain people to be able to open and change a document. The simplest way to do this for an individual document is to assign a password to protect the file so that a person who wants to modify the document must enter a password when opening it to permit changes.

You can assign a password to a document while working in the document or when saving the document. Word offers two levels of password protection:

- **Encrypted** The document is saved in such a way that people who do not know the password cannot open it at all.

- **Unencrypted** The document is saved in such a way that only people who know the password can open it, make changes, and save the file. People who don't know the password can open a read-only version. If they make changes and want to save them, they have to save the document with a different name or in a different location, preserving the original.

Assigning a password to open a document encrypts the document; assigning a password to modify the document does not encrypt it

> **IMPORTANT** Don't use common words or phrases as passwords, and don't use the same password for multiple documents. After assigning a password, make a note of it in a safe place. If you forget it, you won't be able to open the password-protected document.

To recommend against changes to a document

1. Display the **Save As** page of the Backstage view.

2. Using locations in the Places list, the current folder, or recent folders as a starting point, navigate to the folder you want to save the document in. If necessary, click **Browse** to display the **Save As** dialog box.

3. If you want to protect a copy of the document instead of the original, enter a name for the copy in the **File name** box.

4. Near the lower-right corner of the **Save As** dialog box, click the **Tools** button. Then in the **Tools** list, click **General Options**.

5. In the **General Options** dialog box, select the **Read-only recommended** check box, and then click **OK**.

To prevent unauthorized changes by setting a password

1. On the **Save As** page of the Backstage view, navigate to the folder you want to save the password-protected document in. If necessary, click **Browse** to display the **Save As** dialog box.

2. If you want to protect a copy of the document instead of the original, enter a name for the copy in the **File name** box.

3. Near the lower-right corner of the **Save As** dialog box, click the **Tools** button. Then in the **Tools** list, click **General Options**.

4. In the **General Options** dialog box, enter the password you want to assign to the document in the **Password to modify** box. Then click **OK** to display the **Confirm Password** dialog box.

> **TIP** As you enter the password, Word obscures it for security.

5. Enter the same password in the **Reenter password to modify** box, and then click **OK** to set the password.

6. In the **Save As** dialog box, click **Save**. If Word prompts you to overwrite the original document, click **Yes**.

To test the security of a password-protected document

1. Open the document and verify that Word displays the **Password** dialog box.

You can open a read-only version of an unencrypted document but must enter the password to open an encrypted document

2. Enter an incorrect password, click **OK**, and verify that Word denies you access to the document.

To open a password-protected document for reading

1. Open the document.

2. In the **Password** dialog box, click the **Read Only** button to open a read-only version of the document.

TIP When using the default settings, Word opens the document in Read Mode.

To open a password-protected document for editing

1. Open the document.

2. In the **Password** dialog box, enter the password that you assigned to the document, and then click **OK** to open a read/write version of the document.

To remove password protection from an unencrypted document

1. On the **Save As** page of the Backstage view, in the **Current Folder** area, click the current folder.

2. At the bottom of the **Save As** dialog box, in the **Tools** list, click **General Options**.

3. In the **General Options** dialog box, select the contents of the **Password to modify** box, press **Delete**, and then click **OK**.

4. In the **Save As** dialog box, click **Save**.

To prevent document access by setting a password

1. Display the **Info** page of the Backstage view.

2. Click the **Protect Document** button, and then click **Encrypt with Password**.

After you assign the password, you will no longer be able to open the document without it

3. In the **Encrypt Document** dialog box, enter the password you want to assign in the **Password** box, and then click **OK**.

4. In the **Confirm Password** dialog box, enter the same password in the **Password** box, and then click **OK**.

The protected status of the document is displayed on the Info page of the Backstage view

5. Close the document and save your changes.

Or

1. On the **Save As** page of the Backstage view, navigate to the folder you want to save the password-protected document in. If necessary, click **Browse** to display the **Save As** dialog box.

2. If you want to make a password-protected copy of the document, enter a name for the copy in the **File name** box.

3. Near the lower-right corner of the **Save As** dialog box, click the **Tools** button. Then in the **Tools** list, click **General Options**.

4. In the **General Options** dialog box, enter the password you want to assign to the document in the **Password to open** box. Then click **OK** to display the **Confirm Password** dialog box.

5. Enter the same password in the **Reenter password to modify** box, and then click **OK** to set the password.

6. In the **Save As** dialog box, click **Save**. If Word prompts you to overwrite the original document, click **Yes**.

To remove password encryption from a document

1. Open the document and enter the correct password.

2. On the **Info** page of the Backstage view, in the **Protect Document** list, click **Encrypt with Password**.

3. In the **Encrypt Document** dialog box, delete the password from the **Password** box, and then click **OK**.

Restrict access by using rights management

If information rights management (IRM) is configured on your computer, you can control who can view and work with the documents you create. If you have this capability, a Restrict Permission By People option appears in the Protect Document list on the Info page of the Backstage view. Clicking Restrict Permission By People and then Restricted Access displays the Permission dialog box. In this dialog box, you can click Restrict Permission To This Document and then allow specific people to perform specific tasks, such as opening, printing, saving, or copying the document. When this protection is in place, other people cannot perform these tasks. The assigned permissions are stored with the document and apply no matter where the file is stored.

Before you can work on a document to which access has been restricted, you must verify your credentials with a licensing server. You can then download a use license that defines the tasks you are authorized to perform with the document. You need to repeat this process with each restricted document.

IMPORTANT To restrict permissions, your computer must be configured for IRM with a digital certificate that validates your identity. After you configure your computer for IRM, the Protect Document list on the Info page of the Backstage view includes a Restrict Permission By People option.

Coauthor documents

Whether you work for a large organization or a small business, you might need to collaborate with other people on the development of a document. No matter what the circumstances are, it can be difficult to keep track of different versions of a document produced by different people. If you store a document in a shared location such as a SharePoint document library or Microsoft OneDrive folder, multiple people can edit the document simultaneously.

After you save a document to a shared location, you can open and edit the document that is stored on the site just as you would if it were stored on your computer. Other people can also open and edit the document either by browsing to it or from an invitation that you send. This facilitates efficient collaboration between people regardless of location, schedule, or time zone.

When other people open a shared file for editing, Word alerts you by updating the Share button label on the ribbon and in the Share pane.

Dozens of people can work in a document at the same time

Word keeps track of the content that people are editing and locks paragraphs until the changes are shared to other editors. You can choose to automatically share your changes, or share them only when you save the document.

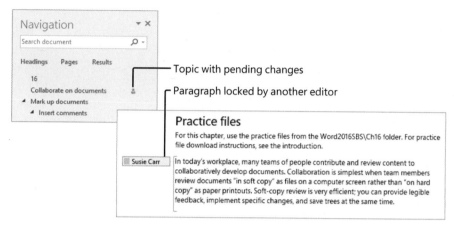

Word indicates the areas of the document that are being edited

If each person working in the document tracks his or her changes, the tracked changes remain available so that the document owner can accept or reject changes when the team has finished working on the document.

To make a document available for coauthoring

1. Save the document to a SharePoint document library or OneDrive folder.

To begin coauthoring a document

1. If the document is stored in a SharePoint document library, do NOT check it out.

2. Open the document directly from the document library or OneDrive folder.

3. Edit the document as you would normally.

To display the Share pane

1. Do either of the following:

   - Click the **Share** button located at the right end of the ribbon.

   - On the **Share** page of the Backstage view, click the **Share with People** button.

To invite other people to edit a shared document

1. Display the **Share** pane.

2. In the **Invite people** box, enter the names or email addresses of the people you want to send a document link to.

3. In the message box, enter any specific message you want to include in the sharing invitation.

4. Click the **Share** button to send an email message that contains a link to the document.

To identify areas locked by other reviewers

1. Display the **Navigation** pane.

2. Scan the **Navigation** pane for icons.

Or

1. Scan the left margin of the document for nametags and paragraph selection brackets.

To display changes made by coauthors

1. Do either of the following:

   - Save the document.

   - On the status bar, click the **Updates Available** button.

The Updates Available button appears on the status bar when other editors save changes

To configure Word to quickly make your changes available to coauthors

1. Display the **Share** pane.

2. In the **Automatically share changes** list, click **Always**.

Or

1. Display the **General** page of the **Word Options** dialog box.

2. In the **Real-time collaboration options** area, in the **When working with others...** list, click **Always**.

> **Real-time collaboration options**
>
> When working with others, I want to automatically share my changes: [Always ⌄]
>
> ☑ Show names on presence flags

If you want to see only that someone is working within a section but don't need to know who, you can clear the Show Names On Presence Flags check box

3. In the **Word Options** dialog box, click **OK**.

Skills review

In this chapter, you learned how to:

- Mark up documents
- Display and review document markup
- Compare and merge documents
- Control content changes
- Coauthor documents

4

Practice tasks

The practice files for these tasks are located in the Office2016SBS\Ch04 folder. You can save the results of the tasks in the same folder.

Mark up documents

Open the TrackChanges document in Word, display the document in Print Layout view, and then perform the following tasks:

1. Turn on change tracking.

2. In the last column of the table, select the words *some good*, and then attach the comment **They carry the new Ultra line.**

3. Configure the review settings to display the All Markup view of changes and to display only comments and formatting in balloons.

4. If necessary, scroll the document to display the table. Perform these tasks in the **Fabrikam** row of the table:

    - In the **Prices** column, delete the word *much* from the phrase *Some much lower.*

    - In the **Service** column, insert **but slow** after the word *Adequate*.

5. Perform these tasks in the **Northwind Traders** row of the table:

    - In the **Quality** column, replace the word *Poor* with **Substandard**.

    - Point to the deleted word and then to the inserted word to display information about the changes in ScreenTips.

6. Configure the review settings to display revisions in balloons instead of inline.

7. Restore the inline revision indicators and remove the balloons.

8. Move the last sentence in the paragraph to the beginning of the paragraph.

9. Turn off change tracking.

10. Configure the review settings to display the Simple Markup view.

11. Save and close the document.

Display and review document markup

Open the ReviewComments document in Word, display the document in Print Layout view, and then perform the following tasks:

1. Configure the review settings to display the **Simple Markup** view of changes.

2. Display only revisions made by Mike Nash.

3. Use the **Next Comment** button to move to the first comment shown in the document, which is attached to the word *competitors*. Delete the comment.

4. Move to the second comment, which is attached to the word *Adequate* in the **Service** column of the table. Point to the word in the table to display a Screen-Tip that contains the name of the person who inserted the comment and the date and time the comment was inserted. Notice that the ScreenTip displays more information than the comment bubble.

5. Click the **Reply to Comment** button in the second comment bubble. In the reply box, enter If you had been a real customer, would you have left?

6. Display the **Revisions** pane on the left side of the app window. Then drag the pane away from the side of the window so that it floats independently.

7. In the **Revisions** pane, expand the detailed summary of revisions and note the types of revisions in the document.

8. Configure the review settings to display revisions made by all reviewers.

9. Scroll through the revisions in the pane, and then close it.

10. Configure the review settings to display the **All Markup** view of changes.

11. Hide all comments in the document.

12. Move between the tracked changes in the document. Accept all the changes in the text paragraph. Process the changes in the table as follows:

    - Reject the table formatting change.

    - Accept the deletion of the word *much*.

    - Reject the changes associated with the addition of the words *but slow*.

    - Accept both of the changes associated with the replacement of *Poor* with *Substandard*.

13. Configure the review settings to display the **No Markup** view of changes. Then change the balloon setting to the one you like best.

14. Save and close the document.

Compare and merge documents

Open a new, blank document in Word, and then perform the following tasks:

1. Compare the MergeDocs1 and MergeDocs2 documents, by using the following settings:

   - Label unmarked changes from MergeDocs2 with your name.

   - Select all available comparison settings.

   - Mark the differences in a separate document.

2. When Word completes the comparison, ensure that the **Revisions** pane is open on the left, the merged document in the center, and the two original documents on the right.

   > **TIP** If the Revisions pane is not open, click the Reviewing Pane button in the Tracking group on the Review tab. If the source documents are not displayed, click the Compare button, click Show Source Documents, and then click Show Both.

3. In the center pane, scroll through the document to review all the revisions, and then in the **Revisions** pane, scroll through the individual revisions.

   Before changes can be accepted in the document, conflicting changes must be resolved.

4. In the **Revisions** pane, locate the deleted instance of *March* and then accept the deletion.

5. Click each change that remains in the **Revisions** pane to display that location in the three document panes.

6. Click the merged document in the center pane to activate it. Then accept all the changes in the document at the same time.

7. Close the **Revisions** pane, and then close the two windows on the right side of the screen.

8. Save the merged document as **MyMergedDocument**, and then close it.

Control content changes

Open the ControlChanges document, and then complete the following tasks:

1. Save a copy of the document, naming the copy **MyControlChanges**, and require the password **P@ssw0rd1** to modify the document but no password to read the document.

2. Configure the document options to recommend that people open a read-only copy of the document.

3. Close the document, and then open a read-only version of it.

4. Attempt to make a change and verify that you can't save the changed document.

5. Close the document, and then use the password to open an editable version of it.

6. Remove the password protection from the document.

7. Encrypt the document and require the password **P@ssw0rd2** to open it.

8. Restrict the formatting in the document to only the recommended minimum styles.

9. Block users from switching schemes or style sets.

10. Turn on the restrictions and remove any formatting and styles that don't meet the requirements you selected. Notice the changes to the document.

11. Configure the editing restrictions so that you can edit only the first paragraph of the document but other people aren't permitted to make any changes.

12. Save and close the document.

Coauthor documents

There is no practice task for this topic because it requires that documents be stored in a shared location.

Merge data with documents and labels

5

Many organizations communicate with customers or members by means of letters, newsletters, and promotional pieces that are sent to everyone on a mailing list. You can use a reasonably simple process called *mail merge* to easily insert specific information from a data source into a Word document to create personalized individual items such as form letters, labels, envelopes, or email messages. You can also use this process to create a directory, catalog, or other listing that incorporates information from the data source.

The primary requirement for a mail merge operation is a well-structured data source. You can pull information from a variety of data sources—even your Outlook address book—and merge it with a starting document or a content template to create the output you want. Word has a wizard that can guide you through the processes, but this chapter provides information about each of the individual processes so you can quickly get started with your merging projects.

This chapter guides you through procedures related to choosing and refining data sources, choosing the output type and starting documents, previewing the results and completing the merge, and creating individual envelopes and labels.

In this chapter

- Understand the mail merge process
- Start the mail merge process
- Choose and refine the data source
- Insert merge fields
- Preview and complete the merge
- Create individual envelopes and labels

Practice files

For this chapter, use the practice files from the Office2016SBS\Ch05 folder. For practice file download instructions, see the introduction.

Understand the mail merge process

The process for creating a mail merge document is quite straightforward and logical. All the tools for performing mail merge operations are available from the Mailings tab. From this tab, you can run the wizard or perform individual steps of the mail merge process on your own.

Mail merge tools are located on the Mailings tab

Three important terms that are used when discussing mail merge processes are:

- **Data source** The file or storage entity that contains the variable information you want to pull into the merge output.

- **Field** A specific category of information, such as a first name, last name, birthdate, customer number, item number, or price.

- **Record** A set of the information that goes in the fields; for example, information about a specific person or transaction. A record doesn't have to contain information for every field, but it must have a placeholder for any missing information.

The mail merge process varies slightly depending on whether you're creating one document per record or one document containing all the records. However, the basic process is this:

1. Identify a data source that contains the records you want to use.

2. Create a document into which you want to merge the records.

3. In the document, identify the fields from the data source that you want to merge into the document.

4. Preview the results and make any necessary adjustments.

5. Merge the data into the document to either create one or more new documents or to print the merge results directly to the printer.

You can perform the mail merge process by using the commands on the Mailings tab of the ribbon, or you can get step-by-step guidance from the Mail Merge wizard. The wizard displays options in a series of panes, and you choose the options you want. If you're new to mail merge, the wizard can provide a helpful framework. If you are comfortable with the mail merge process and know what you want to create, it can be faster to perform the steps manually.

To use the Mail Merge wizard

1. Start Word and display the **Mailings** tab.

2. In the **Start Mail Merge** group, click the **Start Mail Merge** button, and then click **Step-by-Step Mail Merge Wizard**.

3. In each of the six panes of the wizard, select an option or provide the requested information.

4. In the last pane, specify whether to send the merge output directly to the printer or to create one or more documents that you can review and save.

This chapter provides in-depth information about how to get the results that you want from the mail merge process, whether you use the wizard or the commands on the Mailings tab.

Start the mail merge process

For most mail merge projects, you need a starting document that provides structure and common content, and that identifies the locations where you want to insert data. You specify the data to merge into each location by inserting *merge fields*. The merge fields pull data from the data source fields into the starting document. To identify the data fields that are available for the mail merge operation, you must select the data source and import its records into the Mail Merge Recipients list.

The best starting point varies based on the type of output that you want to create. The output categories include letters, email messages, envelopes, labels, and directories.

In this topic, we discuss ways of getting started with a mail merge process based on the output type.

> **TIP** If you find that you need help, you can start the wizard from any point in the process and move back to make changes or forward to keep the work you've done.

Get started with letters

If you're creating a form letter or similar document, you can write the document, connect to the data source, and then insert the merge fields, or you can start with a blank document, connect to the data source, and then insert the merge fields as you write the document. Either way, you can't insert merge fields in a document until you connect to the data source.

If you're creating a document that needs to go through a review process, it's easier to do that before you connect to the data source; otherwise, the document tries to connect to the data source each time a reviewer opens it. When that's the case, you can insert placeholders in the document where you plan to insert merge fields later. You can set off the placeholders from the real text by using brackets or highlighting to indicate to reviewers that the placeholders aren't final content, and to make them easy to locate later.

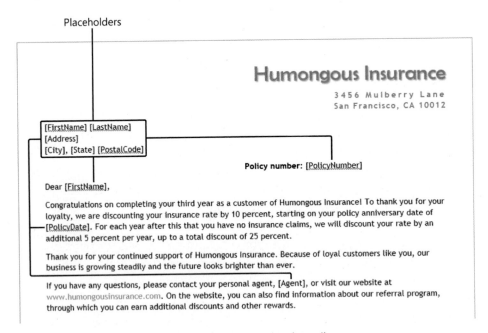

Placeholders

Humongous Insurance

3456 Mulberry Lane
San Francisco, CA 10012

[FirstName] [LastName]
[Address]
[City], [State] [PostalCode]

Policy number: [PolicyNumber]

Dear [FirstName],

Congratulations on completing your third year as a customer of Humongous Insurance! To thank you for your loyalty, we are discounting your insurance rate by 10 percent, starting on your policy anniversary date of [PolicyDate]. For each year after this that you have no insurance claims, we will discount your rate by an additional 5 percent per year, up to a total discount of 25 percent.

Thank you for your continued support of Humongous Insurance. Because of loyal customers like you, our business is growing steadily and the future looks brighter than ever.

If you have any questions, please contact your personal agent, [Agent], or visit our website at www.humongousinsurance.com. On the website, you can also find information about our referral program, through which you can earn additional discounts and other rewards.

It's easiest to write and edit your document before starting the mail merge process

If you need a bit of help creating a document for your intended purpose, you can use any of the Word content templates. A wide variety of templates are available from the New page of the Backstage view.

To start a letter mail merge

1. Open a blank document or a document that contains the static content you want to pull data into.

2. On the **Mailings** tab, in the **Start Mail Merge** group, click the **Start Mail Merge** button.

3. On the **Start Mail Merge** menu, click **Letters**. There is no visible change to the document.

4. To continue and complete the process:

   a. Use the procedures described in "Choose and refine the data source" later in this chapter to identify the data source and available fields.

   b. Create or edit the document content, and use the procedures described in "Insert merge fields" later in this chapter to insert the merge fields.

   c. Use the procedures described in "Preview and complete the merge" later in this chapter to finish creating the letter.

Get started with labels

The mail merge processes for labels are designed not only for stickers but also for name tags, badge inserts, business cards, tab inserts for page dividers, CD labels, postcards, notecards, printable magnets, and anything else that you print onto paper or other sheet-fed media that is divided into fixed areas. Many of these products are available from office supply and craft supply retailers. Common manufacturers of label materials include Avery and 3M, but there are many others.

> **SEE ALSO** For more information about creating mailing labels, see "Create individual envelopes and labels" later in this chapter.

When generating labels from a data source, you're usually printing data from multiple records onto each sheet, but you can also print a full sheet of each record.

When creating labels, you select the manufacturer and product number of the specific printing media, and then Word creates a table that defines the printable area of the label sheet. You insert merge fields into the first cell as a template for all the other cells, format the content as you want it, and then copy the cell content to the other fields. If you're making sheets of labels that pull data from multiple records, each additional field starts with a «Next Record» tag that signals Word to move to the next record.

The starting document and first page of results for a label mail merge

It's important that you select the correct manufacturer and product, because the document page setup is very precisely controlled to match the media.

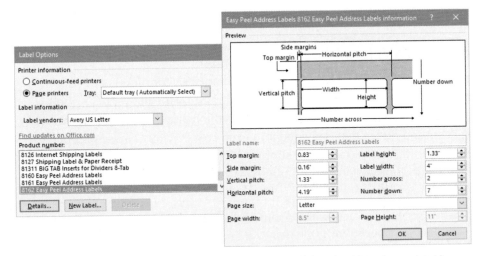

The definition for each label product includes the dimensions of the printable and nonprintable areas of the sheet

To start a label mail merge

1. Open a blank document and display paragraph marks and formatting symbols.

2. On the **Mailings** tab, in the **Start Mail Merge** group, click the **Start Mail Merge** button.

3. On the **Start Mail Merge** menu, click **Labels**. The Label Options dialog box opens.

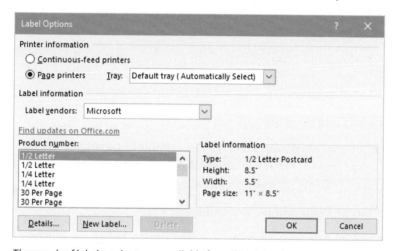

Thousands of label products are available from this dialog box

4. In the **Printer information** area, choose the correct printer type for the label forms and, for standard printers, choose the input tray (or manual feed) for the label sheets.

5. On the label package, identify the manufacturer and product number of the labels you will be using. In the **Label information** area, do the following:

   • In the **Label vendors** list, click the label manufacturer.

   • In the **Product number** list, click the product number.

> ✓ **TIP** To save time, click in the Product Number box and then press the keyboard key corresponding to the first character of the product number to jump to that section of the list. Then scroll to locate the specific product number. If the label product you're using doesn't already appear in the list, click the Find Updates On Office.Com link to refresh the list.

6. In the **Label Options** dialog box, click **OK** to return to the document. Word creates the label form in which you will enter the merge fields and any static content.

Ensure that paragraph symbols and formatting marks are shown before continuing

7. To continue and complete the process:

   a. Use the procedures described in "Choose and refine the data source" later in this chapter to identify the data source and available fields.

   b. Create or edit the static label content, and use the procedures described in "Insert merge fields" later in this chapter to insert the merge fields.

   c. Use the procedures described in "Preview and complete the merge" later in this chapter to finish creating the labels.

Get started with email messages

When you want to send the same information to all the people on a list—for example, all your customers, or all the members of a club or your family—you don't have to print letters and physically mail them. Instead, you can use mail merge to create a personalized email message for each person in a data source. As with a form letter that will be printed, you can either use the Mail Merge wizard or use the buttons on the Mailings tab to insert merge fields into a document. These merge fields will be replaced with information from the specified data source and the starting document will be converted to individual email messages.

Many email messages need no merge fields other than a greeting line.

If you want to edit the custom greeting, right-click the merge field and then click Edit Greeting Line

Because email messages tend to be less formal than printed letters, you might want to start the messages with a custom greeting rather than one of the predefined greeting options (Dear and To).

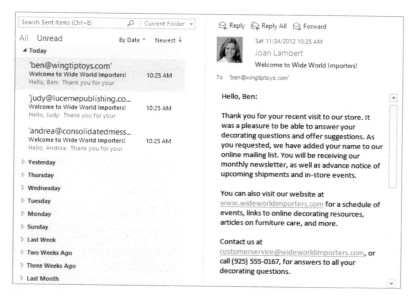

If you send the messages, you can locate them in your Sent Items folder

To start an email mail merge

1. Open a blank document or a document that contains the static content you want to pull data into.

2. On the **Mailings** tab, in the **Start Mail Merge** group, click the **Start Mail Merge** button.

3. On the **Start Mail Merge** menu, click **E-mail Messages**. Word displays the current content in Web view.

> ⊘ **SEE ALSO** For information about the available views, see "Display different views of documents" in Chapter 2, "Create and manage documents," of *Microsoft Word 2016 Step by Step* by Joan Lambert (Microsoft Press, 2015).

4. To continue and complete the process:

    a. Use the procedures described in "Choose and refine the data source" later in this chapter to identify the data source and available fields.

    b. Create or edit the document content, and use the procedures described in "Insert merge fields" later in this chapter to insert the merge fields.

    c. Use the procedures described in "Preview and complete the merge" later in this chapter to finish creating the messages.

Choose and refine the data source

The mail merge process combines variable information from a data source with static information in a starting document. The basic data source requirement is the same regardless of the output format: it must be a container that stores information in a consistent structure.

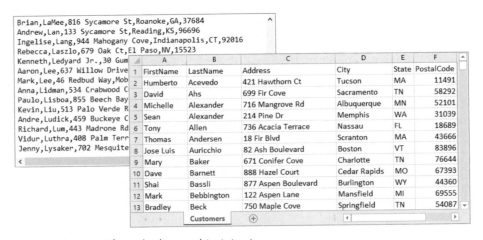

Data sources store information in a consistent structure

Most data source structures store data in a tabular format, with fields identified at the top and records following. The most straightforward example of this, and the one we work with throughout this chapter, is a Microsoft Excel workbook.

Each field in a data source must be identified by a unique name so you can pull data from the field into the starting document. In Excel, the field names are the table headers or column headers.

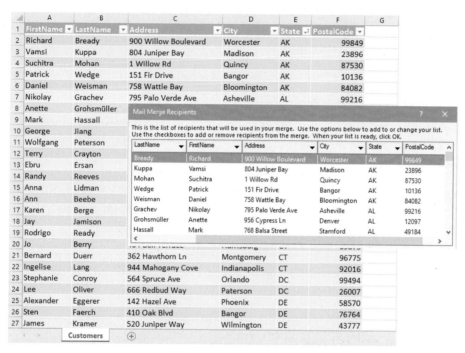

The Mail Merge Recipients dialog box displays all the records from the data source

Select an existing data source

The full list of acceptable data source file types is lengthy. Typical data sources include Excel worksheets and delimited text files, but you can also pull data from tables in Microsoft Word, Access, or SQL Server; from a Microsoft Outlook contact list; or from a variety of other, less common sources.

```
All Data Sources (*.odc;*.mdb;*.mde;*.accdb;*.accde;*.ols;*.udl;*.dsn;*.xlsx;*.xlsm;*.xlsb;*.xls;*.htm;*.html;*.
Office Database Connections (*.odc)
Access Databases (*.mdb;*.mde)
Access 2007 Database (*.accdb;*.accde)
Microsoft Office Address Lists (*.mdb)
Microsoft Office List Shortcuts (*.ols)
Microsoft Data links (*.udl)
ODBC File DSNs (*.dsn)
Excel Files (*.xlsx;*.xlsm;*.xlsb;*.xls)
Web Pages (*.htm;*.html;*.asp;*.mht;*.mhtml)
Rich Text Format (*.rtf)
Word Documents (*.docx;*.doc;*.docm)
All Word Documents (*.docx;*.doc;*.docm;*.dotx;*.dot;*.dotm;*.rtf;*.htm;*.html)
Text Files (*.txt;*.prn;*.csv;*.tab;*.asc)
Database Queries (*.dqy;*.rqy)
OpenDocument Text Files (*.odt)
```

All the file types that are accepted as data sources

> ✓ **TIP** If your company or organization uses another contact-management system, you can probably export information to one of these formats. Delimited text files are the most basic format of structured information storage and should be an export option from any other information storage system.

The data source doesn't have to be stored on your computer; the wizard can link to remotely stored data. If the data source is stored on a server that requires you to log on, you can provide your credentials and, optionally, store your password.

> ✓ **TIP** It isn't necessary for the data source file to be closed during the import operation; you can import records from an open file, edit and save the file, and refresh the list with the changes.

If you use Outlook to manage your email, contacts, and calendar information that is stored in Microsoft Exchange or Exchange Online, you can import data from an Exchange account contact folder to use as a mail merge data source. The Mail Merge wizard polls your Outlook data folders and provides a list of contact folders that you can use. When you choose a contact folder, the wizard imports the contact list.

It's likely that your contact list contains a variety of contacts—clients, employees, friends, relatives, and other people you have corresponded with. Many of these contacts might not be current, and many of them might not be people to whom you want to direct the specific form letter or email message that you're creating. But that's okay—you can import the entire contact list and then use the filtering function in the

Mail Merge Recipients dialog box to identify only those people you want to include in your current mail merge project.

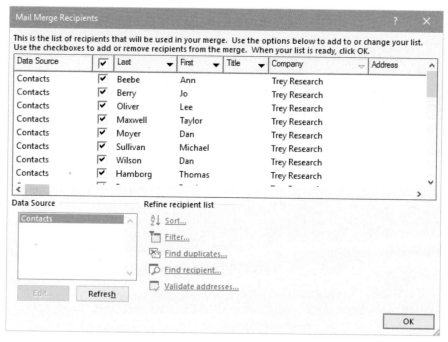

A selected check box indicates that a record will be included in the mail merge

 SEE ALSO For information about filtering records for a mail merge, see "Refine the data source records" later in this topic.

To select an existing data source

1. On the **Mailings** tab, in the **Start Mail Merge** group, click the **Select Recipients** button to display the data source options.

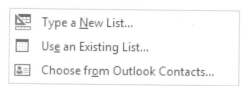

You must choose or create a data source file

2. On the **Select Recipients** menu, do either of the following:

- Click **Use an Existing List**. In the **Select Data Source** dialog box, browse to and select the data source file, and then click **Open**.

- Click **Choose from Outlook Contacts**. If the **Select Contacts** dialog box opens, select the contact folder that you want to import and click **OK**.

Create a new data source

If the information that you want to include in your data source isn't already stored in a file or address list, you can create a "Microsoft Office Address List" while working in the Mail Merge wizard; the wizard saves your list as a table in an Access database (.mdb) file in the My Data Sources subfolder of your Documents folder.

The process of entering information through the Address List interface is somewhat tedious, because you must manually populate each field—so if you have a lot of records, it's easier to enter your data into an Excel worksheet. However, it's fine for an impromptu mail merge process, such as creating a set of name tags for a meeting.

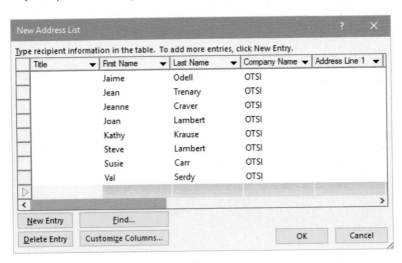

Creating a simple list through the wizard

You're not limited to collecting contact information; you can add, remove, and reorder the fields to store the type of data that is pertinent to your mail merge process.

To create a data source from the Mailings tab

1. On the **Mailings** tab, in the **Start Mail Merge** group, click the **Select Recipients** button, and then click **Type a New List**.

2. In the **New Address List** dialog box, do the following:

   a. Click **Customize Columns**. Add any fields to the column list that you plan to include in the mail merge operation. To keep things tidy, you can remove fields that you don't plan to use.

   b. Enter the information for each record, clicking **New Entry** to create another.

3. When you finish, click **OK**.

4. In the **Save Address List** dialog box, provide a name for the database file, and then click **Save**.

Refine the data source records

The data source you choose doesn't have to be specific to the item you're creating. For example, you could create postcards announcing an in-store sale only for customers who live in that area, or create gift certificates only for people who have birthdays in the next month.

If you don't want to include all the data source records in your mail merge operation, you can now whittle down the list to those you want. You can use the following processes to remove a record from the recipient list:

- **Filter the list on one or more fields** You can filter the list to display only the records that you want to include, or to locate (and then remove) the records that you want to exclude.

- **Remove duplicates** The wizard can help to identify entries that might be duplicates. You can either clear the check boxes for the duplicate versions that you don't want to use, or you can remove the entries from the data source file, save the file, and refresh the recipients list.

- **Manually exclude records** Each record has a check box. Clearing the check box removes the record from the mail merge operation.

Excluding records from the mail merge operation does not remove them from the Mail Merge Recipients list or from the original data source file. They will still be available for you to use in this or another mail merge operation.

In addition to limiting the set of information used in a mail merge, you can also sort the records to specify the order in which they appear in the mail merge document—for example, in postal code order for a bulk mailing.

> ⚠ **IMPORTANT** The Refine Recipient List in the Mail Merge Recipients dialog box includes a Validate Addresses link. At the time of this writing, clicking the link displays a message that an address validation add-in is required. Clicking the link to locate the add-in returns an error. This feature might be fixed by the time you read this book; when it is, you can validate mailing addresses against standards to filter out recipients whose mailing addresses don't appear to be valid per postal regulations.

To display the Mail Merge Recipients list

1. On the **Mailings** tab, in the **Start Mail Merge** group, click **Edit Recipient List**.

To filter the recipients list to display only records you want to include

1. Display the **Mail Merge Recipients** list.

2. In the **Refine recipient list** area, click **Filter** to display the **Filter Records** tab of the **Filter and Sort** dialog box.

3. In the **Field** list, click the field you want to filter by.

4. In the **Comparison** list, click one of the following:

   - Equal to
   - Not equal to
   - Less than
   - Greater than
   - Less than or equal

   - Greater than or equal
   - Is blank
   - Is not blank
   - Contains
   - Does not contain

5. In the **Compare to** list, enter the criterion for the field filter.

6. To apply multiple criteria, click **And** or **Or** in the leftmost list and then enter the additional criteria.

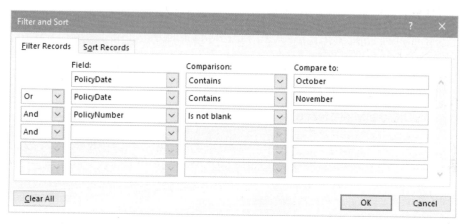

A multi-filter operation that returns only specific insurance policy subscribers

7. In the **Filter and Sort** dialog box, click **OK**. Records that are not displayed in the filtered list are not included in the mail merge operation.

To filter records out of the recipients list

1. Following the instructions in the previous procedure, filter the **Mail Merge Recipients** list to display the records you want to exclude.

2. Click the check box in the column heading area (twice if necessary) to clear the check boxes of all the records returned by the filter operation.

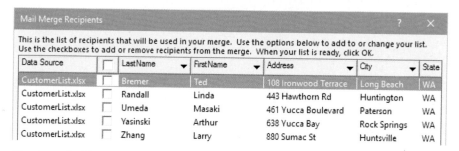

Clearing a check box removes a record from the recipient list but not from the data source

3. In the **Refine recipient list** area, click **Filter** to redisplay the Filter Records tab of the Filter And Sort dialog box.

4. On the **Filter Records** tab, click the **Clear All** button, and then click **OK** to remove the filter. The records that you excluded while the filter was applied are still excluded.

To remove duplicate records from the recipients list

1. Display the **Mail Merge Recipients** list.

2. In the **Refine recipient list** area, click **Find duplicates** to display records that have similar field entries.

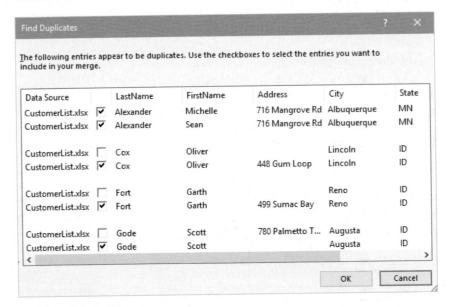

Review possible duplicates

3. In the **Find Duplicates** dialog box, clear the check boxes of any records that you want to exclude from the mail merge operation. Then click **OK**.

To sort records in a data source

1. Display the **Mail Merge Recipients** list.

2. To sort the records by one field, click the field name (the column header) of the field you want to sort by. (Click the field name again to sort in the opposite order.)

   Or

   To sort the records by multiple fields, do the following:

   a. In the **Refine recipient list** area, click **Sort** to display the Sort Records tab of the Filter And Sort dialog box.

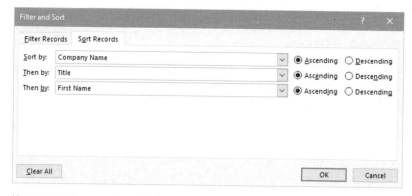

You can sort by up to three fields

   b. In the **Sort by** list, click the first field you want to sort by. Then click the adjacent **Ascending** or **Descending** option to specify the sort order.

   c. In the first **Then by** list, click the second field you want to sort by, and the adjacent **Ascending** or **Descending** option.

   d. In the second **Then by** list, specify the third sort field and order, or click (None).

   e. In the **Filter and Sort** dialog box, click **OK**.

To manually exclude records from the recipients list

1. Display the **Mail Merge Recipients** list.

2. If necessary, sort or filter the list to locate records.

3. Clear the check boxes of any records that you want to exclude from the mail merge operation.

Refresh data

You can save and close the document at any point in the mail merge process. When you reopen the document, if you've already connected to the data source and inserted merge fields, Word prompts you to refresh the data connection.

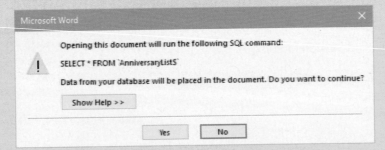

The recipient list reflects changes to the source data when you reopen the document

You can also refresh the data manually at any time from within the document by clicking the Refresh button in the Data Source area of the Mail Merge Recipients dialog box.

Insert merge fields

In the document, merge fields are enclosed in chevrons (« and »). However, you can't simply type the chevrons and the field name; you must insert the merge field by using the commands on the Mailings tab. This creates a link from the merge field to the data source field.

The commands that you use to insert merge fields in a starting document are in the Write & Insert Fields group on the Mailings tab.

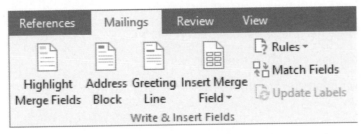

The tools for inserting fields in mail merge documents

Every field in the data source is available to insert as an individual merge field. Additionally, two merge fields are available that can save you a bit of time:

- **Address Block** This merge field inserts elements of a standard address block (the recipient's name, company name, and postal address) that you select so you can insert all the information with one merge field.

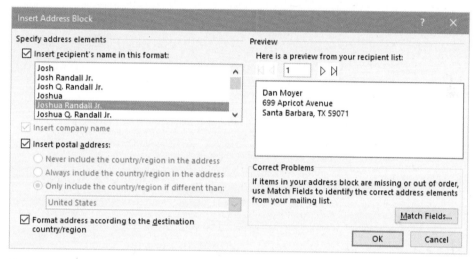

You can customize the Address Block merge field

- **Greeting Line** This merge field inserts a personalized salutation or substitutes a generic salutation for records that are missing the necessary information.

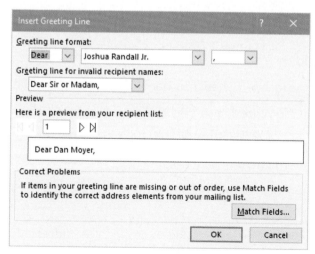

You can select from multiple greetings and name forms

After you insert the first merge field in a document, the Highlight Merge Fields button in the Write & Insert Fields group on the Mailings tab becomes active. Click this button to highlight (in gray) all the merge fields in the document so they're easier to locate.

Humongous Insurance

3456 Mulberry Lane
San Francisco, CA 10012

«AddressBlock»

Policy number: «PolicyNumber»

«GreetingLine»

Congratulations on completing your third year as a customer of Humongous Insurance! To thank you for your loyalty, we are discounting your insurance rate by 10 percent, starting on your policy anniversary date of «PolicyDate». For each year after this that you have no insurance claims, we will discount your rate by an additional 5 percent per year, up to a total discount of 25 percent.

Thank you for your continued support of Humongous Insurance. Because of loyal customers like you, our business is growing steadily and the future looks brighter than ever.

If you have any questions, please contact your personal agent, «Agent», or visit our website at www.humongousinsurance.com. On the website, you can also find information about our referral program, through which you can earn additional discounts and other rewards.

Highlighting the merge fields makes them easier to locate and also verifies that they aren't simply placeholders

> ⚠ **IMPORTANT** Before you can perform the procedures in this topic, you must select a data source. For more information, see "Choose and refine the data source" earlier in this chapter.

To insert a single merge field

1. Position the cursor in the location where you want to insert the merge field.

2. On the **Mailings** tab, in the **Write & Insert Fields** group, click **Insert Merge Field**, and then click the field you want to insert.

To insert an Address Block merge field

1. Position the cursor in the location where you want to insert the Address Block merge field.

2. On the **Mailings** tab, in the **Write & Insert Fields** group, click **Address Block**.

3. In the **Insert Address Block** dialog box, select the address block elements you want to include and select the format for the recipient's name.

4. In the **Preview** box displaying your first data record, check that the address block looks correct. You can move through additional records to check further.

5. When you finish, click **OK**.

To insert a Greeting Line merge field

1. Position the cursor in the location where you want to insert the Greeting Line merge field.

2. On the **Mailings** tab, in the **Write & Insert Fields** group, click **Greeting Line**.

3. In the **Insert Greeting Line** dialog box, select the greeting line elements you want to include and the generic format for records that don't have the elements you specify.

4. In the **Preview** box displaying your first data record, check that the greeting looks correct. You can move through additional records to check further.

5. When you finish, click **OK**.

Preview and complete the merge

After you specify the data source you want to use and enter merge fields in the main document, you can preview the effect of merging the records into the documents, and then perform the actual merge. You can further filter the source data during the preview process. When you're ready, you can either send the merged documents directly to the printer or you can merge them into a new document. If you merge to a new document, you have another chance to review and, if necessary, edit the merged documents before sending them to the printer.

> ⚠ **IMPORTANT** Before you can perform the procedures in this topic, you must select a data source and insert merge fields. For more information, see "Choose and refine the data source" and "Insert merge fields" earlier in this chapter.

To preview merged documents

1. Display the starting document with merge fields in place and the data source attached.

2. On the **Mailings** tab, in the **Preview Results** group, click the **Preview Results** button to display the data source information in place of the merge fields.

3. In the **Preview Results** group, do any of the following:

    - Click the **Next Record** or **Previous Record** button to move through the data source one record at a time.

    - Click the **First Record** or **Last Record** button to move to the first or last record in the data source.

    - Click the **Preview Results** button again to redisplay the merge fields.

To merge the data to a new document

1. On the **Mailings** tab, in the **Finish** group, click the **Finish & Merge** button, and then click **Edit Individual Documents**. The Merge To New Document dialog box opens.

You can limit the merge to one record or a range of records

2. In the **Merge to New Document** dialog box, indicate the record or records that you want to merge, and then click **OK**.

To merge the data and print the resulting file

1. On the **Mailings** tab, in the **Finish** group, click the **Finish & Merge** button, and then click **Print Documents**.

2. In the **Merge to Printer** dialog box, indicate the record or records that you want to merge, and then click **OK**.

3. In the **Print** dialog box, select your printer, configure any additional printer settings that are necessary, and then click **OK**.

To merge the data and email the resulting messages

1. On the **Mailings** tab, in the **Finish** group, click the **Finish & Merge** button, and then click **Send Email Messages**. The Merge To E-mail dialog box opens.

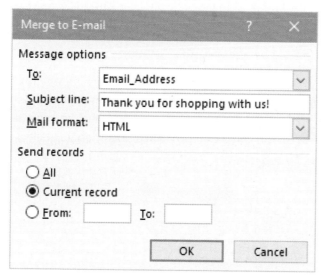

You specify the address field and subject line before sending the messages

2. In the **Message options** area, do the following:

   - In the **To** list, click the field that contains the recipients' email addresses.

   - In the **Subject line** box, enter the message subject you want the email message to display.

   - In the **Mail format** list, click **Attachment**, **Plain text**, or **HTML**.

3. In the **Send records** area, indicate the record or records that you want to merge. Then click **OK**.

Create individual envelopes and labels

If you want to print a lot of envelopes or mailing labels based on data source fields, you can use the mail merge function to create documents, and then print the documents onto envelopes or sheet-fed labels rather than regular paper.

However, you can also use the prominently placed Envelope and Labels functions to create one or more individually addressed envelopes or address labels. Because these functions are related to "mailing" envelopes or packages, they have been (somewhat confusingly) placed on the Mailing tab of the ribbon, which is otherwise home to only the mail merge functionality.

Generate individual envelopes

The Envelope function prints a delivery address and can also print a return address and electronic postage, if you have the necessary software installed. You can manually enter the delivery address or you can pick it up from a document (usually a letter) that contains an address.

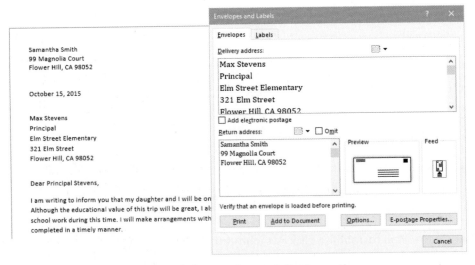

You can edit the address information before creating or printing the envelope

> **TIP** You can save time by storing the return address with your user information. The address then appears by default as the return address in the Envelopes And Labels dialog box.

When creating envelopes, you can specify the envelope size, the address locations, and the fonts for the addresses. You can also specify the paper source, the envelope feed method (horizontally or vertically and face up or face down), and the alignment of the envelope. Then Word configures the page layout options and print options as required for your selections.

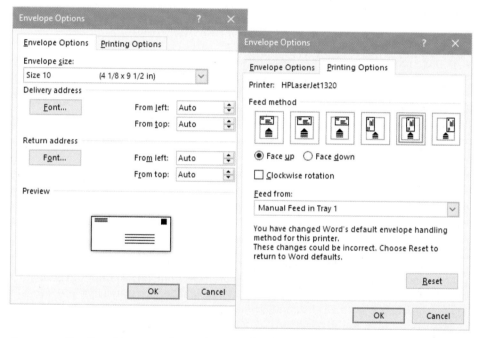

You can position the addresses on the envelope exactly where you want them

When you create an envelope based on an address in a letter, you can print the envelope immediately or add the envelope page to the document, and then print the envelope and letter at a later time.

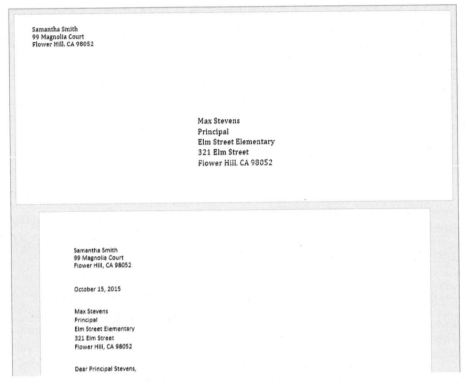

Adding the envelope to the document inserts it as a separate document section with unique page layout settings

> ⚠️ **IMPORTANT** The electronic postage options on the Envelopes tab of the Envelopes And Labels dialog box require the installation of an electronic postage add-in. Clicking the link to locate the add-in returns an error. This feature might be fixed by the time you read this book; when it is, you can print electronic postage directly onto envelopes.

To save your mailing address for use in Word documents

1. Open the **Word Options** dialog box, and then click the **Advanced** tab.

2. On the **Advanced** page, in the **General** section, enter your name and address in the **Mailing Address** box. Then click **OK**.

To set up an envelope with a manually entered address

1. Open any document.

2. On the **Mailings** tab, in the **Create** group, click the **Envelopes** button to open the Envelopes And Labels dialog box.

The Return Address box contains your user name or your mailing address, if you saved that in the Word Options dialog box. (If you saved and then deleted your mailing address, the Return Address box might be blank.)

3. In the **Return address** area, do either of the following:

   - Review the return address information and modify it as necessary.

   - If you plan to print to envelopes that have a preprinted return address, select the **Omit** check box.

4. In the **Delivery address** box, enter the name and address that you want Word to print on the envelope.

5

To set up an envelope from an address in a document

1. Open the document and select the address.

2. On the **Mailings** tab, in the **Create** group, click the **Envelopes** button to open the Envelopes And Labels dialog box with the selected address in the Delivery Address box. The Return Address box contains your user name, and also contains your return address if you've saved that in Word.

3. Review the addresses and make any changes you want. If you plan to print on an envelope that has a preprinted return address, select the **Omit** check box in the **Return address** area.

To configure or confirm the envelope printing options

1. At the bottom of the **Envelopes** tab of the **Envelopes and Labels** dialog box, click the **Options** button to open the Envelope Options dialog box.

2. On the **Envelope Options** tab, set the envelope size, delivery address font and position, and return address font and position.

3. On the **Printing Options** tab, set the feed method, rotation, and paper source.

> ⚠ **IMPORTANT** If the printer shown at the top of the Printing Options tab is not the correct printer, click OK in each of the open dialog boxes to save your settings and return to the source document. Then select the correct printer in the source document and return to the Envelopes And Labels dialog box to finish creating the envelope.

4. Click **OK** to return to the Envelopes And Labels dialog box.

To print or save the envelope

1. After you set up the envelope and configure the envelope printing options, do either of the following:

   - Load an envelope into the printer in the manner configured in the Envelope Options dialog box. Then at the bottom of the **Envelopes and Labels** dialog box, click **Print** to print the envelope.

   - At the bottom of the **Envelopes and Labels** dialog box, click **Add to Document** to insert the envelope content as a separately formatted section at the beginning of the current document.

Generate individual mailing labels

The Labels function is designed to print one address (a delivery address or a return address) onto a sheet of labels, either to create a single label or a full sheet of the same label. Instead of selecting an envelope size, you select a label form by first selecting the label manufacturer and then selecting the specific product number. Word sets up a document to precisely match the content layout areas of the selected form.

Samantha Smith 99 Magnolia Court Flower Hill, CA 98052	Samantha Smith 99 Magnolia Court Flower Hill, CA 98052
Samantha Smith 99 Magnolia Court Flower Hill, CA 98052	Samantha Smith 99 Magnolia Court Flower Hill, CA 98052
Samantha Smith 99 Magnolia Court Flower Hill, CA 98052	Samantha Smith 99 Magnolia Court Flower Hill, CA 98052
Samantha Smith	Samantha Smith

The content cells defined by the table match the printing areas of the label sheets

As discussed in "Get started with labels" earlier in this chapter, the term "labels" refers not only to rectangular stickers, but also to many other things that you print onto sheet-fed media that is divided into fixed areas. You can use the Labels function to print on any of these. It's important that you select the correct form because the print areas are very specifically defined.

To set up individual mailing labels

1. Open any document.

2. On the **Mailings** tab, in the **Create** group, click the **Labels** button to open the Envelopes And Labels dialog box.

3. In the **Address** area, do either of the following:

   - If you've saved your return address information in Word and want to create a return address label, select the **Use return address** check box to insert the saved address into the Address box. Then review the return address information and modify it as necessary.

   - Enter the name and address that you want Word to print on the label.

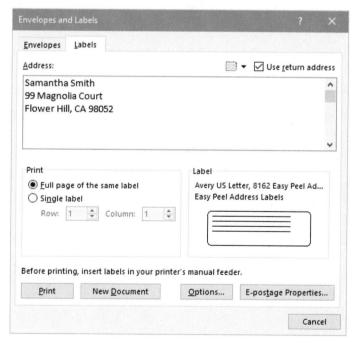

Although the field specifies an address, you can print any text on the labels

4. In the **Print** area, do either of the following to correctly configure the label output:

   - If you want to print one full sheet of labels, click **Full page of the same label**.

   - If you want to print only one label, click **Single label** and then enter the row and column of the position on the sheet of the label you want to print on.

    TIP This feature permits you to easily reuse a partial sheet of blank labels.

5. In the **Label** area, confirm that the label type is the correct one for the printed label forms you are using. If it is not, configure the label settings in the **Label Options** dialog box.

    SEE ALSO For information about configuring label settings, see "Get started with labels" earlier in this chapter.

To print or save the mailing label

1. After you set up the label and configure the label printing options, do either of the following:

   - Load a label form into the printer in the manner configured in the Label Options dialog box. Then at the bottom of the **Envelopes and Labels** dialog box, click **Print** to print the label.

   - At the bottom of the **Envelopes and Labels** dialog box, click **New Document** to generate a new document that contains the merged labels.

Skills review

In this chapter, you learned how to:

- Understand the mail merge process
- Start the mail merge process
- Choose and refine the data source
- Insert merge fields
- Preview and complete the merge
- Create individual envelopes and labels

Practice tasks

The practice files for these tasks are located in the Office2016SBS\Ch05 folder. You can save the results of the tasks in the same folder.

Understand the mail merge process

Start Word, open a new blank document, and then perform the following tasks:

1. Start the Mail Merge wizard and investigate the options provided therein.
2. Using the wizard, create any mail merge item you want to. Use the **CustomerList** workbook from the practice file folder as your data source.
3. If you create a mail merge document, save it as **MyMerge**, and then close it.

Start the mail merge process

Open the StartMerge document from the practice file folder, and then perform the following tasks:

1. Start a letter mail merge. Notice that the document does not change.
2. Next start an email mail merge. Notice that the document view changes to Web Layout.
3. Start a label mail merge, and investigate the options in the Label Options dialog box. Choose a label vendor and product number, and display the label details.
4. Create the label sheet, and allow Word to replace the contents of the StartMerge document when prompted to do so.
5. Close the **StartMerge** document without saving it.

Choose and refine the data source

Open the RefineData document, and then perform the following tasks:

1. Start a letter mail merge. Select the **CustomerList** workbook from the practice file folder as the data source, and select the **Customers$** table of the workbook when prompted to do so.
2. Sort the recipient list alphabetically, in ascending order, by the customers' last names.
3. Remove duplicate records from the recipient list.

4. Filter the list to display only those records for customers who live either in the state of Texas (TX) or the state of Louisiana (LA).

5. Manually exclude all of the Louisiana (LA) records from the recipient list, and then return to the letter.

6. From the **Select Recipients** menu, create a new data source. Add your name and the names of two other people. Add any other information you want, and then save the new list as PracticeList.mdb.

7. Save and close the **RefineData** document.

Insert merge fields

Open the InsertFields document, and then perform the following tasks:

1. Start a letter mail merge. Select the **PolicyholdersList** workbook from the practice file folder as the data source, and select the **PolicyHolders$** table of the workbook when prompted to do so.

2. Replace each placeholder in the document with its corresponding merge field.

3. Save the **InsertFields** document, but don't close it.

4. Create a new blank document and start a new letter mail merge. Use the same data source as in step 1.

5. Open the **Insert Address Block** dialog box. Review the settings and make any changes you want, and then insert the merge field.

6. In the document, two lines below the address block, insert a **Greeting Line** merge field.

7. Save the document as MyFields, and then close it. Leave the **InsertFields** document open for the next set of practice tasks.

Preview and complete the merge

Complete the previous set of practice tasks to modify the InsertFields document. Then perform the following tasks:

1. Use the tools in the **Preview Results** group on the **Mailings** tab to preview the results of completing the mail merge. Then redisplay the merge fields.

2. Merge the data source into the document to create a new document. Save the document as MyLetter, and then close it.

3. Redisplay the **InsertFields** document, and follow the procedure to merge the output directly to the printer. (If you don't want to print the file, click **Cancel** in the final dialog box.)

4. Follow the procedure to merge the output to email messages. Explore the settings, and then click **Cancel**.

5. Save and close the **InsertFields** document.

Create individual envelopes and labels

Open the CreateEnvelopes document, and then perform the following tasks:

1. Open the **Word Options** dialog box, and display the **Advanced** page. In the **General** section, check whether you have saved your mailing address. If you have not, do so now.

2. Open the **Envelopes and Labels** dialog box. Verify that the **Return Address** box contains your saved mailing address.

3. In the **Delivery address** box, enter the name and address of another person. Then add the envelope to the document.

4. In the document, select the letter recipient's name and address, and then open the **Envelopes and Labels** dialog box. Verify that the **Return Address** box contains your mailing address, and the **Delivery Address** box contains the letter recipient's name and address.

5. In the **Envelope Options** dialog box, configure the envelope printing options and then, if you want, load an envelope into your printer, and print the addresses onto the envelope.

6. Save and close the **CreateEnvelopes** document.

7. Create a new blank document.

8. Display the **Labels** tab of the **Envelopes and Labels** dialog box. If your saved mailing address is not already shown in the Address box, select the **Use return address** check box to add your saved information to the **Address** box.

9. Configure the merge output to print one full sheet of labels.

10. If you have a sheet of labels to print to, configure the label settings. Then load a sheet of labels into the printer and print the addresses onto the labels.

11. If you don't have a sheet of labels, generate a new document that contains the merged labels. Then save the document as MyLabels, and close it.

Part 3

Microsoft Excel 2016

Perform calculations on data

Excel 2016 workbooks give you a handy place to store and organize your data, but you can also do a lot more with your data in Excel. One important task you can perform is to calculate totals for the values in a series of related cells. You can also use Excel to discover other information about the data you select, such as the maximum or minimum value in a group of cells. Regardless of your needs, Excel gives you the ability to find the information you want. And if you make an error, you can find the cause and correct it quickly.

Often, you can't access the information you want without referencing more than one cell, and it's also often true that you'll use the data in the same group of cells for more than one calculation. Excel makes it easy to reference several cells at the same time, so that you can define your calculations quickly.

This chapter guides you through procedures related to streamlining references to groups of data on your worksheets and creating and correcting formulas that summarize an organization's business operations.

In this chapter

- Name groups of data
- Define Excel tables
- Create formulas to calculate values
- Summarize data that meets specific conditions
- Set iterative calculation options and enable or disable automatic calculation
- Use array formulas
- Find and correct errors in calculations

Practice files

For this chapter, use the practice files from the Office2016SBS\Ch06 folder. For practice file download instructions, see the introduction.

Name groups of data

When you work with large amounts of data, it's often useful to identify groups of cells that contain related data. For example, you can create a worksheet in which columns of cells contain data summarizing the number of packages handled during a specific time period and each row represents a region.

	A	B	C	D	E	F	G	H	I	J
1										
2										
3			5:00 PM	6:00 PM	7:00 PM	8:00 PM	9:00 PM	10:00 PM	11:00 PM	
4		Northeast	30,825	53,945	44,668	50,670	51,711	43,141	41,705	
5		Atlantic	14,998	7,092	10,650	14,709	14,458	7,714	14,266	
6		Southeast	8,603	9,082	13,995	12,447	12,750	10,216	11,189	
7		North Central	12,480	12,086	12,147	8,102	7,990	9,143	7,117	
8		Midwest	11,639	8,934	7,045	11,869	14,731	14,597	11,205	
9		Southwest	14,528	11,238	12,592	8,418	7,389	8,590	12,220	
10		Mountain West	10,900	14,362	7,951	12,437	11,534	8,462	10,578	
11		Northwest	11,432	7,527	14,753	11,410	7,649	9,730	12,483	
12		Central	7,458	8,567	11,424	14,153	13,565	8,690	11,545	
13										

Worksheets often contain logical groups of data

Instead of specifying the cells individually every time you want to use the data they contain, you can define those cells as a *range* (also called a *named range*). For example, you can group the hourly packages handled in the Northeast region into a group called *NortheastVolume*. Whenever you want to use the contents of that range in a calculation, you can use the name of the range instead of specifying the range's address.

> ✓ **TIP** Yes, you could just name the range *Northeast*, but if you use the range's values in a formula in another worksheet, the more descriptive range name tells you and your colleagues exactly what data is used in the calculation.

If the cells you want to define as a named range have labels in a row or column that's part of the cell group, you can use those labels as the names of the named ranges. For example, if your data appears in worksheet cells B4:I12 and the values in column B are the row labels, you can make each row its own named range.

	A	B	C
1			
2			
3			5:00 PM
4		Northeast	30,825
5		Atlantic	14,998
6		Southeast	8,603
7		North Central	12,480
8		Midwest	11,639
9		Southwest	14,528
10		Mountain West	10,900
11		Northwest	11,432
12		Central	7,458

Select a group of cells to create a named range

If you want to manage the named ranges in your workbook, perhaps to edit a range's settings or delete a range you no longer need, you can do so in the Name Manager dialog box.

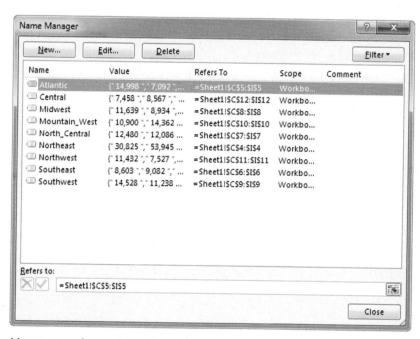

Manage named ranges in the Name Manager dialog box

> ✅ **TIP** If your workbook contains a lot of named ranges, you can click the Filter button in the Name Manager dialog box and select a criterion to limit the names displayed in the dialog box.

To create a named range

1. Select the cells you want to include in the named range.
2. In the **Name** box, which is next to the formula bar, enter the name for your named range.

Or

1. Select the cells you want to include in the named range.
2. On the **Formulas** tab of the ribbon, in the **Defined Names** group, click **Define Name**.
3. In the **New Name** dialog box, enter a name for the named range.
4. Verify that the named range includes the cells you want.
5. Click **OK**.

To create a series of named ranges from worksheet data with headings

1. Select the cells that contain the headings and data cells you want to include in the named ranges.
2. In the **Defined Names** group, click **Create from Selection**.
3. In the **Create Names from Selection** dialog box, select the check box next to the location of the heading text from which you want to create the range names.
4. Click **OK**.

To edit a named range

1. In the **Defined Names** group, click **Name Manager**.
2. Click the named range you want to edit.
3. In the **Refers to** box, change the cells that the named range refers to.

   Or

   Click **Edit**, edit the named range in the **Edit Range** box, and click **OK**.
4. Click **Close**.

To delete a named range

1. Click **Name Manager**.

2. Click the named range you want to delete.

3. Click **Delete**.

4. Click **Close**.

Define Excel tables

With Excel, you've always been able to manage lists of data effectively, so that you can sort your worksheet data based on the values in one or more columns, limit the data displayed by using criteria (for example, show only those routes with fewer than 100 stops), and create formulas that summarize the values in visible (that is, unfiltered) cells. Excel 2016 provides those capabilities, and more, through Excel tables.

6

◢	A	B	C	D
1				
2		Driver ▾	Sorting Minutes ▾	
3		D101	102	
4		D102	162	
5		D103	165	
6		D104	91	
7		D105	103	
8		D106	127	
9		D107	112	
10		D108	137	
11		D109	102	
12		D110	147	
13		D111	163	
14		D112	109	
15		D113	91	
16		D114	107	
17		D115	93	

Manage data by using Excel tables

TIP Sorting, filtering, and summarizing data are all covered elsewhere in this book.

Excel can also create an Excel table from an existing cell range as long as the range has no blank rows or columns within the data and there is no extraneous data in cells immediately below or next to the list. If your existing data has formatting applied to it, that formatting remains applied to those cells when you create the Excel table, but you can have Excel replace the existing formatting with the Excel table's formatting.

 TIP To create an Excel table by using a keyboard shortcut, press Ctrl+L and then click OK.

Entering values into a cell below or to the right of an Excel table adds a row or column to the Excel table. After you enter the value and move out of the cell, the AutoCorrect Options action button appears. If you didn't mean to include the data in the Excel table, you can click Undo Table AutoExpansion to exclude the cells from the Excel table. If you never want Excel to include adjacent data in an Excel table again, click Stop Automatically Expanding Tables.

TIP To stop Table AutoExpansion before it starts, click Options in the Backstage view. In the Excel Options dialog box, click Proofing, and then click the AutoCorrect Options button to open the AutoCorrect dialog box. Click the AutoFormat As You Type tab, clear the Include New Rows And Columns In Table check box, and then click OK twice.

You can resize an Excel table manually by using your mouse. If your Excel table's headers contain a recognizable series of values (such as *Region1*, *Region2*, and *Region3*), and you drag the resize handle to create a fourth column, Excel creates the column with a label that is the next value in the series—in this example, *Region4*.

Excel tables often contain data you can summarize by calculating a sum or average, or by finding the maximum or minimum value in a column. To summarize one or more columns of data, you can add a total row to your Excel table.

◢	A	B	C	D
1				
2		**Driver** ▾	**Sorting Minutes** ▾	
3		D101	102	
4		D102	162	
5		D103	165	
6		D104	91	
7		D105	103	
8		D106	127	
9		D107	112	
10		D108	137	
11		D109	102	
12		D110	147	
13		D111	163	
14		D112	109	
15		D113	91	
16		D114	107	
17		D115	93	
18		Total	1811	

An Excel table with a total row

When you add the total row, Excel creates a formula that summarizes the values in the rightmost Excel table column. You can change the summary function by picking a new one from the partial list displayed in the Excel table or by selecting a function from the full set.

Much as it does when you create a new worksheet, Excel gives your Excel tables generic names such as *Table1* and *Table2*. You can change an Excel table's name to something easier to recognize in your formulas. Changing an Excel table name might not seem important, but it helps make formulas that summarize Excel table data much easier to understand. You should make a habit of renaming your Excel tables so you can recognize the data they contain.

> **SEE ALSO** For more information about using the Insert Function dialog box and about referring to tables in formulas, see "Create formulas to calculate values" later in this chapter.

If for any reason you want to convert your Excel table back to a normal range of cells, you can do so quickly.

To create an Excel table

1. Click a cell in the list of data you want to make into an Excel table.

2. On the **Home** tab, in the **Styles** group, click **Format as Table**.

3. Click the style you want to apply to the table.

4. Verify that the cell range is correct.

5. If necessary, select or clear the **My table has headers** check box, and then click **OK**.

To create an Excel table with default formatting

1. Click a cell in the range that you want to make into an Excel table.

2. Press **Ctrl+L**.

3. Click **OK**.

To add a column or row to an Excel table

1. Click a cell in the row below or the column to the right of the Excel table.

2. Enter the data and press **Enter**.

To expand or contract an Excel table

1. Click any cell in the Excel table.

2. Point to the lower-right corner of the Excel table.

3. When the mouse pointer changes to a diagonal arrow, drag the Excel table's outline to redefine the table.

To add a total row to an Excel table

1. Click any cell in the Excel table.

2. On the **Design** tool tab of the ribbon, in the **Table Style Options** group, select the **Total Row** check box.

To change the calculation used in a total row cell

1. Click any **Total** row cell that contains a calculation.

2. Click the cell's arrow.

3. Select a summary function.

    Or

    Click **More Functions**, use the **Insert Function** dialog box to create the formula, and click **OK**.

To rename an Excel table

1. Click any cell in the Excel table.

2. On the **Design** tool tab, in the **Properties** group, enter a new name for the Excel table in the **Table Name** box.

3. Press **Enter**.

To convert an Excel table to a cell range

1. Click any cell in the Excel table.

2. On the **Design** tool tab, in the **Tools** group, click **Convert to Range**.

3. In the confirmation dialog box that appears, click **Yes**.

Create formulas to calculate values

After you add your data to a worksheet and define ranges to simplify data references, you can create a formula, which is an expression that performs calculations on your data. For example, you can calculate the total cost of a customer's shipments, figure the average number of packages for all Wednesdays in the month of January, or find the highest and lowest daily package volumes for a week, month, or year.

To write an Excel formula, you begin the cell's contents with an equal (=) sign; Excel then knows that the expression following it should be interpreted as a calculation, not text. After the equal sign, you enter the formula. For example, you can find the sum of the numbers in cells C2 and C3 by using the formula =C2+C3. After you have entered a formula into a cell, you can revise it by clicking the cell and then editing the formula in the formula bar. For example, you can change the preceding formula to =C3–C2, which calculates the difference between the contents of cells C2 and C3.

> **IMPORTANT** If Excel treats your formula as text, make sure that you haven't accidentally put a space before the equal sign. Remember, the equal sign must be the first character!

Entering the cell references for 15 or 20 cells in a calculation would be tedious, but in Excel you can easily enter complex calculations by using the Insert Function dialog box. The Insert Function dialog box includes a list of functions, or predefined formulas, from which you can choose.

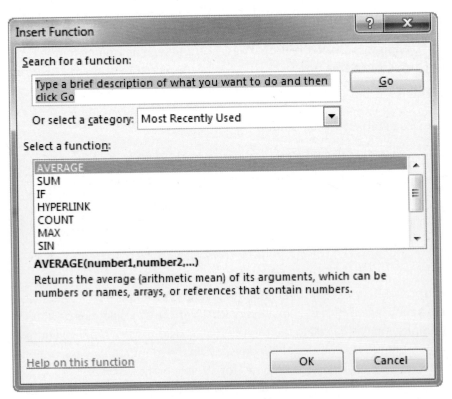

Create formulas with help in the Insert Function dialog box

The following table describes some of the most useful functions in the list.

Function	Description
SUM	Finds the sum of the numbers in the specified cells
AVERAGE	Finds the average of the numbers in the specified cells
COUNT	Finds the number of entries in the specified cells
MAX	Finds the largest value in the specified cells
MIN	Finds the smallest value in the specified cells

Two other functions you might use are the *NOW* and *PMT* functions. The *NOW* function displays the time at which Excel updated the workbook's formulas, so the value will change every time the workbook recalculates. The proper form for this function is *=NOW()*. You could, for example, use the *NOW* function to calculate the elapsed time from when you started a process to the present time.

The *PMT* function is a bit more complex. It calculates payments due on a loan, assuming a constant interest rate and constant payments. To perform its calculations, the *PMT* function requires an interest rate, the number of payments, and the starting balance. The elements to be entered into the function are called *arguments* and must be entered in a certain order. That order is written as *PMT(rate, nper, pv, fv, type)*. The following table summarizes the arguments in the *PMT* function.

Argument	Description
rate	The interest rate, to be divided by 12 for a loan with monthly payments, by 4 for quarterly payments, and so on
nper	The total number of payments for the loan
pv	The amount loaned (*pv* is short for *present value*, or principal)
fv	The amount to be left over at the end of the payment cycle (usually left blank, which indicates 0)
type	0 or 1, indicating whether payments are made at the beginning or at the end of the month (usually left blank, which indicates 0, or the end of the month)

6

If a company wanted to borrow $2,000,000 at a 6 percent interest rate and pay the loan back over 24 months, you could use the *PMT* function to figure out the monthly payments. In this case, you would write the function *=PMT(6%/12, 24, 2000000),* which calculates a monthly payment of $88,641.22.

 TIP The 6-percent interest rate is divided by 12 because the loan's interest is compounded monthly.

You can also use the names of any ranges you defined to supply values for a formula. For example, if the named range *NortheastLastDay* refers to cells C4:I4, you can calculate the average of cells C4:I4 with the formula *=AVERAGE(NortheastLastDay)*. With Excel, you can add functions, named ranges, and table references to your formulas more efficiently by using the Formula AutoComplete capability. Just as AutoComplete offers to fill in a cell's text value when Excel recognizes that the value you're typing matches a previous entry, Formula AutoComplete offers to help you fill in a function, named range, or table reference while you create a formula.

As an example, consider a worksheet that contains a two-column Excel table named *Exceptions*. The first column is labeled *Route*; the second is labeled *Count*.

	A	B
1	Route	Count
2	101	14
3	102	2
4	103	14
5	104	5
6	105	9
7	106	14
8	107	9
9	108	7
10	109	8
11	110	9
12		

Excel tables track data in a structured format

You refer to a table by typing the table name, followed by the column or row name in brackets. For example, the table reference *Exceptions[Count]* would refer to the *Count* column in the *Exceptions* table.

To create a formula that finds the total number of exceptions by using the *SUM* function, you begin by typing =*SU*. When you enter the letter *S*, Formula AutoComplete lists functions that begin with the letter *S*; when you enter the letter *U*, Excel narrows the list down to the functions that start with the letters *SU*.

▲	A	B	C	D	E	F	G	H	I	J
1	**Route** ▼	**Count** ▼		=SU						
2	101	14		*ƒ*ₓ SUBSTITUTE		Replaces existing text with new text in a text string				
3	102	2		*ƒ*ₓ SUBTOTAL						
4	103	14		*ƒ*ₓ SUM						
5	104	5		*ƒ*ₓ SUMIF						
6	105	9		*ƒ*ₓ SUMIFS						
7	106	14		*ƒ*ₓ SUMPRODUCT						
8	107	9		*ƒ*ₓ SUMSQ						
9	108	7		*ƒ*ₓ SUMX2MY2						
10	109	8		*ƒ*ₓ SUMX2PY2						
11	110	9		*ƒ*ₓ SUMXMY2						
12										

Excel displays Formula AutoComplete suggestions to help with formula creation

To add the *SUM* function (followed by an opening parenthesis) to the formula, click *SUM* and then press Tab. To begin adding the table reference, enter the letter *E*. Excel displays a list of available functions, tables, and named ranges that start with the letter *E*. Click *Exceptions*, and press Tab to add the table reference to the formula. Then, because you want to summarize the values in the table's *Count* column, enter an opening bracket, and in the list of available table items, click *Count*. To finish creating the formula, enter a closing bracket followed by a closing parenthesis to create the formula =*SUM(Exceptions[Count])*.

If you want to include a series of contiguous cells in a formula, but you haven't defined the cells as a named range, you can click the first cell in the range and drag to the last cell. If the cells aren't contiguous, hold down the Ctrl key and select all of the cells to be included. In both cases, when you release the mouse button, the references of the cells you selected appear in the formula.

6

◢	A	B	C	D	E	F	G	H	I	J	K
1											
2		Conveyor									
3		350' track	$14,012.00								
4		Catch bin	$ 895.00								
5		Motor	$ 1,249.00			=sum(C3,C6,C14,C17					
6		Chain drive	$ 1,495.00			SUM(number1, [number2], [number3], [number4], [number5], …)					
7		Sorting table	$ 675.00								
8		Subtotal		$ 18,326.00							
9											
10		Loading Dock									
11		Concrete	$ 2,169.00								
12		Labor	$ 4,500.00								
13		Posts	$ 300.00								
14		Excavation	$ 2,500.00								
15		Drain	$ 1,800.00								
16		Rails	$ 495.00								
17		Stairs	$ 1,295.00								
18		Subtotal		$ 13,059.00							
19											
20		Build Total		$ 31,385.00							
21		Labor Percentage		#DIV/0!							
22											

A SUM formula that adds individual cells instead of a continuous range

In addition to using the Ctrl key to add cells to a selection, you can expand a selection by using a wide range of keyboard shortcuts. The following table summarizes many of those shortcuts.

Key sequence	Description
Shift+Right Arrow	Extend the selection one cell to the right.
Shift+Left Arrow	Extend the selection one cell to the left.
Shift+Up Arrow	Extend the selection up one cell.
Shift+Down Arrow	Extend the selection down one cell.
Ctrl+Shift+Right Arrow	Extend the selection to the last non-blank cell in the row.
Ctrl+Shift+Left Arrow	Extend the selection to the first non-blank cell in the row.
Ctrl+Shift+Up Arrow	Extend the selection to the first non-blank cell in the column.

Key sequence	Description
Ctrl+Shift+Down Arrow	Extend the selection to the last non-blank cell in the column.
Ctrl+Shift+8 (Ctrl+*)	Select the entire active region.
Shift+Home	Extend the selection to the beginning of the row.
Ctrl+Shift+Home	Extend the selection to the beginning of the worksheet.
Ctrl+Shift+End	Extend the selection to the end of the worksheet.
Shift+PageDown	Extend the selection down one screen.
Shift+PageUp	Extend the selection up one screen.
Alt+;	Select the visible cells in the current selection.

After you create a formula, you can copy it and paste it into another cell. When you do, Excel tries to change the formula so that it works in the new cells. For instance, suppose you have a worksheet where cell D8 contains the formula =SUM(C2:C6). Clicking cell D8, copying the cell's contents, and then pasting the result into cell D16 writes =SUM(C10:C14) into cell D16. Excel has reinterpreted the formula so that it fits the surrounding cells! Excel knows it can reinterpret the cells used in the formula because the formula uses a relative reference, or a reference that can change if the formula is copied to another cell. Relative references are written with just the cell row and column (for example, C14).

Relative references are useful when you summarize rows of data and want to use the same formula for each row. As an example, suppose you have a worksheet with two columns of data, labeled *Sale Price* and *Rate*, and you want to calculate your sales representative's commission by multiplying the two values in a row. To calculate the commission for the first sale, you would enter the formula =A2*B2 in cell C2.

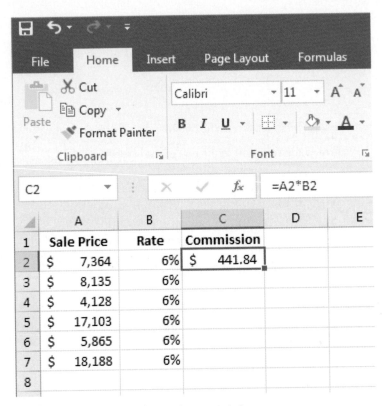

Use formulas to calculate values such as commissions

Selecting cell C2 and dragging the fill handle until it covers cells C2:C7 copies the formula from cell C2 into each of the other cells. Because you created the formula by using relative references, Excel updates each cell's formula to reflect its position relative to the starting cell (in this case, cell C2.) The formula in cell C7, for example, is *=A7*B7*.

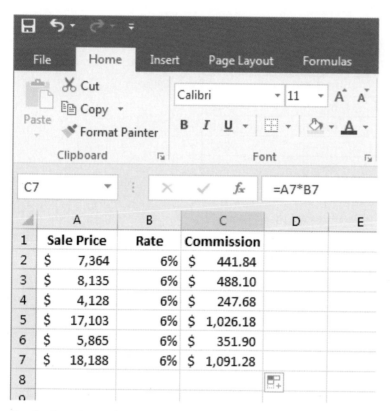

Copying formulas to other cells summarizes additional data

You can use a similar technique when you add a formula to an Excel table column. If the sale price and rate data were in an Excel table and you created the formula =A2*B2 in cell C2, Excel would apply the formula to every other cell in the column. Because you used relative references in the formula, the formulas would change to reflect each cell's distance from the original cell.

◢	A	B	C	D
1	Sale Price ▼	Rate ▼	Commission ▼	
2	$ 7,364	6%	$ 441.84	
3	$ 8,135	6%	$ 488	
4	$ 4,128	6%	$ 248	
5	$ 17,103	6%	$ 1,026	
6	$ 5,865	6%	$ 352	
7	$ 18,188	6%	$ 1,091	
8				

Adding a formula to an Excel table cell creates a calculated column

If you want a cell reference to remain constant when you copy the formula that is using it to another cell, you can use an absolute reference. To write a cell reference as an absolute reference, you enter $ before the row letter and the column number. For example, if you want the formula in cell D16 to show the sum of values in cells C10 through C14 regardless of the cell into which it is pasted, you can write the formula as =SUM($C$10:$C$14).

> ✓ **TIP** Another way to ensure that your cell references don't change when you copy a formula to another cell is to click the cell that contains the formula, copy the formula's text in the formula bar, press the Esc key to exit cut-and-copy mode, click the cell where you want to paste the formula, and press Ctrl+V. Excel doesn't change the cell references when you copy your formula to another cell in this manner.

One quick way to change a cell reference from relative to absolute is to select the cell reference in the formula bar and then press F4. Pressing F4 cycles a cell reference through the four possible types of references:

- Relative columns and rows (for example, C4)

- Absolute columns and rows (for example, $C$4)

- Relative columns and absolute rows (for example, C$4)

- Absolute columns and relative rows (for example, $C4)

To create a formula by entering it in a cell

1. Click the cell in which you want to create the formula.

2. Enter an equal sign (=).

3. Enter the remainder of the formula, and then press **Enter**.

To create a formula by using the Insert Function dialog box

1. On the **Formulas** tab, in the **Function Library** group, click the **Insert Function** button.

2. Click the function you want to use in your formula.

   Or

   Search for the function you want, and then click it.

3. Click **OK**.

4. In the **Function Arguments** dialog box, enter the function's arguments.

5. Click **OK**.

To display the current date and time by using a formula

1. Click the cell in which you want to display the current date and time.

2. Enter =**NOW()** into the cell.

3. Press **Enter**.

To update a *NOW()* formula

1. Press **F9**.

To calculate a payment by using a formula

1. Create a formula with the syntax =*PMT(rate, nper, pv, fv, type)*, where:

   - *rate* is the interest rate, to be divided by 12 for a loan with monthly payments, by 4 for quarterly payments, and so on.

   - *nper* is the total number of payments for the loan.

   - *pv* is the amount loaned.

- *fv* is the amount to be left over at the end of the payment cycle.

- *type* is 0 or 1, indicating whether payments are made at the beginning or at the end of the month.

2. Press **Enter**.

To refer to a named range in a formula

1. Click the cell where you want to create the formula.

2. Enter = to start the formula.

3. Enter the name of the named range in the part of the formula where you want to use its values.

4. Complete the formula.

5. Press **Enter**.

To refer to an Excel table column in a formula

1. Click the cell where you want to create the formula.

2. Enter = to start the formula.

3. At the point in the formula where you want to include the table's values, enter the name of the table.

   Or

   Use Formula AutoComplete to enter the table name.

4. Enter an opening bracket ([) followed by the column name.

   Or

   Enter [and use Formula AutoComplete to enter the column name.

5. Enter]) to close the table reference.

6. Press **Enter**.

To copy a formula without changing its cell references

1. Click the cell that contains the formula you want to copy.

2. Select the formula text in the formula bar.

3. Press **Ctrl+C**.

4. Click the cell where you want to paste the formula.

5. Press **Ctrl+V**.

6. Press **Enter**.

To move a formula without changing its cell references

1. Click the cell that contains the formula you want to copy.

2. Point to the edge of the cell you selected.

3. Drag the outline to the cell where you want to move the formula.

To copy a formula while changing its cell references

1. Click the cell that contains the formula you want to copy.

2. Press **Ctrl+C**.

3. Click the cell where you want to paste the formula.

4. Press **Ctrl+V**.

To create relative and absolute cell references

1. Enter a cell reference into a formula.

2. Click within the cell reference.

3. Enter a **$** in front of a row or column reference you want to make absolute.

   Or

   Press **F4** to advance through the four possible combinations of relative and absolute row and column references.

Operators and precedence

When you create an Excel formula, you use the built-in functions and arithmetic operators that define operations such as addition and multiplication. In Excel, mathematical operators are evaluated in the order listed in the following table.

Operator	Description
-	Negation
%	Percentage
^	Exponentiation
* and /	Multiplication and division
+ and −	Addition and subtraction
&	Concatenation (adding two strings together)

If two operators at the same level, such as + and −, occur in the same equation, Excel evaluates them in left-to-right order. For example, the operations in the formula = 4 + 8 * 3 − 6 would be evaluated in this order:

1. 8 * 3, with a result of 24
2. 4 + 24, with a result of 28
3. 28 − 6, with a final result of 22

You can control the order in which Excel evaluates operations by using parentheses. Excel always evaluates operations in parentheses first. For example, if the previous equation were rewritten as = (4 + 8) * 3 − 6, the operations would be evaluated in this order:

1. (4 + 8), with a result of 12
2. 12 * 3, with a result of 36
3. 36 − 6, with a final result of 30

If you have multiple levels of parentheses, Excel evaluates the expressions within the innermost set of parentheses first and works its way out. As with operations on the same level, such as + and −, expressions in the same parenthetical level are evaluated in left-to-right order.

For example, the formula = 4 + (3 + 8 * (2 + 5)) − 7 would be evaluated in this order:

1. (2 + 5), with a result of 7
2. 7 * 8, with a result of 56
3. 56 + 3, with a result of 59
4. 4 + 59, with a result of 63
5. 63 − 7, with a final result of 56

6

Summarize data that meets specific conditions

Another use for formulas is to display messages when certain conditions are met. This kind of formula is called a conditional formula; one way to create a conditional formula in Excel is to use the *IF* function. Clicking the Insert Function button next to the formula bar and then choosing the *IF* function displays the Function Arguments dialog box with the fields required to create an *IF* formula.

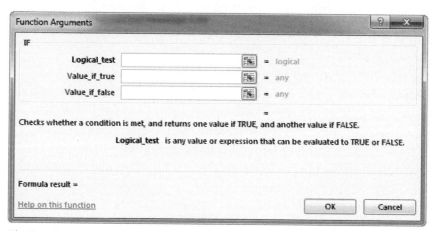

The Function Arguments dialog box for an IF formula

When you work with an *IF* function, the Function Arguments dialog box has three boxes: *Logical_test*, *Value_if_true*, and *Value_if_false*. The *Logical_test* box holds the condition you want to check.

Now you need to have Excel display messages that indicate whether the condition is met or not. To have Excel print a message from an *IF* function, you enclose the message in quotes in the *Value_if_true* or *Value_if_false* box. In this case, you would type *"High-volume shipper—evaluate for rate decrease"* in the *Value_if_true* box and *"Does not qualify at this time"* in the *Value_if_false* box.

Excel also includes several other conditional functions you can use to summarize your data, as shown in the following table.

Function	Description
AVERAGEIF	Finds the average of values within a cell range that meet a specified criterion
AVERAGEIFS	Finds the average of values within a cell range that meet multiple criteria
COUNT	Counts the number of cells in a range that contain a numerical value
COUNTA	Counts the number of cells in a range that are not empty
COUNTBLANK	Counts the number of cells in a range that are empty
COUNTIF	Counts the number of cells in a range that meet a specified criterion
COUNTIFS	Counts the number of cells in a range that meet multiple criteria
IFERROR	Displays one value if a formula results in an error and another if it doesn't
SUMIF	Finds the sum of values in a range that meet a single criterion
SUMIFS	Finds the sum of values in a range that meet multiple criteria

You can use the *IFERROR* function to display a custom error message, instead of relying on the default Excel error messages to explain what happened. For example, you could use an *IFERROR* formula when looking up a value by using the *VLOOKUP* function. An example of creating this type of formula would be to look up a customer's name, found in the second column of a table named *Customers*, based on the customer identification number entered into cell G8. That formula might look like this: *=IFERROR(VLOOKUP(G8,Customers,2,false),"Customer not found")*. If the function finds a match for the CustomerID in cell G8, it displays the customer's name; if it doesn't find a match, it displays the text *Customer not found*.

> **TIP** The last two arguments in the *VLOOKUP* function tell the formula to look in the *Customers* table's second column and to require an exact match. For more information about the *VLOOKUP* function, see "Look up information in a worksheet" in Chapter 8, "Reorder and summarize data."

Just as the *COUNTIF* function counts the number of cells that meet a criterion and the *SUMIF* function finds the total of values in cells that meet a criterion, the *AVERAGEIF* function finds the average of values in cells that meet a criterion. To create a formula that uses the *AVERAGEIF* function, you define the range to be examined for the criterion, the criterion, and, if required, the range from which to draw the values. As an example, consider a worksheet that lists each customer's ID number, name, state, and total monthly shipping bill.

	A	B	C	D
1	**CustomerID**	**CustomerName**	**State**	**Total**
2	OD100	Contoso	WA	$118,476.00
3	OD101	Fabrikam	WA	$125,511.00
4	OD102	Northwind Traders	OR	$103,228.00
5	OD103	Adventure Works	WA	$ 86,552.00

A list of data that contains customer information

If you want to find the average order of customers from the state of Washington (abbreviated in the worksheet as WA), you can create the formula =*AVERAGEIF(C3:C6, "WA", D3:D6)*.

The *AVERAGEIFS*, *SUMIFS*, and *COUNTIFS* functions extend the capabilities of the *AVERAGEIF*, *SUMIF*, and *COUNTIF* functions to allow for multiple criteria. If you want to find the sum of all orders of at least $100,000 placed by companies in Washington, you can create the formula =*SUMIFS(D3:D6, C3:C6, "=WA", D3:D6, ">=100000")*.

The *AVERAGEIFS* and *SUMIFS* functions start with a data range that contains values that the formula summarizes; you then list the data ranges and the criteria to apply to that range. In generic terms, the syntax runs =*AVERAGEIFS(data_range, criteria_range1, criteria1[,criteria_range2, criteria2...])*. The part of the syntax in brackets (which aren't used when you create the formula) is optional, so an *AVERAGEIFS* or *SUMIFS* formula that contains a single criterion will work. The *COUNTIFS* function, which doesn't perform any calculations, doesn't need a data range—you just provide the criteria ranges and criteria. For example, you could find the number of customers from Washington who were billed at least $100,000 by using the formula =*COUNTIFS(D3:D6, "=WA", E3:E6, ">=100000")*.

6

To summarize data by using the *IF* function

1. Click the cell in which you want to enter the formula.

2. Enter a formula with the syntax =*IF(Logical_test, Value_if_true, Value_if_false)* where:

   - *Logical_test* is the logical test to be performed.

   - *Value_if_true* is the value the formula returns if the test is true.

   - *Value_if_false* is the value the formula returns if the test is false.

To create a formula by using the Insert Function dialog box

1. To the left of the formula bar, click the **Insert Function** button.

2. In the **Insert Function** dialog box, click the function you want to use in your formula.

3. Click **OK**.

4. In the **Function Arguments** dialog box, define the arguments for the function you chose.

5. Click **OK**.

To count cells that contain numbers in a range

1. Click the cell in which you want to enter the formula.

2. Create a formula with the syntax =*COUNT(range)*, where *range* is the cell range in which you want to count cells.

To count cells that are non-blank

1. Click the cell in which you want to enter the formula.

2. Create a formula with the syntax =*COUNTA(range)*, where *range* is the cell range in which you want to count cells.

To count cells that contain a blank value

1. Click the cell in which you want to enter the formula.

2. Create a formula with the syntax =*COUNTBLANK(range)*, where *range* is the cell range in which you want to count cells.

To count cells that meet one condition

1. Click the cell in which you want to enter the formula.

2. Enter a formula of the form *=COUNTIF(range, criteria)* where:

   - *range* is the cell range that might contain the criteria value.

   - *criteria* is the logical test used to determine whether to count the cell or not.

To count cells that meet multiple conditions

1. Click the cell in which you want to enter the formula.

2. Enter a formula of the form *=COUNTIFS(criteria_range, criteria,...)* where for each *criteria_range* and *criteria* pair:

   - *criteria_range* is the cell range that might contain the *criteria* value.

   - *criteria* is the logical test used to determine whether to count the cell or not.

To find the sum of data that meets one condition

1. Click the cell in which you want to enter the formula.

2. Enter a formula of the form *=SUMIF(range, criteria, sum_range)* where:

   - *range* is the cell range that might contain the *criteria* value.

   - *criteria* is the logical test used to determine whether to include the cell or not.

   - *sum_range* is the range that contains the values to be included if the *range* cell in the same row meets the criterion.

To find the sum of data that meets multiple conditions

1. Click the cell in which you want to enter the formula.

2. Enter a formula of the form *=SUMIFS(sum_range, criteria_range, criteria,...)* where:

   - *sum_range* is the range that contains the values to be included if all *criteria_range* cells in the same row meet all criteria.

   - *criteria_range* is the cell range that might contain the *criteria* value.

   - *criteria* is the logical test used to determine whether to include the cell or not.

6

To find the average of data that meets one condition

1. Click the cell in which you want to enter the formula.

2. Enter a formula of the form *=AVERAGEIF(range, criteria, average_range)* where:

   - *range* is the cell range that might contain the *criteria* value.

   - *criteria* is the logical test used to determine whether to include the cell or not.

   - *average_range* is the range that contains the values to be included if the *range* cell in the same row meets the criterion.

To find the average of data that meets multiple conditions

1. Click the cell in which you want to enter the formula.

2. Enter a formula of the form *=AVERAGEIFS(average_range, criteria_range, criteria,...)* where:

   - *average_range* is the range that contains the values to be included if all *criteria_range* cells in the same row meet all criteria.

   - *criteria_range* is the cell range that might contain the *criteria* value.

   - *criteria* is the logical test used to determine whether to include the cell or not.

To display a custom message if a cell contains an error

1. Click the cell in which you want to enter the formula.

2. Enter a formula with the syntax *=IFERROR(value, value_if_error)* where:

   - *value* is a cell reference or formula.

   - *value_if_error* is the value to be displayed if the *value* argument returns an error.

Set iterative calculation options and enable or disable automatic calculation

Excel formulas use values in other cells to calculate their results. If you create a formula that refers to the cell that contains the formula, you have created a circular reference. Under most circumstances, Excel treats circular references as a mistake for two reasons. First, the vast majority of Excel formulas don't refer to their own cell, so a circular reference is unusual enough to be identified as an error. The second, more serious consideration is that a formula with a circular reference can slow down your workbook. Because Excel repeats, or iterates, the calculation, you need to set limits on how many times the app repeats the operation.

You can control your workbook's calculation options by using the controls on the Formulas page of the Excel Options dialog box.

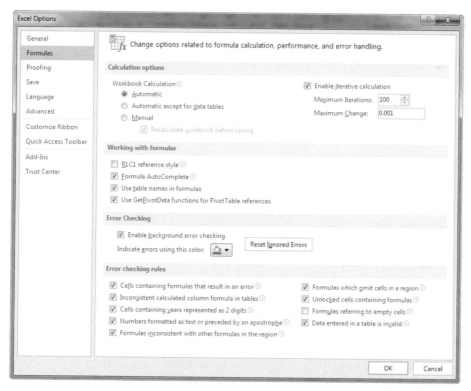

Set iterative calculation options on the Formulas page of the Excel Options dialog box

The Calculation Options section of the Excel Options dialog box has three available settings:

- **Automatic** The default setting; recalculates a worksheet whenever a value affecting a formula changes

- **Automatic except for data tables** Recalculates a worksheet whenever a value changes, but doesn't recalculate data tables

- **Manual** Requires you to press F9 or, on the Formulas tab, in the Calculation group, click the Calculate Now button to recalculate your worksheet

You can also use options in the Calculation Options section to allow or disallow iterative calculations. If you select the Enable Iterative Calculation check box, Excel repeats calculations for cells that contain formulas with circular references. The default Maximum Iterations value of 100 and Maximum Change of 0.001 are appropriate for all but the most unusual circumstances.

 TIP You can also control when Excel recalculates its formulas by clicking the Formulas tab on the ribbon, clicking the Calculation Options button, and selecting the behavior you want.

To recalculate a workbook

1. Display the workbook you want to recalculate.

2. Press **F9**.

    Or

    On the **Formulas** tab, in the **Calculation** group, click **Calculate Now**.

To recalculate a worksheet

1. Display the worksheet you want to recalculate.

2. In the **Calculation** group, click the **Calculate Sheet** button.

To set worksheet calculation options

1. Display the worksheet whose calculation options you want to set.

2. In the **Calculation** group, click the **Calculate Options** button.

3. Click the calculation option you want in the list.

To set iterative calculation options

1. Display the Backstage view, and then click **Options**.

2. In the **Excel Options** dialog box, click **Formulas**.

3. In the **Calculation options** section, select or clear the **Enable iterative calculation** check box.

4. In the **Maximum Iterations** box, enter the maximum iterations allowed for a calculation.

5. In the **Maximum Change** box, enter the maximum change allowed for each iteration.

6. Click **OK**.

Use array formulas

Most Excel formulas calculate values to be displayed in a single cell. For example, you could add the formulas =B1*B4, =B1*B5, and =B1*B6 to consecutive worksheet cells to calculate shipping insurance costs based on the value of a package's contents.

	A	B	C	D
1	**Insurance Rate**	2.50%		
2				
3	**PackageID**	**Value**	**Premium**	
4	PK000352	$ 591.00		
5	PK000353	$1,713.00		
6	PK000354	$3,039.00		
7				

A worksheet with data to be summarized by an array formula

Rather than add the same formula to multiple cells one cell at a time, you can add a formula to every cell in the target range at the same time by creating an array formula. To create an array formula, you enter the formula's arguments and press Ctrl+Shift+Enter to identify the formula as an array formula. To calculate package insurance rates for values in the cell range B4:B6 and the rate in cell B1, you would select a range of cells with the same shape as the value range and enter the formula

=B1*B4:B6. In this case, the values are in a three-cell column, so you must select a range of the same shape, such as C4:C6.

	A	B	C	D
1	**Insurance Rate**	2.50%		
2				
3	**PackageID**	**Value**	**Premium**	
4	PK000352	$ 591.00	=B1*B4:B6	
5	PK000353	$1,713.00		
6	PK000354	$3,039.00		
7				

A worksheet with an array formula ready to be entered

 IMPORTANT If you enter the array formula into a range of the wrong shape, Excel displays duplicate results, incomplete results, or error messages, depending on how the target range differs from the value range.

When you press Ctrl+Shift+Enter, Excel creates an array formula in the selected cells. The formula appears within a pair of braces to indicate that it is an array formula.

IMPORTANT You can't add braces to a formula to make it an array formula—you must press Ctrl+Shift+Enter to create it.

In addition to creating an array formula that combines a single cell's value with an array, you can create array formulas that use two separate arrays. For example, a company might establish a goal to reduce sorting time in each of four distribution centers.

	A	B	C	D
1	Center	Previous Time	Target Percentage	Target Time
2	North	145	85%	
3	South	180	90%	
4	East	195	75%	
5	West	205	70%	
6				

A worksheet with data for an array formula that multiplies two arrays

This worksheet stores the previous sorting times in minutes in cells B2:B5, and the percentage targets in cells C2:C5. The array formula to calculate the targets for each of the four centers is *=B2:B5*C2:C5* which, when entered into cells D2:D5 by pressing Ctrl+Shift+Enter, would appear as *{= B2:B5*C2:C5}*.

To edit an array formula, you must select every cell that contains the array formula, click the formula bar to activate it, edit the formula in the formula bar, and then press Ctrl+Shift+Enter to re-enter the formula as an array formula.

 TIP Many operations that used to require an array formula can now be calculated by using functions such as *SUMIFS* and *COUNTIFS*.

To create an array formula

1. Select the cells into which you want to enter the array formula.

2. Enter your array formula.

3. Press **Ctrl+Shift+Enter**.

To edit an array formula

1. Select the cells that contain the array formula.

2. Edit your array formula.

3. Press **Ctrl+Shift+Enter**.

Find and correct errors in calculations

Including calculations in a worksheet gives you valuable answers to questions about your data. As is always true, however, it is possible for errors to creep into your formulas. With Excel, you can find the source of errors in your formulas by identifying the cells used in a specific calculation and describing any errors that have occurred. The process of examining a worksheet for errors is referred to as auditing.

Excel identifies errors in several ways. The first way is to display an error code in the cell holding the formula generating the error.

9			
10	**Loading Dock**		
11	Concrete	$ 2,169.00	
12	Labor	$ 4,500.00	
13	Posts	$ 300.00	
14	Excavation	$ 2,500.00	
15	Drain	$ 1,800.00	
16	Rails	$ 495.00	
17	Stairs	$ 1,295.00	
18	*Subtotal*		$ 13,059.00
19			
20	**Build Total**		$ 31,385.00
21	**Labor Percentage**	◈	#DIV/0!
22			
23			
24			
25			

FirstBid ⊕

A worksheet with an error code displayed

When a cell with an erroneous formula is the active cell, an Error button is displayed next to it. If you point to the Error button Excel displays an arrow on the button's right edge. Clicking the arrow displays a menu with options that provide information about the error and offer to help you fix it.

The table on the following page lists the most common error codes and what they mean.

Error code	Description
#####	The column isn't wide enough to display the value.
#VALUE!	The formula has the wrong type of argument (such as text in a cell where a numerical value is required).
#NAME?	The formula contains text that Excel doesn't recognize (such as an unknown named range).
#REF!	The formula refers to a cell that doesn't exist (which can happen whenever cells are deleted).
#DIV/0!	The formula attempts to divide by zero.

Another technique you can use to find the source of formula errors is to ensure that the appropriate cells are providing values for the formula. You can identify the source of an error by having Excel trace a cell's precedents, which are the cells with values used in the active cell's formula. You can also audit your worksheet by identifying cells with formulas that use a value from a particular cell. Cells that use another cell's value in their calculations are known as dependents, meaning that they depend on the value in the other cell to derive their own value.

9		
10	**Loading Dock**	
11	Concrete	$ 2,169.00
12	Labor	$ 4,500.00
13	Posts	$ 300.00
14	Excavation	$ 2,500.00
15	Drain	$ 1,800.00
16	Rails	$ 495.00
17	Stairs	$ 1,295.00
18	*Subtotal*	$ 13,059.00
19		
20	**Build Total**	$ 31,385.00
21	**Labor Percentage**	14%
22		

A worksheet with a cell's dependents indicated by tracer arrows

If the cells identified by the tracer arrows aren't the correct cells, you can hide the arrows and correct the formula.

If you prefer to have the elements of a formula error presented as text in a dialog box, you can use the Error Checking dialog box to move through the formula one step at a time, to choose to ignore the error, or to move to the next or the previous error.

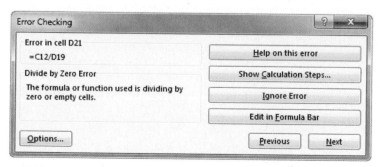

Identify and manage errors by using the Error Checking dialog box

> **TIP** You can have the Error Checking tool ignore formulas that don't use every cell in a region (such as a row or column) by modifying this option in the Excel Options dialog box. To do so, on the Formulas tab of the dialog box, if you clear the Formulas Which Omit Cells In A Region check box, you can create formulas that don't add up every value in a row or column (or rectangle) without Excel marking them as an error.

For times when you just want to display the results of each step of a formula and don't need the full power of the Error Checking tool, you can use the Evaluate Formula dialog box to move through each element of the formula. The Evaluate Formula dialog box is much more useful for examining formulas that don't produce an error but aren't generating the result you expect.

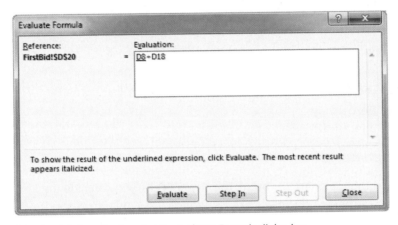

Step through formulas by using the Evaluate Formula dialog box

Finally, you can monitor the value in a cell regardless of where in your workbook you are by opening a Watch Window that displays the value in the cell. For example, if one of your formulas uses values from cells in other worksheets or even other workbooks, you can set a watch on the cell that contains the formula and then change the values in the other cells.

As soon as you enter the new value, the Watch Window displays the new result of the formula. When you're done watching the formula, you can delete the watch and hide the Watch Window.

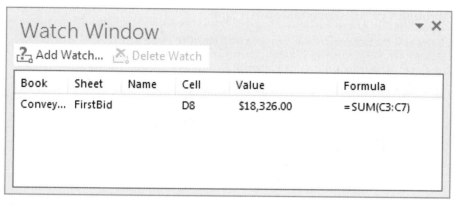

Follow cell values by using the Watch Window

To display information about a formula error

1. Click the cell that contains the error.

2. Point to the error indicator next to the cell.

   Or

   Click the error indicator to display more information.

To display arrows identifying formula precedents

1. On the **Formulas** tab, in the **Formula Auditing** group, click the **Trace Precedents** button.

To display arrows identifying cell dependents

1. In the **Formula Auditing** group, click the **Trace Dependents** button.

To remove tracer arrows

1. Do either of the following:

   • In the **Formula Auditing** group, click the **Remove Arrows** button (not its arrow).

   • Click the **Remove Arrows** arrow and select the arrows you want to remove.

To move through a calculation one step at a time

1. Click the cell that contains the formula you want to evaluate.

2. In the **Formula Auditing** group, click the **Evaluate Formula** button.

3. In the **Evaluate Formula** dialog box, click **Evaluate**.

4. Click **Step In** to move forward by one calculation.

   Or

   Click **Step Out** to move backward by one calculation.

5. Click **Close**.

To change error display options

1. Display the Backstage view, and then click **Options**.

2. In the **Excel Options** dialog box, click **Formulas**.

3. In the **Error Checking** section, select or clear the **Enable background error checking** check box.

4. Click the **Indicate errors using this color** button and select a color.

5. Click **Reset Ignored Errors** to return Excel to its default error indicators.

6. In the **Error checking rules** section, select or clear the check boxes next to errors you want to indicate or ignore, respectively.

To watch the values in a cell range

1. Click the cell range you want to watch.

2. In the **Formula Auditing** group, click the **Watch Window** button.

3. In the **Watch Window** dialog box, click **Add Watch**.

4. Click **Add**.

To delete a watch

1. Click the **Watch Window** button.

2. In the **Watch Window** dialog box, click the watch you want to delete.

3. Click **Delete Watch**.

Skills review

In this chapter, you learned how to:

- Name groups of data
- Create formulas to calculate values
- Define Excel tables
- Summarize data that meets specific conditions
- Set iterative calculation options and enable or disable automatic calculation
- Use array formulas
- Find and correct errors in calculations

6

Practice tasks

The practice files for these tasks are located in the Office2016SBS\Ch06 folder. You can save the results of the tasks in the same folder.

Name groups of data

Open the CreateNames workbook in Excel, and then perform the following tasks:

1. Create a named range named **Monday** for the V_101 through V_109 values (found in cells **C4:C12**) for that weekday.

2. Edit the **Monday** named range to include the V_110 value for that column.

3. Select cells **B4:H13** and create named ranges for V_101 through V_110, drawing the names from the row headings.

4. Delete the **Monday** named range.

Create formulas to calculate values

Open the BuildFormulas workbook in Excel, and then perform the following tasks:

1. On the **Summary** worksheet, in cell **F9**, create a formula that displays the value from cell **C4**.

2. Edit the formula in cell **F9** so it uses the *SUM* function to find the total of values in cells **C3:C8**.

3. In cell **F10**, create a formula that finds the total expenses for desktop software and server software.

4. Edit the formula in **F10** so the cell references are absolute references.

5. On the **JuneLabor** worksheet, in cell **F13**, create a *SUM* formula that finds the total of values in the **JuneSummary** table's **Labor Expense** column.

Define Excel tables

Open the CreateExcelTables workbook in Excel, and then perform the following tasks:

1. Create an Excel table from the list of data on the **Sort Times** worksheet.

2. Add a row of data to the Excel table for driver **D116**, and assign a value of **100** sorting minutes.

3. Add a **Total** row to the Excel table, and then change the summary function to **Average**.

4. Rename the Excel table to **SortTimes**.

˙ ˙ ᵈᵃᵗᵃ ᵗʰᵃᵗ meets specific conditions

ok in Excel, and then perform the

s whether the value in **F3** is greater than
st discount; if not, display **No discount**

ange **G4:G14**.

e average cost of all expenses in cells
s the value *Box*.

e sum of all expenses in cells **F3:F14**
alue *Envelope* and the **Destination**
al.

and enable or disable

Excel, and then perform the following

ion group, click the **Calculation Options**
button, and ...

2. In cell **B6**, enter the formula **=B7*B9**, and then press **Enter**.

Note that this result is incorrect because the Gross Savings minus the Savings Incentive should equal the Net Savings value, which it does not.

3. Press **F9** to recalculate the workbook and read the message box indicating you have created a circular reference.

4. Click **OK**.

5. Use options in the **Excel Options** dialog box to enable iterative calculation.

6. Close the **Excel Options** dialog box and recalculate the worksheet.

7. Change the workbook's calculation options to **Automatic**.

Use array formulas

Open the CreateArrayFormulas workbook in Excel, and then perform the following tasks:

1. On the **Fuel** worksheet, select cells **C11:F11**.

2. Enter the array formula =C3*C9:F9 in the selected cells.

3. Edit the array formula you just created to read =C3*C10:F10.

4. Display the **Volume** worksheet.

5. Select cells **D4:D7**.

6. Create the array formula =B4:B7*C4:C7.

Find and correct errors in calculations

Open the AuditFormulas workbook in Excel, and then perform the following tasks:

1. Create a watch that displays the value in cell **D20**.

2. Click cell **D8**, and then display the formula's precedents.

3. Remove the tracer arrows from the worksheet.

4. Click cell **A1**, and then use the **Error Checking** dialog box to identify the error in cell **D21**.

5. Show the tracer arrows for the error.

6. Remove the arrows, then edit the formula in cell **D21** so it is =C12/D20.

7. Use the **Evaluate Formula** dialog box to evaluate the formula in cell **D21**.

8. Delete the watch you created in step 1.

Manage worksheet data

With Excel 2016, you can manage huge data collections, but storing more than 1 million rows of data doesn't help you make business decisions unless you have the ability to focus on the most important data in a worksheet. Focusing on the most relevant data in a worksheet facilitates decision making. Excel includes many powerful and flexible tools with which you can limit the data displayed in your worksheet. When your worksheet displays the subset of data you need to make a decision, you can perform calculations on that data. You can discover what percentage of monthly revenue was earned in the 10 best days in the month, find your total revenue for particular days of the week, or locate the slowest business day of the month.

Just as you can limit the data displayed by your worksheets, you can also create validation rules that limit the data entered into them. When you set rules for data entered into cells, you can catch many of the most common data entry errors, such as entering values that are too small or too large, or attempting to enter a word in a cell that requires a number. If you add a validation rule after data has been entered, you can circle any invalid data so that you know what to correct.

This chapter guides you through procedures related to limiting the data that appears on your screen, manipulating list data, and creating validation rules that limit data entry to appropriate values.

In this chapter

- Limit data that appears on your screen
- Manipulate worksheet data
- Define valid sets of values for ranges of cells

Practice files

For this chapter, use the practice files from the Office2016SBS\Ch07 folder. For practice file download instructions, see the introduction.

Limit data that appears on your screen

Excel worksheets can hold as much data as you need them to, but you might not want to work with all the data in a worksheet at the same time. For example, you might want to look at the revenue figures for your company during the first third, second third, and final third of a month. You can limit the data shown on a worksheet by creating a filter, which is a rule that selects rows to be shown in a worksheet.

> **⚠ IMPORTANT** When you turn on filtering, Excel treats the cells in the active cell's column as a range. To ensure that the filtering works properly, you should always have a label at the top of the column you want to filter. If you don't, Excel treats the first value in the list as the label and doesn't include it in the list of values by which you can filter the data.

When you turn on filtering, a filter arrow appears to the right of each column label in the list of data. Clicking the filter arrow displays a menu of filtering options and a list of the unique values in the column. Each item has a check box next to it, which you can use to create a selection filter. Some of the commands vary depending on the type of data in the column. For example, if the column contains a set of dates, you will get a list of commands specific to that data type.

> **TIP** In Excel tables, filter arrows are turned on by default.

> **TIP** When a column contains several types of data, the filter command for it is Number Filters.

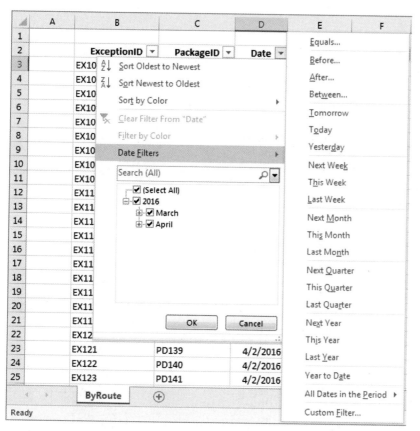

Use filters to limit the data that appears in a worksheet

When you click a filtering option, Excel displays a dialog box in which you can define the filter's criteria. As an example, you could create a filter that displays only dates after 3/31/2016.

◢	A	B	C	D	E	F	G
1							
2		ExceptionID ▼	PackageID ▼	Date �	Center ▼	Route ▼	
16		EX114	PD132	4/1/2016	Midwest	RT436	
17		EX115	PD133	4/1/2016	Midwest	RT758	
18		EX116	PD134	4/1/2016	Midwest	RT529	
19		EX117	PD135	4/1/2016	Northeast	RT243	
20		EX118	PD136	4/1/2016	Northeast	RT189	
21		EX119	PD137	4/1/2016	Northwest	RT714	
22		EX120	PD138	4/2/2016	Central	RT151	
23		EX121	PD139	4/2/2016	Midwest	RT543	
24		EX122	PD140	4/2/2016	Southwest	RT208	
25		EX123	PD141	4/2/2016	South	RT145	
26		EX124	PD142	4/2/2016	Central	RT250	
27		EX125	PD143	4/2/2016	Midwest	RT852	
28							

Columns with a filter applied display a funnel icon on their filter arrows

If you want to display the highest or lowest values in a data column, you can create a Top 10 filter. You can choose whether to show values from the top or bottom of the list, define the number of items you want to display, and choose whether that number indicates the actual number of items or the percentage of items to be shown when the filter is applied.

 TIP Top 10 filters can be applied only to columns that contain number values.

Excel 2016 includes a capability called the search filter, which you can use to enter a search string that Excel uses to identify which items to display in an Excel table or a data list. Enter the character string you want to search for, and Excel limits your data to values that contain that string.

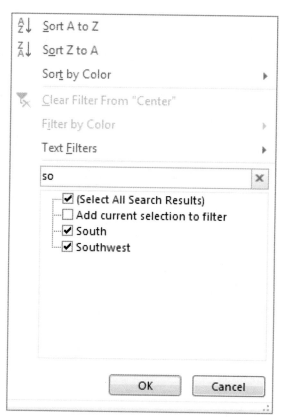

Applying a search filter limits the items that appear in the selection list

When you create a custom filter, you can define a rule that Excel uses to decide which rows to show after the filter is applied. For instance, you can create a rule that determines that only days with package volumes of less than 100,000 should be shown in your worksheet. With those results in front of you, you might be able to determine whether the weather or another factor resulted in slower business on those days.

Excel indicates that a column has a filter applied by changing the appearance of the column's filter arrow to include an icon that looks like a funnel. After you finish examining your data by using a filter, you can clear the filter or turn off filtering entirely and hide the filter arrows.

To turn on filter arrows

1. Click any cell in the list of data you want to filter.

2. On the **Home** tab of the ribbon, in the **Editing** group, click **Sort & Filter**, and then click **Filter**.

To create a selection filter

1. Click **Sort & Filter**, and then click **Filter**.

2. Click the filter arrow for the column by which you want to filter your data.

3. Clear the check boxes next to the items you want to hide.

   Or

   Clear the **Select All** check box and select the check boxes next to the items you want to display.

4. Click **OK**.

To create a filter rule

1. Display the filter arrows for your list of data.

2. Click the filter arrow for the field by which you want to filter your data.

3. Point to the *Type* **Filters** item to display the available filters for the column's data type.

4. Click the filter you want to create.

5. Enter the arguments required to define the rule.

6. Click **OK**.

To create a Top 10 filter

1. Display the filter arrows for your list of data.

2. Click the filter arrow for a column that contains number values, point to **Number Filters**, and then click **Top 10**.

3. In the **Top 10 AutoFilter** dialog box, click the arrow for the first list box, and select whether to display the top or bottom values.

4. Click the arrow for the last list box, and select whether to base the rule on the number of items or the percentage of items.

5. Click in the middle box and enter the number or percentage of items to display.

6. Click **OK**.

To create a search filter

1. Display the filter arrows for your list of data.

2. Click the filter arrow for the field by which you want to filter your data.

3. Enter the character string that should appear in the values you want to display in the filter list.

4. Click **OK**.

To clear a filter

1. Click the filter arrow for the field that has the filter you want to clear.

2. Click **Clear Filter From** *Field*.

To turn off the filter arrows

1. Click any cell in the list of data.

2. Click **Sort & Filter**, and then click **Filter**.

Manipulate worksheet data

Excel includes a wide range of tools you can use to summarize worksheet data. This topic describes how to select rows at random by using the *RAND* and *RANDBETWEEN* functions, how to summarize worksheet data by using the *SUBTOTAL* and *AGGREGATE* functions, and how to display a list of unique values within a data set.

Select list rows at random

In addition to filtering the data that is stored in your Excel worksheets, you can choose rows at random from a list. Selecting rows randomly is useful for choosing which customers will receive a special offer, deciding which days of the month to audit, or picking prize winners at an employee party.

To choose rows randomly, you can use the *RAND* function, which generates a random decimal value between 0 and 1, and compare the value it returns with a test value included in a formula. If you recalculate the *RAND* function 10 times and check each time to find out whether the value is below 0.3, it's very unlikely that you would get exactly three instances where the value is below 0.3. Just as flipping a coin can result in the same result 10 times in a row by chance, so can the *RAND* function's results appear to be off if you only recalculate it a few times. However, if you were to recalculate the function 10,000 times, it is extremely likely that the number of *values less than 0.3* would be very close to 30 percent.

TIP Because the *RAND* function is a volatile function (that is, it recalculates its results every time you update the worksheet), you should copy the cells that contain the *RAND* function in a formula and paste the formulas' values back into their original cells. To do so, select the cells that contain the *RAND* formulas and paste them back into the same cells as values.

The *RANDBETWEEN* function generates a random whole number within a defined range. For example, the formula =*RANDBETWEEN(1,100)* would generate a random integer value from 1 through 100, inclusive. The *RANDBETWEEN* function is very useful for creating sample data collections for presentations. Before the *RANDBETWEEN* function was introduced, you had to create formulas that added, subtracted, multiplied, and divided the results of the *RAND* function, which are always decimal values between 0 and 1, to create data.

To use *RAND* or *RANDBETWEEN* to select a row, create an *IF* formula that tests the random values. If you want to check 30 percent of the rows, a formula such as =*IF(cell_address<0.3, "TRUE", "FALSE")* would display *TRUE* in the formula cells for any value of 0.3 or less and *FALSE* otherwise.

Summarize data in worksheets that have hidden and filtered rows

The ability to analyze the data that's most vital to your current needs is important, but there are some limitations to how you can summarize your filtered data by using functions such as *SUM* and *AVERAGE*. One limitation is that any formulas you create that include the *SUM* and *AVERAGE* functions don't change their calculations if some of the rows used in the formula are hidden by the filter.

Excel provides two ways to summarize just the visible cells in a filtered data list. The first method is to use AutoCalculate. To use AutoCalculate, you select the cells you want to summarize. When you do, Excel displays the average of the values in the cells, the sum of the values in the cells, and the number of visible cells (the count) in the selection. You'll find the display on the status bar at the lower edge of the Excel window.

When you use AutoCalculate, you aren't limited to finding the sum, average, and count of the selected cells. You can add or remove calculations to suit your needs; a check mark appears next to a function's name if that function's result appears on the status bar.

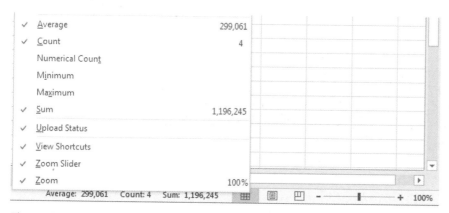

The status bar displays summary values when you select more than one cell that contains numeric data

AutoCalculate is great for finding a quick total or average for filtered cells, but it doesn't make the result available in the worksheet. Formulas such as *=SUM(C3:C26)* always consider every cell in the range, regardless of whether you hide a cell's row manually or not, so you need to create a formula by using either the *SUBTOTAL* function or the *AGGREGATE* function to summarize just those values that are visible in your worksheet. The *SUBTOTAL* function lets you choose whether to summarize every value in a range or summarize only those values in rows you haven't manually hidden. The *SUBTOTAL* function has this syntax: =*SUBTOTAL(function_num, ref1, ref2, ...)*. The *function_num* argument holds the number of the operation you want to use to summarize your data. (The operation numbers are summarized in a table later in this section.) The *ref1, ref2,* and further arguments represent up to 29 ranges to include in the calculation.

As an example, assume you have a worksheet where you hid rows 20-26 manually. In this case, the formula =*SUBTOTAL(9, C3:C26, E3:E26, G3:G26)* would find the sum of all values in the ranges C3:C26, E3:E26, and G3:G26, regardless of whether that range contained any hidden rows. The formula =*SUBTOTAL(109, C3:C26, E3:E26, G3:G26)* would find the sum of all values in cells C3:C19, E3:E19, and G3:G19, ignoring the values in the manually hidden rows.

> ⚠ **IMPORTANT** Be sure to place your *SUBTOTAL* formula in a row that is even with or above the headers in the range you're filtering. If you don't, your filter might hide the formula's result!

The following table lists the summary operations available for the *SUBTOTAL* formula. Excel displays the available summary operations as part of the Formula AutoComplete functionality, so you don't need to remember the operation numbers or look them up in the Help system.

Operation number (includes hidden values)	Operation number (ignores values in manually hidden rows)	Function	Description
1	101	AVERAGE	Returns the average of the values in the range
2	102	COUNT	Counts the cells in the range that contain a number
3	103	COUNTA	Counts the nonblank cells in the range
4	104	MAX	Returns the largest (maximum) value in the range

Operation number (includes hidden values)	Operation number (ignores values in manually hidden rows)	Function	Description
5	105	*MIN*	Returns the smallest (minimum) value in the range
6	106	*PRODUCT*	Returns the result of multiplying all numbers in the range
7	107	*STDEV.S*	Calculates the standard deviation of values in the range by examining a sample of the values
8	108	*STDEV.P*	Calculates the standard deviation of the values in the range by using all the values
9	109	*SUM*	Returns the result of adding all numbers in the range together
10	110	*VAR.S*	Calculates the variance of values in the range by examining a sample of the values
11	111	*VAR.P*	Calculates the variance of the values in the range by using all of the values

7

As the preceding table shows, the *SUBTOTAL* function has two sets of operations. The first set (operations 1–11) represents operations that include hidden values in their summary, and the second set (operations 101–111) represents operations that summarize only values visible in the worksheet. Operations 1–11 summarize all cells in a range, regardless of whether the range contains any manually hidden rows. By contrast, operations 101–111 ignore any values in manually hidden rows. What the *SUBTOTAL* function doesn't do, however, is change its result to reflect rows hidden by using a filter.

> ⚠ **IMPORTANT** Excel treats the first cell in the data range as a header cell, so it doesn't consider the cell as it builds the list of unique values. Be sure to include the header cell in your data range!

The *AGGREGATE* function extends the capabilities of the *SUBTOTAL* function. With it, you can select from a broader range of functions and use another argument to determine which, if any, values to ignore in the calculation. *AGGREGATE* has two possible syntaxes, depending on the summary operation you select. The first syntax is =AGGREGATE(function_num, options, ref1...), which is similar to the syntax of the *SUBTOTAL* function. The other possible syntax, =AGGREGATE(function_num, options, array, [k]), is used to create *AGGREGATE* functions that use the *LARGE*, *SMALL*, *PERCENTILE.INC*, *QUARTILE.INC*, *PERCENTILE.EXC*, and *QUARTILE.EXC* operations.

The following table summarizes the summary operations available for use in the *AGGREGATE* function.

Number	Function	Description
1	AVERAGE	Returns the average of the values in the range.
2	COUNT	Counts the cells in the range that contain a number.
3	COUNTA	Counts the nonblank cells in the range.
4	MAX	Returns the largest (maximum) value in the range.
5	MIN	Returns the smallest (minimum) value in the range.
6	PRODUCT	Returns the result of multiplying all numbers in the range.

Number	Function	Description
7	STDEV.S	Calculates the standard deviation of values in the range by examining a sample of the values.
8	STDEV.P	Calculates the standard deviation of the values in the range by using all the values.
9	SUM	Returns the result of adding all numbers in the range together.
10	VAR.S	Calculates the variance of values in the range by examining a sample of the values.
11	VAR.P	Calculates the variance of the values in the range by using all of the values.
12	MEDIAN	Returns the value in the middle of a group of values.
13	MODE.SNGL	Returns the most frequently occurring number from a group of numbers.
14	LARGE	Returns the k-th largest value in a data set; k is specified by using the last function argument. If k is left blank, Excel returns the largest value.
15	SMALL	Returns the k-th smallest value in a data set; k is specified by using the last function argument. If k is left blank, Excel returns the smallest value.
16	PERCENTILE.INC	Returns the k-th percentile of values in a range, where k is a value from 0 to 1, inclusive.
17	QUARTILE.INC	Returns the quartile value of a data set, based on a percentage from 0 to 1, inclusive.
18	PERCENTILE.EXC	Returns the k-th percentile of values in a range, where k is a value from 0 to 1, exclusive.
19	QUARTILE.EXC	Returns the quartile value of a data set, based on a percentage from 0 to 1, exclusive.

7

You use the second argument, *options*, to select which items the *AGGREGATE* function should ignore. These items can include hidden rows, errors, and *SUBTOTAL* and *AGGREGATE* functions. The following table summarizes the values available for the *options* argument and the effect they have on the function's results.

Number	Description
0	Ignore nested *SUBTOTAL* and *AGGREGATE* functions
1	Ignore hidden rows and nested *SUBTOTAL* and *AGGREGATE* functions
2	Ignore error values and nested *SUBTOTAL* and *AGGREGATE* functions
3	Ignore hidden rows, error values, and nested *SUBTOTAL* and *AGGREGATE* functions
4	Ignore nothing
5	Ignore hidden rows
6	Ignore error values
7	Ignore hidden rows and error values

To summarize values by using AutoCalculate

1. Select the cells in your worksheet.

2. View the summaries on the status bar.

To change the AutoCalculate summaries displayed on the status bar

1. Right-click the status bar.

2. Click a summary operation without a check mark to display it.

   Or

   Click a summary operation with a check mark to hide it.

To create a *SUBTOTAL* formula

1. In a cell, enter a formula that uses the syntax *=SUBTOTAL(function_num, ref1, ref2, ...)*. The arguments in the syntax are as follows:

   - The *function_num* argument is the reference number of the function you want to use.

   - The *ref1*, *ref2*, and subsequent *ref* arguments refer to cell ranges.

To create an *AGGREGATE* formula

1. Do one of the following:

   - Create a formula of the syntax =*AGGREGATE(function_num, options, ref1...)*. The arguments in the syntax are as follows:

     - The *function_num* argument is the reference number of the function you want to use.

     - The *options* argument is the reference number for the options you want.

     - The *ref1, ref2*, and subsequent *ref* arguments refer to cell ranges.

   Or

   - Create a formula with the syntax =*AGGREGATE(function_num, options, array, [k])*. The arguments in the syntax are as follows:

     - The *function_num* argument is the reference number of the function you want to use.

     - The *options* argument is the reference number for the options you want to use.

     - The *array* argument represents the cell range (array) that provides data for the formula.

     - The optional *k* argument, used with the *LARGE, SMALL, PERCENTILE.INC, QUARTILE.INC, PERCENTILE.EXC*, and *QUARTILE.EXC*, indicates which value, percentile, or quartile to return.

Find unique values within a data set

Summarizing numerical values can provide valuable information that helps you run your business. It can also be helpful to know how many different values appear within a column. For example, you might want to display all of the countries and regions in which Consolidated Messenger has customers. If you want to display a list of the unique values in a column, you can do so by creating an advanced filter.

Use the Advanced Filter dialog box to find unique records in a list

All you need to do is identify the rows that contain the values you want to filter and indicate that you want to display unique records so that you get only the information you want.

To find unique values within a data set

1. Click any cell in the range for which you want to find unique values.

2. On the **Data** tab of the ribbon, in the **Sort & Filter** group, click **Advanced**.

3. Click **Filter the list, in place**.

    Or

    Click **Copy to another location**.

4. Verify that the address of your data range appears in the **List range** box.

5. If necessary, click in the **Copy to** box and select the cells where you want the filtered list to appear.

6. Select the **Unique records only** check box.

7. Click **OK**.

Define valid sets of values for ranges of cells

Part of creating efficient and easy-to-use worksheets is to do what you can to ensure that the data entered into your worksheets is as accurate as possible. Although it isn't possible to catch every typographical or transcription error, you can set up a validation rule to make sure that the data entered into a cell meets certain standards. For example, you can specify the type of data you want, the range of acceptable values, and whether blank values are allowed. Setting accurate validation rules can help you and your colleagues avoid entering a customer's name in the cell designated to hold the phone number or setting a credit limit above a certain level.

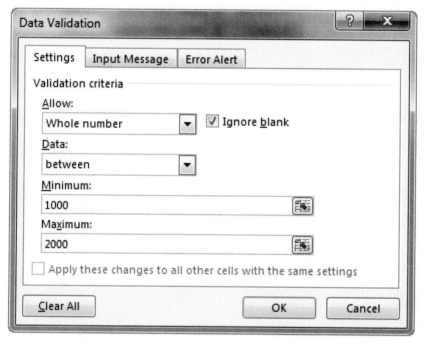

Create data validation rules to ensure that appropriate data is entered into worksheet cells

You can select the cells where you want to add a validation rule, even if those cells already contain data. Excel doesn't tell you whether any of those cells contain data that violates your rule at the moment you create the rule, but you can find out by having Excel circle any worksheet cells that contain data that violates the cell's valida-tion rule. When you're done, you can have Excel clear the validation circles or have Excel turn off data validation for those cells entirely.

	D	E	F	G	H	I	J
	CustomerName	Address	City	State	ZIP	Phone	Limit
	Contoso	11020 Microsoft Way	Redmond	WA	98073	(425) 555-0101	$ 26,000.00
	Fabrikam	1480 Microsoft Way	Redmond	WA	98073	(425) 555-0173	$ 7,500.00
	Northwind Traders	891A Microsoft Way	Redmond	WA	98073	(425) 555-0145	$ 15,000.00

Validation circles indicate data previously entered into a worksheet that violates data validation rules

To add a validation rule to a cell

1. On the **Data** tab, in the **Data Tools** group, click **Data Validation**.

2. In the **Data Validation** dialog box, on the **Settings** tab, click the **Allow** arrow, and then click the type of values to allow.

3. Use the controls to define the rule.

4. Select the **Ignore blank** check box to allow blank values.

   Or

   Clear the **Ignore blank** check box to require a value be entered.

5. On the **Input Message** tab, enter an input message for the cell.

6. On the **Error Alert** tab, create an error alert message for values that violate the rule.

7. Click **OK**.

To edit a validation rule

1. Select one or more cells that contain the validation rule.

2. Click **Data Validation**.

3. On the **Settings** tab, select the **Apply these changes to all other cells with the same settings** check box to affect other cells with the same rule.

   Or

   Leave the **Apply these changes to all other cells with the same settings** check box cleared to affect only the selected cells.

4. Use the controls in the dialog box to edit the rule, input message, and error alert.

5. Click **OK**.

To circle invalid data in a worksheet

1. Click the **Data Validation** arrow.
2. Click **Circle Invalid Data**.

To remove validation circles

1. Click the **Data Validation** arrow.
2. Click **Clear Validation Circles**.

Skills review

In this chapter, you learned how to:

- Limit data that appears on your screen
- Manipulate worksheet data
- Define valid sets of values for ranges of cells

7

Practice tasks

The practice files for these tasks are located in the Office2016SBS\Ch07 folder. You can save the results of the tasks in the same folder.

Limit data that appears on your screen

Open the LimitData workbook in Excel, and then perform the following tasks:

1. Create a filter that displays only those package exceptions that happened on **RT189**.

2. Clear the previous filter, and then create a filter that shows exceptions for the **Northeast** and **Northwest** centers.

3. With the previous filter still in place, create a filter that displays only those exceptions that occurred before April 1, 2016.

4. Clear the filter that shows values related to the **Northeast** and **Northwest** centers.

5. Turn off filtering for the list of data.

Manipulate worksheet data

Open the SummarizeValues workbook in Excel, and then perform the following tasks:

1. Combine the *IF* and *RAND* functions into formulas in cells **H3:H27** that display *TRUE* if the value is less than 0.3 and *FALSE* otherwise.

2. Use AutoCalculate to find the *SUM*, *AVERAGE*, and *COUNT* of cells **G12:G16**.

3. Remove the *COUNT* summary from the status bar and add the *MINIMUM* summary.

4. Create a *SUBTOTAL* formula that finds the average of the values in cells **G3:G27**.

5. Create an *AGGREGATE* formula that finds the maximum of values in cells **G3:G27**.

6. Create an advanced filter that finds the unique values in cells **F3:F27**.

Define valid sets of values for ranges of cells

Open the ValidateData workbook in Excel, and then perform the following tasks:

1. Create a data validation rule in cells **J4:J7** that requires values entered into those cells be no greater than $25,000.

2. Attempt to type the value **30000** in cell **J7**, observe the message that appears, and then cancel data entry.

3. Edit the rule you created so it includes an input message and an error alert.

4. Display validation circles to highlight data that violates the rule you created, and then hide the circles.

Reorder and summarize data

One of the most important uses of business information is to record when something happens. Whether you ship a package to a client or pay a supplier, tracking when you took those actions, and in what order, helps you analyze your performance. Sorting your information based on the values in one or more columns helps you discover useful trends, such as whether your sales are generally increasing or decreasing, whether you do more business on specific days of the week, or whether you sell products to lots of customers from certain regions of the world.

Microsoft Excel has capabilities you might expect to find only in a database program—the ability to organize your data into levels of detail you can show or hide, and formulas that let you look up values in a list of data. Organizing your data by detail level lets you focus on the values you need to make a decision, and looking up values in a worksheet helps you find specific data. If a customer calls to ask about an order, you can use the order number or customer number to discover the information that customer needs.

This chapter guides you through procedures related to sorting your data by using one or more criteria, calculating subtotals, organizing your data into levels, and looking up information in a worksheet.

In this chapter

- Sort worksheet data
- Sort data by using custom lists
- Organize data into levels
- Look up information in a worksheet

Practice files

For this chapter, use the practice files from the Office2016SBS\Ch08 folder. For practice file download instructions, see the introduction.

Sort worksheet data

Although Excel makes it easy to enter your business data and to manage it after you've saved it in a worksheet, unsorted data will rarely answer every question you want to ask it. For example, you might want to discover which of your services generates the most profits, or which service costs the most for you to provide. You can discover that information by sorting your data.

When you sort data in a worksheet, you rearrange the worksheet rows based on the contents of cells in a particular column or set of columns. For instance, you can sort a worksheet to find your highest-revenue services.

You can sort a group of rows in a worksheet in a number of ways, but the first step is to identify the column that will provide the values by which the rows should be sorted. In the revenue example, you could find the highest revenue totals by sorting on the cells in the Revenue column. You can do this by using the commands available from the Sort & Filter button on the Home tab of the ribbon.

> **TIP** The exact set of values that appears in the Sort & Filter list changes to reflect the data in your column. If your column contains numerical values, you'll get the options Sort Largest To Smallest, Sort Smallest To Largest, and Custom List. If your column contains text values, the options will be Sort A To Z (ascending order), Sort Z To A (descending order), and Custom List. And if your column contains dates, you'll get Sort Newest To Oldest, Sort Oldest To Newest, and Custom List.

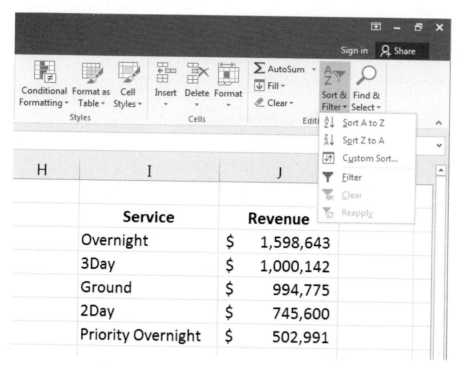

Revenue sorted in descending order

The Sort Smallest To Largest and Sort Largest To Smallest options let you sort rows in a worksheet quickly, but you can use them only to sort the worksheet based on the contents of one column, even though you might want to sort by two columns. For example, you might want to order the worksheet rows by service category and then by total so that you can tell which service categories are used most frequently.

H	I	J
Customer	**Service**	**Revenue**
Contoso	2Day	$ 745,600
Fabrikam	2Day	$ 562,245
Tailspin Toys	2Day	$ 41,894
Contoso	3Day	$ 1,000,142
Fabrikam	3Day	$ 274,659
Tailspin Toys	3Day	$ 41,830
Contoso	Ground	$ 994,775
Fabrikam	Ground	$ 338,168
Tailspin Toys	Ground	$ 87,590
Contoso	Overnight	$ 1,598,643
Fabrikam	Overnight	$ 583,589
Tailspin Toys	Overnight	$ 38,682
Contoso	Priority Overnight	$ 502,991
Fabrikam	Priority Overnight	$ 455,643
Tailspin Toys	Priority Overnight	$ 25,202

Sort a list of data by more than one column

You can sort rows in a worksheet by the contents of more than one column by using the Sort dialog box, in which you can pick any number of columns to use as sort criteria and choose whether to sort the rows in ascending or descending order. If you want to create two similar rules, perhaps changing just the field to which the rules are applied, you can create a rule for one field, copy it within the Sort dialog box, and change the field name.

If your data cells have fill colors applied to them, perhaps representing cells with values you want your colleagues to notice, you can sort your list of data by using those colors. In addition, you can create more detailed sorting rules, change the order in which rules are applied, and edit and delete rules by using the controls in the Sort dialog box.

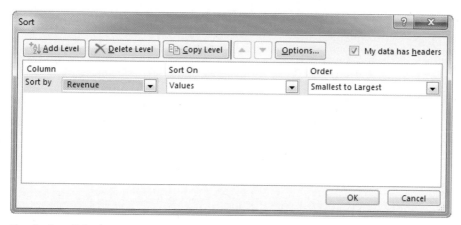

Use the Sort dialog box to create detailed sorting rules

To sort worksheet data based on values in a single column

1. Click a cell in the column that contains the data by which you want to sort.

2. On the **Home** tab of the ribbon, in the **Editing** group, click the **Sort & Filter** button to display a menu of sorting and filtering choices.

3. Click **Sort A to Z** to sort the data in ascending order.

   Or

   Click **Sort Z to A** to sort the data in descending order.

To sort worksheet data based on values in multiple columns

1. Click a cell in the list of data you want to sort.

2. On the **Sort & Filter** menu, click **Custom Sort**.

3. If necessary, select the **My data has headers** check box.

4. In the **Sort by** list, select the first field; in the **Sort On** list, select the option by which you want to sort the data (Values, Cell Color, Font Color, or Cell Icon). Then, in the **Order** list, select an order for the sort operation.

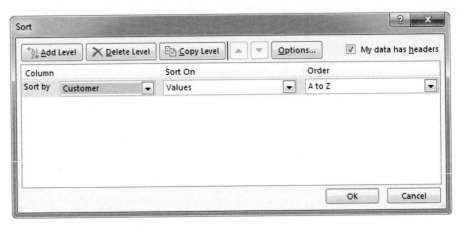

You can create up to 64 sorting levels in Excel 2016

5. Click the **Add Level** button.

6. In the **Then by** list, create another rule by using the techniques described in step 4.

7. When you are done creating sort levels, click **OK** to sort the values.

Customer	Season	Revenue
Contoso	Spring	$201,438.00
Contoso	Winter	$183,651.00
Contoso	Fall	$118,299.00
Contoso	Summer	$114,452.00
Fabrikam	Fall	$255,599.00
Fabrikam	Summer	$183,632.00
Fabrikam	Spring	$139,170.00
Fabrikam	Winter	$100,508.00
Northwind Traders	Fall	$188,851.00
Northwind Traders	Winter	$174,336.00
Northwind Traders	Summer	$129,732.00
Northwind Traders	Spring	$120,666.00

A list of data that has had sorting rules applied to it

To sort by cell color

1. Select a cell in the list of data.

2. On the **Sort & Filter** menu, click **Custom Sort**.

3. If necessary, select the **My data has headers** check box.

4. In the **Sort by** list, select the field by which you want to sort.

5. In the **Sort On** list, select **Cell Color**.

6. In the **Order** list, select the cell color on which you want to sort.

7. In the last list box, select the position you want for the color you identified (On Top or On Bottom).

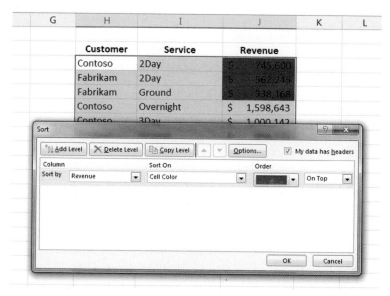

Sort lists of data by using cell fill colors as a criterion

8. When you are done creating sorting rules, click **OK** to sort the values.

To copy a sorting level

1. Select a cell in the list of data.

2. On the **Sort & Filter** menu, click **Custom Sort**.

3. Select the sorting level you want to copy.

4. Click the **Copy Level** button, and edit the rule as needed.

5. Click **OK**.

To move a sorting rule up or down in priority

1. On the **Sort & Filter** menu, click **Custom Sort**.

2. Select the sorting rule you want to move.

3. Click the **Move Up** button to move the rule up in the order.

   Or

   Click the **Move Down** button to move the rule down in the order.

4. Click **OK**.

To delete a sorting rule

1. On the **Sort & Filter** menu, click **Custom Sort**.

2. Select the sorting level you want to delete.

3. Click the **Delete Level** button.

4. Click **OK**.

Sort data by using custom lists

The default setting for Excel is to sort numbers according to their values and to sort words in alphabetical order, but that pattern doesn't work for some sets of values. One example in which sorting a list of values in alphabetical order would yield incorrect results is the months of the year. In an "alphabetical" calendar, April is the first month and September is the last! Fortunately, Excel recognizes a number of special lists, such as days of the week and months of the year. You can have Excel sort the contents of a worksheet based on values in a known list; if needed, you can create your own list of values. For example, the default lists of weekdays in Excel start with Sunday. If you keep your business records based on a Monday–Sunday week, you can create a new list with Monday as the first day and Sunday as the last.

You can create a new custom list by using controls that are reached through the Excel Options dialog box, which gives you the choice of entering the values yourself or importing them from a cell range in your workbook.

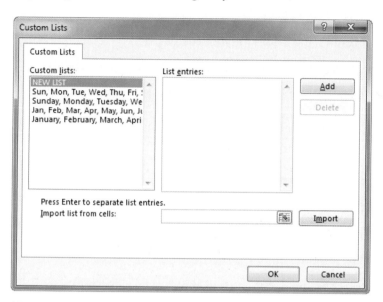

Manage your lists by using the Custom Lists dialog box

> ✓ **TIP** Another benefit of creating a custom list is that dragging the fill handle of a list cell that contains a value causes Excel to extend the series for you. For example, if you create the list Spring, Summer, Fall, Winter, and then enter Summer in a cell and drag the cell's fill handle, Excel extends the series as Fall, Winter, Spring, Summer, Fall, and so on.

To define a custom list by entering its values

1. On the **File** tab, click **Options**.

2. In the **Excel Options** dialog box, click the **Advanced** category.

3. Scroll down to the **General** area, and then click the **Edit Custom Lists** button.

4. In the **Custom Lists** dialog box, enter a list of items in the **List entries** area.

5. Click **Add**.

6. Click **OK**, and then click **OK** to close the **Excel Options** dialog box.

To define a custom list by copying values from a worksheet

1. Select the cells that contain the values for your custom list.

2. In the **Excel Options** dialog box, click the **Advanced** category.

3. Scroll down to the **General** area, and click the **Edit Custom Lists** button.

4. In the **Custom Lists** dialog box, click the **Import** button.

5. Click **OK**, and then click **OK** to close the **Excel Options** dialog box.

To sort worksheet data by using a custom list

1. Click a cell in the list of data you want to sort.

2. On the **Home** tab, click the **Sort & Filter** button, and then click **Custom Sort**.

3. If necessary, select the **My data has headers** check box.

4. In the **Sort by** list, select the field that contains the data by which you want to sort.

5. If necessary, in the **Sort On** list, select **Values**.

6. In the **Order** list, select **Custom List**.

7. In the **Custom Lists** dialog box, select the list you want to use.

8. Click **OK**.

Organize data into levels

After you have sorted the rows in an Excel worksheet or entered the data so that it doesn't need to be sorted, you can have Excel calculate subtotals (totals for a portion of the data). In a worksheet with sales data for three different product categories, for example, you can sort the products by category, select all the cells that contain data, and then open the Subtotal dialog box.

Apply subtotals to data by using the Subtotal dialog box

In the Subtotal dialog box, you can choose the column on which to base your subtotals (such as every change of value in the Week column), the summary calculation you want to perform, and the column or columns with values to be summarized. After you define your subtotals, they appear in your worksheet.

1 2 3		A	B	C	D
	1	Year	Quarter	Month	Package Volume
	2	2014	1	January	5,213,292
	3	2014	1	February	2,038,516
	4	2014	1	March	2,489,601
	5	2014	2	April	9,051,231
	6	2014	2	May	5,225,156
	7	2014	2	June	3,266,644
	8	2014	3	July	2,078,794
	9	2014	3	August	1,591,434
	10	2014	3	September	8,518,985
	11	2014	4	October	1,973,050
	12	2014	4	November	7,599,195
	13	2014	4	December	9,757,876
	14	2014 Total			58,803,774
	15	2015	1	January	5,304,039
	16	2015	1	February	5,465,096
	17	2015	1	March	1,007,799
	18	2015	2	April	4,010,287
	19	2015	2	May	4,817,070
	20	2015	2	June	8,155,717
	21	2015	3	July	6,552,370
	22	2015	3	August	2,295,635
	23	2015	3	September	7,115,883
	24	2015	4	October	1,362,767

A list of data with Subtotal outlining applied

When you add subtotals to a worksheet, Excel also defines groups based on the rows used to calculate a subtotal. The groupings form an outline of your worksheet based on the criteria you used to create the subtotals. For example, all the rows representing months in the year 2014 could be in one group, rows representing months in 2015 in another, and so on. The outline area at the left of your worksheet holds controls you can use to hide or display groups of rows in your worksheet.

1 2 3		A	B	C	D
	1	Year	Quarter	Month	Package Volume
+	14	2014 Total			58,803,774
	15	2015	1	January	5,304,039
	16	2015	1	February	5,465,096
	17	2015	1	March	1,007,799
	18	2015	2	April	4,010,287
	19	2015	2	May	4,817,070
	20	2015	2	June	8,155,717
	21	2015	3	July	6,552,370
	22	2015	3	August	2,295,635
	23	2015	3	September	7,115,883
	24	2015	4	October	1,362,767
	25	2015	4	November	8,935,488
	26	2015	4	December	9,537,077
−	27	2015 Total			64,559,228
−	28	Grand Total			123,363,002
	29				

A list of data with details for the year 2014 hidden

When you hide a group of rows, the button displayed next to the group changes to a Show Detail button (the button with the plus sign). Clicking a group's Show Detail button restores the rows in the group to the worksheet.

The level buttons are the other buttons in the outline area of a worksheet with sub-totals. Each button represents a level of organization in a worksheet; clicking a level button hides all levels of detail below that of the button you clicked. The following table describes the data contained at each level of a worksheet with three levels of organization.

Level	Description
1	Grand total
2	Subtotals for each group
3	Individual rows in the worksheet

8

1 2 3		A	B	C	D
	1	Year	Quarter	Month	Package Volume
+	14	2014 Total			58,803,774
+	27	2015 Total			64,559,228
−	28	Grand Total			123,363,002
	29				

A list of data with details hidden at level 2

If you want, you can add levels of detail to the outline that Excel creates. For example, you might want to be able to hide revenues from January and February, which you know are traditionally strong months. You can also delete any groupings you no longer need, or remove subtotals and outlining entirely.

> **TIP** If you want to remove all subtotals from a worksheet, open the Subtotal dialog box, and click the Remove All button.

To organize data into levels

1. Click a cell in the group of data you want to organize.

2. On the **Data** tab of the ribbon, in the **Outline** group, click the **Subtotal** button.

3. In the **Subtotal** dialog box, in the **At each change in** list, select the field that controls when subtotals appear.

4. In the **Use function** list, select the summary function you want to use for each subtotal.

5. In the **Add subtotal to** group, select the check box next to any field you want to summarize.

6. Click **OK**.

To show or hide detail in a list with a subtotal summary

1. Do either of the following:

   - Click a **Hide Detail** control to hide a level of detail.

   - Click a **Show Detail** control to show a level of detail.

To create a custom group in a list that has a subtotal summary

1. Select the rows you want to include in the group.

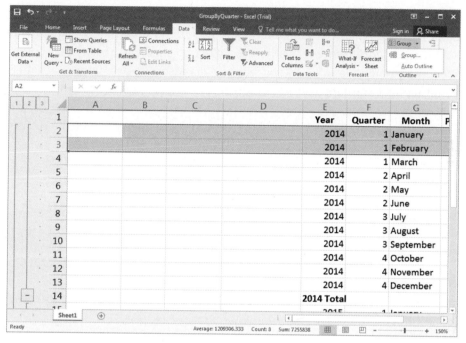

A data list with rows selected to create a custom group

2. Click the **Group** button.

To remove a custom group in a list that has a subtotal summary

1. Select the rows you want to remove from the group.

2. Click the **Ungroup** button.

To remove subtotals from a data list

1. Click any cell in the list.

2. Click the **Subtotal** button.

3. In the **Subtotal** dialog box, click **Remove All**.

Look up information in a worksheet

Whenever you create a worksheet that holds information about a list of distinct items, such as products offered for sale by a company, you should ensure that at least one column in the list contains a unique value that distinguishes that row (and the item the row represents) from every other row in the list. Assigning each row a column that contains a unique value means that you can associate data in one list with data in another list. For example, if you assign every customer a unique identification number, you can store a customer's contact information in one worksheet and all orders for that customer in another worksheet. You can then associate the customer's orders and contact information without writing the contact information in a worksheet every time the customer places an order.

In technical terms, the column that contains a unique value for each row is known as the primary key column. When you look up information in an Excel worksheet, it is very useful to position the primary key column as the first column in your list of data.

If you know an item's primary key value, it's no trouble to look through a list of 20 or 30 items to find it. If, however, you have a list of many thousands of items, looking through the list to find one would take quite a bit of time. Instead, you can use the VLOOKUP function to find the value you want.

	A	B	C	D	E	F
1						
2		ShipmentID	Destination			
3						
4						
5		ShipmentID	CustomerID	Date	OriginationPostalCode	DestinationPostalCode
6		SH210	CI384471	5/21/2015	59686	77408
7		SH211	CI495231	5/22/2015	24348	91936
8		SH212	CI429120	5/23/2015	70216	83501
9		SH213	CI418125	5/24/2015	84196	21660
10		SH214	CI782990	5/25/2015	13193	92518
11		SH215	CI102300	5/26/2015	27910	76842
12		SH216	CI560742	5/27/2015	73820	21393
13		SH217	CI483289	5/28/2015	34245	33975
14		SH218	CI762179	5/29/2015	87569	11471
15						

An Excel table for use with VLOOKUP

The VLOOKUP function finds a value in the leftmost column of a named range, such as a table, and then returns the value from the specified cell to the right of the cell with the found value. A properly formed VLOOKUP function has four arguments (data that is passed to the function), as shown in the following definition:
=VLOOKUP(lookup_value, table_array, col_index_num, range_lookup).

The following table summarizes the values Excel expects for each of these arguments.

Argument	Expected value
lookup_value	The value to be found in the first column of the named range specified by the *table_array* argument. The *lookup_value* argument can be a value, a cell reference, or a text string.
table_array	The multicolumn range or name of the range or data table to be searched.
col_index_num	The number of the column in the named range that has the value to be returned.
range_lookup	A TRUE or FALSE value, indicating whether the function should find an approximate match (TRUE) or an exact match (FALSE) for the *lookup_value*. If this argument is left blank, the default value for it is TRUE.

> **IMPORTANT**   When *range_lookup* is left blank or set to TRUE, for VLOOKUP to work properly, the rows in the named range specified in the *table_array* argument must be sorted in ascending order based on the values in the leftmost column of the named range.

The VLOOKUP function works a bit differently depending on whether the *range_lookup* argument is set to TRUE or FALSE. The following list summarizes how the function works based on the value of *range_lookup*:

- If the *range_lookup* argument is left blank or set to TRUE, and VLOOKUP doesn't find an exact match for *lookup_value*, the function returns the largest value that is less than *lookup_value*.

- If the *range_lookup* argument is left blank or set to TRUE, and *lookup_value* is smaller than the smallest value in the named range, an #N/A error is returned.

- If the *range_lookup* argument is left blank or set to TRUE, and *lookup_value* is larger than all values in the named range, the largest value in the named range is returned.

- If the *range_lookup* argument is set to FALSE, and VLOOKUP doesn't find an exact match for *lookup_value*, the function returns an #N/A error.

As an example of a VLOOKUP function, consider the following data, which shows an Excel table with its headers in row 2 and the first column in column B of the worksheet.

CustomerID	Customer
CU01	Fabrikam
CU02	Northwind Traders
CU03	Tailspin Toys
CU04	Contoso

If the =*VLOOKUP (E3, B3:C6, 2, FALSE)* formula is used, when you enter CU03 in cell E3 and press Enter, the VLOOKUP function searches the first column of the table, finds an exact match, and returns the value Tailspin Toys to cell F3.

A VLOOKUP formula that looks up a customer name when a customer ID is provided

> **TIP** The related HLOOKUP function matches a value in a column of the first row of a table and returns the value in the specified row number of the same column. The letter *H* in the HLOOKUP function name refers to the horizontal layout of the data, just as the *V* in the VLOOKUP function name refers to the data's vertical layout. For more information on using the HLOOKUP function, click the Excel Help button, enter HLOOKUP in the search terms box, and then click Search.

> **IMPORTANT** Be sure to give the cell in which you type the VLOOKUP formula the same format as the data you want the formula to display. For example, if you create a VLOOKUP formula in cell G14 that finds a date, you must apply a date cell format to cell G14 for the result of the formula to display properly.

To look up worksheet values by using VLOOKUP

1. Ensure that the data list includes a unique value in each cell of the leftmost column and that the values are sorted in ascending order.

2. In the cell where you want to enter the VLOOKUP formula, enter a formula of the form =*VLOOKUP(lookup_value, table_array, col_index_num, range_lookup)*.

3. Enter **TRUE** for the *range_lookup* argument to allow an approximate match.

   Or

   Enter **FALSE** for the *range_lookup* argument to require an exact match.

4. Enter a lookup value in the cell named in the VLOOKUP formula's first argument, and press **Enter**.

Skills review

In this chapter, you learned how to:

8

- Sort worksheet data
- Sort data by using custom lists
- Organize data into levels
- Look up information in a worksheet

Practice tasks

The practice files for these tasks are located in the Office2016SBS\Ch08 folder. You can save the results of the tasks in the same folder.

Sort worksheet data

Open the SortData workbook in Excel, and then perform the following tasks:

1. Sort the data in the list in ascending order based on the values in the Revenue column.

2. Sort the data in the list in descending order based on the values in the Revenue column.

3. Sort the data in the list in ascending order based on a two-level sort where the first sorting level is the Customer column and the second is the Season column.

4. Change the order of the fields in the previous sort so that the first criterion is the Season column and the second is the Customer column.

5. Sort the data so that the cells in the Revenue column that have a red fill color are at the top of the list.

Sort data by using custom lists

Open the SortCustomData workbook in Excel, and then perform the following tasks:

1. Create a custom list by using the values in cells **G4:G7**.

2. Sort the data in the cell range **B3:D14** by the values in the Season column based on the custom list you just created.

3. Create a two-level sort by using the values in the Customer column, in ascending order, as the first criterion, and the custom list–based sort for the Season column as the second.

Organize data into levels

Open the OrganizeData workbook in Excel, and then perform the following tasks:

1. Outline the data list in cells **A1:D25** to find the subtotal for each year.

2. Hide the details of rows for the year 2015.

3. Create a new group consisting of the rows showing data for June and July 2014.

4. Hide the details of the group you just created.

5. Show the details of all months for the year 2015.

6. Remove the subtotal outline from the entire data list.

Look up information in a worksheet

Open the LookupData workbook in Excel, and then perform the following tasks:

1. Sort the values in the first table column in ascending order.

2. In cell C3, create a formula that finds the CustomerID value for a ShipmentID entered into cell B3.

3. Edit the formula so that it finds the DestinationPostalCode value for the same package.

Analyze alternative data sets

9

When you store data in an Excel 2016 workbook, you can use that data, either by itself or as part of a calculation, to discover important information about your organization. You can summarize your data quickly by using the Quick Analysis Lens to create charts, calculate totals, or apply conditional formatting.

The data in your worksheets is great for answering "what-if" questions, such as, "How much money would we save if we reduced our labor to 20 percent of our total costs?" You can always save an alternative version of a workbook and create formulas that calculate the effects of your changes, but you can do the same thing in your existing workbooks by defining one or more alternative data sets. You can also create a data table that calculates the effects of changing one or two variables in a formula, find the input values required to generate the result you want, and describe your data statistically.

This chapter guides you through procedures related to examining data by using the Quick Analysis Lens, defining an alternative data set, defining multiple alternative data sets, analyzing data by using data tables, varying data to get a specific result by using Goal Seek, finding optimal solutions by using Solver, and analyzing data by using descriptive statistics.

In this chapter

- Examine data by using the Quick Analysis Lens
- Define an alternative data set
- Define multiple alternative data sets
- Analyze data by using data tables
- Vary your data to get a specific result by using Goal Seek
- Find optimal solutions by using Solver
- Analyze data by using descriptive statistics

Practice files

For this chapter, use the practice files from the Office2016SBS\Ch09 folder. For practice file download instructions, see the introduction.

Examine data by using the Quick Analysis Lens

One useful tool in Excel 2016 is the Quick Analysis Lens, which brings the most commonly used formatting, charting, and summary tools into one convenient location. After you select the data you want to summarize, clicking the Quick Analysis action button displays the tools you can use to analyze your data.

	A	B	C
1	Region	Packages	
2	Northeast	440,971	
3	Atlantic	304,246	
4	Southeast	444,006	
5	North Central	466,687	
6	Midwest	400,713	
7	Southwest	402,456	
8	Mountain Wes	370,176	
9	Northwest	209,013	
10	Central	234,993	
11			
12			

Click the Quick Analysis action button to display analysis tools

TIP To display the Quick Analysis toolbar by using a keyboard shortcut, press Ctrl+Q.

The Quick Analysis toolbar makes a wide range of tools available, including the ability to create an Excel table or PivotTable, insert a chart, or add conditional formatting. You can also add total columns and rows to your data range.

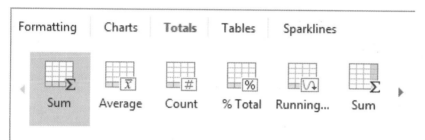

Select from several categories of analysis tools

You can use the tools on the Totals tab of the Quick Analysis toolbar to add summary operations to your data. You can add one summary column and one summary row to each data range. If you select a new summary column or row when one exists, Excel displays a confirmation dialog box to verify that you want to replace the existing summary.

9

To add formatting by using the Quick Analysis Lens

1. Select the cells you want to analyze.

2. Click the **Quick Analysis** action button.

3. If necessary, click the **Formatting** tab.

4. Click the button that represents the formatting you want to apply.

To add totals by using the Quick Analysis Lens

1. Select the cells you want to analyze.

2. Click the **Quick Analysis** action button.

3. If necessary, click the **Totals** tab.

4. Click the button that represents the total you want to apply.

To add tables by using the Quick Analysis Lens

1. Select the cells you want to analyze.

2. Click the **Quick Analysis** action button.

3. If necessary, click the **Tables** tab.

4. Click the button that represents the type of table you want to create.

Define an alternative data set

When you save data in an Excel worksheet, you create a record that reflects the characteristics of an event or object. That data could represent the number of deliveries in an hour on a particular day, the price of a new delivery option, or the percentage of total revenue accounted for by a delivery option. After the data is in place, you can create formulas to generate totals, find averages, and sort the rows in a worksheet based on the contents of one or more columns. However, if you want to perform a what-if analysis or explore the impact that changes in your data would have on any of the calculations in your workbooks, you need to change your data.

The problem with manipulating data that reflects an event or item is that when you change any data to affect a calculation, you run the risk of destroying the original data if you accidentally save your changes. You can avoid ruining your original data by creating a duplicate workbook and making your changes to it, but you can also create an alternative data set, or scenario, within an existing workbook.

When you create a scenario, you give Excel alternative values for a list of cells in a worksheet. You can use the Scenario Manager to add, delete, and edit scenarios.

Track and change scenarios by using the Scenario Manager

When you're ready to add a scenario, you start by providing its name and, if you want, a comment describing the scenario.

> ✓ **TIP** Adding a comment gives you and your colleagues valuable information about the scenario and your purpose for creating it. Many Excel users create scenarios without comments, but comments are extremely useful when you work on a team or revisit a workbook after several months.

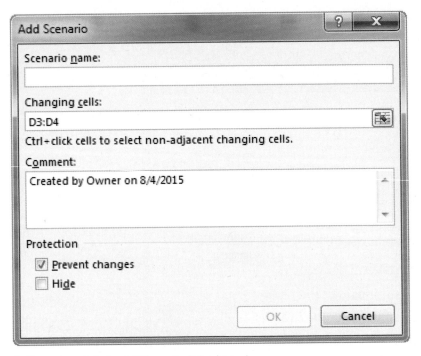

Define a scenario in the Add Scenario dialog box

After you name your scenario, you can define its values.

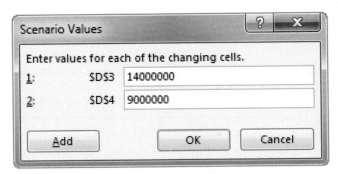

Enter alternative data in the Scenario Values dialog box

After you have created your scenario, clicking the Show button in the Scenario Manager replaces the values in the original worksheet with the alternative values you just defined in the scenario. Any formulas that reference cells with changed values will recalculate their results. You can then remove the scenario by clicking the Undo button on the Quick Access Toolbar.

> ⚠️ **IMPORTANT** If you save and close a workbook while a scenario is in effect, those values become the default values for the cells changed by the scenario! You should seriously consider creating a scenario that contains the original values of the cells you change or creating a scenario summary worksheet (a subject covered in the next topic).

The tools available in the Scenario Manager also let you edit your scenarios and delete the ones you no longer need.

To define an alternative data set by creating a scenario

1. On the **Data** tab, in the **Forecast** group, click the **What-If Analysis** button to display a menu of the what-if choices, and then click **Scenario Manager**.

2. In the **Scenario Manager** dialog box, click **Add**.

3. In the **Scenario name** box, enter a name for the scenario.

4. Click in the **Changing cells** box, and then select the cells you want to change.

5. Click **OK**.

6. In the **Scenario Values** dialog box, enter new values for each of the changing cells.

7. Click **OK**.

8. Click **Close** to close the **Scenario Manager** dialog box.

To display an alternative data set

1. On the **What-if Analysis** menu, click **Scenario Manager**.

2. In the **Scenario Manager** dialog box, click the scenario you want to display.

3. Click **Show**.

4. If you want to close the **Scenario Manager** dialog box, click **Close**.

To edit an alternative data set

1. On the **What-If Analysis** menu, click **Scenario Manager**.

2. In the **Scenario Manager** dialog box, click the scenario you want to edit.

3. Click **Edit**.

9

4. In the **Edit Scenario** dialog box, change the values in the **Scenario name**, **Changing cells**, or **Comment** box.

5. Click **OK**.

6. In the **Scenario Values** dialog box, enter new values for each of the changing cells.

7. Click **OK**.

8. Click **Close** to close the **Scenario Manager** dialog box.

To delete an alternative data set

1. On the **What-if Analysis** menu, click **Scenario Manager**.

2. In the **Scenario Manager** dialog box, click the scenario you want to delete.

3. Click **Delete**.

4. Click **Close** to close the **Scenario Manager** dialog box.

Define multiple alternative data sets

One great feature of Excel scenarios is that you're not limited to creating one alternative data set—you can create as many scenarios as you want and apply them by using the Scenario Manager.

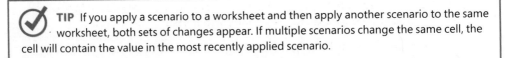 **TIP** If you apply a scenario to a worksheet and then apply another scenario to the same worksheet, both sets of changes appear. If multiple scenarios change the same cell, the cell will contain the value in the most recently applied scenario.

Applying multiple scenarios alters the values in your worksheets. You can see how those changes affect your formulas, but Excel also lets you create a record of your different scenarios by using the Scenario Summary dialog box. From within the dialog box, you can choose the type of summary worksheet you want to create and the cells you want to display in the summary worksheet.

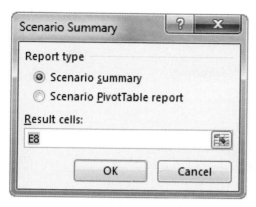

Summarize scenarios by using the Scenario Summary dialog box

> **IMPORTANT** Make sure you don't have any scenarios applied to your workbook when you create the summary worksheet. If you do have an active scenario, Excel will record the scenario's changed values as the originals, and your summary will be inaccurate.

It's a good idea to create an "undo" scenario named *Normal* that holds the original values of the cells you're going to change before you change them in other scenarios. For example, if you create a scenario that changes the values in three cells, your *Normal* scenario restores those cells to their original values. That way, even if you accidentally modify your worksheet, you can apply the *Normal* scenario and not have to reconstruct the worksheet from scratch.

> **IMPORTANT** Each scenario can change a maximum of 32 cells, so you might need to create more than one scenario to ensure that you can restore a worksheet.

To apply multiple alternative data sets

1. On the **Data** tab, in the **Forecast** group, click the **What-If Analysis** button to display a menu of the what-if choices, and then click **Scenario Manager**.

2. In the **Scenario Manager** dialog box, click the scenario you want to display.

3. Click **Show**.

4. Repeat steps 2 and 3 for any additional scenarios you want to display.

5. Click **Close**.

9

To create a scenario summary worksheet

1. On the **What-if Analysis** menu, click **Scenario Manager**.

2. In the **Scenario Manager** dialog box, click **Summary**.

3. In the **Scenario Summary** dialog box, click **Scenario summary**.

4. Click **OK**.

Analyze data by using data tables

When you examine business data in Excel, you will often want to discover what the result of a formula would be with different input values. In Excel 2016, you can calculate the results of those changes by using a data table. To create a data table with one variable, you create a worksheet that contains the data required to calculate the variations in the table.

	A	B	C	D	E
1	**Revenue Increases**			Revenue	
2	Year	2016		$ 2,102,600.70	
3	Increase	0%	2%		
4	Package Count	237,582	5%		
5	Rate	$ 8.85	8%		
6					

Perform data analysis by changing one variable

 IMPORTANT You must lay out the data and formulas in a rectangle so the data table you create will appear in the lower-right corner of the cell range you select.

For example, you can put the formula used to summarize the base data in cell D2, the cells with the changing values in the range C3:C5, and the cells to contain the calculations based on those values in D3:D5. Given the layout of this specific worksheet, you would select cells C2:D5, which contain the summary formula, the changing values, and the cells where the new calculations should appear.

After you select the data and the formula, you can use the Data Table dialog box to perform your analysis.

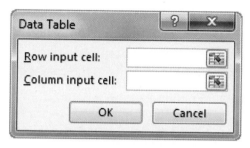

Identify input cells for your data table

To change a single variable, you identify the cell that contains the summary formula's value that will change in the data table's cells. In this example, that cell is B3. Because the target cells D3:D5 are laid out as a column, you would identify that range as the column input cell.

> **TIP** If your target cells were laid out as a row, you would enter the address of the cell containing the value to be changed in the Row Input Cell box.

When you click OK, Excel fills in the results of the data table, using the replacement values in cells C3:C5 to provide the values for cells D3:D5.

	A	B	C	D
1	**Revenue Increases**			Revenue
2	Year	2016		$ 2,102,600.70
3	Increase	0%	2%	$ 2,107,352.34
4	Package Count	237,582	5%	$ 2,114,479.80
5	Rate	$ 8.85	8%	$ 2,121,607.26
6				

A completed one-variable data table

To create a two-variable data table, you lay your data out with one set of replacement values as row headers and the other set as column headers.

	A	B	C	D	E
1	**Revenue Increases**		Revenue		
2	Year	2016	$ 2,102,600.70	260,000	300,000
3	Increase	0%	2%		
4	Package Count	237,582	5%		
5	Rate	$ 8.85	8%		
6			10%		
7					

Two-variable data tables replace both row and column values

In this example, you would select the cell range C2:E5 and create the data table. Because you're creating a two-variable data table, you need to enter cell addresses for both the *column input cell* and *row input cell*. The column input cell is B3, which represents the rate increase, and the row input cell is B4, which contains the package count. When you're done, Excel creates your data table.

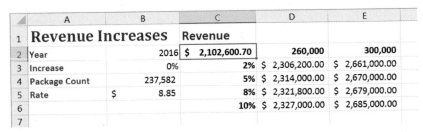

	A	B	C	D	E
1	**Revenue Increases**		Revenue		
2	Year	2016	$ 2,102,600.70	260,000	300,000
3	Increase	0%	2%	$ 2,306,200.00	$ 2,661,000.00
4	Package Count	237,582	5%	$ 2,314,000.00	$ 2,670,000.00
5	Rate	$ 8.85	8%	$ 2,321,800.00	$ 2,679,000.00
6			10%	$ 2,327,000.00	$ 2,685,000.00
7					

Replacing both row and column values generates multiple outcomes

 TIP For a two-value data table, the summary formula should be the top-left cell in the range you select before creating the data table.

To create a one-variable data table

1. Create a worksheet with a summary formula, the input values that the summary formula uses to calculate its value, and a series of adjacent cells that contain alternative values for one of the summary formula's input values.

2. Select the cells representing the summary formula and the changing values, and the cells where the alternative summary formula results should appear.

3. On the **Data** tab, in the **Forecast** group, click the **What-If Analysis** button to display a menu of the what-if choices, and then click **Data Table**.

4. In the **Data Table** dialog box, do either of the following:

   - If the changing values appear in a row, in the **Row input cell** box, enter the cell address of the changing value.

   - If the changing values appear in a column, in the **Column input cell** box, enter the cell address of the changing value.

5. Click **OK**.

To create a two-variable data table

1. Create a worksheet with a summary formula, the input values that the summary formula uses to calculate its value, and two series of adjacent cells (one in a row, one in a column) that contain alternative values for two of the summary formula's input values.

2. Select the cells representing the summary formula and the changing values, and the cells where the alternative summary formula results should appear.

3. On the **What-If Analysis** menu, click **Data Table**.

4. In the **Data Table** dialog box, in the **Row input cell** box, enter the cell address of the cell that has alternative values that appear in a worksheet row.

5. In the **Column input cell** box, enter the cell address of the cell that has alternative values that appear in a worksheet column.

6. Click **OK**.

Vary your data to get a specific result by using Goal Seek

9

When you run an organization, you must track how every element performs, both in absolute terms and in relation to other parts of the organization. There are many ways to measure your operations, but one useful technique is to limit the percentage of total costs contributed by a specific item.

As an example, consider a worksheet that contains the actual costs and percentage of total costs for several production input values.

	A	B	C	D	E	F	G
1							
2			Labor	Transportation	Taxes	Facilities	Total
3		Cost	$ 18,000,382.00	$ 35,000,000.00	$ 7,000,000.00	$ 19,000,000.00	$ 79,000,382.00
4		Share	22.79%	44.30%	8.86%	24.05%	
5							

A worksheet that calculates the percentage of total costs for each of four categories

Under the current pricing structure, Labor represents 22.79 percent of the total costs for the product. If you'd prefer that Labor represent no more than 20 percent of total costs, you can change the cost of Labor manually until you find the number you want. Rather than do it manually, though, you can use Goal Seek to have Excel find the solution for you.

When you use Goal Seek, you identify the cell that contains the formula you use to evaluate your data, the target value, and the cell you want to change to generate that target value.

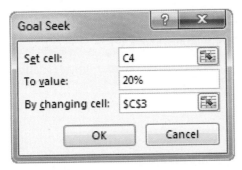

Identify the cell that contains the formula you want to use to generate a target value

Clicking OK tells Excel to find a solution for the goal you set. When Excel finishes its work, the new values appear in the designated cells, and the Goal Seek Status dialog box opens.

 IMPORTANT If you save a workbook with the results of a Goal Seek calculation in place, you will overwrite the values in your workbook.

	A	B	C	D	E	F	G
1							
2			Labor	Transportation	Taxes	Facilities	Total
3		Cost	$ 15,224,031.93	$ 35,000,000.00	$ 7,000,000.00	$ 19,000,000.00	$ 76,224,031.93
4		Share	19.97%	45.92%	9.18%	24.93%	
5							
6							
7							
8							
9							
10							
11							
12							

A worksheet where Goal Seek found a solution to a problem

TIP Goal Seek finds the closest solution it can without exceeding the target value.

To find a target value by using Goal Seek

1. On the **Data** tab, in the **Forecast** group, click the **What-If Analysis** button, and then click **Goal Seek**.

2. In the **Goal Seek** dialog box, in the **Set cell** box, enter the address of the cell that contains the formula you want to use to produce a specific value.

3. In the **To value** box, enter the target value for the formula you identified.

4. In the **By changing cell** box, enter the address of the cell that contains the value you want to vary to produce the result you want.

5. Click **OK**.

Find optimal solutions by using Solver

Goal Seek is a great tool for finding out how much you need to change a single input value to generate a specific result from a formula, but it's of no help if you want to find the best mix of several input values. For more complex problems that seek to maximize or minimize results based on several input values and constraints, you need to use Solver.

	A	B	C	D	E	F	G	H	I	J
1		Boxes						Constraints		
2			Maple	Elm	Ash	Total Boxes		Product	Available	
3		Apples	1	1	1	3		Apples	50	
4		Pears	1	1	1	3		Pears	45	
5		Strawberries	1	1	1	3		Strawberries	80	
6		Blueberries	1	1	1	3		Blueberries	100	
7		Blackberries	1	1	1	3		Blackberries	100	
8		Total Boxes	5	5	5					
9								Market	Maximum	
10		Sale Price						Maple	40	
11			Maple	Elm	Ash					
12		Apples	$ 14.95	$ 12.95	$ 12.95					
13		Pears	$ 9.95	$ 10.95	$ 10.95					
14		Strawberries	$ 8.95	$ 8.95	$ 8.95					
15		Blueberries	$ 8.95	$ 8.95	$ 10.95					
16		Blackberries	$ 8.95	$ 10.95	$ 9.95					
17										
18						Total Revenue				
19						$ 158.25				
20										

Use Solver to select a product distribution to maximize revenue

TIP It helps to spell out every aspect of your problem so that you can identify the cells you want Solver to use in its calculations.

If you performed a complete installation when you installed Excel on your computer, the Solver button will appear on the Data tab in the Analyze group. If not, you can install the Solver add-in from the Add-Ins page of the Excel Options dialog box. After the installation is complete, Solver appears on the Data tab, in the Analyze group, and you can create your model.

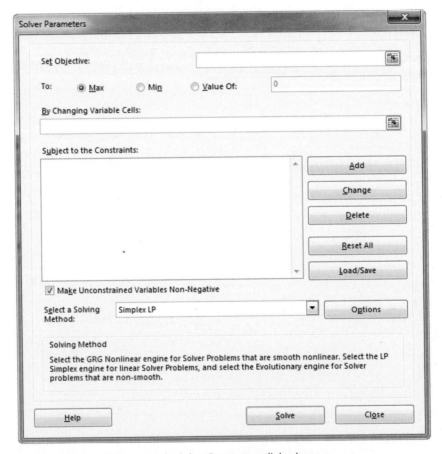

Create a Solver model by using the Solver Parameters dialog box

The first step in setting up your Solver problem is to identify the cell that contains the summary formula you want to establish as your objective, followed by indicating whether you want to minimize the cell's value, maximize the cell's value, or make the cell take on a specific value. Next, you select the cells Solver should vary to change the value in the objective cell. You can, if you want, require Solver to find solutions that use only integer values (that is, values that are whole numbers and have no decimal component).

> ⚠️ **IMPORTANT** Finding integer-only solutions, or *integer programming*, is much harder than finding solutions that allow decimal values. It might take Solver several minutes to find a solution or to discover that a solution using just integer values isn't possible.

Next, you create constraints that will set the limits for the values Solver can use. The best way to set your constraints is to specify them in your worksheet. Basing Solver constraints on worksheet cell values lets you add labels and explanatory text in neighboring cells and change the constraints quickly, without opening the Solver Parameters dialog box.

> ✅ **TIP** After you run Solver, you can use the commands in the Solver Results dialog box to save the results as changes to your worksheet or create a scenario based on the changed data.

Finally, you need to select the solving method that Solver will use to look for a solution to your problem. There are three options, each of which works best for a specific type of problem:

- **Simplex LP** Used to solve problems where all of the calculations are linear, meaning they don't involve exponents or other non-linear elements.

- **GRG Nonlinear** Used to solve problems where the calculations involve exponents or other non-linear mathematical elements.

- **Evolutionary** Uses genetic algorithms to find a solution. This method is quite complex and can take far longer to run than either of the other two engines, but if neither the Simplex LP or GRG Nonlinear engines can find a solution, the Evolutionary engine might be able to.

> ✅ **TIP** If you're using the Simplex LP engine and Solver returns an error immediately, indicating that it can't find a solution, try using the GRG Nonlinear engine.

9

To add Solver to the ribbon

1. Click the **File** tab, and then in the Backstage view, click **Options**.

2. In the **Excel Options** dialog box, click the **Add-Ins** category.

3. If necessary, in the **Manage** list, click **Excel Add-ins**. When **Excel Add-ins** appears in the **Manage** box, click **Go**.

4. In the **Add-Ins** dialog box, select the **Solver Add-in** check box.

5. Click **OK**.

To open the Solver Parameters dialog box

1. On the **Data** tab, in the **Analyze** group, click **Solver**.

To identify the objective cell of a model

1. Click **Solver**.

2. In the **Solver Parameters** dialog box, click in the **Set Objective** box.

3. Click the cell that includes the formula you want to optimize.

To specify the type of result your Solver model should return

1. In the **Solver Parameters** dialog box, do any of the following:

   - Select **Max** to maximize the objective cell's value.

   - Select **Min** to minimize the objective cell's value.

   - Select **Value Of** and enter the target value in the box to the right to generate a specific result.

To identify the cells with values that can be changed

1. In the **Solver Parameters** dialog box, click in the **By Changing Variable Cells** box.

2. Select the cells you will allow Solver to change to generate a solution.

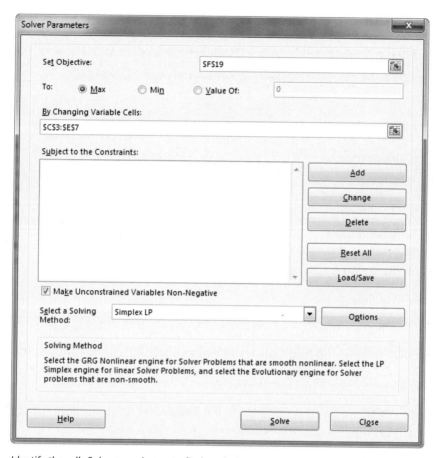

Identify the cells Solver can change to find a solution

To add a constraint to your Solver model

1. In the **Solver Parameters** dialog box, click **Add**.

2. In the **Add Constraint** dialog box, in the **Cell Reference** box, identify the cells to which you want to apply the constraint.

3. In the middle list box, click the arrow, and then click the type of constraint you want to apply.

4. Click in the **Constraint** box and do either of the following:

   - Enter the address of the cell that contains the constraint's comparison value.

   - Select the cell that contains the constraint's comparison value.

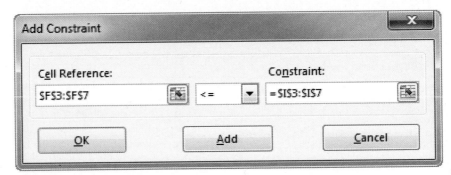

Add constraints to reflect the specified circumstances of your business

5. Click **Add** to create a new constraint.

   Or

   Click **OK** to close the **Add Constraint** dialog box.

To require a value to be a binary number (0 or 1)

1. In the **Add Constraint** dialog box, in the **Cell Reference** box, identify the cells to which you want to apply the constraint.

2. In the middle list box, click the arrow, and then click **bin**.

3. Click **OK**.

To require a value to be an integer

1. In the **Add Constraint** dialog box, in the **Cell Reference** box, identify the cells to which you want to apply the constraint.

2. In the middle list box, click the arrow, and then click **int**.

3. Click **OK**.

To edit a constraint

1. In the **Solver Parameters** dialog box, click the constraint you want to edit.

2. Click **Change**.

3. In the **Change Constraint** dialog box, in the **Cell Reference** box, identify the cells to which you want to apply the constraint.

4. In the middle list box, click the arrow, and then click the type of constraint you want to apply.

5. Click in the **Constraint** box and do either of the following:

   - Enter the address of the cell that contains the constraint's comparison value.

   - Select the cell that contains the constraint's comparison value.

6. Click **OK**.

To delete a constraint

1. In the **Solver Parameters** dialog box, click the constraint you want to delete.

2. Click **Delete**.

To require changing cells to contain non-negative values

1. In the **Solver Parameters** dialog box, select the **Make Unconstrained Variables Non-Negative** check box.

To select a solving method

1. In the **Solver Parameters** dialog box, click the **Select a Solving Method** arrow.

2. Click the method you want to use.

To reset the Solver model

1. In the **Solver Parameters** dialog box, click **Reset All**.

2. Click **OK**.

3. Click **Close**.

Analyze data by using descriptive statistics

Experienced business people can tell a lot about numbers just by looking at them to determine if they "look right." That is, the sales figures are approximately where they're supposed to be for a particular hour, day, or month; the average seems about right; and sales have increased from year to year. When you need more than an informal assessment, however, you can use the tools in the Analysis ToolPak.

If the Data Analysis button, which displays a set of analysis tools when clicked, doesn't appear in the Analyze group on the Data tab, you can install it by using tools available on the Excel Options dialog box Add-Ins page. After you complete its installation, the Data Analysis button appears in the Analyze group on the Data tab.

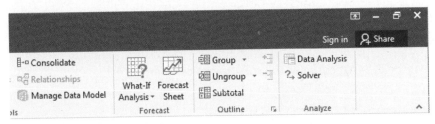

Adding Data Analysis, Solver, or both adds the Analyze group to the Data tab

To add the Data Analysis button to the ribbon

1. In the Backstage view, click **Options**.

2. In the **Excel Options** dialog box, click the **Add-Ins** category.

3. If necessary, click the **Manage** arrow and then click **Excel Add-ins**. When **Excel Add-ins** appears in the **Manage** box, click **Go**.

4. In the **Add-Ins** dialog box, select the **Analysis ToolPak** check box.

5. Click **OK**.

To analyze your data by using descriptive statistics

1. On the **Data** tab, in the **Analyze** group, click **Data Analysis**.

2. In the **Data Analysis** dialog box, click **Descriptive Statistics**.

3. Click **OK**.

4. Click in the **Input Range** box, and then select the cells that contain the data you want to summarize.

5. Select the **Summary statistics** check box.

6. Click **OK**.

Skills review

In this chapter, you learned how to:

- Examine data by using the Quick Analysis Lens
- Define an alternative data set
- Define multiple alternative data sets
- Analyze data by using data tables
- Vary your data to get a specific result by using Goal Seek
- Find optimal solutions by using Solver
- Analyze data by using descriptive statistics

9

Practice tasks

The practice files for these tasks are located in the Office2016SBS\Ch09 folder. You can save the results of the tasks in the same folder.

Examine data by using the Quick Analysis Lens

Open the PerformQuickAnalysis workbook in Excel, and then perform the following tasks:

1. Select cells **B2:B10**.

2. Use the **Quick Analysis** action button to add a total row to the bottom of the selected range.

3. Use the **Quick Analysis** action button to add a running total column to the right of the selected range.

Define an alternative data set

Open the CreateScenarios workbook in Excel, and then perform the following tasks:

1. Create a scenario called **Overnight** that changes the **Base Rate** value for **Overnight** and **Priority Overnight** packages (in cells **C6** and **C7**) to **$18.75** and **$25.50**.

2. Apply the scenario.

3. Undo the scenario application by pressing **Ctrl+Z**.

4. Close the **Scenario Manager** dialog box.

Define multiple alternative data sets

Open the ManageMultipleScenarios workbook in Excel, and then perform the following tasks:

1. Create a scenario called **HighVolume** that increases **Ground** packages to **17,000,000** and **3Day** to **14,000,000**.

2. Create a second scenario called **NewRates** that increases the **Ground** rate to **$9.45** and the **3Day** rate to **$12**.

3. Open the **Scenario Manager** and create a summary worksheet.

4. Apply the **HighVolume** scenario, and then apply the **NewRates** scenario.

5. Close the **Scenario Manager** dialog box.

Analyze data by using data tables

Open the DefineDataTables workbook in Excel, and then perform the following tasks:

1. On the **RateIncreases** worksheet, select cells **C2:D5**.

2. Use the **What-If Analysis** button to start creating a data table.

3. In the **Column input cell** box, enter **B3**.

4. Click **OK**.

5. On the **RateAndVolume** worksheet, select cells **C2:E6**.

6. On the **What-If Analysis** menu, click **Data Table**.

7. In the **Row input cell** box, enter **B4**.

8. In the **Column input cell** box, enter **B3**.

9. Click **OK**.

Vary your data to get a specific result by using Goal Seek

Open the PerformGoalSeekAnalysis workbook in Excel, and then perform the following tasks:

1. Click cell **C4**.

2. Open the **Goal Seek** dialog box.

3. Verify that **C4** appears in the **Set cell** box.

4. In the **To value** box, enter **20%**.

5. In the **By changing cell** box, enter **C3**.

6. Click **OK**.

Find optimal solutions by using Solver

Open the BuildSolverModel workbook in Excel, and then perform the following tasks:

1. Click cell **F19**, and then open the **Solver Parameters** dialog box.

2. Verify that cell **F19** appears in the **Set Objective** box, and then select **Max**.

3. In the **By Changing Variable Cells** box, select cells **C3:E7**.

4. Add a constraint to require cell **C8** to be less than or equal to the value in cell **I10**.

5. Add a constraint that requires the values in cells **F3:F7** to be less than or equal to the values in cells **I3:I7**.

6. Make the unconstrained variables non-negative.

7. Solve the model by using the **GRG Nonlinear** engine.

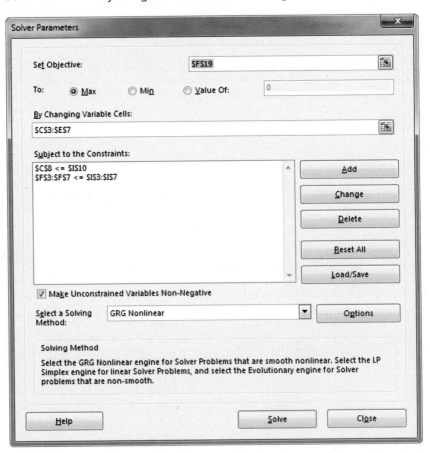

Define your solution by using the Solver Parameters dialog box

8. Click **OK** to close the **Solver Results** dialog box and examine the result.

	A	B	C	D	E	F	G	H	I	J
1		Boxes						Constraints		
2			Maple	Elm	Ash	Total Boxes		Product	Available	
3		Apples	40	0	10	50		Apples	50	
4		Pears	0	25.80462	19.19538	45		Pears	45	
5		Strawberries	0	0	80	80		Strawberries	80	
6		Blueberries	0	0	100	100		Blueberries	100	
7		Blackberries	0	100	0	100		Blackberries	100	
8		Total Boxes	40	125.8046	209.1954					
9								Market	Maximum	
10		Sale Price						Maple	40	
11			Maple	Elm	Ash					
12		Apples	$ 14.95	$ 12.95	$ 12.95					
13		Pears	$ 9.95	$ 10.95	$ 10.95					
14		Strawberries	$ 8.95	$ 8.95	$ 8.95					
15		Blueberries	$ 8.95	$ 8.95	$ 10.95					
16		Blackberries	$ 8.95	$ 10.95	$ 9.95					
17										
18						Total Revenue				
19						$ 4,126.25				
20										

Solver generates a solution without integer constraints

9. Reopen the **Solver Parameters** dialog box and add another constraint that requires the values in cells **C3:E7** to be integers.

10. Click **Solve**, close the **Solver Parameters** dialog box, and note how the solution has changed.

Analyze data by using descriptive statistics

Open the UseDescriptiveStatistics workbook in Excel, and then perform the following tasks:

1. Open the **Data Analysis** dialog box.

2. Click **Descriptive Statistics**, and then click **OK**.

3. In the **Descriptive Statistics** dialog box, click in the **Input Range** box and select cells **C3:C17**.

4. Select the **Summary statistics** check box, and then click **OK**.

Part 4

Microsoft PowerPoint 2016

Create and manage slides

When you create a presentation from a design template, the only slide that is immediately available is the title slide. It's up to you to add more slides for the content that you want the presentation to include. You can create slides based on slide templates that are designed to hold specific types of content, or you can copy existing slides from other presentations.

When the presentation you're developing has multiple slides, you can organize them into sections. Sections are not visible to the audience, but they make it easier to work with slide content in logical segments. A logical presentation and an overall consistent look, punctuated by variations that add weight exactly where it is needed, can enhance the likelihood that your intended audience will receive the message you want to convey.

This chapter guides you through procedures related to adding, copying, and importing slides; importing slide content; hiding and deleting slides; dividing presentations into sections; rearranging slides and sections; applying themes; and changing slide backgrounds.

In this chapter

- Add and remove slides
- Divide presentations into sections
- Rearrange slides and sections
- Apply themes
- Change slide backgrounds

Practice files

For this chapter, use the practice files from the Office2016SBS\Ch10 folder. For practice file download instructions, see the introduction.

> **TIP** The content in this chapter is about slides in general, rather than the content of the slides. Chapters 11 and 12 of this book are about working with the various types of slide content.

Add and remove slides

The appearance and structure of slides is defined by the slide layouts associated with the design template. Slide layouts define the elements on specific types of slides, such as:

- Slide backgrounds and incorporated graphics.

- Text box locations, sizes, and formats.

- Default paragraph and character formats for each text box location.

- Standard headers or footers.

> **TIP** Text boxes can contain static content that can't be changed by the presentation author (for example, a company logo), or they can serve as placeholders that define the default formatting of content entered within the text box.

A template could have only one slide layout, but most have unique slide layouts for slides that display the presentation title, section titles, and various combinations of slide titles and content, and a blank slide with only the background. Each slide layout is named; the name suggests the primary application of the slide layout, but you aren't limited to that suggestion; you can enter any type of content in any slide layout and modify the layout of any slide. The slide layouts that are available in a presentation are displayed on the New Slide menu.

> **SEE ALSO** For information about working with slide masters and slide layouts, see Chapter 12, "Create custom presentation elements," of *Microsoft PowerPoint 2016 Step by Step* by Joan Lambert (Microsoft Press, 2015).

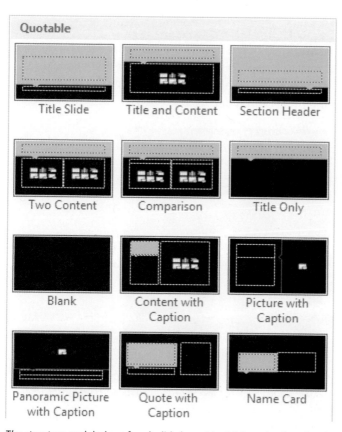

The structure and design of each slide layout is visible on its thumbnail

You can modify the built-in slide layouts, create your own slide layouts, or create entirely new sets of slide layouts called slide masters, and you can reset slides to match their slide layouts, or apply different slide layouts to existing slides.

10

Insert new slides

When you create a new slide, PowerPoint inserts it after the currently active slide. In a new presentation based on a standard PowerPoint template, a slide you add after the title slide has the Title And Content layout, and a slide added after a slide other than the title slide has the layout of the preceding slide.

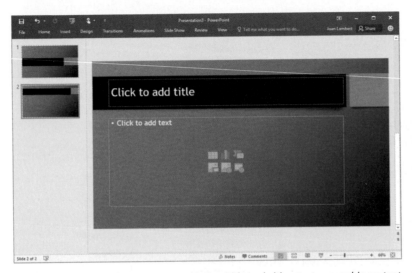

The Title And Content layout accommodates a title and either text or graphic content—a table, chart, diagram, picture, clip art image, or media clip

If you want to add a slide that has a different layout, you can select the layout when you insert the slide or you can change the slide layout at any time after you create the slide.

To add a slide based on the default slide layout

1. Select the slide after which you want to add the new slide.

2. Do either of the following:

   - On the **Home** tab, in the **Slides** group, click the **New Slide** button (not its arrow).

   - Press **Ctrl+M**.

> ✓ **TIP** You can also add new Title And Content slides by pressing keyboard shortcuts while you're entering text in the Outline pane. For more information, see "Enter text in placeholders" in Chapter 4, "Enter and edit text on slides," of *Microsoft PowerPoint 2016 Step by Step* by Joan Lambert (Microsoft Press, 2015).

To add a slide based on any slide layout

1. Select the slide after which you want to add the new slide.

2. On the **Home** tab, in the **Slides** group, click the **New Slide** arrow to display the **New Slide** gallery and menu.

3. In the gallery, click a slide layout thumbnail to add a slide based on that slide layout.

Copy and import slides and content

You can reuse slides from one presentation in another, in one of two ways: you can copy the slides from the original presentation to the new presentation, or you can use the Reuse Slides tool, which displays the content of an original presentation and allows you to choose the slides you want to insert in the new presentation.

Within a presentation, you can duplicate an existing slide to reuse it as the basis for a new slide. You can then customize the duplicated slide instead of having to create it from scratch.

If you frequently include a certain type of slide in your presentations, such as a slide that introduces you to the audience, you don't have to re-create the slide for each presentation. You can easily reuse a slide from one presentation in a different presentation. (You can use the same techniques to reuse a slide from someone else's presentation to standardize the appearance or structure of slide content with other members of your organization.) The slide takes on the formatting of its new presentation unless you specify otherwise.

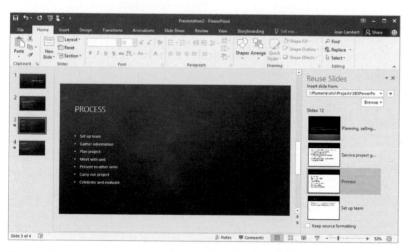

PowerPoint automatically applies the new theme to reused slides

If the content of your presentation exists in a document, you can configure that content in outline format and then import the outline into PowerPoint. For the import process to work smoothly, format the document content that you want to port into the presentation as headings. PowerPoint converts some styles into slide headings, converts some styles into bullet points, and ignores other styles.

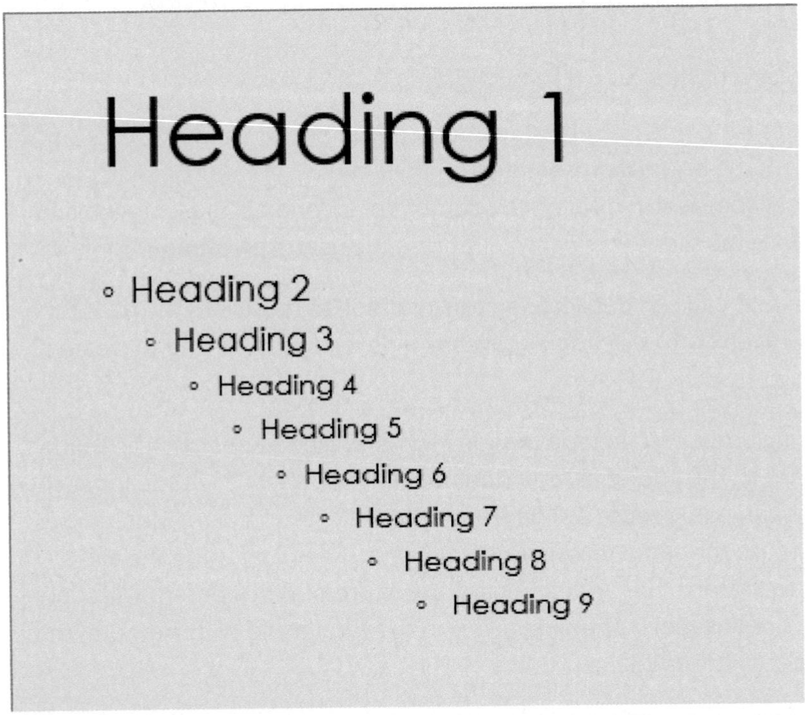

Heading 1

- Heading 2
  - Heading 3
    - Heading 4
      - Heading 5
        - Heading 6
          - Heading 7
            - Heading 8
              - Heading 9

A slide created from an imported outline

The following table illustrates how PowerPoint converts Word document styles to PowerPoint slide elements.

Word document style	PowerPoint presentation style
Title, Subtitle, Heading 1, any bulleted list level, or any numbered list level	Slide title
Heading 2	First-level bulleted list item
Heading 3	Second-level bulleted list item

Word document style	PowerPoint presentation style
Heading 4	Third-level bulleted list item
Heading 5	Fourth-level bulleted list item
Heading 6	Fifth-level bulleted list item
Heading 7	Sixth-level bulleted list item
Heading 8	Seventh-level bulleted list item
Heading 9	Eighth-level bulleted list item

To select a single slide

1. Do any of the following:

   - In Normal view, click the slide in the **Thumbnails** pane.

   - In Outline view, click the slide header in the **Outline** pane.

   - In Slide Sorter view, click the slide in the **Slide** pane.

To select multiple slides

1. In Normal view, Outline view, or Slide Sorter view, click the first slide you want to select.

2. Do either of the following:

   - To select a contiguous series of slides, press and hold the **Shift** key, and then click the last slide you want to select.

   - To select noncontiguous slides, press and hold the **Ctrl** key, and then click each additional slide you want to select.

To insert a copy of a slide immediately following the original slide

1. Display the presentation in Normal view.

2. In the **Thumbnails** pane, right-click the slide that you want to copy, and then click **Duplicate Slide**.

10

To insert a copy of one or more slides anywhere in a presentation

1. Display the presentation in Normal view or Slide Sorter view.

2. Do either of the following:

   - Select the thumbnail or thumbnails of the slide or slides you want to copy, and then press **Ctrl+C** or, on the **Home** tab, in the **Clipboard** group, click the **Copy** button.

   - Right-click the thumbnail of the slide that you want to copy, and then click **Copy**.

3. Do either of the following:

   - Click the thumbnail that you want to insert the slide copy or copies after, or click the empty space after the thumbnail. Then press **Ctrl+V** or, on the **Home** tab, in the **Clipboard** group, click the **Paste** button.

   - Right-click after an existing thumbnail where you want to insert the slide copy or copies, and then, in the **Paste Options** section of the short-cut menu, click the **Use Destination Theme** button or the **Keep Source Formatting** button.

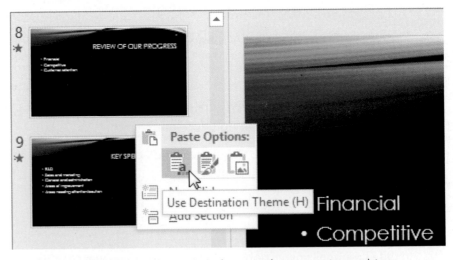

You can match the destination theme, retain the source theme, or paste as a picture

 TIP When PowerPoint displays the paste options, press H to use the destination style or K to use the source style.

TIP Repeat step 3 to paste additional copies of the slide or slides into the presentation.

To insert a slide from another presentation

1. Open the source and destination presentations in PowerPoint. Display each presentation in Normal view or Slide Sorter view.

2. Display the two PowerPoint windows side by side.

3. In the source presentation, select the slide or slides you want to copy.

4. Drag the selection to the destination presentation. A horizontal line between slide thumbnails in Normal view or a vertical line between thumbnails in Slide Sorter view indicates the location at which PowerPoint will insert the slides.

   PowerPoint creates copies of the slides and applies the destination theme to the copies.

Or

1. Display the destination presentation in Normal view.

2. On the **Home** tab or **Insert** tab, in the **Slides** group, click the **New Slide** arrow.

3. On the **New Slide** menu, below the gallery, click **Reuse Slides** to open the **Reuse Slides** pane on the right side of the screen.

4. Click the **Browse** button, and then click **Browse File**. In the **Browse** dialog box, browse to the folder that contains the presentation you want to use slides from, and then double-click the presentation.

 TIP If you've previously connected to the presentation you want to import slides from, you can click the down arrow in the Insert Slide From box to expand the list, and then click the presentation in the list, or click the presentation file name in the Open section of the Reuse Slide pane.

Or

Click the **Browse** button, and then click **Browse Slide** Library. In the **Select a Slide Library** window, browse to the slide library that contains the slide or slides you want to insert.

SEE ALSO For information about slide libraries, see the sidebar "SharePoint slide libraries" in this topic.

The Reuse Slides pane displays thumbnails of the available slides.

5. In the **Reuse Slides** pane, click the thumbnail of each slide you want to use to insert that slide into your presentation.

 TIP The reused slide takes on the design of the presentation in which it is inserted. If you want the slide to retain the formatting from the source presentation instead, select the Keep Source Formatting check box at the bottom of the Reuse Slides pane.

6. Close the **Reuse Slides** pane.

SharePoint slide libraries

If your organization uses a version of Microsoft SharePoint that supports slide libraries, you and your colleagues can store individual slides or entire presentations in a slide library so they are available for use by anyone who has access to the library. At the time of this writing, the current versions of SharePoint (SharePoint Server 2013 and SharePoint Online 2013) don't support the creation of new slide libraries but you can publish slides to and insert slides from legacy libraries.)

To store slides in a slide library, follow these steps:

1. On the **Share** page of the Backstage view, click **Publish Slides**, and then click the **Publish Slides** button.

2. In the **Publish Slides** dialog box, select the check box of each slide you want to publish. (Click the **Select All** button to select the entire presentation.)

3. In the **Publish To** box, enter or paste the URL of the slide library (or click the **Browse** button and browse to the slide library).

To prepare a source document to import as a presentation

1. Enter the content that you want to appear on the slides (and any other content) in a document.

2. Review the styles applied to the content you want to include in the presentation.

   - Title, Subtitle, Heading 1, and any list items will convert to slide titles.

   - Heading 2 through Heading 8 will convert to bulleted list items.

3. Save and close the document.

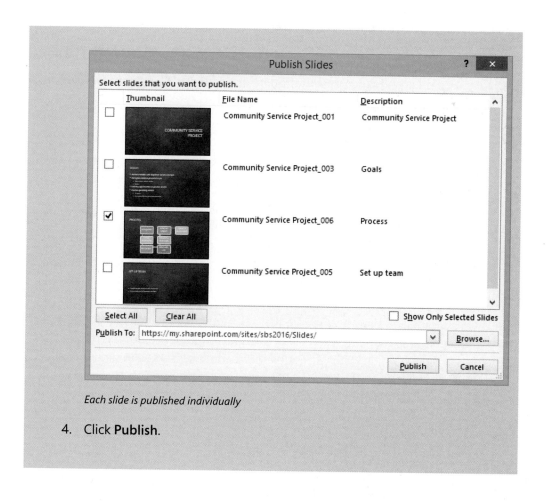

Each slide is published individually

4. Click **Publish**.

To create a presentation by importing a Word document

1. On the **Open** page of the Backstage view, click **Browse**.

2. In the file type list, click **All Files (*.*)**.

3. Browse to the folder that contains the Word document that contains the slide title and bullet point information.

4. Double-click the document to create a new presentation.

5. Select all the slides in the new presentation, and then on the **Home** tab, in the **Slides** group, click the **Reset** button.

6. Apply the design template you want.

> **SEE ALSO** For information about applying design templates to presentations, see "Create presentations" in Chapter 2, "Create and manage presentations," of *Microsoft PowerPoint 2016 Step by Step* by Joan Lambert (Microsoft Press, 2015).

To create slides in an existing presentation by importing a Word document

1. Select the slide after which you want to insert the new slides.

2. On the **Home** tab or **Insert** tab, in the **Slides** group, click the **New Slide** arrow.

3. On the **New Slide** menu, below the gallery, click **Slides from Outline** to open the **Insert Outline** dialog box, which resembles the **Open** dialog box.

4. Use standard Windows techniques to browse to the folder that contains the Word document you want to use for the slide titles and content.

5. Double-click the document to insert slides based on its content.

Hide and delete slides

If you create a slide and then later realize that you don't need it, you can delete it. If you don't need the slide for a presentation to a specific audience but might need it later, you can hide the slide instead. Hidden slides aren't presented in slide shows. They remain available from the Thumbnails pane, but their thumbnails are dimmed and slide numbers crossed through with a backslash.

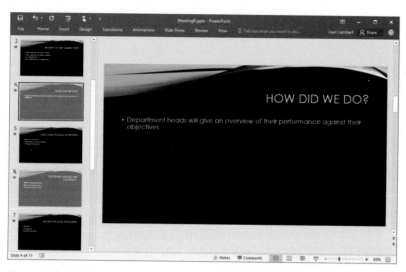

You can edit the content of hidden slides

When you select a hidden slide, the Hide Slide button on the Slide Show tab is shaded to indicate that the command is in effect. You can edit a hidden slide in the Slide pane just as you can any other, so you might use this feature to keep a slide that you're still working on hidden until it's final. You can unhide a slide to include it in the slide show.

To hide or unhide slides

1. Right-click a single slide, and then click **Hide Slide**.

Or

1. Select the slide or slides you want to hide or unhide.

2. Do either of the following:

   • Right-click the selection, and then click **Hide Slide**.

   • On the **Slide Show** tab, in the **Set Up** group, click the **Hide Slide** button.

> **TIP** The name of the Hide Slide command and button doesn't change; when a hidden slide is active, the command and button are shaded.

To delete slides

1. Right-click a single slide, and then click **Delete Slide**.

Or

1. Select the slide or slides you want to delete.

2. Do any of the following:

   - Right-click the selection, and then click **Delete Slide**.

   - On the **Home** tab, in the **Clipboard** group, click **Cut**.

   - Press the **Delete** key.

 TIP When you add or delete slides, PowerPoint renumbers all the subsequent slides.

Divide presentations into sections

To make it easier to organize and format a longer presentation, you can divide it into sections. In both Normal view and Slide Sorter view, sections are designated by titles above their slides. They do not appear in other views, and they do not create slides or otherwise interrupt the flow of the presentation.

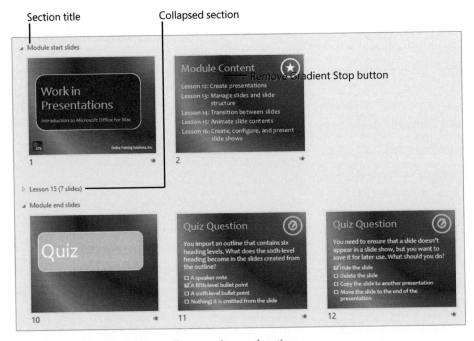

You can rename, remove, move, collapse, and expand sections

Because you can collapse entire sections to leave only the section titles visible, the sections make it easier to focus on one part of a presentation at a time.

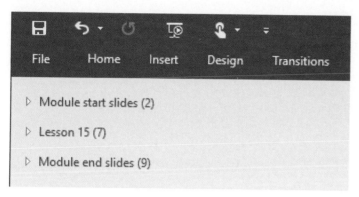

You can collapse sections to provide an "outline" of long presentations, with the number of slides in each section displayed in parentheses

 TIP If you're collaborating with other people on the development of a presentation, sections are a convenient way of assigning slides to different people.

Some templates include a slide layout, similar to the title slide layout, that is specifically designed for section divider slides. If you divide a long presentation into sections based on topic, you might want to transfer your section titles to these slides to provide guidance to the audience or to mark logical points in the presentation to take breaks or answer questions.

To create a section

1. In Normal view or Slide Sorter view, select the slide that you want to be first in the new section.

2. On the **Home** tab, in the **Slides** group, click the **Section** button, and then click **Add Section** to insert a section title named *Untitled Section* before the selected slide.

10

To rename a section

1. In Normal view or Slide Sorter view, do either of the following to open the
   Rename Section dialog box:

   - Right-click the section title you want to change, and then click **Rename
     Section**.

   - On the **Home** tab, in the **Slides** group, click the **Section** button, and then
     click **Rename Section**.

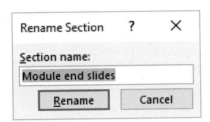

The current section name is selected so that you can easily replace it

2. In the **Section name** box, replace or edit the existing section name, and then
   click the **Rename** button.

To collapse or expand one slide section

1. In Normal view or Slide Sorter view, click the arrow that precedes the section
   title.

    TIP A right-pointing arrow indicates a collapsed section, an arrow that points to
   the lower-right corner indicates an expanded section.

To collapse or expand all slide sections

1. Do either of the following:

   - On the **Home** tab, in the **Slides** group, click the **Section** button, and then
     click **Collapse All** or **Expand All**.

   - Right-click any section name, and then click **Expand All** or **Collapse All**.

Rearrange slides and sections

After you have added several slides to a presentation, you might want to rearrange their order so that they more effectively communicate your message.

You can rearrange a presentation by moving individual slides or entire sections of slides.

To move a slide within a presentation

1. In Normal view or Slide Sorter view, drag the slide thumbnail to its new position. Notice as you drag that the other thumbnails move to indicate where the selected slide will appear when you release the mouse button.

Or

1. Select the slide thumbnail, and then press **Ctrl+X** or on the **Home** tab, in the **Clipboard** group, click **Cut**.

2. Do either of the following:

   - Click the slide thumbnail that you want to insert the cut slide after, and then press **Ctrl+V** or, in the **Clipboard** group, click **Paste**.

   - Click between the other slide thumbnails to insert a thin red marker (horizontal in Normal view or vertical in Slide Sorter view) where you want to move the slide. Then press **Ctrl+V** or, in the **Clipboard** group, click **Paste**.

Or

1. Right-click the slide thumbnail, and then click **Cut**.

2. Right-click between the other slide thumbnails where you want to move the slide.

> **TIP** The thin red destination marker appears only when you click between thumbnails, not when you right-click between thumbnails.

3. In the **Paste Options** section of the shortcut menu, click the **Use Destination Theme** button or the **Keep Source Formatting** button.

> **TIP** When PowerPoint displays the paste options, press H to use the destination style or K to use the source style.

10

To move a section within a presentation

1. Click the title of the section of slides you want to move, to select all the slides in the section.

2. Drag the section to its new location.

Or

1. Right-click the section title, and then click **Move Section Up** or **Move Section Down** to move the section and all its slides before the preceding section or after the following section.

 TIP The Move Section commands aren't available on the Section menu; they are available only on the shortcut menu that appears when you right-click a section title.

To merge a section into the preceding section by removing the section divider

1. Click the title of the section of slides you want to ungroup.

2. On the **Home** tab, in the **Slides** group, click the **Section** button, and then click **Remove Section**.

Or

1. Right-click the section title, and then click **Remove Section**.

To merge all sections by removing all section dividers

1. On the **Home** tab, in the **Slides** group, click the **Section** button, and then click **Remove All Sections**.

To delete a section of slides

1. Click the title of the section of slides you want to delete, to select all the slides in the section.

2. Press the **Delete** key.

Or

1. Right-click the section title, and then click **Remove Section & Slides**.

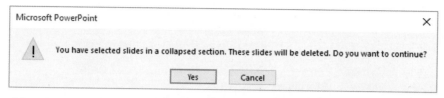

If the selected section is collapsed, PowerPoint prompts you to confirm the deletion

2. If PowerPoint prompts you to confirm the deletion, click **Yes** to delete the section title and all the slides in the section.

 TIP The Remove Section & Slides command isn't available on the Section menu; it is available only on the shortcut menu that appears when you right-click a section title.

Apply themes

The appearance of every presentation that you create is governed by a theme—a combination of colors, fonts, effect styles, and background graphics or formatting that coordinates the appearance of all the presentation elements. Even a blank presentation has a theme: the Office theme, which has a white slide background, a standard set of text and accent colors, and the Office font set, which uses Calibri Light for headings and Calibri for body text.

PowerPoint and the other Office 2016 apps share a common set of themes and theme elements. This enables you to easily produce coordinated print and presentation materials. Approximately 30 of these themes are available to you from the PowerPoint Themes gallery. Many of the themes come with predefined variants, which have a different color scheme or background graphic.

10

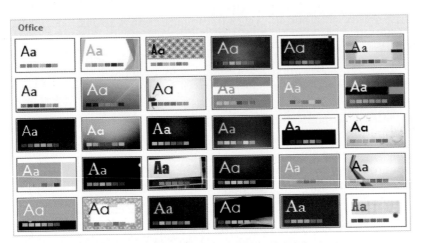

The built-in Office themes for PowerPoint

Each thumbnail in the PowerPoint Themes gallery displays a sample of the font set in the form of an uppercase and lowercase letter A (*Aa*) and the color scheme in the form of colored blocks over the default title slide. Title slides frequently have background graphics that set the tone for the presentation. The standard slides associated with the theme will often have a more-subtle background graphic that coordinates with the title slide background. You can choose to hide the background graphic and use only a colored background if you want to.

You can change the theme that is applied to an entire presentation or to only one section of the presentation. If you like the colors of one theme, the fonts of another, and the effects of another, you can mix and match theme elements. You can also create your own themes.

> **SEE ALSO** For information about creating theme and custom theme elements, see "Create themes, color sets, and font sets" in Chapter 12, "Create custom presentation elements," of *Microsoft PowerPoint 2016 Step by Step* by Joan Lambert (Microsoft Press, 2015).

When you're working in Normal view you can use the Live Preview feature to see how your presentation would look with a different theme applied. Simply point to any theme and pause. PowerPoint temporarily applies the selected formatting to the slide in the Slide pane. This makes it easy to try different themes and theme elements until you find the ones you want.

To apply a standard theme to a presentation

1. Display the presentation in Normal view.

2. On the **Design** tab, in the **Themes** group, click the **More** button (below the scroll arrows) to display the menu that includes the **Office** theme gallery.

> **TIP** The menu displays the currently applied template and any custom Office templates on your computer above the Office themes.

3. Point to thumbnails in the gallery to display the theme names in tooltips and preview the effect of applying the themes to your presentation.

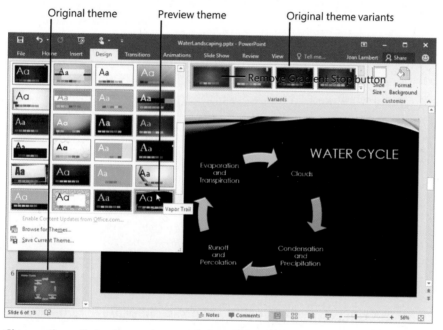

Choose a theme that enhances the content of your presentation

4. Click a **theme** thumbnail to apply that theme to the entire presentation.

To change the color scheme of the presentation

1. On the **Design** tab, in the **Variants** group, click a variant thumbnail.

Or

1. On the **Design** tab, in the **Variants** group, click the **More** button (below the scroll arrows) to expand the **Variants** menu.

2. On the **Variants** menu, click **Colors**.

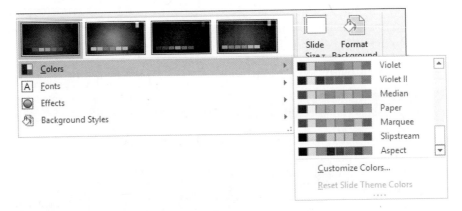

Choose from the dozens of standard color schemes

3. On the **Colors** menu, click the color set you want to apply.

> **TIP** Changing the color scheme, font set, or effect style of a presentation doesn't change the theme that is applied to the presentation.

To change the font set of the presentation

1. On the **Design** tab, in the **Variants** group, click the **More** button (below the scroll arrows) to expand the **Variants** menu.

2. On the **Variants** menu, click **Fonts**.

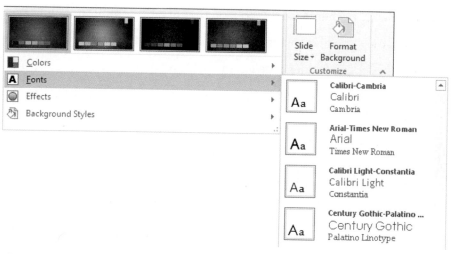

Choose from same-font or complementary-font heading/body font combinations

3. On the **Fonts** menu, click the font set you want to apply.

To change the effect style of the presentation

1. On the **Design** tab, in the **Variants** group, click the **More** button (below the scroll arrows) to expand the **Variants** menu.

2. On the **Variants** menu, click **Effects**.

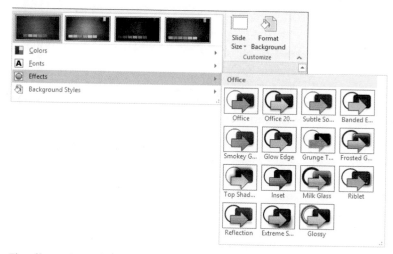

The effect style preview color coordinates with the current color scheme

3. On the **Effects** menu, click the effect style you want to apply.

To apply a theme or theme variant to only part of a presentation

1. Create a section that contains the slides you want to have a different theme.

2. Click the section header to select the section.

3. Apply the theme or theme element.

Change slide backgrounds

The presentation theme includes a standard background. The background might be a color or it might include a background graphic.

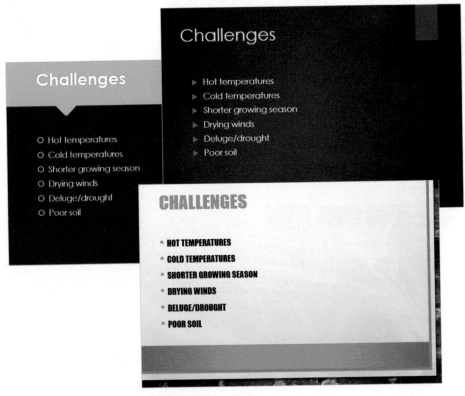

A variety of thematic background graphics

You can customize slide backgrounds by removing the background graphic and filling the slide background with a solid color, a color gradient, a texture, a pattern, or a picture of your choice. You make these changes in the Format Background pane.

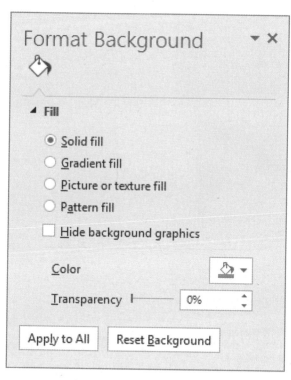

You can control the color, texture, pattern, or picture in the background of one or all slides

Each of the options in the Format Background pane has specific settings that appear when you select the option.

A solid color background is a good choice for readability, but if you want to add some interest without a lot of distraction, you can use a color gradient in which a solid color gradually changes to another. PowerPoint offers several light-to-dark and dark-to-light gradient patterns based on the color scheme. You can also create custom gradients of two, three, or more colors. Each change in color within a gradient is controlled by a gradient stop. For each gradient stop, you can specify the location and specific color (including the transparency and brightness of the color). A color gradient can have from 2 to 10 gradient stops.

A gradient can include up to 10 color changes

If you want something fancier than a solid color or a color gradient, you can give the slide background a texture or pattern. PowerPoint comes with several built-in textures that you can easily apply to the background of slides.

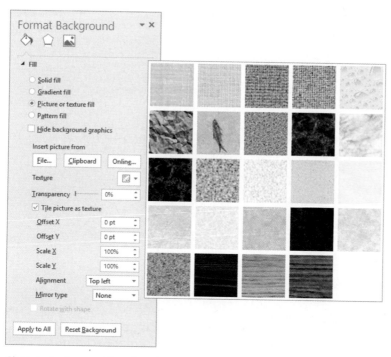

Choose a background that doesn't overpower your presentation

If none of these meets your needs, you might want to use a picture of a textured surface. For a dramatic effect, you can even incorporate a picture of your own, although these are best reserved for small areas of the slide rather than the entire background.

If you prefer to use a simple pattern rather than a texture, you can choose from 48 patterns and set the background and foreground color to your liking.

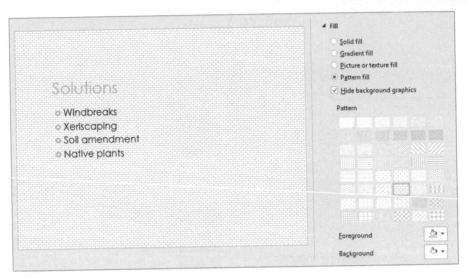

Click any pattern to preview it on the slide

To display the Format Background pane

1. On the **Design** tab, in the **Customize** group, click the **Format Background** button.

To close the Format Background pane

1. Do either of the following:
   - In the upper-right corner of the pane, click the **Close** button (the X).
   - To the right of the pane name, click the down arrow, and then click **Close**.

To apply a background change to all slides

1. In the **Format Background** pane, configure the slide background formatting you want.

2. At the bottom of the pane, click the **Apply to All** button.

To remove the slide background graphic applied by a theme

1. Display the **Format Background** pane.

2. In the **Format Background** pane, select the **Hide background graphics** check box.

To apply a solid background color to one or more slides

1. In the **Format Background** pane, click **Solid fill**.

2. Click the **Color** button to display the color palette.

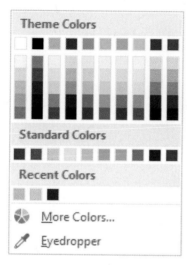

The color palette displays theme colors, standard colors, and recently used colors

 SEE ALSO For information about the colors you can use, see the sidebar "Non-theme colors" later in this topic.

3. Click a theme color variant, a solid color, or a recent color, or click **More Colors** and select a custom color.

4. Move the **Transparency** slider to adjust the background color transparency, or set a specific transparency percentage.

SEE ALSO For information about printing slides without background colors and images, see "Preview and print presentations" in Chapter 9, "Review presentations," of *Microsoft PowerPoint 2016 Step by Step* by Joan Lambert (Microsoft Press, 2015).

To apply a gradient background color to one or more slides

1. In the **Format Background** pane, click **Gradient fill**.

2. Click the **Preset gradients** button, and then click a gradient option based on the current color palette.

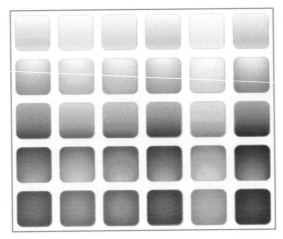

Preset color gradients offer linear and radial variants of the theme accent color

Or

1. In the **Type** list, click **Linear**, **Radial**, **Rectangular**, **Path**, or **Shade from title**.

2. In the **Direction** list, click the direction you want the gradient to flow.

3. If you chose the **Linear** type, you can specify the angle you want the gradient to move along. Enter the angle in the **Angle** box.

4. If you want to add gradient stops, do either of the following in the **Gradient Stops** area:

   - Click the **Add gradient stop** button, and then reposition the marker that appears on the slider.

   - Click the slider in the approximate location where you want to insert the gradient stop.

Add Gradient Stop button

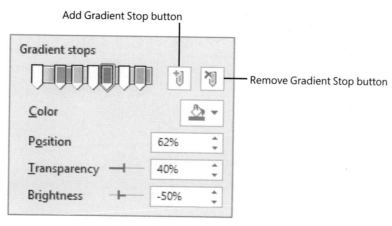

Remove Gradient Stop button

You can precisely control a color by adjusting the transparency and brightness

5. If you want to remove gradient stops, do either of the following in the **Gradient Stops** area:

   - On the slider, click the marker for the gradient stop you want to remove. Then click the **Remove gradient stop** button.

   - Drag the gradient stop marker off of the slider.

6. In the **Gradient stops** area, set the color, position, transparency, and brightness for each color in the gradient. Note the following:

   - You can select a color swatch or match an existing color by using the eye-dropper tool to select a color.

   - You can change the transparency and brightness by moving the markers on the sliders, by entering specific percentages, or by scrolling the dials.

To apply a textured background to one or more slides

1. In the **Format Background** pane, click **Picture or texture fill**.

2. Click the **Texture** button to display the texture gallery. You can select from a variety of textures, including fabric, marble, granite, wood grain, and Formica-like textures in various colors.

3. In the texture gallery, click the texture you want to apply.

4. Move the **Transparency** slider to adjust the background color transparency, or set a specific transparency percentage.

10

Non-theme colors

Although using themes enables you to create presentations with a color-coordinated design, you can also use colors that aren't part of the theme. Whenever you apply a color to any presentation element, you can choose from among these options:

- Six shades of each of the 10 theme colors
- Ten standard colors that are available in all Office documents, regardless of the theme
- Non-standard colors that you've used recently
- The Standard color palette that offers permutations of primary, secondary, and tertiary colors in a hexagonal color wheel

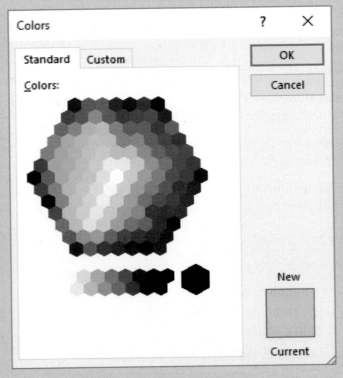

Colors from the Standard color wheel remain the same in any Office document regardless of the color scheme

- A custom color model on which you can select from permutations of primary and secondary colors or specify colors by RGB (Red, Green, and Blue) or HSL (Hue, Saturation, and Luminescence) values

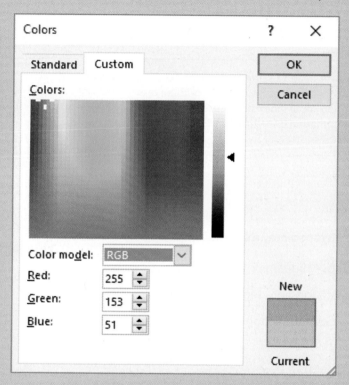

Choose a color by clicking the rainbow, sliding the shade scale, or entering an RGB or HSL value

If you want to make a selected element the same color as one that is used elsewhere on the same slide, display the color menu, click Eyedropper, and then click the color you want.

To apply a patterned background to one or more slides

1. In the **Format Background** pane, click **Pattern fill**.

2. In the **Pattern** palette, click one of the 48 pattern swatches.

3. Click the **Foreground** button, and then select the primary pattern color.

4. Click the **Background** button, and then select the secondary pattern color.

> **TIP** If you want to add a watermark, such as the word *Draft* or *Confidential*, to the background of your slides, you need to add the text to the background of the slide master. For information about slide masters, see "Display and change slide masters" in Chapter 12, "Create custom presentation elements," of *Microsoft PowerPoint 2016 Step by Step* by Joan Lambert (Microsoft Press, 2015).

Skills review

In this chapter, you learned how to:

- Add and remove slides
- Divide presentations into sections
- Rearrange slides and sections
- Apply themes
- Change slide backgrounds

Practice tasks

The practice files for these tasks are located in the Office2016SBS\Ch10 folder. You can save the results of the tasks in the same folder.

Add and remove slides

Open the AddRemoveSlides presentation in PowerPoint, and then perform the following tasks:

1. Add two slides after the title slide. First, add a slide that has the default **Title and Content** layout. Then add a slide that has the **Two Content** layout.

2. Add 7 more slides, so you have a total of 10 slides. Use each slide layout at least once.

3. In Normal view, delete slide **3**.

4. Switch to Slide Sorter view, and then delete slides **5** through **8**. The presentation now contains five slides.

5. Add seven slides to the end of the presentation by inserting the content of the **ImportOutline** document.

6. Use the **Reuse Slides** feature to insert the first slide from the **ReuseSlides** presentation as slide **2** in the **AddRemoveSlides** presentation. Then close the **Reuse Slides** pane.

7. Insert a duplicate copy of slide **2** as slide **3**.

8. Hide slide **2**, and then delete slide **8**.

9. Close and save the presentation.

Divide presentations into sections

Open the CreateSections presentation in Normal view, and then perform the following tasks:

1. Divide the presentation into two sections:

   - A section that contains slides **1** through **3**

   - A section that contains slides **4** through **12**

2. Change the name of the first section to **Introduction**.

3. Switch to Slide Sorter view, and then change the name of the second section to **Process**.

4. Collapse both sections, and then expand only the **Process** section.

5. Close and save the presentation.

Rearrange slides and sections

Open the RearrangeSlides presentation in Normal view, and then perform the following tasks:

1. Move the first slide in the **Step 1** section so that it is the third slide in the Introduction section. Then delete the last slide in the Introduction section.

2. Switch to **Slide Sorter** view and scroll through the presentation, noticing the sections.

3. Collapse the sections, and then rearrange them so that the sections for steps 1 through 7 are in order and the End section is at the end of the presentation.

4. Merge the **End** section into the **Step 7** section.

5. Close and save the presentation.

Apply themes

Open the ApplyThemes presentation in Normal view, and then perform the following tasks:

1. On slide **1**, click the slide title. On the **Home** tab, in the **Font** group, notice that the title font is blue-gray, 44-point, Times New Roman.

2. Apply the **Ion** theme to the presentation. On the **Home** tab, in the **Font** group, notice that the title font is now white, 72-point, Century Gothic.

3. Switch to **Slide Sorter** view, and adjust the magnification to display all the slides.

4. Apply the **Circuit** theme to the presentation. Notice that the slide background is blue.

5. Apply the **gray** variant of the Circuit theme to the **Past** section of the presentation.

6. Apply the **red** variant of the Circuit theme to the **Present** section of the presentation.

7. Apply the **green** variant of the Circuit theme to the **Future** section of the presentation.

8. Close and save the presentation.

Change slide backgrounds

Open the ChangeBackgrounds presentation, and then perform the following tasks:

1. Apply a gradient fill background to slide **1**.

2. Change the gradient type to **Rectangular** and set the direction to **From Top Left Corner**.

3. Configure the gradient to have the following four gradient stops:

Stop	Color	Position	Transparency	Brightness
1	Light Green	5%	0%	-10%
2	White	45%	0%	90%
3	Light Blue	75%	0%	0%
4	Purple	100%	20%	0%

4. Apply the custom gradient fill to all slides in the presentation.

5. Change the background of only slide **1** to the **Water droplets** texture, and set the **Transparency** of the texture to **25%**.

6. Close and save the presentation.

Insert and manage simple graphics

With the ready availability of professionally designed templates, presentations have become more visually sophisticated and appealing. Gone (ideally) are the days of presenters reading a list of bullet points to the audience; successful presentations are likely to have fewer words and more graphic elements. You can use images, diagrams, animations, charts, tables, and other visual elements to graphically reinforce your spoken message (which can be conveniently documented in the speaker notes attached to the slides).

The term *graphics* generally refers to several kinds of visual objects, including photos, "clip art" images, diagrams, charts, and shapes. You can insert all these types of graphics as objects on a slide and then size, move, and copy them. Because elements on a PowerPoint slide float independently, it is simpler to creatively present information on PowerPoint slides than in Word documents.

This chapter guides you through procedures related to inserting, moving, and resizing pictures; editing and formatting pictures; drawing and modifying shapes; capturing and inserting screen clippings; and creating a photo album.

In this chapter

- Insert, move, and resize pictures
- Edit and format pictures
- Draw and modify shapes
- Capture and insert screen clippings
- Create a photo album

Practice files

For this chapter, use the practice files from the Office2016SBS\Ch11 folder. For practice file download instructions, see the introduction.

Insert, move, and resize pictures

You can place digital photographs and images created and saved in other programs on slides in your PowerPoint 2016 presentations. Collectively, these types of images are referred to as *pictures*. You can use pictures to make slides more visually interesting, but in a PowerPoint presentation, you're more likely to use pictures to convey information in a way that words cannot.

Pictures can help to illustrate a concept

You can insert a picture onto a slide either from your computer or from an online source, such as the Internet or your cloud storage drive.

> ✓ **TIP** Pictures you acquire from the web are often copyrighted, meaning that you cannot use them without the permission of the image's owner. Sometimes owners will grant permission if you give them credit. Professional photographers usually charge a fee to use their work. Always assume that pictures are copyrighted unless the source clearly indicates that they are license free.

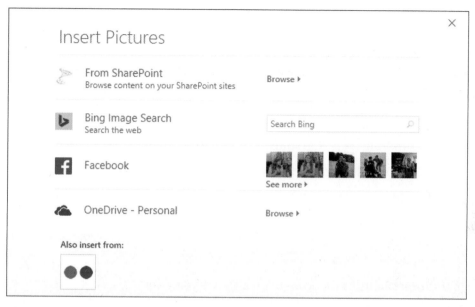

Choose an online storage location or search for an image

After you insert a picture, you can make it larger or smaller and position it anywhere you want on the slide.

Inserting or selecting a picture activates its sizing handles and the Format tool tab in the Picture Tools tab group. This tab contains commands for formatting the appearance of a picture and controlling its position relative to text, images, and other page elements.

> ✔ **TIP** You can save PowerPoint slides as pictures that you can insert in other types of documents. For more information, see "Preview and print presentations" in Chapter 9, "Review presentations," of *Microsoft PowerPoint 2016 Step by Step* by Joan Lambert (Microsoft Press, 2015).

11

To insert a picture from your computer

1. Do either of the following to open the Insert Picture dialog box:

    -   If the slide has a content placeholder, click the **Pictures** button in the placeholder.

    -   If the slide doesn't have a content placeholder, on the **Insert** tab, in the **Images** group, click the **Pictures** button.

2. In the **Insert Picture** dialog box, browse to and select the picture (or pictures) you want to insert. Then click the **Insert** button.

> **TIP** If a picture might change, you can ensure that the slide is always up to date by clicking the Insert arrow and then clicking Link To File to insert a link to the picture, or by clicking Insert And Link to insert the picture and link it to its graphic file.

The inserted picture is surrounded by a frame to indicate that it is selected. You can use the handles around the frame to size and rotate the picture.

To insert a picture from an online source

1. Do either of the following to open the Insert Pictures window:

   - If the slide has a content placeholder, click the **Online Pictures** button in the placeholder.

   - If the slide doesn't have a content placeholder, on the **Insert tab**, in the **Images group**, click the **Online Pictures button**.

2. In the **Insert Pictures** window, click the source you want to use, or enter a search term in the search box.

3. Browse to and select the picture you want to insert. Then click the **Insert** button.

To select a picture for editing

1. Click the picture once.

To move a picture

1. Point to the image. When the cursor changes to a four-headed arrow, drag the picture to its new location.

> **TIP** As you drag, red dotted lines, called *smart guides*, might appear on the slide to help you align the picture with other elements.

To resize a picture

1. Select the picture, and then do any of the following:

   - To change only the width of the picture, drag the left or right size handle.

   - To change only the height of the picture, drag the top or bottom size handle.

   - To change both the height and the width of the picture without changing its aspect ratio, drag a corner size handle or set the **Height** or **Width** measurement in the **Size** group on the **Format** tool tab, and then press **Enter**.

Graphic formats

Many common graphic formats store graphics as a series of dots, or *pixels*. Each pixel is made up of bits. The number of bits per pixel (bpp) determines the number of distinct colors that can be represented by a pixel.

The mapping of bits to colors isn't 1:1; it's 2^{bpp}. In other words:

- 1 bpp = 2 colors
- 2 bpp = 4 colors
- 4 bpp = 16 colors
- 8 bpp = 256 colors

- 16 bpp = 65,536 colors
- 32 bpp = 4,294,967,296 colors
- 64 bpp = 18,446,744,073,709,551,616 colors

Image files that you will use in a PowerPoint presentation are usually in one of the following file formats:

- **BMP (bitmap)** There are different qualities of BMPs.

- **GIF (Graphics Interchange Format)** This format is common for images that appear on webpages, because the images can be compressed with no loss of information and groups of them can be animated. GIFs store at most 8 bits per pixel, so they are limited to 256 colors.

- **JPEG (Joint Photographic Experts Group)** This compressed format works well for complex graphics such as scanned photographs. Some information is lost in the compression process, but often the loss is imperceptible to the human eye. Color JPEGs store 24 bits per pixel. Grayscale JPEGs store 8 bits per pixel.

- **PNG (Portable Network Graphic)** This format has the advantages of the GIF format but can store colors with 24, 32, 48, or 64 bits per pixel and grayscales with 1, 2, 4, 8, or 16 bits per pixel. A PNG file can also specify whether each pixel blends with its background color and can contain color correction information so that images look accurate on a broad range of display devices. Graphics saved in this format are smaller, so they display faster.

Of the commonly available file formats, PNG images are usually the best choice because they provide high quality images with a small file size, and support transparency.

11

Edit and format pictures

From time to time in this book, we have alluded to the modern trend away from slides with bullet points and toward presentations that include more graphics. Successful presenters have learned that most people can't listen to a presentation while they are reading slides. So these presenters make sure most of their slides display graphics that represent the point they are making, giving the audience something to look at while they focus on what is being said. PowerPoint gives you the tools you need to create graphic-intensive rather than text-intensive presentations.

After you insert any picture into a presentation, you can modify it by using the commands on the Format tool tab. For example, you can do the following:

- Remove the background by designating either the areas you want to keep or those you want to remove.

- Sharpen or soften the picture, or change its brightness or contrast.

- Enhance the picture's color.

- Make one of the picture's colors transparent.

- Choose an effect, such as Pencil Sketch or Paint Strokes.

- Apply effects such as shadows, reflections, and borders; or apply combinations of these effects.

- Add a border consisting of one or more solid or dashed lines of whatever width and color you choose.

- Rotate the picture to any angle, either by dragging the rotating handle or by choosing a rotating or flipping option.

- Crop away the parts of the picture that you don't want to show on the slide. (The picture itself is not altered—parts of it are simply covered up.)

- Minimize the presentation's file size by specifying the optimum resolution for where or how the presentation will be viewed—for example, on a webpage or printed page. You can also delete cropped areas of a picture to reduce file size.

All these changes are made to the representation of the picture that is on the slide and do not affect the original picture.

To crop a picture

1. Select the picture. On the **Format** tool tab, in the **Size** group, click the **Crop** button to display thick black handles on the sides and in the corners of the picture.

2. Drag the handles to define the area you want to crop to. The areas that will be excluded from the cropped picture are shaded.

Cropping a photo

 TIP When you select a crop handle, be careful to not drag the picture sizing handles instead—they're very close to each other.

3. When you finish defining the area, click away from the picture, or click the **Crop** button again to apply the crop effect.

 TIP To redisplay the uncropped picture at any time, select it and click the Crop button.

Or

1. Select the picture. On the **Format** tool tab, in the **Size** group, click the **Crop** arrow, and then do one of the following:

   - Click **Crop to Shape**, and then click a shape.

   - Click **Aspect Ratio**, and then click an aspect ratio.

   PowerPoint crops the picture to meet your specifications.

11

You can crop photos to shapes

To frame a picture

1. Select the picture. On the **Format** tool tab, in the **Picture Styles** group, click the **More** button to display the Picture Styles gallery.

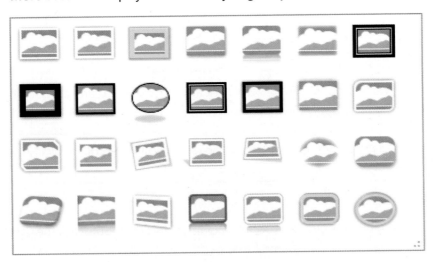

Picture styles can add frames, shadows, reflections, and more

2. Point to each picture style in turn to display a live preview of the frame applied to your picture. Click the picture style you want to apply.

There are a lot of picture styles, so experiment with them to identify those you like

To remove a background from a picture

1. Select the picture. On the **Format** tool tab, in the **Adjust** group, click the **Remove Background** button to display the Background Removal tool tab and apply purple shading to the areas of the picture that the tool thinks you want to remove.

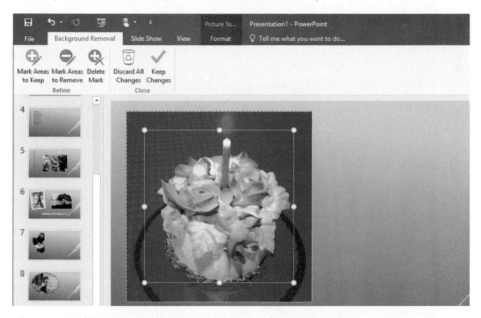

The accuracy of the estimate depends on the intricacy of the background

2. Drag the white handles to define the area that you want to keep. The Background Removal tool updates its shading as you do.

11

3. On the **Background Removal** tool tab, click **Mark Areas to Keep**, and then click any areas of the photo that are shaded, that you'd like to expose and keep.

4. On the **Background Removal** tool tab, click **Mark Areas to Remove**, and then click any areas of the photo that aren't shaded, that you'd like to remove.

5. Depending on the simplicity of the picture, you might need to make a lot of adjustments or only a few.

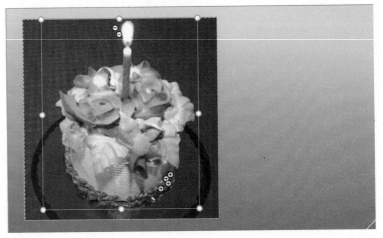

The Background removal tool updates the shading when you indicate areas to keep or remove

6. When you finish, click the **Keep Changes** button to display the results. You can return to the Background Removal tool tab at any time to make adjustments.

A floating cake!

To apply an artistic effect to a picture

1. Select the picture. On the **Format** tool tab, in the **Adjust** group, click the **Artistic Effects** button to display the Artistic Effects gallery.

2. Point to each effect to display a live preview of the effect on the selected photo.

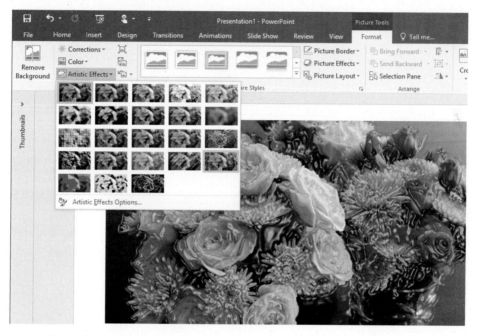

Try out all the effects

3. Click the effect that you want to apply.

Draw and modify shapes

An extensive library of shapes is available in PowerPoint. Shapes can be simple, such as lines, circles, or squares; or more complex, such as stars, hearts, and arrows. Some shapes are three-dimensional (although most are two-dimensional). Some of the shapes have innate meanings or intentions, and others are simply shapes.

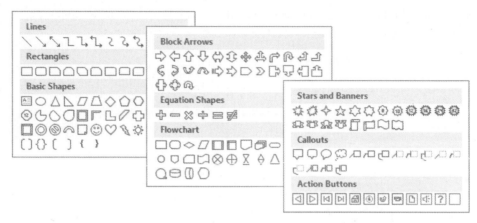

Simple representations of the shapes you can insert on a slide

Pointing to any shape in the gallery displays a ScreenTip that contains the shape name.

Draw and add text to shapes

After you select a shape that you want to add to your slide, you drag to draw it on the slide. Shapes are also text boxes, and you can enter text directly into them. You can format the text in shapes just as you would regular text.

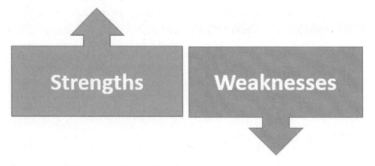

Shapes can help to visually reinforce a concept

With a little imagination, you'll soon discover ways to create images by combining shapes. You can use these images to illustrate a concept on a slide, or you can animate the drawings to convey actions or draw attention to specific elements.

 SEE ALSO For information about animating shapes and text on slides, see "Animate text and pictures on slides" in Chapter 12, "Add sound and movement to slides."

To create a shape on a slide

1. On the **Insert** tab, in the **Illustrations** group, click the **Shapes** button and then, on the **Shapes** menu, click the shape you want to insert.

    TIP If you click a shape button and then change your mind about drawing the shape, you can release the shape by pressing the Esc key.

2. When the cursor changes to a plus sign, do either of the following:

   - Click on the slide to create a shape of the default size.

   - Drag diagonally on the slide to specify the upper-left and lower-right corners of the rectangle that surrounds the shape (the drawing canvas).

    TIP To draw a shape that has the same height and width (such as a circle or square), hold down the Shift key while you drag.

To add text to a shape

1. Select the shape, and then enter the text you want to display on the shape. There is no cursor to indicate the location of the text; simply start typing and it appears on the shape.

11

Locate additional formatting commands

You control the area of the shape that is available for text by formatting the Text Box margins of the shape. This setting is gathered with many others in the Format Shape pane, which you can display by clicking the dialog box launcher (the small diagonal arrow) in the lower-right corner of the Shape Styles, WordArt Styles, or Size group on the Format tool tab.

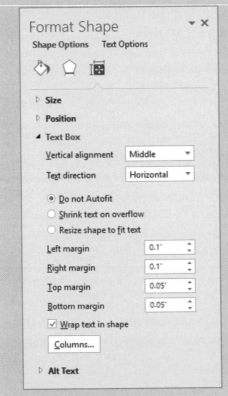

You can display different pages of settings by clicking the text and icons at the top of the pane

In PowerPoint 2016, the most frequently used formatting commands are located on the ribbon. If additional commands are available, the ribbon group includes a dialog box launcher. Clicking the dialog box launcher displays either a dialog box or a control pane.

Move and modify shapes

You can change the size, angles, outline and fill colors, and effects applied to the shape. You can apply different colors to the outline and inside (fill) of a shape.

When you first draw a shape and any time you select it thereafter, it has a set of handles.

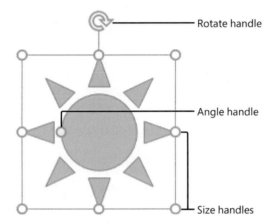

You can easily modify the shape, size, and angle of an image

You can use the handles to manipulate the shape in the following ways:

- Drag the side or corner handles (hollow circles) to change the size or aspect ratio of the shape.

- Drag the angle handles (yellow circles) to change the angles or curves of the text within the shape. Not all shapes have angle handles.

- Drag the rotate handle (circling arrow) to rotate the shape on the slide.

11

Nine shapes arranged to create a recognizable image

To select a shape for editing

1. Click the shape once.

To select multiple shapes

1. Do either of the following:

   - Click a shape, hold down the **Shift** or **Ctrl** key, and click each other shape.

   - Drag to encompass all the shapes you want to select.

To resize a shape

1. Select the shape, and then do any of the following:

   - To change only the width of the shape, drag the left or right size handle.

   - To change only the height of the shape, drag the top or bottom size handle.

   - To change both the height and the width of the shape, drag a corner size handle.

   - To resize a shape without changing its aspect ratio, hold down the **Shift** key and drag a corner size handle or press an arrow key.

To move a shape on a slide

1. Select the shape that you want to move.

2. Drag the shape or press the arrow keys to move it to the new location.

To rotate or flip a shape

1. Select the shape.

2. On the **Format** tool tab, in the **Arrange** group, click the **Rotate Objects** button.

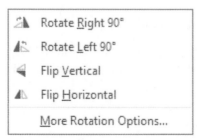

The menu illustrates the rotate and flip options

3. On the **Rotate Objects** menu, click the Rotate or Flip option you want.

> **TIP** You can rotate or flip any type of image. Rotating turns a shape 90 degrees to the right or left; flipping turns a shape 180 degrees horizontally or vertically.

Or

1. Select the shape.

2. Drag the **Rotate** handle in a clockwise or counterclockwise direction until the shape is at the angle of rotation you want.

To change a shape to another shape

1. Select the shape you want to change.

2. On the **Format** tool tab, in the **Insert Shapes** group, click the **Edit Shape** button, click **Change Shape**, and then click the new shape.

    Changing the shape doesn't affect the shape formatting or text.

Format shapes

When a shape is selected, the Format tool tab in the Drawing Tools tab group appears on the ribbon. You can use the commands on the Format tool tab to do the following:

- Replace the shape with another without changing the formatting.

- Change the fill and outline colors of the shape, and the effects applied to the shape.

- Separately, change the fill and outline colors and effects of any text that you add to the shape.

- Arrange, layer, and group multiple shapes on a slide.

Having made changes to one shape, you can easily apply the same attributes to another shape, or you can to apply the attributes to all future shapes you draw on the slides of the active presentation.

11

A happy fan cheering her team to victory!

When you have multiple shapes on a slide, you can group them so that you can copy, move, and format them as a unit. You can change the attributes of an individual shape—for example, its color, size, or location—without ungrouping the shapes.

To format a shape

1. Select the shape that you want to format.

2. On the **Format** tool tab, in the **Shape Styles** groups, click the **More** button to display the Shape Styles gallery.

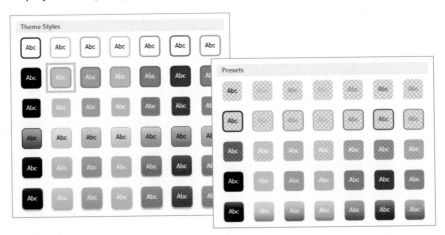

The shape style color options reflect the current color scheme

3. Point to thumbnails to display live previews of their effects, and then select a style thumbnail to apply the selected style.

To format text on a shape

1. Select the shape.

2. On the **Format** tool tab, in the **WordArt Styles** group, modify the style, text fill, text outline, or text effects.

Or

1. Select the text on the shape.

2. Do either of the following:

    •   On the **Format** tool tab, in the **WordArt Styles** group, modify the style, text fill, text outline, or text effects.

    •   On the **Home** tab, in the **Font** and **Paragraph** groups, use the standard text formatting commands.

To copy formatting from one shape to another

1. Select the formatting source shape.

2. On the **Home** tab, in the **Clipboard** group, click the **Format Painter** button.

3. Click the shape you want to copy the formatting to.

To set formatting as the default for the active presentation

1. Right-click the formatting source shape, and then click **Set as Default Shape**.

 TIP The Set As Default Shape command doesn't actually set a default shape; it sets only the default shape formatting.

To group shapes together as one object

1. Select all the shapes on a slide that you want grouped together.

2. On the **Format** tool tab, in the **Arrange** group, click the **Group** button (when you point to this button, the ScreenTip that appears says Group Objects) and then, in the list, click **Group**.

11

Grouped objects have a common set of handles

To move an entire group

1. Point to any shape in the group.

2. When the pointer changes to a four-headed arrow, drag the group to the new location.

To ungroup shapes

1. Select the group.

2. On the **Format** tool tab, in the **Arrange** group, click the **Group** button, and then click **Ungroup**.

To regroup shapes

1. Select any one shape from the former group.

2. On the **Format** tool tab, in the **Arrange** group, on the **Group** menu, click **Regroup**.

Connect shapes

If you want to show a relationship between two shapes, you can connect them with a line by joining special handles called *connection points*.

To connect shapes, follow these steps:

1. On the **Insert** tab, in the **Illustrations** group, click the **Shapes** button. In the **Lines** area of the **Shapes** gallery, click a **Connector** shape.

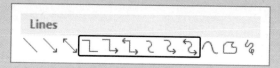

   You can identify connectors by the word Connector in their names

2. Point to the first shape that you want to connect.

3. When a set of small black connection points appears, point to a connection point, press and hold the mouse button, and then drag to the other shape (don't release the mouse button).

4. When connection points appear on the other shape, point to a connection point, and release the mouse button.

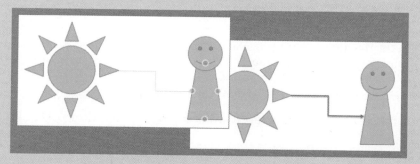

   When you move a shape, the connector line adapts to the change

TROUBLESHOOTING The connector has green handles when the shapes are connected. If a handle is white, drag it to a connection point.

After you draw a connector, you can adjust its shape by dragging a yellow handle and format it by changing its color and weight. If you move a connected shape, the connector moves with it, maintaining the relationship between the shapes.

11

Capture and insert screen clippings

Many people rely on the web as a source of information. At times, there might be information that you want to include in a PowerPoint presentation. For example, you might display an image of a page of a client's website in a sales presentation. PowerPoint 2016 provides a screen-clipping tool that you can use to easily capture an image of anything that is visible on your computer screen. After you capture the image, you can edit it just as you can other graphics.

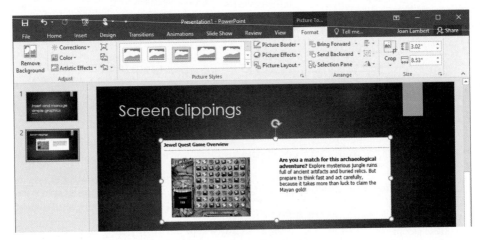

You can format a screen clipping just as you can any other image

> **TIP** You aren't limited to capturing screen clippings with the Office tools; you can also use the Windows Snipping Tool (available in the Windows Accessories folder) to capture an image and add it to your Screenshot list.

To insert an image of an on-screen window

1. Display the window that you want to capture and size it to display its contents as you want to show them.

2. Switch to PowerPoint and display the slide you want to insert the screen content on.

3. On the **Insert** tab, in the **Images** group, click **Screenshot**. The Screenshot menu displays thumbnails of all the windows on your screen that are currently available to insert.

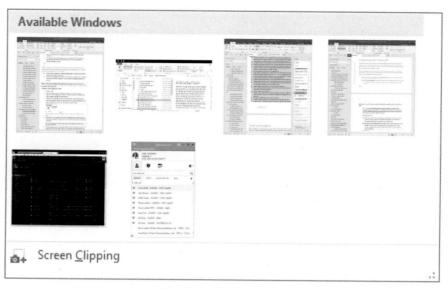

Some open windows aren't available from this menu and must be captured as clippings

> ⚠ **IMPORTANT** At the time of this writing, the Screenshot menu displays only desktop app windows; it doesn't display Store app windows.

4. On the **Screenshot** menu, click the window you want to insert an image of on the slide.

5. Resize the inserted image to suit your needs.

To capture a screen clipping from PowerPoint

1. Display the content that you want to capture.

2. Switch to PowerPoint and display the slide you want to insert the screen content on.

3. On the **Insert** tab, in the **Images** group, click **Screenshot**.

4. On the **Screenshot** menu, click **Screen Clipping**. The PowerPoint menu minimizes to the taskbar, and a translucent white layer covers the entire display.

> ✓ **TIP** If you change your mind about capturing the screen clipping, press the Esc key to remove the white layer.

11

5. When the cursor changes to a plus sign, point to the upper-left corner of the area you want to capture, and then drag down and to the right to define the screen clipping borders.

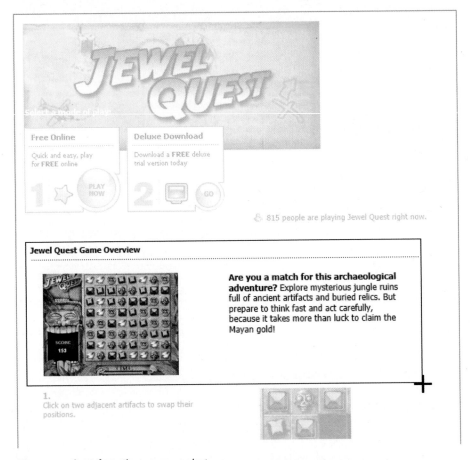

The screen clears from the area you select

When you release the mouse button, PowerPoint captures the clipping, restores the window, and inserts the clipping in the center of the slide.

 SEE ALSO For information about formatting pictures, see "Insert, move, and resize pictures" and "Edit and format pictures" earlier in this chapter.

Create a photo album

When you want to display a dynamic array of pictures in a presentation, you can use a photo album template to do the initial layout and then customize the album by adding frames of different shapes, in addition to captions.

A PowerPoint photo album

The first step in creating a photo album is to choose the pictures you want to include. After you know the album contents, you can configure the album options.

When creating a photo album, you have several choices. The primary choice is the slide layout. You can choose from seven layouts that display one, two, or four pictures per slide. The pictures can optionally have titles. The default layout is Fit To Slide, which creates one slide per photo. The photo album uses the layout you select on all pages of the album.

A basic preview of the selected layout is available in the Photo Album dialog box while you're creating the album. When you choose a layout, a slide number appears next to the first picture that will be on that slide. If you want to group pictures differently, you can reorder the photos before creating the album.

11

You can insert a text box on a photo album page, where it takes the place of a picture. You can use the text boxes to display comments about the pictures on that page, or you can leave them blank to control the layout. The total number of text boxes and pictures on a slide is the same as the layout that you choose. (In other words, if you choose a four-picture layout, the slide can display any combination of pictures and text boxes for a total of four objects.)

When you choose any layout other than Fit To Slide, you can opt to display captions below all the pictures. It isn't necessary to specify the captions when you select the photos for the album; if you choose the option to have captions, PowerPoint creates placeholders for them.

You can choose from these seven picture frame styles:

- Rectangle
- Rounded Rectangle
- Simple Frame, White
- Simple Frame, Black
- Compound Frame, Black
- Center Shadow Rectangle
- Soft Edge Rectangle

PowerPoint applies the same frame to all the pictures in the album.

You can choose a theme for the album when you're creating it, but it's easier to create the album and then apply the theme separately, because you can't preview the theme in the Photo Album dialog box.

You can also choose to render all the pictures in the album in black and white rather than their native colors.

You can make these changes when creating the album, or you can create an album and then edit its settings to make changes.

> **TIP** To integrate the slide layouts from a photo album template into a more traditional presentation, create the photo album and then import its slides into the other presentation by clicking Reuse Slides at the bottom of the New Slide gallery. For information about reusing slides, see "Copy and import slides and content" in Chapter 10, "Create and manage slides."

To create a photo album

1. Start PowerPoint and display any blank or existing presentation. (PowerPoint creates the photo album as an entirely separate file.)

2. On the **Insert** tab, in the **Images** group, click the **Photo Album** button to open the Photo Album dialog box.

3. In the **Insert picture from** area, click **File/Disk** to open the Insert New Pictures dialog box.

4. Browse to the folder that contains the pictures you want to use, and select the photos. Then click **Insert** to add the selected files to the Pictures In Album list in the Photo Album dialog box.

> ✓ **TIP** If you want to include all the pictures in a folder in your photo album, browse to the folder, click one picture, and press Ctrl+A to select all the folder contents. Then click Insert to add all the files to the photo album.

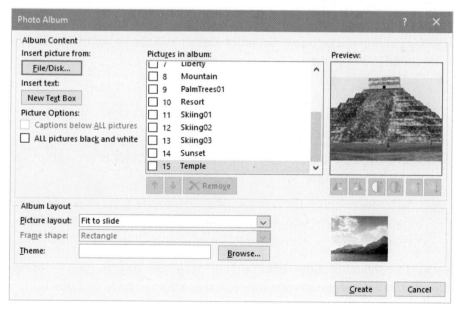

Default photo album settings

5. Next, configure the album layout. In the **Picture layout** list, click the layout you want to use. A generic preview of the layout appears to the right of the list. The numbers preceding the photo file names change to reflect the slide number the photo appears on.

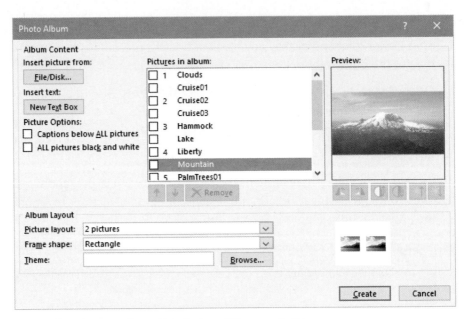

The numbers change to show which pictures will be on each slide

6. Now confirm the picture order and slide content. Do any of the following in the **Pictures in album** list:

   - To preview a picture, click its file name (not its check box).

   - To move a picture to an earlier position, select its check box, and then click the **Move Up** button.

   - To move a picture to a later position, select its check box, and then click the **Move Down** button.

   - To rotate or adjust the coloring of a picture, select its check box, and then click the buttons below the preview to rotate it, or to increase or decrease the contrast or brightness.

   - To insert a blank text box in a picture position, click the picture that you want to precede the text box, and then click the **New Text Box** button.

   - To remove a photo from the album, select its check box, and then click the **Remove** button.

7. Next, if the picture layout is set to something other than Fit To Slide, choose the picture frame. In the **Frame shape** list, click the frame you want to use.

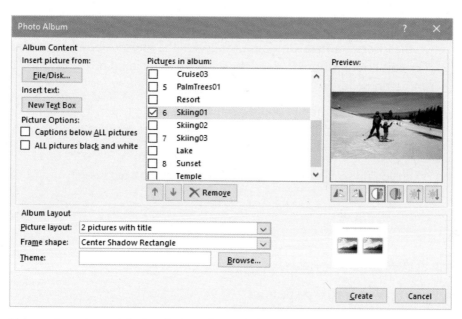

The generic preview updates to reflect your frame choice

8. Finally, do any of the following:

    •   If you want to display captions below the photos, select the **Captions below ALL pictures** check box.

    •   If you want to display grayscale versions of the photos, select the **ALL pictures black and white** check box.

    •   If you know the theme you want to apply to the photo album, click the **Browse** button to the right of the **Theme** box, and then double-click the theme you want to use.

9. To create the photo album, click **Create**.

10. Review the photo album, and do any of the following:

    •   Change the photo album title from the generic *Photo Album* to something more meaningful.

    •   If you added titles, captions, or text boxes, insert appropriate content in the placeholders.

    •   If you didn't choose a theme, or don't like the theme you chose, choose an appropriate theme from the **Themes** gallery on the **Design** tab.

11. Save the photo album.

11

To edit photo album settings

1. On the **Insert** tab, in the **Images** group, click the **Photo Album** arrow, and then click **Edit Photo Album** to open the Photo Album dialog box with all the current settings.

2. Add, remove, and modify photos; change the photo order; insert or remove text boxes; change the picture layout or frame; add or remove captions; or make any other changes you want.

3. When you finish, click the **Update** button to apply your changes.

Skills review

In this chapter, you learned how to:

- Insert, move, and resize pictures

- Edit and format pictures

- Draw and modify shapes

- Capture and insert screen clippings

- Create a photo album

Practice tasks

The practice files for these tasks are located in the Office2016SBS\Ch11 folder. You can save the results of the tasks in the same folder.

Insert, move, and resize pictures

Open the InsertPictures presentation, and then perform the following tasks:

1. Display slide **5**.

2. In the content placeholder, click the **Pictures** icon. Browse to the practice file folder, and insert the **Flowers01** picture.

3. From the **Size** group on the **Format** pane, resize the picture to a width of **4"**. Ensure that the aspect ratio doesn't change.

4. Move the picture on the slide to identify locations in which the smart guides appear—for example, the edges of the content space, and below the slide title. Align the picture with the upper-right corner of the content area as defined by the smart guides.

5. On the **Insert** tab, in the **Images** group, click **Online Pictures**. In the **Insert Pictures** window that opens, enter the word **flowers** in the **Bing** search box, and then press **Enter**.

6. Review the search results and locate a picture that you like. Insert the picture onto the slide.

7. Resize the picture to a width of **4"**, and align it with the right side of the content area, near the bottom of the slide (a smart guide might not appear at the bottom of the slide). Note that the pictures overlap near the center of the slide.

8. Close the presentation, saving your changes if you want to.

Edit and format pictures

Open the EditPictures presentation, and then perform the following tasks:

1. Display slide **5**.

2. Select the picture that is located on the right side of the slide.

3. On the **Format** tool tab, in the **Adjust** group, click **Corrections**, and then point to the thumbnails to identify one that will brighten the picture to make it similar to the picture on the left. Click that thumbnail to apply the correction.

4. Click the **Crop** arrow, point to **Aspect Ratio**, and then click **1:1**. Adjust the picture so the flowers are in the center, and then complete the cropping process.

5. Display the **Picture Styles** gallery, and point to the thumbnails in the gallery to find one that you like. Click the thumbnail to apply the picture style.

6. Select the picture that is located on the left side of the slide.

7. Remove the neutral background from the selected picture.

8. Close the presentation, saving your changes if you want to.

Draw and modify shapes

Open the DrawShapes presentation, and then perform the following tasks:

1. Display slide **5**.

2. Draw a **5-Point Star** shape (in the **Stars and Banners** category of the **Shapes** gallery) near the center of the slide.

3. Draw a small arrow (in the **Block Arrows** category of the **Shapes** gallery) to the right of the star.

4. Drag a copy of the arrow to the left of the star, and align it with the right arrow. Then flip the left arrow so that it points away from the star.

5. Adjacent to the left arrow, add a scroll shape, and then adjacent to the right arrow, add a heart shape.

6. Paste a copy of the heart shape on top of the original, and make the second heart smaller than the first.

7. In the star, enter the word **ME**. Then increase the font size to make it prominent.

8. Repeat task 7 to add the word **Education** to the scroll shape and **Family** to the heart shape. Then resize the shapes as necessary to make all the words fit on one line.

9. Select the scroll, star, and heart shapes (don't select the text), and apply the style **Intense Effect – Light Blue, Accent 6**.

10. Suppose you have completed your education and entered the workforce. Change the scroll shape to the **Up Arrow** (in the **Block Arrows** category) to reflect your new status.

11. In the up arrow shape, change the word *Education* to **Job**. Then adjust the size and position of the shape so that it balances with the other shapes on the slide, using the smart guides to help align the shapes.

12. Group all the shapes together as one object, and apply a purple outline.

13. Move the entire group until the shapes are centered and balanced with the slide title.

14. Change the fill color of the left and right arrows to Purple.

15. Close the presentation, saving your changes if you want to.

Capture and insert screen clippings

Open the InsertScreens presentation, and then perform the following tasks:

1. Display slide **4**.

2. Open a web browser window and locate a webpage that has information about tablets.

3. Return to PowerPoint. Then capture and insert a screen clipping of part of the webpage.

4. Close the presentation, saving your changes if you want to.

Create a photo album

Start PowerPoint, and then perform the following tasks:

1. From the **Insert** tab, create a new photo album. Select photos from the practice file folder, or select your own photos.

2. While creating the album, do the following:

   - Experiment with the different picture layouts and frame shapes.

   - Change the order of the pictures in the album.

   - Insert text boxes to make spaces between photos.

   - Apply a theme.

3. After you create the album, experiment with the changes you can make from within PowerPoint. For example:

   - Replace placeholder text.

   - Change the theme.

   - Resize pictures.

4. If you want to, click the **Edit photo album** command to return to the Photo Album dialog box and make additional changes.

5. Save your photo album as **MyPhotoAlbum**, and then close it.

Add sound and movement to slides

A PowerPoint presentation might be designed to provide ancillary information for a live presentation, or to stand alone as an information source. Regardless of the method of delivery, a presentation has no value if it doesn't keep the attention of the audience. An element that can make the difference between an adequate presentation and a great presentation is the judicious use of animated content, sound, and videos. By incorporating these dynamic effects, you can grab and keep the attention of your audience. You can emphasize key points, control the focus of the discussion, and entertain in ways that will make your message memorable.

With PowerPoint 2016, you have so many opportunities to add pizzazz to your slides that it is easy to end up with a presentation that looks more like an amateur experiment than a professional slide show. When you first start adding animations, sound, and videos to your slides, it is best to err on the conservative side. As you gain more experience, you'll learn how to mix and match effects to get the results you want for a particular audience.

This chapter guides you through procedures related to animating text and pictures on slides, customizing animation effects, adding audio content to slides, adding video content to slides, and optimizing and compressing media.

In this chapter

- Animate text and pictures on slides
- Customize animation effects
- Add audio content to slides
- Add video content to slides
- Compress media to decrease file size

Practice files

For this chapter, use the practice files from the Office2016SBS\Ch12 folder. For practice file download instructions, see the introduction.

Animate text and pictures on slides

In the context of PowerPoint, *animation* refers to the movement of an element on a slide. When used appropriately, animated slide elements can both capture the audience's attention and effectively convey information. You can animate any individual objects on a slide, including text containers, pictures, and shapes. (You can't animate objects that are part of the slide background or slide master, other than as part of the transition between slides.)

> **SEE ALSO** For information about the movement that occurs between slides, see "Add and manage slide transitions" in Chapter 9, "Review presentations," of *Microsoft PowerPoint 2016 Step by Step* by Joan Lambert (Microsoft Press, 2015).

Thoughtfully designed animations can be very informative, particularly for audience members who are more receptive to visual input than to auditory input. Animations have the added benefit of providing a consistent message with or without a presenter to discuss or externally illustrate a process.

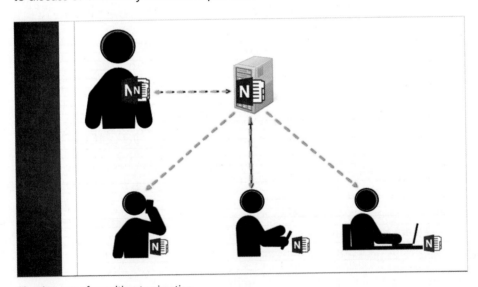

The elements of a multipart animation

You can configure four types of animations: the appearance, movement, emphasis, and disappearance of objects on the slide. There are multiple options within these four categories. The options are categorized as Basic, Subtle, Moderate, and Exciting (although you might have a different concept of "exciting" than the PowerPoint developer who categorized the effects). A few more animation effects are available for text than for other slide objects.

Here's a breakdown of the animation effects that are available in PowerPoint 2016:

- **Entrance animations** An object with an animated entrance is not visible when the slide first appears. (It is visible during the development process, but not when you present the slide show.) It then appears on the slide in the manner specified by the entrance effect. Some entrance effects are available in the Animation gallery. They're illustrated in green, and their icons provide some idea of the movement associated with the effect.

Have fun experimenting with the different effects

Clicking More Entrance Effects at the bottom of the Animation menu opens a dialog box that displays all the available entrance animations by category to help you choose an appropriate effect.

Basic

★ Appear	★ Blinds
★ Box	★ Checkerboard
★ Circle	★ Diamond
★ Dissolve In	★ Fly In
★ Peek In	★ Plus
★ Random Bars	★ Split
★ Strips	★ Wedge
★ Wheel	★ Wipe

Subtle

★ Expand	★ Fade
★ Swivel	★ Zoom

Moderate

★ Basic Zoom	★ Center Revolve
★ Compress	★ Float Down
★ Float Up	★ Grow & Turn
★ Rise Up	★ Spinner
★ Stretch	

Exciting

★ Basic Swivel	★ Boomerang
★ Bounce	★ Credits
★ Curve Up	★ Drop
★ Flip	★ Float
★ Pinwheel	★ Spiral In
★ Whip	

The entrance animation effects available for text

12

■ **Emphasis animations** These effects animate an object that is already visible on the slide to draw attention to it, without changing its location. The emphasis effects that are available in the Animation gallery are illustrated in yellow.

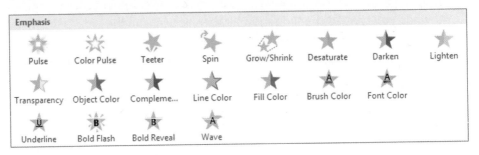

Effects range from subtle to bold

Clicking More Emphasis Effects at the bottom of the Animation menu opens a dialog box that displays all the available emphasis animations by category.

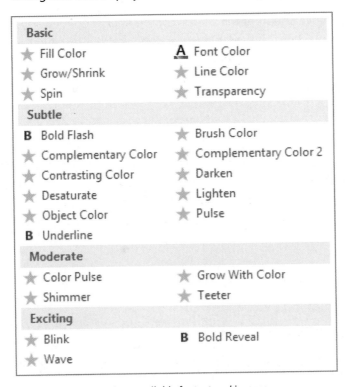

The emphasis animations available for text and images

- **Motion Path animations** These effects move an object along a path that you specify, over a period of time that you specify. A few simple motion paths are available from the Animation gallery, but a surprisingly large variety is available from the dialog box that opens when you click More Motion Paths at the bottom of the Animation menu.

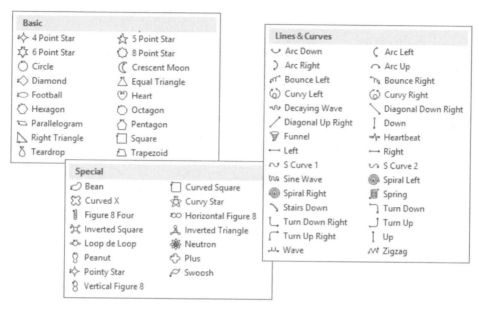

The motion path animations available for text

- **Exit animations** These effects take an existing object through a process that results in the object no longer being visible on the slide. The exit effects that are available in the Animation gallery are illustrated in red.

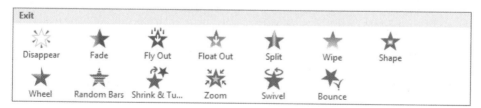

Choose an effect that suits the style of your presentation

Additional exit effects are available from the Change Exit Effect dialog box.

12

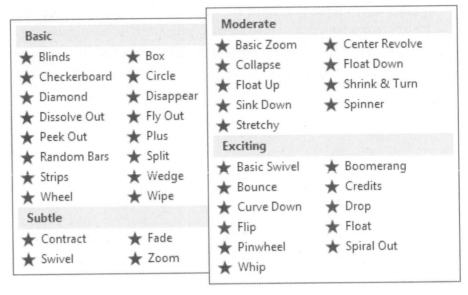

The exit animations available for text

Animations can be very simple, or very complex. Many animations have options that you can configure, such as the direction, speed, size, or color. For example, when you configure an entrance effect for a bulleted list, you can specify whether to have the entire list enter the slide at the same time, or to have only one bulleted item enter at a time. After you choose an effect, the applicable options are available on the Effect Options menu.

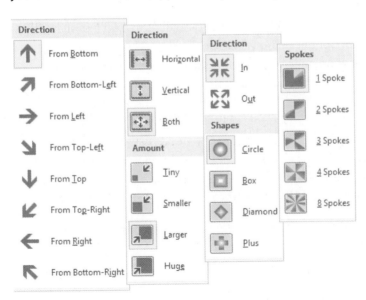

Some animations have options, and others don't

You can apply multiple animation effects (for example, an entrance effect and an emphasis effect) to a single object. As you assign animations to slide objects, numbers appear on the objects to specify the order of the animation effects. The numbers are visible only when the Animation tab is active.

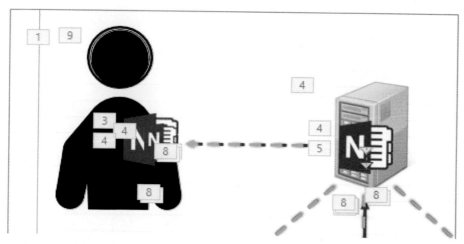

Each number represents one animation

As you build an animated slide, you can add and animate individual elements, or you can add all the elements to the slide first, and then animate them. Regardless of the process you choose, position the objects on the slide as follows:

- **Entrance effects** Position the object where you want it to end up after it enters the slide.

- **Emphasis effects** Position the object where it will be before and after the effect.

- **Exit effects** Position the object where it will be before it leaves the slide.

After all the elements are in place, animate them in the order you want the animations to occur. (If you're animating multiple objects, it might be helpful to write out a description of the process before starting.) If you animate something out of order, don't worry—you can reorder the animations from within the Animation Pane.

12

Animate this

Animations can greatly enrich presentation content. However, incorporating a "dazzling" array of animation effects into a presentation can be distracting or confusing to the audience. Ensure that the time you put into creating an animation has value to you and to your audience members.

Consider using animations to provide subliminal information—for example, in a multipart presentation, use one consistent entrance effect for the part opener titles to draw the attention of the audience members and cue them to a change of subject.

An excellent use of animation is to create "build slides" that add information in layers and essentially culminate in a review slide. Simple examples of build slides include:

- A bulleted list that adds one item to the list at a time. For greater impact, display an image related to the current list item, and replace the image as each new list item appears.

- A pie chart that displays each chart wedge individually, and finishes with the complete pie. Make this even more informative by displaying a detailed breakdown of the chart data for each category as you display its chart wedge.

You could achieve these effects by creating series of separate slides, but it's much simpler to animate the list or chart object.

A more difficult but often worthwhile use of slide object animation is to provide a visual image of a process as you describe it. You can narrate the animation in person or, if you're going to distribute the presentation electronically, you can record the narration and synchronize the animations with the relevant wording.

To animate an object on a slide

1. Display the slide in the **Slide** pane, and select the object that you want to animate, or its container. (For example, if you want to animate the entrance of a bulleted list, select the text box that contains the bulleted list.)

2. On the **Animations** tab, in the **Animation** group, click the **More** button to display the **Animation** menu and gallery.

> **TIP** If the menu expands to cover the slide content, you can drag the handle in the lower-right corner of the menu to resize it.

The Animation gallery and menu

12

3. Do either of the following:

- In the **Animation** gallery, click the icon that represents the animation you want to apply.

- On the **Animation** menu, click the **More** command for the type of animation you want to apply, and then in the **Change *Type* Effect** dialog box, click the animation you want.

PowerPoint displays a live preview of the selected animation effect and adds an animation number adjacent to the object. A star appears next to the slide thumbnail to indicate that the slide contains either an animation or a transition.

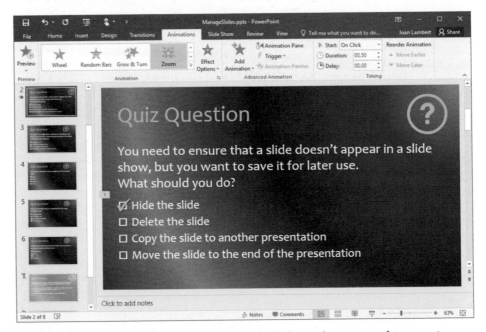

In the Thumbnails pane, the star below the slide number indicates the presence of movement on the slide

> **TIP** When you apply an animation, PowerPoint automatically previews (plays) the animation. If this is distracting to you, you can turn off this feature by clicking the Preview arrow (in the Preview group on the Animations tab) and then clicking AutoPreview to remove the check mark that indicates the option is turned on.

To select an applied animation

1. On the slide or in the **Animation Pane**, click the animation number.

To display or hide the Animation Pane

1. On the **Animations** tab, in the **Advanced Animation** group, click the **Animation Pane** button.

 TIP You can expand and collapse sets of animation effects in the Animation Pane to help you focus on those you want to work with.

To configure animation options

1. Apply the animation, or select a previously applied animation.

2. On the **Animations** tab, in the **Animation** group, click the **Effect Options** button. (If the button is unavailable, the animation has no configurable options.)

   The Effect Options menu has one titled section for each option that you can configure.

3. On the **Effect Options** menu, click one option in each section.

To apply multiple animation effects to one object

1. Apply the first animation effect and configure any options.

2. Select the object (not the animation). The existing animation information is highlighted on the Animations tab and in the Animation Pane.

3. On the **Animations** tab, in the **Advanced Animation** group, click the **Add Animation** button. In the **Add Animation** gallery, click the additional animation you want to apply.

To copy a set of animation effects from one object to another object

1. Select the source object.

2. On the **Animations** tab, in the **Advanced Animation** group, click the **Animation Painter** button.

3. Point to the object you want to format. When a paintbrush appears to the right of the cursor, click the object to apply the formatting.

12

> **TIP** The Animation Painter is similar to the Format Painter. If you click the Animation Painter button one time, you can copy the formatting to one other object. If you double-click the Animation Painter button, you can copy the formatting to many other objects, until you click the button again or press Esc to deactivate it.

To preview animations

1. Do any of the following:

   - To preview all animations on a slide in order, on the **Animations** tab, in the **Preview** group, click the **Preview** button.

   - To preview a specific animation and those that follow, in the **Animation Pane**, click the first animation, and then click the **Play From** button.

   - To preview one animation, select the animation on the slide and then, in the **Animation Pane**, click the **Play Selected** button.

To remove animation effects from slide objects

1. Do either of the following in the **Animation Pane**:

   - To remove one animation, right-click the animation, and then click **Remove**.

   - To remove all animations, click any animation, press **Ctrl+A** to select all the animations, and then press **Delete**.

Customize animation effects

Many presentations don't require much in the way of animation, and you might find that transitions and ready-made animation effects will meet all your animation needs. However, for those occasions when you want a presentation with pizzazz, you can customize the animation effects.

> **TIP** Animations can be useful for self-running presentations, where there is no presenter to lead the audience from one concept to another.

After you apply an animation effect, you can fine-tune its action in the following ways:

- Specify the direction, shape, or sequence of the animation. (The options vary depending on the type of animation you apply.)

- Specify what action will trigger the animation. For example, you can specify that clicking a different object on the slide will animate the selected object.

- As an alternative to clicking the mouse button to build animated slides, have PowerPoint build the slide for you.

- Control the implementation speed (duration) of each animation, or delay an animation effect.

- Change the order of the animation effects.

Entrance and exit effects cause objects to appear and disappear when you're previewing or presenting a slide. However, all the objects are visible while you're working in the Slide pane. A very helpful tool when managing multiple animated objects on a slide is the Animation Pane. Each numbered animation on the slide has a corresponding entry in the Animation Pane that provides information and options for managing the animations.

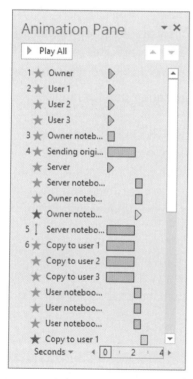

Manage all aspects of animations from the Animation Pane

12

The color coding of the Entrance, Emphasis, and Exit effects is visible in the Animation Pane, and a timeline is available at the bottom of the pane. The visual indicators to the right of each object name represent the type, starting point, and duration of each animation event, as follows:

- The indicator color represents the animation type (green for Entrance, yellow for Emphasis, blue for Motion Path, and red for Exit).

- The left side of the indicator aligns with the animation starting point. If the left sides of two indicators align, those animations start at the same time. If the left side of an indicator aligns with the right side of the previous indicator, the animations run in order.

- The width of the indicator is the animation duration as it relates to the timeline at the bottom of the Animation Pane.

- The right side of the indicator is either triangular or square. A square indicates that the animation has a fixed duration; a triangular edge indicates that the duration is set to Auto.

Each animation is an individual event. By default, each animation starts immediately "on click," meaning when you switch to the slide, click the mouse button, tap the screen, or press an arrow key—any action that would otherwise move to the next slide. You can change the animation "trigger" either to run with or after another event, to run it after a certain length of time, or to run it when you click a specific screen element or reach a bookmark in an audio or video clip. You control these settings either from the Advanced Animation and Timing groups on the Animations tab, or from the Animation Pane.

Clicking an animation in the Animation Pane selects the animation and displays an arrow to the right of the animation timing indicators. Clicking the arrow displays a menu of actions. Some of these actions are available from the Animations tab, but the effect options available from this menu are more complex than those on the Effect Options menu in the Animation group.

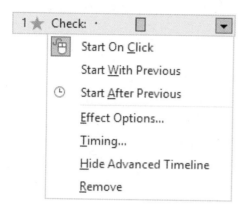

You can configure these actions from the Animation Pane to customize an animation

Clicking Effect Options on the shortcut menu provides access to an effect-specific dialog box where you can refine that type of animation in the following ways:

- Specify whether the animation should be accompanied by a sound effect.

- Dim or hide the element after the animation, or have it change to a specific color.

- If the animation is applied to text, animate all the text at once or animate it word by word or letter by letter.

- Repeat an animation and specify what triggers its action.

- If a slide has more than one level of bullet points, animate different levels separately.

- If an object has text, animate the object and the text together (the default) or separately, or animate one but not the other.

12

The dialog box title is the animation type, and the options available in the dialog box are specific to that type of animation.

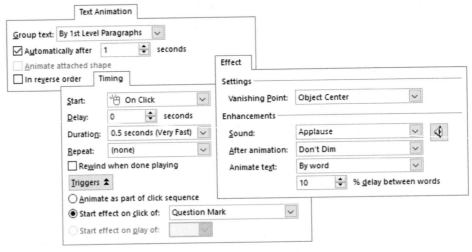

Some of the settings available through the Animation Pane Effect Options menu

To open the effect-specific dialog box for an animation

1. Do either of the following in the **Animation Pane**:

   - Point to the animation, click the arrow, and then click **Effect Options**.

   - Double-click the animation.

To change the order of animation effects on a slide

1. On the slide or in the **Animation Pane**, select the animation you want to reorder.

2. On the **Animations** tab, in the **Timing** group, click **Move Earlier** or **Move Later**.

Or

1. In the **Animation Pane**, select the animation or animations that you want to move.

2. Drag the selection to the new position in the **Animation Pane**. The animation numbers change to reflect the new positions.

 TIP After reordering animations, it's a good idea to preview the animations to ensure that the actions happen in a logical order.

To set the trigger for a selected animation

> **TIP** Many of the following settings can be configured on the Animations tab, in the Animation Pane, or in the effect-specific options dialog box. We've provided one path to the setting, but use the interface that you're most comfortable with.

1. Do any of the following in the **Timing** group on the **Animations** tab:

   - To start the animation manually, click the **Start** list, and then click **On Click**.

   - To start the animation based on the previous animation, click the **Start** list, and then click **With Previous** or **After Previous**.

   - To start the animation a specific period of time after the trigger, specify the **Delay** in seconds.

Or

1. Do either of the following in the **Advanced Animation** group on the **Animations** tab:

   - To start the animation when you click an object on the slide, click the **Trigger** button, click **On Click of**, and then click a trigger object on the slide.

   - To start the animation at a specific point during the playback of an audio clip or video clip, in the **Trigger** list, click **On Bookmark**, and then click a bookmark that you've set in an audio or video clip.

   > **SEE ALSO** For information about setting bookmarks, see the sidebar "Bookmark points of interest in media clips" later in this chapter.

Or

1. In the **Animation Pane**, drag the colored indicator bar to the starting point you want.

To set the duration of a selected animation

1. Do either of the following:

   - On the **Animations** tab, in the **Timing** group, specify the **Duration** in seconds.

   - In the **Animation Pane**, drag the right side of the colored indicator bar to set the duration in accordance with the timeline at the bottom of the pane.

12

To add a sound effect to an animation

1. In the **Animation Pane**, double-click the animation to open the animation-specific effect options dialog box.

2. On the **Effect** tab, click the **Sound** list, and then click the sound effect you want to assign to the animation.

3. Click the speaker icon to the right of the **Sound** list to display the volume slider, and set the volume level of the sound effect.

4. Click **OK** to close the dialog box.

Bookmark points of interest in media clips

Bookmarks are a useful new feature for PowerPoint users who incorporate audio, video, and animation into presentations. You can insert bookmarks into audio and video clips to identify locations either that you want to be able to quickly get to or that you want to use as triggers for other events.

For example, you could create an animation that visually describes a process, and record a narration that verbally describes the process. Instead of setting up a series of timing points to synchronize the narration and animation, you could insert bookmarks at key points in the narrative audio clip that trigger specific segments of the animation to play.

As another example, you could embed a video on a slide, and record audio comments about certain parts of the video. Then you can insert bookmarks at those points of the video to trigger the playback of the relevant audio comments.

When you insert bookmarks in audio and video clips within PowerPoint, those bookmarks exist only in PowerPoint and don't affect the original recording.

To insert a bookmark in an audio or video clip, follow these steps:

1. Display the slide in Normal view and select the audio or video clip to display the Audio Tools or Video Tools tab group.

2. Play the clip by clicking the **Play** button on the playback toolbar or in the **Preview** group on the **Playback** tool tab.

3. At the point that you want to insert a bookmark, click the **Add Bookmark** button in the **Bookmarks** group on the **Playback** tool tab.

4. To insert additional bookmarks, repeat steps 2 and 3.

Bookmarks in audio or video clips are indicated by circles on the playback toolbar. Pointing to a bookmark on the toolbar displays a ScreenTip that includes the bookmark name. You can select a bookmark as the starting point for an animation, from the Trigger list on the Animations tab.

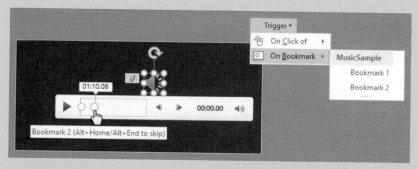

Adding a bookmark to a media clip makes it available as a trigger

If you create a bookmark but then don't need it, you can remove it by selecting it and then clicking the Remove Bookmark button in the Bookmarks group on the Playback tool tab.

12

Add audio content to slides

You can enhance presentations by adding sound to slide transitions, to animated content, to an individual slide, or to the presentation as a whole. For example, you could run a presentation that provides basic information and icebreakers during the time leading up to your actual presentation. You can add a pleasant royalty-free soundtrack that loops while the presentation plays, to avoid the discomfort of a room full of people who don't want to break the silence.

If you plan to distribute a presentation electronically for people to watch on their own, you might want to add audio narration to an animation, or provide narration for the entire presentation.

> **SEE ALSO** For information about adding sound effects to animations, see "Customize animation effects" earlier in this chapter. For information about adding sound effects to slide transitions, see "Add and manage slide transitions" in Chapter 9, "Review presentations," of *Microsoft PowerPoint 2016 Step by Step* by Joan Lambert (Microsoft Press, 2015).

You can add prerecorded audio content to a presentation, or record your own content directly within PowerPoint. PowerPoint supports the most common audio formats—MP3, MP4, Windows audio (.wav) and Windows Media audio (.wma), and more specialized formats such as ADTS, AU, FLAC, MIDI, and MKA audio.

> **TIP** The Insert Online Audio feature that was present in earlier versions of PowerPoint is not available in PowerPoint 2016. However, you can download royalty-free audio music and sound effects from many online sources. Some of these require that you credit the website as the source, so be sure to read the website fine print. When you locate an audio clip that you want to use, you can download it to your computer and follow the instructions in this topic to use it in a PowerPoint presentation.

When you add audio to a slide (rather than to an animation or transition), the audio icon (shaped like a speaker) and an accompanying trigger icon appear on the slide, and the trigger event appears in the Animation Pane.

The trigger is created and added to the Animation Pane automatically

When the audio icon is selected, the Audio Tools tab group, which includes the Format and Playback tool tabs, appears on the ribbon, and audio playback controls appear on the slide.

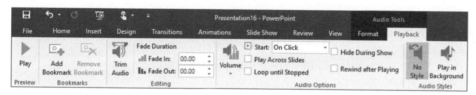

The playback controls are simple but provide sufficient options

You can start audio content on a slide automatically or from the playback controls. The playback controls are visible only when the audio icon is selected. The icon isn't obtrusive, but you can disguise or hide it if you want to.

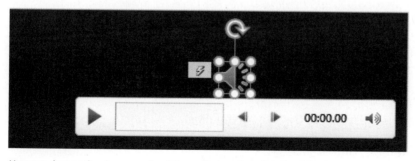

You can change the size or angle of the audio icon by using the sizing handles or rotation handle

12

You can customize the audio content by using commands on the Playback tool tab, as follows:

- Edit the audio content so that only part of it plays.

- Make the sound gradually increase and decrease in volume.

- Adjust the volume or mute the sound.

- Specify whether the audio content plays:

    - Automatically when the slide appears.

    - Only if you click its icon.

- Make the audio object invisible while the presentation is displayed in Reading view or Slide Show view.

- Specify that the audio content should play continuously until you stop it.

- Ensure that the audio content starts from the beginning each time it is played.

To insert an audio clip onto a slide

1. Save the audio clip on your computer or on a network-connected location.

2. On the **Insert** tab, in the **Media** group, click the **Audio** button, and then click **Audio on My PC** to open the Insert Audio dialog box.

3. In the **Insert Audio** dialog box, browse to and select the audio file, and then click the **Insert** button.

Or

1. In File Explorer, open the folder that contains the audio file.

2. Arrange the File Explorer and PowerPoint windows on your screen so that both are visible.

3. Drag the audio file from File Explorer to the slide.

To record audio directly onto a slide

1. On the **Insert** tab, in the **Media** group, click the **Audio** button, and then click **Record Audio** to open the Record Sound dialog box.

2. In the **Name** box, enter a name to uniquely identify the recording. Then click the **Record** button (labeled with a red circle).

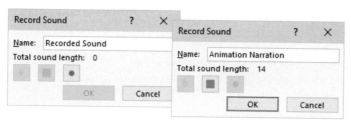

The Record Sound dialog box

3. Speak or otherwise provide the audio that you want to record. When you finish, click the **Stop** button (labeled with a blue square). The audio icon and an accompanying trigger icon appear in the center of the slide, and the trigger event appears in the Animation Pane.

> **TIP** If you record multiple clips, the audio icons stack up in the same location on the slide. It might be necessary to move one or more out of the way to get to an earlier clip.

To restrict the playback of an audio clip to a specific segment

1. Select the audio icon. On the **Playback** tool tab, in the **Editing** group, click the **Trim Audio** button to open the Trim Audio dialog box.

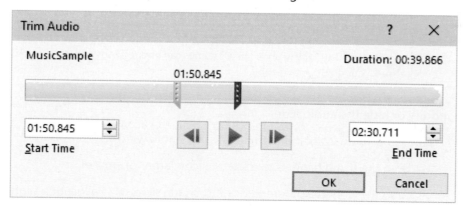

You can trim audio from the beginning and end of the clip, but not from the middle

2. In the **Trim Audio** dialog box, do any of the following:

    *   Click the **Play** button to play the clip, and then click the **Pause** button to pause when you locate a point that you want to mark.

    *   Drag the green **Start** marker to specify a playback starting point other than the beginning of the clip. (If you drag the marker near the point at which you paused the playback, the marker snaps to that location.)

- Drag the red **End** marker to specify a playback end point other than the end of the clip.

- Select the **Start** or **End** marker, and then click the **Previous Frame** or **Next Frame** button to move the selected marker back or forward 0.1 seconds (one-tenth of a second).

3. When you finish, click **OK** to close the Trim Audio dialog box.

> **TIP** Trimming the audio affects only the playback of the audio on the slide, not the original audio clip. You can re-trim or restore the audio clip at any time. For information about discarding trimmed content, see "Compress media to decrease file size" later in this chapter.

To fade into or out of an audio clip

1. Select the audio icon. On the **Playback** tool tab, in the **Editing** group, do the following:

   - In the **Fade In** box, specify the length of time over which you want to increase the audio to full volume.

   - In the **Fade Out** box, specify the number of seconds at the end of the audio clip over which you want to decrease the audio volume.

> **TIP** The Fade In and Fade Out times can be specified precisely down to a hundredth of a second.

To modify or hide the audio icon

1. Select the audio icon, and then do any of the following:

   - Drag the sizing handles to make the icon larger or smaller.

   - Drag the icon to a different location on the slide, or to a location slightly off the slide but still on the development canvas.

   - Use the commands on the **Format** tool tab to change the icon's appearance.

   - Replace the default icon with a different image (such as a picture or logo).

To manually start audio playback

1. Do any of the following:

   - In Normal view, Reading view, or Slide Show view, point to the audio icon. When the playback controls appear, click the **Play** button.

   - In Normal view, click the audio icon, and then click the **Play** button on the playback toolbar or in the **Preview** group on the **Playback** tool tab.

   - In Slide Show view, after the audio icon has had focus, press **Alt+P**.

 TIP To play sounds and other audio content, you must have a sound card and speakers installed.

To automatically start audio playback

1. On the **Playback** tool tab, in the **Audio Options** group, in the **Start** list, click **Automatically**. Then select the **Loop until Stopped** check box.

 TIP If your presentation might be viewed by people using assistive technologies such as screen readers or text-to-speech tools, you should avoid starting audio clips or files automatically. Instead, allow the user to play the audio content after the tool has finished communicating the slide content.

To prevent an audio clip from stopping when the slide changes

1. On the **Playback** tool tab, do either of the following:

   - To play to the end of the audio and then stop, in the **Audio Options** group, select the **Play Across Slides** check box.

   - To loop the audio until the end of the slide show regardless of other audio tracks, in the **Audio Styles** group, click the **Play in Background** button.

12

To loop (repeat) an audio clip

1. On the **Playback** tool tab, in the **Audio Options** group, select the **Loop until Stopped** check box.

> **TIP** To automatically start and continuously play an audio clip through an entire slide show, configure the settings as follows: On the Playback tool tab, in the Audio Options group, change the Start setting to Automatically. Then select the Play Across Slides, Loop Until Stopped, and Hide During Show check boxes.

Add video content to slides

Sometimes the best way to ensure that your audience understands your message is to show a video. For example, if your company has developed a short advertising video, it makes more sense to include the video in a presentation about marketing plans than to try to describe it by using bullet points or even pictures. To save you the trouble of switching between PowerPoint and a video player, you can embed a video recording directly onto a slide, and then play the video as part of presenting the slide show. This is a much smoother way of presenting information from multiple sources than switching between them.

You can insert a video onto a slide from your computer or a connected local storage device, from your Facebook account, from YouTube, or from a website that provides an "embed code" (basically, an address that you can link to).

> **TIP** If a publicly posted video clip has an "embed code" available, you can link to the online video rather than embedding it in the slide show. PowerPoint uses the embed code to locate and play the video. As long as the video remains available in its original location (and you have an active Internet connection), you will be able to access and play the video from the slide at any time.

After you insert the video, you can format its representation on the slide in all the ways that you can other imagery. You can move and resize it, display it in a frame of your choice, and even adjust the brightness or color contrast.

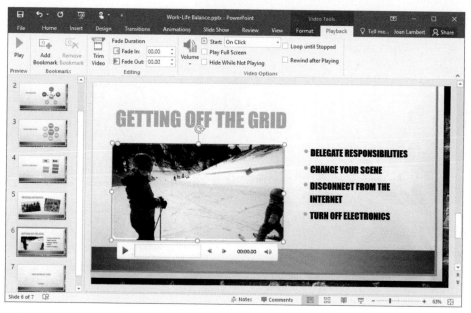

You can resize the video frame

> **TIP** The changes that you make to an image on a slide also affect the video playback. So, for example, if you change the aspect ratio of the video representation on the slide, imagery in the video might appear to be skewed.

When working with local videos that you embed rather than online videos that you link to, you can fade into and out from the video playback, and manage the content of the video by trimming it to play only a specific portion. You can insert bookmarks to use as triggers for other events (for example, you might display a list of selling points as each is presented in the advertising video).

Set your start and end times to focus on the specific content you want to highlight

When you're previewing or presenting a slide show, you can play (and pause) embedded audio or video, move around within the recording, and control the volume by using the controls that appear when the audio icon or video placeholder image is active. When playing back a video, you can display it at the embedded size or full screen.

Many of the processes for managing video clips are the same as those for managing audio clips:

- Restricting the playback of a video clip to a specific segment
- Fading into or out of a video clip
- Manually or automatically starting video playback
- Preventing a video clip from stopping when the slide changes
- Looping a video clip

 SEE ALSO For additional information related to the preceding processes, see "Add audio content to slides" earlier in this chapter.

To insert a video clip onto a slide

1. On a slide that includes a content placeholder, click the **Insert Video** button in the content placeholder to display the Insert Video window that contains links to all the video sources you've configured Office to connect to.

You can insert video clips from a variety of sources

2. In the **Insert Video** window, click the source of the video that you want to insert, and then follow the process to insert a video from the selected source.

Or

1. On any slide, on the **Insert** tab, in the **Media** group, click the **Insert Video** button, and then do either of the following:

   • Click **Online Video** to open the Insert Video window. In the **Insert Video** window, click the source of the video that you want to insert, and then follow the process to insert a video from the selected source.

   • Click **Video on My PC** to open the Insert Video dialog box. In the **Insert Video** dialog box, browse to and select the video file, and then click the **Insert** button.

12

To select an embedded video

1. Click the video image one time. Selection handles appear around the video image, the playback toolbar appears below it, and the Video Tools tab group appears on the ribbon.

To move the video image on the slide

1. Select the video, and then do either of the following:

   - Drag the video to the new location. Smart guides might appear on the slide to help you align the video with other objects.

   - Press the arrow keys to move the video by small amounts.

To resize the video image on the slide and retain its aspect ratio

1. Do either of the following:

   - Drag any corner handle. Smart guides appear on the slide to help you align the video with other objects.

   - On the **Format** tool tab, in the **Size** group, set a specific **Video Height** or **Video Width**, and then press **Enter** to change both settings.

To format the video image on the slide

1. Select the video, and then apply formatting from the **Format** tool tab just as you would for a picture.

> **SEE ALSO** For information about formatting pictures, see "Edit and format pictures" in Chapter 11, "Insert and manage simple graphics."

To configure an embedded video to play back at full screen size

1. Select the video.

2. On the **Playback** tool tab, in the **Video Options** group, select the **Play Full Screen** check box.

To set the relative volume of a video soundtrack

1. Select the video.

2. On the **Playback** tool tab, in the **Video Options** group, click the **Volume** button.

3. In the **Volume** list, click **Low**, **Medium**, **High**, or **Mute**.

Compress media to decrease file size

Trimming an audio or video clip affects only the playback of the media on the slide, not the original media clip. The original media clip is stored in its entirety as part of the presentation, and you can re-trim or restore the media clip at any time.

You can decrease the size of a PowerPoint file that contains trimmed media clips by discarding the unused portions of the clips. PowerPoint 2016 offers three compression configurations designed to balance size and quality.

 Presentation Quality
Save space while maintaining overall audio and video quality.

 Internet Quality
Quality will be comparable to media which is streamed over the Internet.

 Low Quality
Use when space is limited, such as when sending presentations via e-mail.

Choose the size and quality that best fits your needs

When you save and close the file after compressing the media, the trimmed portions of the videos are discarded and no longer available. You can reverse the compression operation until you save and close the file.

12

To compress media files

1. Save the PowerPoint presentation, and then display the **Info** page of the Backstage view.

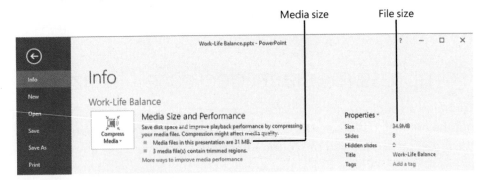

Info page of the Backstage view

2. Note the total size of the presentation, the size of the media files in the presentation, and the number of files that have been trimmed.

3. On the **Info** page, click the **Compress Media** button, and then click the level of compression you want. In the Compress Media window, PowerPoint itemizes the media elements and their compression levels, and reports the total space savings.

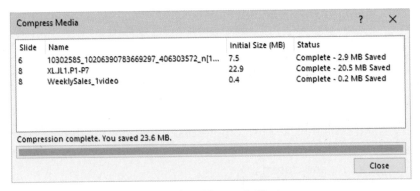

Compressing media files can make a big difference in file size

4. In the **Compress Media** window, click the **Close** button. In the Media Size And Performance area of the Info page, the Compress Media button is active to indicate that media has been compressed, and specifics about the compression are available.

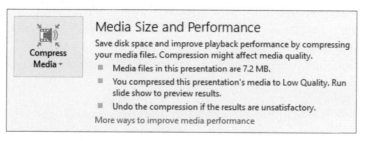

You can undo the compression if you don't like the results

5. Play the presentation to assess the quality, and then save the file if the quality is acceptable.

To reverse the compression of media files

1. On the **Info** page, click the **Compress Media** button, and then click **Undo**. PowerPoint immediately reverts to the uncompressed files.

Skills review

In this chapter, you learned how to:

- Animate text and pictures on slides
- Customize animation effects
- Add audio content to slides
- Add video content to slides
- Compress media to decrease file size

12

Hyperlink to additional resources

Presentations often include URLs of websites that provide additional information related to the presentation topic. When a presentation will be viewed electronically, the URLs can be formatted as hyperlinks so that the websites can be accessed directly from the presentation. Hyperlinks can also provide access to information that might be on a hidden slide in the presentation, or in a separate file.

TIP If you use Microsoft Outlook, you can also use a hyperlink to open an email message window so that people viewing the presentation can easily contact you.

Hyperlinks are most frequently in text format, but you can attach a hyperlink to any object—for example, an image such as a shape, logo, or picture. Clicking the hyperlinked object then takes you directly to the linked location. Editing the object does not disrupt the hyperlink; however, deleting the object also deletes the hyperlink.

The simplest method of creating a hyperlink is to enter a URL in a text box and then press the Enter key. PowerPoint automatically inserts the hyperlink and formats the URL so that people recognize it as a hyperlink.

If you want the same hyperlink to appear on every slide in a presentation, attach the hyperlink to text or an object on the presentation's primary slide master. For information about slide masters, see "Display and change slide masters" in Chapter 12, "Create custom presentation elements," of *Microsoft PowerPoint 2016 Step by Step* by Joan Lambert (Microsoft Press, 2015).

To attach a hyperlink to an object, follow these steps:

1. Select the object that you want to hyperlink from.

2. Open the **Insert Hyperlink** box by doing either of the following:

   - On the **Insert** tab, in the **Links** group, click **Hyperlink**.

   - Press **Ctrl+K**.

3. In the **Link to** list, click the type of target you're linking to. Often this is a webpage or another place in the file.

You can link to internal, local, and online locations

4. If you're linking to a webpage, enter the URL in the **Address** box. If you're linking to a slide or heading in the current file, click it in the **Select a place in this document** pane. Then click **OK**.

12

Practice tasks

The practice files for these tasks are located in the Office2016SBS\Ch12 folder. You can save the results of the tasks in the same folder.

Animate text and pictures on slides

Open the AnimateSlides presentation, and then perform the following tasks:

1. On slide **1**, apply the **Shape** entrance animation to the slide title and then to the subtitle. Notice that the animation numbers 1 and 2 appear to the left of the animated objects.

2. Display slide **2**, and apply the **Shape** entrance animation to the left content placeholder. Notice that boxes containing the numbers 1 through 3 appear to the left of the bullet points to indicate the order of their animations.

3. Repeat task 2 for the placeholder on the right.

4. Preview all the animations on slide **2**.

5. Display slide **3**. Apply the **Shape** entrance animation to the frog photo, and then add the **Pulse** emphasis animation.

6. Copy the animations from the frog photo to the crow photo and to the cat photo.

7. Preview the animations on the slide, and then preview the entire presentation.

8. Return to Normal view.

9. Save and close the presentation.

Customize animation effects

Open the CustomizeAnimation presentation, and then perform the following tasks:

1. On slide **1**, apply the **Diamond** entrance effect to the slide title. Set the direction to **Out**.

2. Copy the animation from the slide title to the subtitle. Then change the timing of the subtitle animation to **After Previous**.

3. Switch to Reading view, and preview the animation effects on slide **1**.

4. Switch back to Normal view, display slide **2**, and then click anywhere in the bulleted list on the left.

5. Display the **Animation Pane**. Right-click animation **1**, and then click **Effect Options** to open the Circle dialog box.

6. In the **Circle** dialog box, do the following:

   - Apply the **Chime** sound.

   - Dim the text color to **Red** after the animation.

   - Animate the text by letter.

   - Set the duration to **3 seconds (Slow)**.

7. Watch the effects of your changes to the animation effects.

   The Shape animation doesn't work very well with the selected effect options, so let's adjust them.

8. On the slide, click the left content placeholder. Notice that in the Animation Pane, all the animations for the bullet points in the placeholder are selected.

9. Apply the **Float In** entrance animation to the entire placeholder, and then display the effect options.

10. In the **Float Up** dialog box, do the following:

    - Apply the **Chime** sound.

    - Dim the text color to **Red** after the animation.

    - Animate text by letter.

    - Set the duration to **1 seconds (Fast)**.

11. Preview the animations, and make any additional adjustments you want to your custom animation effects.

12. Copy the animation effects of the bullet points on the left to those on the right.

13. Switch to Reading view, and then click the **Next** button to display the animated bullet points on slide 2.

14. When all the bullet points are visible and dimmed to red, press the **Esc** key to return to Normal view.

15. Save and close the presentation.

Add audio content to slides

Open the AddAudio presentation, display slide 1, and then perform the following tasks:

1. On the **Insert** tab, in the **Media** group, click the **Audio** button, and then click **Audio on My PC** to open the Insert Audio dialog box.

2. In the **Insert Audio** dialog box, browse to the practice file folder, and double-click the **SoundTrack** file to insert the audio clip on the slide.

3. On the **Playback** tool tab, in the **Audio Options** group, change the **Start** setting to **Automatically**. Then select the **Play Across Slides**, **Loop until Stopped**, and **Hide During Show** check boxes.

4. Switch to Reading view, and listen to the audio file as the presentation moves from slide to slide.

5. Press **Esc** to stop the presentation and return to Normal view.

6. Save and close the presentation.

Add video content to slides

Open the AddVideo presentation, and then perform the following tasks:

1. In the left content placeholder, insert the **Butterfly** video from the practice file folder.

2. On the playback toolbar, click the **Play/Pause** button, and then watch the video.

3. Insert the **Wildlife** video from the practice file folder into the content place-holder on the right, and then play the video.

4. With the **Wildlife** video selected, open the **Trim Video** dialog box, and drag the green start marker until it sits at about the **00:17.020** mark. Then, frame-by-frame, adjust the starting point until the first marmot frame comes into view at about the **00:17.292** mark.

5. Drag the red stop marker until it sits at about the **00:20.900** mark. Then, frame-by-frame, adjust the ending point until the last marmot frame comes into view at about the **00:20.790** mark.

6. Play the trimmed video, and then click **OK** to close the Trim Video dialog box.

7. Change the height of the **Butterfly** video representation to 3".

8. Change the height of the **Wildlife** video representation to **3**", and then crop it to a width of **4**".

9. Drag the video representations until they are evenly spaced on the slide and center-aligned with each other.

10. Apply the **Reflected Bevel, Black** (in the **Intense** area of the **Video Styles** gallery) video style to both video objects.

11. Set up the **Butterfly** video to play back on mute, to start automatically, and to loop until stopped.

12. Set up the **Wildlife** video to play back on mute, to start on click, and to loop until stopped.

13. Preview and pause the **Butterfly** video. Then preview and pause the **Wildlife** video.

14. Return to Normal view.

15. Save and close the presentation.

Compress media to decrease file size

There are no practice tasks for this topic.

Part 5

Microsoft Outlook 2016

Send and receive email messages

Although Microsoft Outlook 2016 is an excellent tool for managing your schedule, contact records, and task lists, the primary reason most people use Outlook is to send and receive email messages. Over the past decade, email has become an important method of communication for both business and personal purposes. Outlook provides all the tools you need to send, respond to, organize, find, filter, sort, and otherwise manage email messages for one or more email accounts.

When creating email messages in Outlook, you can format the text, include images, attach files, and set message options such as voting buttons, importance, sensitivity, reminders, and message receipts.

Outlook has many features that make it easy to display and track information about the people you correspond with, particularly if your organization uses technologies that interact with Outlook such as Microsoft Exchange, SharePoint, and Skype for Business. These features include presence icons that indicate whether a person is online and available, and information cards that provide a convenient starting point for many kinds of contact.

This chapter guides you through procedures related to creating, sending, and displaying messages and message attachments; displaying message participant information; and responding to messages.

In this chapter

- Create and send messages
- Attach files and Outlook items to messages
- Display messages and message attachments
- Display message participant information
- Respond to messages

Practice files

For this chapter, use the practice file from the Office2016SBS\Ch13 folder. For practice file download instructions, see the introduction.

Create and send messages

If you have an Internet connection, you can send email messages to people within your organization and around the world by using Outlook, regardless of the type of email account you have. Outlook can send and receive email messages in three message formats:

- **HTML** Supports paragraph styles (including numbered and bulleted lists), character styles (such as fonts, sizes, colors, weight), and backgrounds (such as colors and pictures). Most (but not all) email programs support the HTML format. Programs that don't support HTML display these messages as Plain Text.

- **Rich Text** Supports more paragraph formatting options than HTML, including borders and shading, but is compatible only with Outlook and Exchange Server. Outlook converts Rich Text messages to HTML when sending them outside of an Exchange network.

- **Plain Text** Does not support the formatting features available in HTML and Rich Text messages, but is supported by all email programs.

Email message content isn't limited to simple text. You can create almost any type of content in an email message that you can in a Microsoft Word document. Because Outlook 2016 and Word 2016 share similar commands, you might already be familiar with many processes for formatting content.

You can personalize your messages by using an individual font style or color and add a professional touch by inserting your contact information in the form of an email signature. (You can apply other formatting, such as themes and page backgrounds, but these won't always appear to email recipients as you intend them to, and they can make your communications appear less professional.)

> ✓ **TIP** You can specify different email signatures for new messages and for replies and forwarded messages. For example, you might want to include your full name and contact information in the signature that appears in new messages, but only your first name in the signature that appears in replies and forwarded messages. For more information, see "Create and use automatic signatures" in Chapter 4, "Enhance message content," of *Microsoft Outlook 2016 Step by Step* by Joan Lambert (Microsoft Press, 2015).

You can format the text of your message to make it more readable by including headings, lists, or tables, and you can represent information graphically by including charts, pictures, and other types of graphics. You can attach files to your message and link to other information, such as files or webpages.

> **SEE ALSO** For information about attaching files and other content to email messages, see "Attach files and Outlook items to messages" later in this chapter.

For the purposes of this book, I assume that you know how to enter, edit, and format content by using standard Word techniques, so I don't discuss all of them in this book.

> **SEE ALSO** For extensive information about entering and editing content and about formatting content by using character and paragraph styles, Quick Styles, and themes, refer to *Microsoft Word 2016 Step by Step*, by Joan Lambert (Microsoft Press, 2015).

Creating an email message is a relatively simple process. You will usually provide information in the following fields:

- **To** Enter the email address of the primary message recipient(s) in this field. This is the only field that is absolutely required to send a message.

- **Subject** Enter a brief description of the message contents or purpose in this field. The subject is not required, but it is important to provide information in this field, both so that you and the recipient can identify the message and so that the message isn't blocked as suspected junk mail by a recipient's email program. Outlook will warn you if you try to send a message with no subject.

- **Message body** Enter your message to the recipient in this field, which is a large text box. You can include many types of information, including formatted text, hyperlinks, and graphics in the message body.

> **TIP** In this chapter and throughout this book, for expediency's sake, I sometimes refer to email messages simply as *messages*. When referring to other types of messages I use full descriptions such as *instant messages* or *text messages* to avoid confusion.

Create messages

Addressing an email message is easy: just insert the intended recipient's email address (or name, if he or she is in your address book) into an address box in the message header of a message composition window.

13

You can enter email recipients into any of three address boxes:

- **To** Use for primary message recipients. Usually, these are the people you want to respond to the message. Each message must have at least one address in the To box.

- **Cc** Use for "courtesy copy" recipients. These are usually people you want to keep informed about the subject of the email message but from whom you don't require a response.

- **Bcc** Use for "blind courtesy copy" recipients. These are people you want to keep informed, but whom you want to keep hidden from other message recipients. Bcc recipients are not visible to any other message recipients and therefore aren't included in message responses unless specifically added to one of the address boxes in the response message.

The To and Cc address boxes are always displayed in the message header. The Bcc address box is not displayed by default. You can display it in the message header by clicking the Bcc button, located in the Show Fields group on the Options tab of the message composition window.

> **TIP** Replying to or forwarding a received message automatically fills in one or more of the address boxes in the new message window. For information, see "Respond to messages" later in this chapter.

If your email account is part of a Microsoft Exchange network, you can send messages to another person on the same network by entering only his or her email alias—for example, *joan*; the at symbol (@) and domain name aren't required. If you enter only the name of a person whose email address is in your address book, Outlook associates the name with the corresponding email address, a process called *resolving the address*, before sending the message.

> **TIP** Press Ctrl+K to initiate address resolution. For more information about keyboard shortcuts, see "Keyboard shortcuts" at the end of this book.

Depending on the method you use to enter a message recipient's name or email address into an address box, Outlook either resolves the name or address immediately (if you chose it from a list of known names) or resolves it when you send the message.

The resolution process for each name or address has one of two results:

- If Outlook successfully resolves the name or address, an underline appears below it. If the name or address matches one stored in an address book, Outlook replaces your original entry with the content of the Display As field in the contact record, and then underlines it.

> **SEE ALSO** For information about contact record fields, see "Save and update contact information" in Chapter 7, "Store and access contact information," of *Microsoft Outlook 2016 Step by Step* by Joan Lambert (Microsoft Press, 2015).

- If Outlook is unable to resolve the name or address, the Check Names dialog box opens, asking you to select the address you want to use.

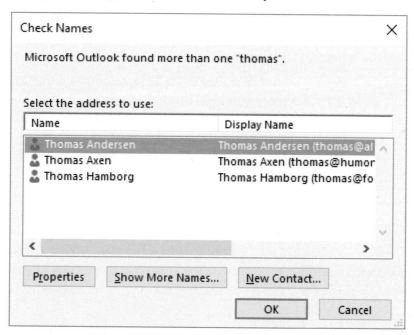

The Check Names dialog box might display No Suggestions, names that match the entry, or saved contact options

In the Check Names dialog box, you can select from the suggested options, or do any of the following:

- Click **Properties** to learn more about the selected option.
- Click **Show More Names** to display your default address book.
- Click **New Contact** to create a new contact record in your default address book, directly from the dialog box.

To open an email message composition window

1. Do either of the following:

   - In any module, on the **Home** tab, in the **New** group, click the **New Items** button, and then click **E-mail Message**.

   - In the Mail module, on the **Home** tab, in the **New** group, click the **New Email** button.

To enter an email address into an address box

1. In the message composition window, click in the **To**, **Cc**, or **Bcc** box, and then do any of the following:

   - Enter the entire address.

   - Enter part of a previously used address and then select the address from the **Auto-Complete List** that appears.

   - Click the address box label to display the Select Names dialog box, in which you can select one or more addresses from your address book(s).

> **SEE ALSO** For information about the Auto-Complete List, see "Troubleshoot message addressing" later in this topic. For information about address books, see "Save and update contact information" in Chapter 7, "Store and access contact information," of *Microsoft Outlook 2016 Step by Step* by Joan Lambert (Microsoft Press, 2015).

To enter a subject for an email message

1. In the message composition window, in the **Subject** box, enter the subject of the email message.

To enter content for an email message

1. In the message composition window, in the message body field, enter the content of the email message.

To format the content of an email message

1. In the message composition window, in the message body field, select the content you want to format.

2. Apply basic font and paragraph formatting from the **Mini Toolbar** that appears when you select the content, or from the **Basic Text** group on the **Message** tab.

Basic text formats   Dialog box launcher   Mini Toolbar

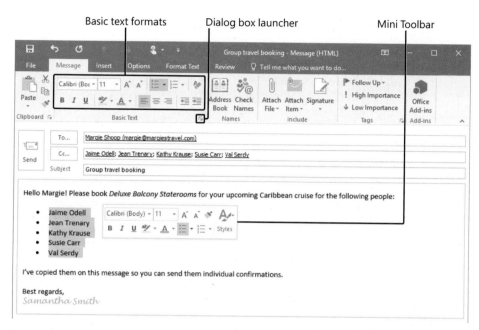

You can format message content in the message composition window just as you can in Word

Or

Do any of the following:

- Apply an extended range of font and paragraph formats from the **Format Text** tab.

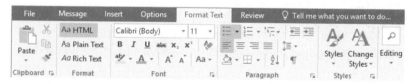

The Format Text tab provides additional font and paragraph formatting options

- On the **Message** tab, click the **Basic Text** dialog box launcher, or on the **Format Text** tab, click the **Font** dialog box launcher to open the Font dialog box. Apply the full range of font formatting, including character spacing, from this dialog box.

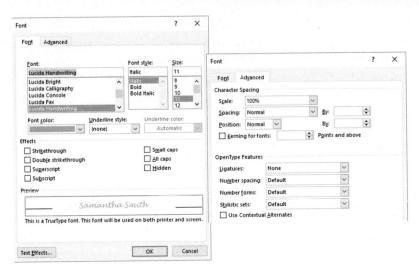

Advanced options include expanding and condensing space between characters

Troubleshoot message addressing

Outlook 2016 includes many features intended to simplify the process of addressing messages to recipients. As with any tool, these features can sometimes be more difficult to use than you'd like. In this topic, I discuss troubleshooting tips for some common problems.

Troubleshoot the Auto-Complete List

As you enter a name or an email address into the To, Cc, or Bcc box, Outlook displays matching addresses in a list. You can insert a name or address from the list into the address box by clicking it or by pressing the arrow keys to select it and then pressing Tab or Enter.

You can insert a recipient for the message from the Auto-Complete List

Sometimes the Auto-Complete List might contain incorrect or outdated addresses—for example, if you have previously sent a message to an incorrect email address, or if a person changes his or her email address. The list might also contain people with whom you no longer correspond. If you don't remove incorrect or outdated addresses from the list, it can be easy to mistakenly accept Outlook's suggestion and send a message to the wrong address.

You can modify the Auto-Complete List settings in the Outlook Options dialog box.

Troubleshoot address lists

When resolving email addresses, Outlook first searches your Global Address List (the corporate directory provided with an Exchange account, if you're working with one), and then searches the contact records stored in the People module of your default account.

If you have multiple address lists, such as those in custom contact folders that you create or associated with additional email accounts that are configured in Outlook, you can specify the order in which Outlook searches for names and addresses, or you can exclude an address list from the search if you don't want to accidentally resolve to an email address from that list.

Troubleshoot multiple recipients

By default, Outlook requires that you separate multiple email addresses with semicolons. If you separate multiple addresses by pressing the spacebar or the Enter key, Outlook replaces the space or return with a semicolon before sending the message. If you separate multiple addresses by using a comma (which might seem to be the more natural action), Outlook treats the addresses as one address and displays an error message when you try to send the message.

You can instruct Outlook to accept commas as address separators in the Outlook Options dialog box.

> **SEE ALSO** For more information, see "Configure Office and Outlook options" in Chapter 12, "Customize Outlook," of *Microsoft Outlook 2016 Step by Step* by Joan Lambert (Microsoft Press, 2015).

13

To remove a name or email address from the Auto-Complete List

1. In the **To**, **Cc**, or **Bcc** box, enter the first letter or letters of a name or email address to display the Auto-Complete List of matching names and addresses.

2. In the list, point to the name or address you want to remove.

3. Click the **Delete** button (the X) that appears to the right of the name or address.

To open the Outlook Options dialog box

1. In any module, click the **File** tab to display the Backstage view, and then click **Options**.

To change the Auto-Complete List settings

1. Open the **Outlook Options** dialog box, and then click the **Mail** tab.

2. On the **Mail** page, scroll to the **Send messages** section.

3. Do any of the following:

   - To prevent the Auto-Complete List from appearing when you enter an address, clear the **Use Auto-Complete List to suggest names...** check box.

   - To remove all entries from the Auto-Complete List (and start the list from scratch) click the **Empty Auto-Complete List** button, and then click **Yes** in the dialog box that appears.

4. Click **OK** to apply the changes and close the dialog box.

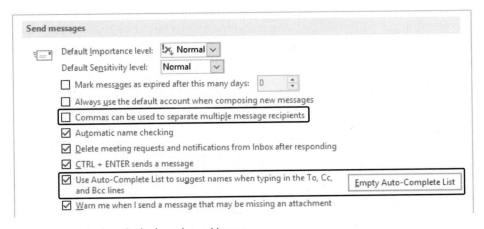

You can customize how Outlook resolves addresses

To use commas as a separator between email addresses

1. Open the **Outlook Options** dialog box, and then click the **Mail** tab.

2. On the **Mail** page, scroll to the **Send messages** section.

3. Select the **Commas can be used to separate multiple message recipients** check box.

4. Click **OK** to apply the changes and close the dialog box.

To change the order in which Outlook searches the address books

1. On the **Home** tab of any module, in the **Find** group, click **Address Book** to open the Address Book displaying your default address list.

2. In the **Address Book** window, on the **Tools** menu, click **Options**.

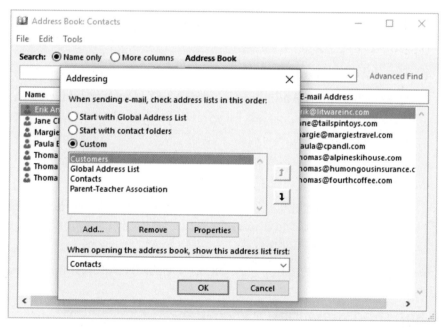

You can designate the order in which Outlook searches for contacts in existing address books

13

3. In the **Addressing** dialog box, do one of the following:

   - Click **Start with Global Address List** to have Outlook search first in your default Exchange account directory.

   - Click **Start with contact folders** to have Outlook search first in the contact records in the People module of your default account.

   - Click **Custom**, and then reorder address lists by clicking the list and then clicking the **Move Up** or **Move Down** button, to specify a custom search order.

4. In the **Addressing** dialog box, click **OK**. Then close the **Address Book** window.

To modify the address lists that Outlook searches

1. On the **Home** tab of any module, in the **Find** group, click **Address Book**.

2. In the **Address Book** window, on the **Tools** menu, click **Options**.

3. In the **Addressing** dialog box, click **Custom** to activate the buttons below the list. Then do any of the following:

   - To search additional address lists, click **Add**. In the **Add Address List** dialog box, click the address list you want to add, click **Add**, and then click **Close**.

   - To prevent Outlook from searching an address list, click the address list, and then click **Remove**.

   - If you're uncertain of the source of an address list, click the address list, and then click **Properties** to display the server address or account name and folder name of the address list.

4. In the **Addressing** dialog box, click **OK**. Then close the **Address Book** window.

Save and send messages

At regular intervals while you're composing a message (every three minutes, by default), Outlook saves a copy of the message in the Drafts folder. This is intended to protect you from losing messages that are in progress. If you close a message that hasn't yet had a draft saved, Outlook gives you the option of saving one. You can manually save a message draft at any time, and you can resume working on it later, either in its own window or directly in the Reading Pane. When you save a draft, the number in the unread message counter to the right of the Drafts folder in the Folder Pane increases. If the draft is in response to a received message, [Draft] appears in the message header of the received message.

Locate a message draft in the Drafts folder or message list

When you send a message, Outlook deletes the message draft, if one exists, and moves the message temporarily to the Outbox. After successfully transmitting the message, Outlook moves it from the Outbox to the Sent Items folder. If a connectivity issue prevents Outlook from transmitting the message, it remains in your Outbox.

> **TIP** Each account you access from Outlook has its own Drafts folder and its own Sent Items folder. Outlook automatically saves draft messages and sent messages in the folders associated with the email account in which you compose or send the message. You can change the location in which Outlook saves message drafts from the Mail page of the Outlook Options dialog box. For more information, see "Configure Office and Outlook options" in Chapter 12, "Customize Outlook," of *Microsoft Outlook 2016 Step by Step* by Joan Lambert (Microsoft Press, 2015).

13

Send from a specific account

If you have configured Outlook to connect to multiple email accounts, a From button appears in the header area of the message composition window. The active account appears to the right of the From button.

By default, Outlook assumes that you intend to send a message from the account you're currently working in. If you begin composing a message while viewing the Inbox of your work account, for example, Outlook selects the work account as the message-sending account. If you reply to a message received by your personal account, Outlook selects the personal account as the message-sending account.

To change the active account when you're composing a message, click the From button, and then click the account from which you want to send the message.

The From list displays all types of email accounts

TIP If Outlook is configured to connect to only one account, you can display the From button by clicking From in the Show Fields group on the Options tab of a message composition window.

If you have permission to send messages from an account that you haven't configured in Outlook—for example, a generic Customer Service email account for your company—you can click Other E-mail Address in the From list, enter the email address you want to send the message from, and click OK.

Clicking the From button displays the Address Book window in which you can choose a sending address

To save a draft of an email message

1. In the message composition window, do either of the following to save a draft without closing the message:

   - On the **Quick Access Toolbar**, click the **Save** button.

   - Press **Ctrl+S**.

Or

1. At the right end of the title bar, click the **Close** button.

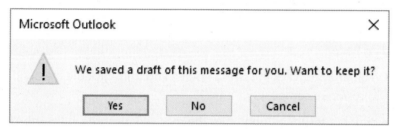

If you close a message before sending it, Outlook prompts you to save a draft

2. In the **Microsoft Outlook** message box, click **Yes** to save a draft and close the message window.

To change how often Outlook automatically saves email message drafts

1. Open the **Outlook Options** dialog box, and then click the **Mail** tab.

2. On the **Mail** page, scroll to the **Save messages** section.

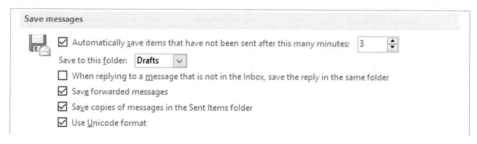

You can customize how often and where Outlook saves message drafts

13

3. Do either of the following:

    -   In the **Automatically save items that have not been sent after this many minutes** box, change the number of minutes.

    -   Clear the **Automatically save items that have not been sent after this many minutes** check box to turn off automatic saving of message drafts.

4. Click **OK** to apply the changes and close the dialog box.

To modify an email message draft

1. Do either of the following in the Mail module to display the message draft in the Reading Pane:

    -   In the **Folder Pane**, click the **Drafts** folder, and then click the message you want to continue composing.

    -   If the draft is a response, right-click the received message in the **Inbox**, click **Find Related**, and then click **Messages in this Conversation**. Then click the message draft in the search results.

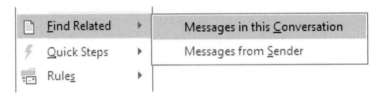

You can find messages that are related to the selected message by conversation or sender

 TIP If you have a lot of message drafts in your Drafts folder, this can be the simplest method of locating a specific draft.

When you click the message in either message list, the message becomes active for editing in the Reading Pane, and a Message tool tab appears on the ribbon.

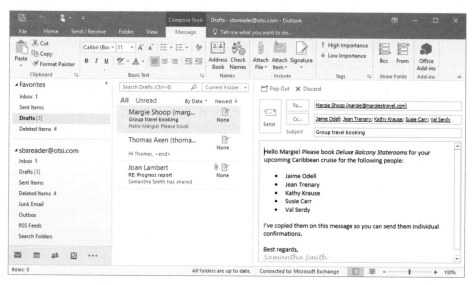

You can edit message drafts directly in the Reading Pane

2. Do any of the following:

   - Edit the message in the **Reading Pane**. The Message tool tab contains the most frequently used commands from the message composition window ribbon.

   - In the upper-left corner of the **Reading Pane**, click the **Pop Out** button to open the message in a message composition window (with the full ribbon).

   - In the message list, double-click the message header to open the message in a message composition window.

3. After you edit the message, you can send it or close it. If you close the message, it remains in the Drafts folder.

To send an email message

1. In the message composition window, do either of the following:

   - In the message header, click the **Send** button.

   - Press **Ctrl+Enter**. (The first time you press this key combination, Outlook asks whether you want to designate this as the keyboard shortcut for sending messages.)

2. The message window closes and the message is sent. If the message was saved in the Drafts folder, sending it removes it from the Drafts folder.

To verify that an email message was sent

1. In the **Folder Pane** of the Mail module, click the **Sent Items** folder to verify that the message is in the folder.

2. If the message is not in the Sent Items folder, check the **Outbox** folder.

> ✅ **TIP** If you want to send personalized copies of the same email message to several people, you can use the mail merge feature of Word 2016. For more information, refer to *Microsoft Word 2016 Step by Step*, by Joan Lambert (Microsoft Press, 2015).

Attach files and Outlook items to messages

A convenient way to distribute a file (such as a Microsoft PowerPoint presentation, Excel workbook, Word document, or picture) is by attaching the file to an email message. Message recipients can preview or open the file from the Reading Pane, open it from the message window, forward it to other people, or save it to their computers.

When Outlook is set to your default email app, you can email files by using several different methods:

- **From Outlook** You can create a message, and then attach the file to the message. If the file you attach is stored in a shared location such as a OneDrive folder or SharePoint library, you have the option of sending a link rather than a copy of the file.

- **From an Office app** You can send a document from Word, a workbook from Excel, or a presentation from PowerPoint while you're working in the file. You have the option of sending a copy of the file as a message attachment or, if the file is stored in a shared location, you can send a link to the file.

- **From File Explorer** You can send any file as an attachment directly from File Explorer. When sending pictures from File Explorer, you have the option of resizing the pictures to reduce the file size.

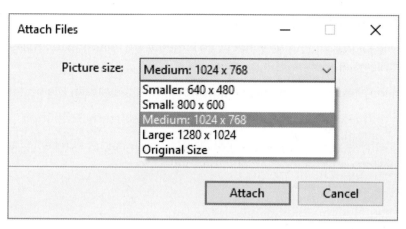

The picture size options are always the same, so they might be larger or smaller than your original picture

After you attach a file to an email message by using any of these methods, and before you send the message, you can modify or remove the attachments. When you attach files that are from shared locations, a cloud symbol on the file icon indicates that the attachment is a link, rather than a copy of the file. If you want to send a copy of the online file, you can easily do so.

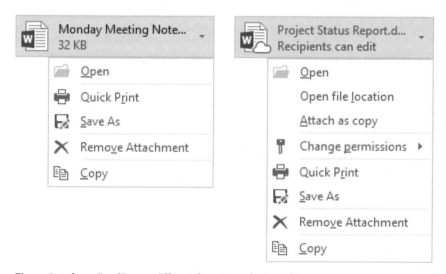

The options for online files are different from those for local files

In addition to sending files, you can send Outlook items, such as email messages or contact records.

To attach a file to an outgoing email message

1. In the message composition window, do either of the following to display the Attach File menu:

   - On the **Message** tab, in the **Include** group, click the **Attach File** button.

   - On the **Insert** tab, in the **Include** group, click the **Attach File** button.

   The Attach File menu includes a list of files you've worked with recently, and that are stored in locations Outlook can connect to.

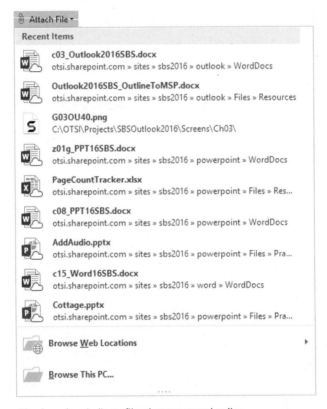

Cloud overlays indicate files that are stored online

2. On the **Attach File** menu, do any of the following:

- If the file you want to attach is in the list, click the file.

- At the bottom of the **Insert File** menu, click **Browse Web Locations**, and then click a connected online storage location to open the Insert File dialog box displaying the storage structure of that location. Browse to the file you want to attach, select it, and then click **Insert**.

- At the bottom of the **Insert File** menu, click **Browse This PC** to open the Insert File dialog box displaying your local storage structure. Browse to the file you want to attach, select it, and then click **Insert**.

The attached file or files appear at the bottom of the message header. If the file that you attached is stored online, the file icon includes a cloud.

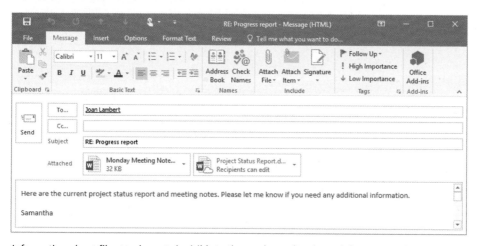

Information about file attachments is visible to the sender and to the recipient

To create an email message with an attachment from within an Office file

1. In the document, workbook, or presentation, click the **File** tab to display the Backstage view.

2. On the **Share** page of the Backstage view, click **Email** to display the email options.

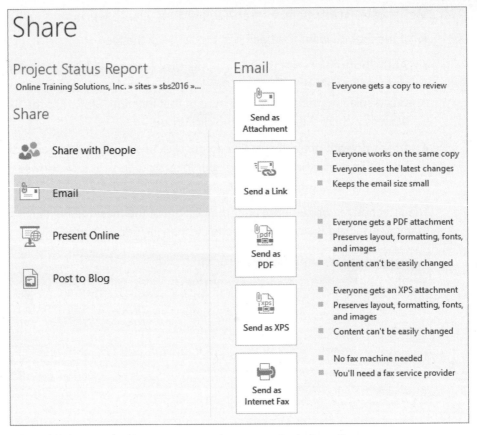

Share

Project Status Report

Online Training Solutions, Inc. » sites » sbs2016 »...

Share

Share with People

Email

Present Online

Post to Blog

Email

Send as Attachment
- Everyone gets a copy to review

Send a Link
- Everyone works on the same copy
- Everyone sees the latest changes
- Keeps the email size small

Send as PDF
- Everyone gets a PDF attachment
- Preserves layout, formatting, fonts, and images
- Content can't be easily changed

Send as XPS
- Everyone gets an XPS attachment
- Preserves layout, formatting, fonts, and images
- Content can't be easily changed

Send as Internet Fax
- No fax machine needed
- You'll need a fax service provider

You can share an Office document as an attachment to an Outlook email message

3. In the **Email** pane, click **Send As Attachment**, **Send a Link**, **Send as PDF**, or **Send as XPS** to create an email message and attach the specified version of the file.

> **TIP** If you have an account with a fax service provider that permits the transmission of fax messages by email, you can click the Send As Internet Fax option and provide the fax number to address the message in the format required by the fax service. For example, if your fax service provider is Contoso and the fax number is (425)555-0199, the email might be addressed to 14255551212@contoso.com. The fax service relays the message electronically to the recipient's fax number.

To create an email message with an attachment from File Explorer

1. Select the file or files you want to send.

2. Right-click the selected file or files you want to email, click **Send to**, and then click **Mail recipient**.

3. If the files are pictures, the Attach Files dialog box opens and provides the opportunity to reduce the file size. In the **Picture size** list, click a size to display an estimate of the total file size of the pictures at those maximum dimensions.

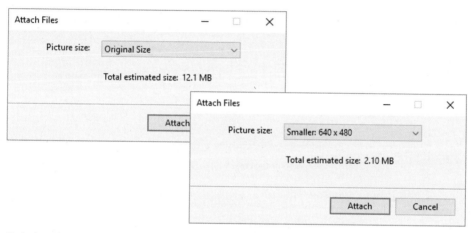

Reducing picture size can significantly reduce the attachment size

4. After you specify the picture size if necessary, click **Attach** to create the message.

To attach a copy of an online file

1. Attach the file to the email message.

2. In the **Attached** area, point to the file attachment, click the arrow that appears, and then click **Attach as copy** to download a temporary copy of the file to your computer and attach that copy to the message.

To remove an attachment from an outgoing email message

1. In the **Attached** area, point to the file attachment, click the arrow that appears, and then click **Remove Attachment**.

13

To attach an Outlook item to an outgoing email message

1. In the message composition window, do either of the following to open the Insert Item dialog box:

   - On the **Message** tab, in the **Include** group, click the **Attach Item** button, and then click **Outlook Item**.

   - On the **Insert** tab, in the **Include** group, click the **Outlook Item** button.

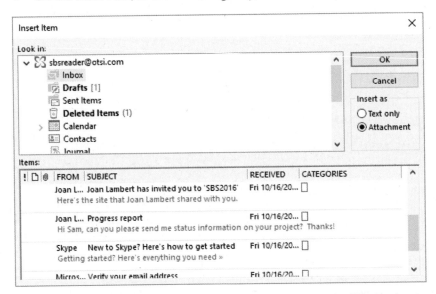

The Insert Item dialog box displays all the items in the folder, so it can be difficult to locate a specific item by using this method

2. In the **Insert Item** dialog box, browse to the message, calendar item, contact record, note, or task you want to send.

3. Click the item, and then click **OK**.

Or

1. In the Outlook program window, locate the item you want to send.

2. Right-click the item, and then click **Forward**.

> **SEE ALSO** For information about sending calendar information by email, see "Share calendar information" in Chapter 10, "Manage your calendar," of *Microsoft Outlook 2016 Step by Step* by Joan Lambert (Microsoft Press, 2015).

New mail notifications

When new messages, meeting requests, or task assignments arrive in your Inbox, Outlook alerts you in several ways so that you can be aware of email activity if you're using another application or you've been away from your computer.

These are the default notifications:

- A chime sounds.

- A desktop alert appears on your screen for a few seconds, displaying the sender's information, the message subject, and the first few words of the message.

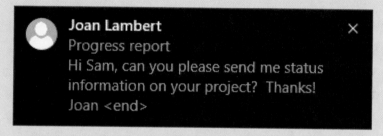

You can open the message by clicking the desktop alert

- A closed envelope icon appears on the Outlook taskbar button and, in versions of Windows earlier than Windows 10, in the notification area of the taskbar.

- In Windows 10, the Action Center icon in the notification area changes from hollow to white, and the new message is available in the Action Center.

You can configure the notification options from the Mail page of the Outlook Options dialog box. The only optional notification that isn't turned on by default is for Outlook to briefly change the shape of the mouse pointer to an envelope.

SEE ALSO For information about modifying new mail notifications, see "Configure Office and Outlook options" in Chapter 12, "Customize Outlook," of *Microsoft Outlook 2016 Step by Step* by Joan Lambert (Microsoft Press, 2015).

13

Display messages and message attachments

Each time you start Outlook and connect to your email server, any new messages received since the last time you connected appear in your Inbox. Depending on your settings, Outlook downloads either the entire message to your computer or only the message header, which provides basic information about the message, such as:

- The item type (message, meeting request, task assignment, and so on)
- Who sent it
- When you received it
- The subject

Icons displayed in the message header indicate optional information such as:

- The most recent response action taken
- Whether files are attached
- If the message has been digitally signed or encrypted
- If the sender marked the message as being of high or low importance

The message list displays the message header information. You can open messages from the message list or display message content in the Reading Pane.

> **SEE ALSO** For information about changing the display of the message list or configuration of the program window elements, see "Work in the Mail module" in Chapter 2, "Explore Outlook modules," of *Microsoft Outlook 2016 Step by Step* by Joan Lambert (Microsoft Press, 2015).

Display message content

You can display the content of a message by opening it in a message window. However, you can save time by reading and working with messages (and other Outlook items) in the Reading Pane. You can display the Reading Pane to the right of or below the module content pane.

If a message contains external content, which many marketing email messages do, the external content will be automatically downloaded only if your security settings are configured to permit this. Otherwise, you must give permission to download the external content.

> **TIP** If you find it difficult to read the text in the Reading Pane at its default size, you can change the magnification level of the Reading Pane content by using the Zoom controls located at the right end of the program window status bar. Changing the Zoom level is temporary and lasts only until you switch to a different message. The Zoom controls are available only for message content; they're unavailable when you preview an attachment in the Reading Pane.

> **SEE ALSO** For information about modifying Reading Pane functionality, see "Configure Office and Outlook options" in Chapter 12, "Customize Outlook," of *Microsoft Outlook 2016 Step by Step* by Joan Lambert (Microsoft Press, 2015).

To display the content of a message

1. In the Mail module, do any of the following:

   - Open a message in its own window by double-clicking its header in the message list.

   - Read a message without opening it by clicking its header once in the message list to display the message in the Reading Pane.

   - Display the first three lines of each unread message under the message header by using the Preview feature.

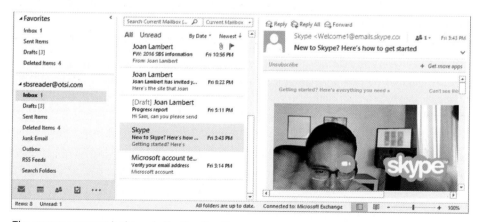

The message content is shown in the Reading Pane

To move through message content in the Reading Pane

1. In the Reading Pane, do any of the following:

   - Scroll at your own pace by dragging the vertical scroll bar that appears at the right side of the Reading Pane.

   - Move up or down one line at a time by clicking the scroll arrows.

   - Move up or down one page at a time by clicking above or below the scroll box.

   - Move up or down one page at a time by pressing the **Spacebar**. When you reach the end of a message by using this feature, called *Single Key Reading*, pressing the Spacebar again displays the first page of the next message. This option is very convenient if you want to read through several consecutive messages in the Reading Pane, or if you find it easier to press the Spacebar than to use the mouse.

Display attachment content

If a message has attachments, you can open or download them from the message window or Reading Pane. Outlook can also display interactive previews of many types of attachments, including Word documents, Excel workbooks, PowerPoint presentations, Visio diagrams, text files, XPS files, and image files.

If a preview app for a file type hasn't been installed, Outlook won't be able to preview a file of that type in the Reading Pane. You can display the apps that are used to preview files from the Attachment Handling page of the Trust Center window, which you open from the Outlook Options dialog box.

> **SEE ALSO** For information about Trust Center settings, see "Configure Office and Outlook options" in Chapter 12, "Customize Outlook," of *Microsoft Outlook 2016 Step by Step* by Joan Lambert (Microsoft Press, 2015).

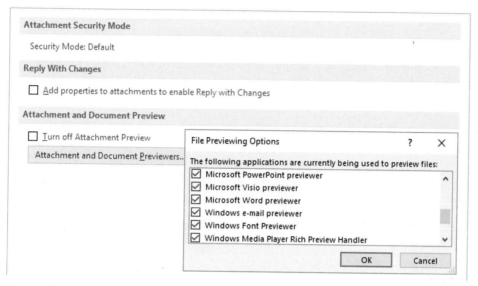

You can view which apps are used to preview files in the Reading Pane, or turn off the Attachment Preview feature

Clicking certain types of attachments displays a warning message asking you to confirm that the content comes from a trusted source. You can approve the content on a case-by-case basis or give Outlook permission to skip the warning message for files of this type.

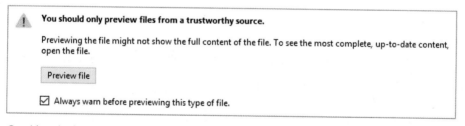

Consider whether it is safe to dismiss warnings for the file type

13

Previewing a file can save you a great deal of time. You can interact with the preview in many ways, to the point that you might not have to take the time to open the file at all.

If you suspect that an attachment might contain a virus, and you have a reputable anti-malware program installed, you might want to download the file and scan it for viruses before you open it.

To preview the content of a message attachment

1. In the open message window or **Reading Pane**, click the attachment once. The **Attachments** tool tab appears on the ribbon, and a preview of the attachment appears in the message content pane or Reading Pane.

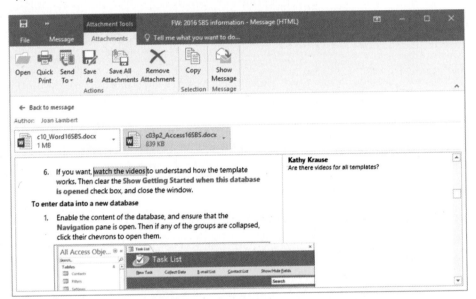

You use the same techniques to preview and open attachments in the message window and Reading Pane

To work with attachment content in the preview

1. Display the attachment preview, and then do any of the following:

   - Scroll vertically or horizontally through content.

   - Point to comment markup in a Word document to display the full comment.

   - Click worksheet tabs at the bottom of the preview area to switch between worksheets in an Excel workbook.

- Scroll vertically or click the **Next** button to move through slides in a Power-Point presentation. Transitions and animations function in the preview area.

- When previewing a PowerPoint presentation, click the slides in the preview area to advance through the presentation, including all transitions and animations; or click the **Next** button (the arrow) at the bottom of the vertical scroll bar to advance through the presentation without displaying the animated elements.

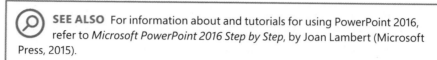

> **SEE ALSO** For information about and tutorials for using PowerPoint 2016, refer to *Microsoft PowerPoint 2016 Step by Step*, by Joan Lambert (Microsoft Press, 2015).

- Click hyperlinks to open the target webpages or files, or click mailto links to create email messages.

To return from the attachment preview to the message content

1. Do either of the following:

   - In the upper-left corner of the message header, click **Back to message**.

   - On the **Attachments** tool tab, in the **Message** group, click the **Show Message** button. (The ScreenTip that appears when you point to the button says *Return to Message*.)

To open an attachment in the default app for that file type

1. In the message window or **Reading Pane**, do either of the following:

   - In the message header, double-click the attachment.

   - In the message header, click the attachment to display a preview. Then on the **Attachments** tool tab, in the **Actions** group, click **Open**.

To save an attachment to a storage drive

1. From the message window or **Reading Pane**, do either of the following:

   - Point to the attachment, click the arrow that appears, and then click **Save As**.

   - On the **Attachments** tool tab, in the **Actions** group, click the **Save As** button.

2. In the **Save As** dialog box, browse to the folder in which you want to save the file, and then click **Save**.

13

To save multiple attachments to a storage drive

1. From the message window or **Reading Pane**, do either of the following to display a list of all the files that are attached to the message:

   - Point to any attachment, click the arrow that appears, and then click **Save All Attachments**.

   - On the **Attachments** tool tab, in the **Actions** group, click the **Save All Attachments** button.

2. In the **Save All Attachments** list, all the attached files are selected by default. If you want to save only some of the files, click one file that you want to save, and then do either of the following:

   - Press **Shift+click** to select contiguous files.

   - Press **Ctrl+click** to select noncontiguous files.

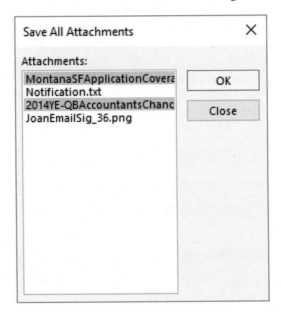

You can choose which attached files you want to save

3. When the files you want to save are selected in the list, click **OK**.

4. In the **Save All Attachments** dialog box, browse to the folder in which you want to save the files, and then click **OK**.

Display message participant information

After you receive a message (or after Outlook validates a recipient's name in a message that you're sending), you have access to contact information and a history of your communications with that person. There are three sources of information available in a message window: presence icons, contact cards, and the People Pane.

Outlook uses presence information provided by central administration server programs such as Office 365. If presence information is available, a square presence icon appears in the Reading Pane or message window to the left of each message participant's name, and a rectangular icon to the left of each contact picture, when shown in a message.

The presence icon (casually referred to as a *jelly bean* or *chiclet*) is color-coded to indicate the availability or online status of the message participant as follows:

- **Green** The person is online and available.
- **Red** The person is busy, in a conference call, or in a meeting.
- **Dark red with a white bar** The person does not want to be disturbed.
- **Yellow** The person is away or has not been active online for a certain length of time (usually five minutes).
- **Gray** The person is offline.
- **White** The person's presence information is not known.

> **TIP** This same set of presence icons is used in all Microsoft Office apps and on Microsoft SharePoint sites, to provide a consistent user experience. I don't display the presence icons in all the graphics in this book, but I do display some in this topic.

13

Pointing to a message participant's name displays an interactive contact card of information that includes options for contacting the person by email, instant message, or phone; for scheduling a meeting; and for working with the person's contact record.

Presence indicators   Communication options   Open Contact Card

You can initiate many types of communication from the contact card

Clicking the Open Contact Card button displays additional contact information and interaction options, and links to a more extensive range of information. From the expanded contact card, you can view the contact's position within the organization and which distribution lists he or she is a member of.

More information   Pin Contact Card

Pinning the contact card keeps it open even if you send or close the email message

> **TIP** A distribution list is a membership group created through Exchange and available from an organization's Global Address List. You can't create distribution lists, but you can create contact groups, which are membership groups saved in the Outlook Contacts module. For more information, see "Create contact groups" in Chapter 8, "Manage contact records," of *Microsoft Outlook 2016 Step by Step* by Joan Lambert (Microsoft Press, 2015).

Clicking any of the blue links initiates contact with the person through the stored phone number or email address, initiates a meeting request, or, if the person is in your address book, opens his or her contact record.

The Organization tab displays information about the person's manager and direct reports. The What's New tab displays social updates. The Membership tab displays information about distribution lists the contact is a member of. This information is available only for Exchange accounts.

The People Pane is an optional pane that displays information about conversation participants and your past communications with them, at the bottom of the message window or Reading Pane. In Outlook 2016, the People Pane is hidden by default; you can display it by clicking Normal or Minimized in the People Pane list on the View tab of any module.

In its minimized state, the People Pane displays small thumbnails that represent each message participant. If a person's contact record includes a photograph, the photo appears in the People Pane. If no photograph is available, a silhouette of one person represents an individual message participant, and a silhouette of three people represents a distribution list.

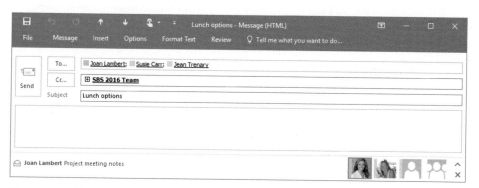

The minimized People Pane shows small thumbnails of the conversation participants

13

You can expand the People Pane to display either large thumbnails or a tabbed breakdown of communications for each message participant.

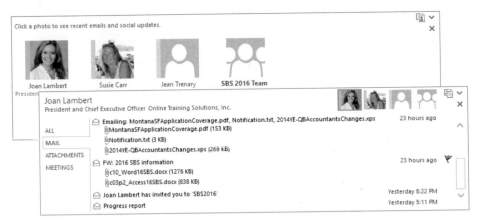

The expanded People Pane displays either participant images or a history of interactions with the selected participant

The All Items tab of the detailed view displays all your recent Outlook interactions with the selected person. If you're looking for a specific item, such as a meeting request or a document attached to a message, you can filter the item list.

The People Pane displays past interactions only when the Cached Exchange Mode feature is enabled. If the expanded People Pane doesn't display past information when you're viewing an Exchange account message, the likely problem is that Cached Exchange Mode is not enabled.

 TIP The detailed People Pane is available for all types of email accounts. The images in this book depict the People Pane for an Exchange account.

To display a message participant's contact information

1. Point to the person's name to display a simple contact card.

2. In the contact card, click the **Open Contact Card** button to display a more extensive range of information and interaction options.

To initiate contact from a contact card

1. In the basic contact card, do any of the following:

   - Click the **Instant Message** icon to initiate a Skype for Business message.

- Click the **Phone** icon to initiate a phone call through Skype for Business or your connected enterprise phone system.

- Click the **Video** icon to initiate a Skype for Business video chat.

- Click the **Email** icon to create a preaddressed email message form.

2. In the expanded contact card, click any blue link.

To expand the People Pane

1. Do any of the following:

   - Click the **Expand** button at the right end of the pane.

   - Drag the horizontal bar at the top of the pane.

   - On the **View** tab of any module, in the **People Pane** list, click **Normal**.

> ✓ **TIP** The People Pane can occupy only a certain percentage of the message window, so the amount you can manually adjust the height of the People Pane to is dependent on the height of the message window.

To switch between detailed and simple views of the People Pane

1. Near the right end of the expanded People Pane header, click the **Toggle** button.

To filter the All Items list

1. Click the **Mail**, **Attachments**, or **Meetings** tab to display only interactions of that type.

To enable Cached Exchange Mode

1. On the **Info** page of the Backstage view of the Outlook program window, click **Account Settings**, and then in the list that appears, click **Account Settings**.

2. On the **E-mail** tab of the **Account Settings** dialog box, click your Exchange account, and then click **Change**.

3. On the **Server Settings** page of the **Change Account** wizard, select the **Use Cached Exchange Mode** check box, click **Next**, and then on the wizard's final page, click **Finish**.

4. Exit and restart Outlook to implement the change.

13

Respond to messages

You can respond to most email messages that you receive by clicking a response button either in the Reading Pane, in the message window, or in the Respond group on the Message tab. You can respond to a message by replying to the sender, replying to all the message participants, replying with a meeting request, replying with an instant message, or forwarding the message.

When you choose one of the following options, Outlook creates a new message based on the original message and fills in one or more of the address boxes for you:

- **Reply** Creates an email message, addressed to only the original message sender, that contains the original message text.

- **Reply All** Creates an email message, addressed to the message sender and all recipients listed in the To and Cc boxes, that contains the original message text. The message is not addressed to recipients of blind courtesy copies (Bcc recipients).

- **Reply with Meeting** Creates a meeting invitation addressed to all message recipients. The message text is included in the meeting window content pane. Outlook suggests the current date and an upcoming half-hour time slot for the meeting.

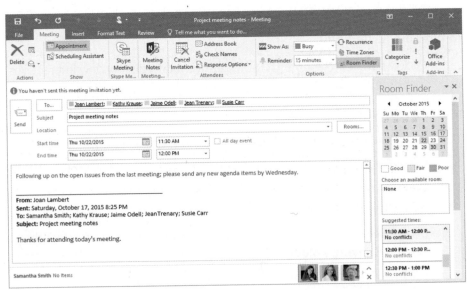

A meeting invitation created from a message

Message replies include the original message header and text, preceded by a space in which you can respond. Replies do not include any attachments from the original message.

You can add, change, and delete recipients from any reply email before sending it.

> ✓ **TIP** When responding to an email message, take care to use good email etiquette. For example, if your response is not pertinent to all the original recipients of a message, don't reply to the entire recipient list, especially if the message was addressed to a distribution list that might include hundreds of members. You can prevent other people from replying to all recipients of a message you send by addressing the message to yourself and entering other recipients in the Bcc box. Then the recipient list will not be visible to anyone.

You can forward a received message to any email address (regardless of whether the recipient uses Outlook) provided the message was not sent with restricted permissions. Outlook 2016 has the following message-forwarding options:

- **Forward** Creates a new message that contains the text of the original, and retains any attachments from the original message.

- **Forward As Attachment** Creates a blank message that contains no text but includes the original message as an attachment. The original message text and any attachments are available to the new recipient when he or she opens the attached message.

Both types of forwarded messages include the original message header and text, preceded by a space in which you can add information. Forwarded messages include attachments from the original message.

When you forward a message, Outlook does not fill in the recipient boxes for you.

If you reply to or forward a received message from within the message window, the original message remains open after you send your response. You can instruct Outlook to close original messages after you respond to them—you'll probably be finished working with the message at that point.

13

If your organization has the necessary unified communications infrastructure, you may also have these additional response options:

- **Call or Call All** Initiates a Voice over IP (VoIP) call from your computer to the phone number of the original message sender or sender and other message recipients.

- **Reply with IM or Reply All with IM** Opens an instant messaging window with the message sender or sender and other recipients as the chat participants. You must enter and send the first message to start the IM session.

> **TIP** The response options available in your Outlook installation might vary from those described here. The available response options for your installation are available from the Respond group that is on the Message tab of the message window and on the Home tab of the program window.

Nonstandard messages have alternative response options, such as the following:

- A meeting request includes options for responding to the request.

- A task assignment includes options for accepting or declining the assignment.

- If a message contains voting buttons, you can respond by opening the message, clicking the Vote button in the Respond group on the Message tab, and then clicking the response you want to send. Or you can click the InfoBar (labeled *Click here to vote*) in the Reading Pane and then click the response you want.

> **SEE ALSO** For information about meeting requests, see "Respond to meeting requests" in Chapter 15, "Manage scheduling." For information about polling other Outlook users in your organization, see "Change message settings and delivery options" in Chapter 4, "Enhance message content," of *Microsoft Outlook 2016 Step by Step* by Joan Lambert (Microsoft Press, 2015). For information about task assignments, see "Manage task assignments" in Chapter 11, "Track tasks," of the same book.

To reply to an email message

1. At the top of the **Reading Pane** or in the **Respond** group on the **Message** tab, do either of the following:

   - Click the **Reply** button to create a response already addressed to the original sender. If the message had been sent to any other people, the reply would not include them.

   - Click the **Reply All** button to create a response already addressed to the original sender. If the message had been sent to any other people, the reply also includes them.

   The *RE:* prefix appears at the beginning of the message subject to indicate that this is a response to an earlier message. The original message, including its header information, appears in the content pane, separated from the new content by a horizontal line.

> **TIP** Note that a Reply or Reply All response does not include attachments, even if there were attachments in the original message. (In fact, there is no indication that the original message had any.)

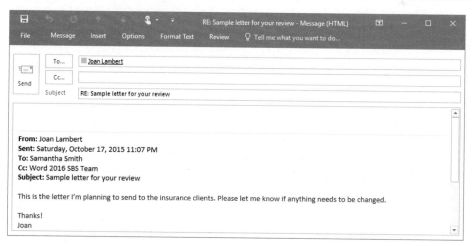

Replying to a message generates a new message addressed to the original sender

2. At the top of the content pane, enter the text of your reply.

3. In the response header, click the **Send** button to send the reply. The original message remains open on your screen.

Resending and recalling messages

If you want to send a new version of a message you've already sent—for example, a status report in which you update details each week—you can *resend* the message. Resending a message creates a new version of the message with none of the extra information that might be attached to a forwarded message. To resend a message, follow these steps:

1. From your **Sent Items** folder, open the message you want to resend. (Or, if you copied yourself on the message, you can open it from your **Inbox**.)

2. On the **Message** tab, in the **Move** group, click the **Actions** button (the ScreenTip that appears when you point to it says *More Move Actions*), and then in the list, click **Resend This Message**.

Outlook creates a new message form identical to the original. You can change the message recipients, subject, attachments, or content before sending the new version of the message.

If, after sending a message, you realize that you shouldn't have sent it—for example, if the message contained an error or was sent to the wrong people—you can *recall* it by instructing Outlook to delete or replace any unread copies of the message. If a recipient has already opened a message, it can't be recalled.

The message recall operation works only for recipients with Exchange accounts. Recipients with Internet email accounts or those who have already opened the original message will end up with both the original message and the recall notification or replacement message.

IMPORTANT You might want to test the message recall functionality within your organization before you have occasion to need it so that you can feel confident about the way it works.

To recall a message, follow these steps:

1. From your **Sent Items** folder, open the message you want to recall.

2. On the **Message** tab, in the **Move** group, click the **Actions** button, and then click **Recall This Message**. The Recall This Message dialog box offers options for handling the recalled message.

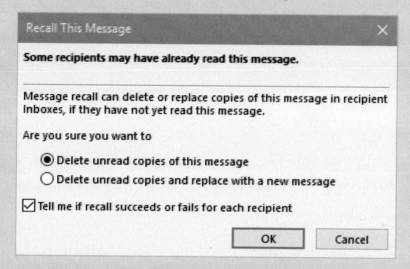

You can delete or replace a message you've sent if it hasn't been read yet

3. In the **Recall This Message** dialog box, click an option to indicate whether you want to delete or replace the sent message, and whether you want to receive an email notification of the success or failure of each recall. Then click **OK**.

4. If you choose to replace the message, a new message window opens. Enter the content that you want to include in the replacement message, and then send it.

13

To forward an email message

1. At the top of the **Reading Pane** or in the **Respond** group on the **Message** tab, click the **Forward** button to create a new version of the message that is not addressed to any recipient. The FW: prefix at the beginning of the message subject indicates that this is a forwarded message.

> **TIP** Any files that were attached to the original message appear in the Attached box. The message is otherwise identical to the earlier response. You address and send a forwarded message as you would any other.

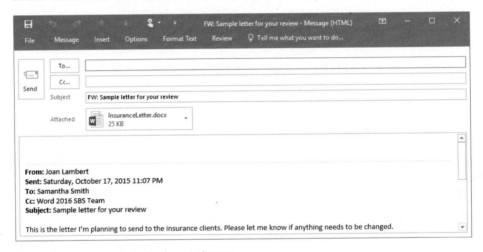

Forwarding a message includes the attachments

2. At the top of the content pane, enter the text of your reply.

3. In the response header, click the **Send** button to send the reply. The original message remains open on your screen.

To have Outlook close messages after responding

1. Open the **Outlook Options** dialog box, and then click the **Mail** tab.

2. On the **Mail** page, scroll to the **Replies and forwards** section.

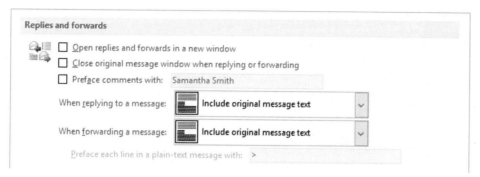

You can customize how Outlook opens, closes, and formats replies and forwards

3. Select the **Close original message window when replying or forwarding** check box.

4. Click **OK** to apply the changes and close the dialog box.

Skills review

In this chapter, you learned how to:

- Create and send messages
- Attach files and Outlook items to messages
- Display messages and message attachments
- Display message participant information
- Respond to messages

13

Practice tasks

The practice file for these tasks is located in the Office2016SBS\Ch13 folder. You can save the results of the tasks in the same folder.

> ⚠️ **IMPORTANT** As you work through the practice tasks in this book, you will create Outlook items that might be used as practice files for tasks in later chapters. If you haven't created specific items that are referenced in later chapters, you can substitute items of your own.

Create and send messages

Start Outlook, and then perform the following tasks:

1. Start a new email message. Begin entering your name or address in the **To** box, and notice the results that the Auto-Complete List provides. If you want to, remove one or more names or addresses from the list. (They'll be added to the list again the next time you send messages to them.)

2. Create a new email message, and do the following:

   - Address the message to yourself.

   - In the **Subject** box, enter **SBS Test**.

   - In the content pane, enter **Welcome to Outlook!**

   - Format the word *Welcome* in bold font and the word *Outlook* in blue font.

3. Close the message window, and have Outlook save a draft copy of the message.

4. Open the **Outlook Options** dialog box. Locate the Auto-Complete List, comma separator, and AutoSave settings discussed in this chapter and make any changes that you want to the standard configuration. Then close the dialog box.

5. Display the **Drafts** folder, and edit your draft in the **Reading Pane**. Append **Sincerely,** and your name on separate lines at the end of the message. Then send the message.

6. Display the Address Book and find out what contact lists are available to you. If you want to, follow the procedures described in this chapter to change the order in which Outlook searches the address books. Then close the Address Book.

7. Display the **Sent Items** folder and verify that the *SBS Test* message was sent.

Attach files and Outlook items to messages

Start File Explorer, browse to the practice file folder, and then perform the following tasks:

1. From the practice file folder, open the **AttachFiles** document in Word. Enter your name in the **Contact Information** section and save the file. Then save a copy of the file in the same folder with the name **AttachCopy**.

2. In the **AttachCopy** document, display the **Share** page of the Backstage view. Send a PDF copy of the document to yourself. Then close the document.

3. Display your Outlook Inbox. Create a new email message, and do the following:

   - Address the message to yourself.

   - In the **Subject** box, enter **SBS Attachment from Outlook**.

4. In the message window, display the **Attach File** menu. Notice that the two files you worked with in Word are at the top of the list. Attach the **AttachFiles** document to your message. Then send the message to yourself.

5. Display the contents of the practice file folder in File Explorer. Select the **Attach-Files** and **AttachCopy** messages. Right-click the selection, click **Send to**, and then click **Mail recipient** to create a new message.

6. Address the message to yourself, and enter **SBS Attachments from Explorer** as the message subject. Then send the message.

Display messages and message attachments

Display your Inbox, and then perform the following tasks:

1. In your Inbox, locate the **SBS Test** message that you sent to yourself in an earlier practice task.

2. Display the message content in the **Reading Pane**, and magnify the Reading Pane content.

3. In your Inbox, locate the **SBS Attachments from Explorer** message.

4. Click the **AttachFiles** attachment to preview its content in the **Reading Pane**. Scroll through the document by using the tools that are available in the **Reading Pane**, and by pressing keyboard keys.

5. Return from the attachment preview to the message content.

6. Save the **AttachFiles** attachment from the message to the practice files folder with the name **AttachCopy2**.

Display message participant information

Display your Inbox, and then perform the following tasks:

1. In your Inbox, locate an email message from another person (preferably some-one in your organization or who you have saved contact information for). Display the message in the **Reading Pane**.

2. In the **Reading Pane**, point to the sender's name or email address. Notice the information that is displayed in the contact card. Then expand the contact card to display more information.

3. From the contact card, initiate an email message to the person. Then close the message window without sending it.

4. If you want to, turn on the display of the **People Pane**. Then experiment with the display of the People Pane in the **Reading Pane** and in received and outgo-ing message windows.

Respond to messages

Display your Inbox, and then perform the following tasks:

1. In your Inbox, locate the **SBS Attachment from Outlook** message that you sent to yourself in an earlier set of practice tasks. Using this email message, do both of the following:

    - Reply to the message. Enter **Test of replying** in the message content, and then send it.

    - Forward the message to yourself. Enter **Test of forwarding** in the message content, and then send it.

2. Open each of the received messages from your Inbox. Notice the difference between the message subjects, and that only the forwarded message contains the original attachment.

3. If you want to, follow the procedures in this chapter to change the way that Outlook handles received messages after you respond to them.

Organize your Inbox

You can use Outlook 2016 to manage multiple email accounts, including multiple Microsoft Exchange Server accounts and their associated contacts, calendars, and other elements. Even if you use Outlook only for sending and receiving email messages, it can be challenging to keep track of them and to locate specific information that you're looking for. Fortunately, Outlook provides many simple yet useful features that you can use to organize messages and other Outlook items and to quickly find information you need.

By default, the message list displays the email messages you receive in order by time and date of receipt (from newest to oldest). You can arrange, group, and sort messages in Outlook to keep conversation threads together and to help you quickly determine which are the most important, decide which can be deleted, and locate any that need an immediate response.

You can simplify the process of organizing Outlook items of all kinds by assigning categories to related items. You can then arrange, sort, filter, and search for Outlook items by category.

This chapter guides you through procedures related to working with Conversation view, arranging messages by specific attributes, organizing items by using color categories, and organizing messages in folders.

In this chapter

- Display and manage conversations
- Arrange messages by specific attributes
- Categorize items
- Organize messages in folders

Practice files

No practice files are necessary to complete the practice tasks in this chapter.

Display and manage conversations

When a recipient replies to an email message, the exchange of multiple messages creates a *conversation*. Conversations that involve multiple recipients and responses can contain many messages. Conversation view is an alternative arrangement of messages grouped by subject. All the messages with the same subject appear together in your Inbox (or other message folder) under one conversation header.

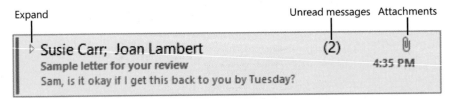

Until you expand the conversation header, the entire conversation takes up only as much space in your Inbox as a single message would

The conversation header provides information about the messages within the conversation, including the number of unread messages and whether one or more messages includes an attachment, is categorized, or is flagged for follow up.

You can display differing levels of messages within a conversation, as follows:

- Click the conversation header or the Expand button once to display the most recent message in the Reading Pane and to display all the unique messages in the conversation (the most recent message in each thread) in the message list. Reading only these messages will give you all the information that exists in the conversation.

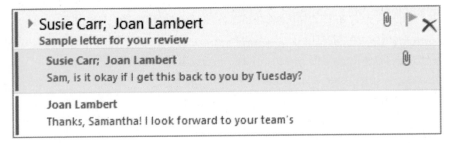

When a conversation is expanded to display unique messages, the conversation header displays recent participants and subjects

- Click the Expand button again to display all messages in the conversation, including messages from your Sent Items folder.

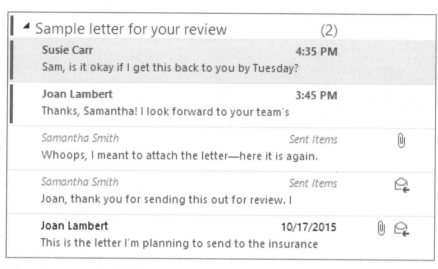

When the conversation is fully expanded, the conversation header displays only the subject

> ✓ **TIP** When an email conversation involves more than two people, particularly if the email was addressed to a large distribution list, often more than one person responds to the same message, and other people respond to each of those messages. Multiple conversations that emerge from the primary conversation are referred to as branches.

Benefits of displaying messages as conversations include the following:

- When you receive a message that is part of a conversation, the entire conversation moves to the top of your Inbox and the new message appears when you click the conversation header.

  A blue vertical line and bold blue subject indicate that a conversation includes unread messages. If there are multiple unread messages, the number is indicated in parentheses following the subject. The senders of the unread messages are listed below the subject.

- Sent messages are available from within the conversation. (They remain stored in the Sent Items folder, but you can read and open them from the Inbox.) This is particularly convenient when you need to access sent attachments that aren't available in the replies.

- You can manage all the messages that are part of a conversation as a group. Clicking the conversation headers selects all the messages in the conversation. You can move or categorize all the messages as a unit.

14

You can modify the way Conversation view displays messages to suit the way you work by turning the following display settings on or off:

- **Show Messages from Other Folders** By default, Conversation view displays messages stored in any folder, including sent messages that are stored in the Sent Items folder. (Within an expanded conversation, sent messages are indicated by an italic font.) You can turn off this setting to display only messages from the current folder.

- **Show Senders Above the Subject** By default, when a conversation is collapsed, the conversation header displays the names of all the conversation participants above the conversation subject; when the conversation is fully expanded, the conversation header displays only the subject. This setting reverses the order of the information in the conversation header; the names of the conversation participants are displayed above the conversation subject. In some cases, such as when Outlook displays a message on the second line, the subject might not be visible at all.

- **Always Expand Conversations** This setting causes Outlook to display all messages in a conversation when you click the Expand Conversation button or conversation header once.

- **Use Classic Indented View** This setting causes Outlook to indent older messages within individual message threads to show the progression of the thread. This setting is not as effective as the default setting for displaying split conversations, because a message might be at the root of multiple branches but can appear only once in the message list.

Outlook tracks conversations by subject regardless of whether you display the messages in Conversation view. You can use the following features to manage conversations:

- **Ignore Conversation** This command moves the selected conversation and any related messages you receive in the future directly to the Deleted Items folder.

> **TIP** Be cautious when using the Ignore Conversation command. Outlook identifies conversations based on message subjects. If you receive unrelated messages in the future that have the same message subject as a conversation that you've chosen to ignore, you won't receive those messages.

- **Clean Up Conversation** This command deletes redundant messages—messages whose text is wholly contained within later messages—from a conversation or folder. By default, Outlook doesn't clean up categorized, flagged, or digitally signed messages. You can modify conversation clean-up settings when you clean up conversations, on the Mail page of the Outlook Options dialog box. For information about modifying mail settings, see "Configure Office and Outlook options" in Chapter 12, "Customize Outlook," of *Microsoft Outlook 2016 Step by Step* by Joan Lambert (Microsoft Press, 2015).

 TIP Because Conversation view displays only unique messages until you fully expand the conversation, a specific message that you're looking for might not be immediately visible. If this happens, you can temporarily disable Conversation view by choosing a different message arrangement. For more information, see "Arrange messages by specific attributes" later in this chapter.

To turn Conversation view on or off for one or all folders

⚠ **IMPORTANT** Conversation view is available only when messages are arranged by date.

1. Do either of the following:

   - On the **View** tab, in the **Messages** group, select or clear the **Show as Conversations** check box.

   - Click the message list header, and then on the menu, click **Show as Conversations**.

Specify the scope of the change

2. In the **Microsoft Outlook** message box, indicate the scope of the change by clicking **All mailboxes** or **This folder**.

 TIP When you arrange a folder by an attribute other than date, Conversation view is temporarily disabled. For more information, see "Arrange messages by specific attributes" later in this chapter.

14

To display the messages within a conversation

1. Click the conversation header or the **Expand** button once to display the unique messages in the conversation.

2. Click the **Expand** button again to display all messages in the conversation.

To select all the messages in a conversation

1. Click the conversation header once.

To change the way conversations are displayed in the message list

1. On the **View** tab, in the **Messages** group, click **Conversation Settings**. On the Conversation Settings menu, a check mark indicates that an option is turned on.

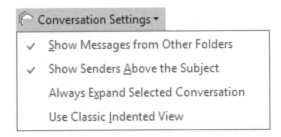

Change the default display settings

2. On the **Conversation Settings** menu, click a setting to turn it on or off.

To remove redundant messages from a conversation

1. Select any message in the conversation.

2. On the **Home** tab, in the **Delete** group, click **Clean Up**, and then on the menu, click **Clean Up Conversation**.

You can change the location to which Outlook moves messages when cleaning up

3. If the Clean Up Conversation message box opens, do the following:

   a. If you want to instruct Outlook to clean up conversations without request-ing confirmation, select the **Don't show this message again** check box.

   b. If you want to change the conversation clean-up settings, click **Settings** to display the Mail page of the Outlook Options dialog box. Scroll to the **Conversation Clean Up** section, and change any of the settings you want to. Then click **OK**.

   Conversation Clean Up

   Cleaned-up items will go to this folder: [   ] Browse...
   Messages moved by Clean Up will go to their account's Deleted Items.
   ☐ When cleaning sub-folders, recreate the folder hierarchy in the destination folder
   ☐ Don't move unread messages
   ☑ Don't move categorized messages
   ☑ Don't move flagged messages
   ☑ Don't move digitally-signed messages
   ☑ When a reply modifies a message, don't move the original

   ---

   You can retain specific categories of messages

   c. Click **Clean Up**.

To remove redundant messages from a folder

1. Select any message in the folder.

2. On the **Home** tab, in the **Delete** group, click **Clean Up**, and then on the menu, click **Clean Up Folder** or **Clean Up Folder & Subfolders**.

3. If the Clean Up Folder message box opens, do the following:

   a. If you want to instruct Outlook to clean up folders without requesting confirmation, select the **Don't show this message again** check box.

   b. If you want to change the conversation clean-up settings, click **Settings** to display the Mail page of the Outlook Options dialog box. Scroll to the **Conversation Clean Up** section, and change any of the settings you want to. Then click **OK**.

   c. Click **Clean Up Folder**.

14

To ignore a conversation

1. Select any message in the conversation, and then do either of the following:

   - On the **Home** tab, in the **Delete** group, click **Ignore**.

   - Press **Ctrl+Del**.

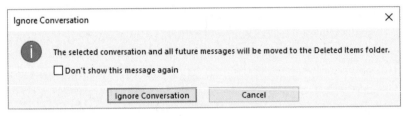

Automatically delete future messages in the conversation

2. If the Ignore Conversation message box opens, do the following:

   a. If you want to instruct Outlook to ignore conversations without requesting confirmation, select the **Don't show this message again** check box.

   b. Click **Ignore Conversation**.

To stop ignoring a conversation

1. Display the **Deleted Items** folder.

2. Locate and select any item in the ignored conversation.

3. On the **Home** tab, in the **Delete** group, the Ignore button is active for a conversation that is being ignored. Click the **Ignore** button to turn it off.

Arrange messages by specific attributes

By default, Outlook displays messages arranged by date, from newest to oldest. Alternatively, you can arrange items by any of the following attributes:

- **Account** Messages are grouped by the email account to which they were sent. This is useful if you receive messages for more than one email account in your Inbox (for example, if you receive messages sent to your POP3 account within your Exchange account mailbox).

- **Attachments** Messages are grouped by whether they have attachments and secondarily by date received.

- **Categories** Messages are arranged by the category you assign to them. Messages without a category appear first. Messages with multiple categories assigned to them appear in each of those category groups.

- **Flag: Start Date or Due Date** Unflagged messages and messages without specific schedules appear first. Messages that you've added to your task list with specific start or due dates are grouped by date.

- **From** Messages appear in alphabetical order by the message sender's display name. If you receive messages from a person who uses two different email accounts, or who sends messages from two different email clients (for example, from Outlook and from Windows Mail), the messages will not necessarily be grouped together.

- **Importance** Messages are grouped by priority: High (indicated by a red exclamation point), Normal (the default), or Low (indicated by a blue downward-pointing arrow).

- **To** Messages are grouped alphabetically by the primary recipients (the addresses or names on the To line). The group name exactly reflects the order in which addresses appear on the To line. Therefore, a message addressed to *Bart Duncan; Lukas Keller* is not grouped with a message addressed to *Lukas Keller; Bart Duncan*.

- **Size** Messages are grouped by size of the message, including any attachments. Groups include Huge (1–5 MB), Very Large (500 KB–1 MB), Large (100–500 KB), Medium (25–100 KB), Small (10–25 KB), and Tiny (less than 10 KB). This feature is useful if you work for an organization that limits the size of your Inbox, because you can easily locate large messages and delete them or move them to a personal folder.

- **Subject** Messages are arranged alphabetically by their subjects and then by date. This is similar to arranging by conversation except that the messages aren't threaded.

- **Type** Items in your Inbox (or other folder) are grouped by the type of item—for example, messages, encrypted messages, message receipts, meeting requests and meeting request responses, tasks, Microsoft InfoPath forms, and server notifications.

After arranging the items in your message list, you can change the sort order of the arrangement. The message list header displays the current sort order and arrangement of the message list.

14

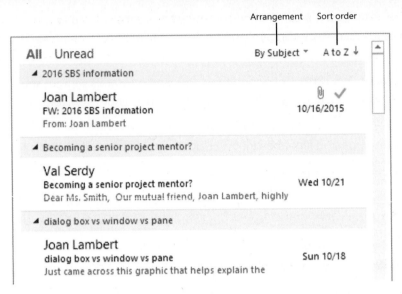

Numbers come before letters when sorting from A to Z

By default, the messages within each arrangement are in groups specific to that category. For example, when messages are arranged by date, they are grouped by date; groups include each day of the current week, Last Week, Two Weeks Ago, Three Weeks Ago, Last Month, and Older. Each group has a header. You can collapse a group so that only the header is visible, or select and process messages by group.

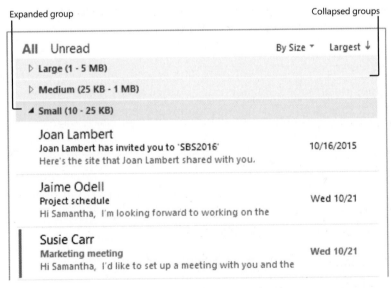

Collapsing groups of messages displays only the group headers

In Single view or Preview view, you can sort messages by any visible column. If you want to sort by an attribute that isn't shown, you can add that column to the view.

To arrange messages by a specific attribute

1. Do any of the following:

   - In any view: On the **View** tab, in the **Arrangement** gallery, click the message attribute.

   - In Compact view: In the message list header, click the current arrangement, and then click the message attribute.

   - In Single view or Preview view: Right-click any column header, click **Arrange By**, and then click the message attribute.

To reverse the default sort order of the message list arrangement

1. Do any of the following:

   - In any view: On the **View** tab, in the **Arrangement** group, click **Reverse Sort**.

   - In Compact view: In the message list header, click the current sort order.

   - In Single view or Preview view: Right-click any column header, and then click **Reverse Sort**.

 TIP In a list view, you can sort by any column by clicking the column header, and reverse the sort order by clicking the column header again.

To group or ungroup messages

1. Do any of the following:

   - In any view: On the **View** tab, in the **Arrangement** gallery, click **Show in Groups**.

   - In Compact view: Click the message list header, and then on the menu, click **Show in Groups**.

   - In Single view or Preview view: Right-click the header of the column you want to group by, and then click **Group By This Field**.

To select a group of messages

1. Click the group header.

14

To expand the current message group

1. Do any of the following:

   - Click the arrow at the left end of the group header.

   - Press the **Right Arrow** key.

   - On the **View** tab, in the **Arrangement** group, click the **Expand/Collapse** button, and then click **Expand This Group**.

To collapse the current message group

1. Do any of the following:

   - Click the arrow at the left end of the group header.

   - Press the **Left Arrow** key.

   - On the **View** tab, in the **Arrangement** group, click the **Expand/Collapse** button, and then click **Collapse This Group**.

To expand or collapse all message groups

1. On the **View** tab, in the **Arrangement** group, click the **Expand/Collapse** button, and then click **Expand All Groups** or **Collapse All Groups**.

To reset the message arrangement (and other view settings)

1. On the **View** tab, in the **Current View** group, click the **Reset View** button.

2. In the **Microsoft Outlook** dialog box, click **Yes**.

Categorize items

To help you more easily locate Outlook items associated with a specific subject, project, person, or other common factor, you can create a category specific to that attribute and assign the category to any related items. You can assign a category to any type of Outlook item, such as a message, an appointment, or a contact record. For example, you might have categories for different people, clients, interest groups, or occasions.

Each category has an associated color, which provides a visual indicator in the item windows and in the module content views. More importantly, the category is a property that you can use to search, sort, and filter items within or across all the Outlook modules.

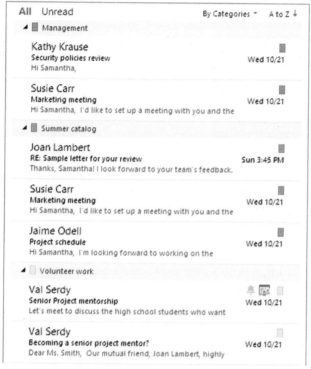

Messages that have multiple categories assigned appear in multiple category groups

Outlook 2016 comes with six starter categories named for their associated colors. You can rename these six categories to suit your needs. If you don't rename a standard color category before assigning it for the first time, Outlook gives you the option of renaming the category the first time you use it.

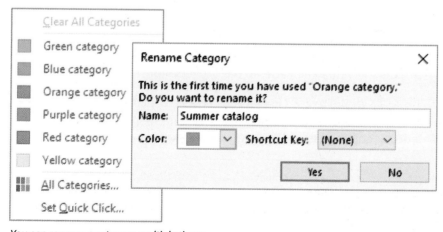

You can rename a category multiple times

14

You can create new categories as you need them. Each category can have the following elements:

- **Name** The category name can be one simple word or a long, descriptive phrase. The first 32 characters of the category name are visible in the Color Categories dialog box, but pointing to a truncated name displays the entire name in a ScreenTip.

- **Shortcut key** You can assign any of the 11 available keyboard shortcut combinations (Ctrl+F2 through Ctrl+F12) to the individual color categories.

- **Color** You can assign any of the 25 available colors to a category, or you can choose not to assign a color and to rely only on the name to distinguish between categories. When you assign a category that doesn't have an associated color to an Outlook item, the color block or color bar is shown as white. You can assign a color to multiple color categories.

Categories that you assign are represented by color blocks in a content list view, and by color bars in the open item window and in the Reading Pane.

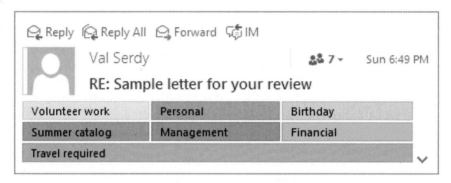

You can assign multiple categories to a message or other item

When Conversation view is on, the conversation header displays all the color category blocks assigned to the individual messages in the conversation.

You can designate one category as the Quick Click category. When displaying items in a view that includes a Categories column—such as Single view or Preview view— clicking the Categories column assigns the Quick Click category.

> **TIP** You can instruct Outlook to automatically assign a category to an incoming message that meets specific criteria by creating a rule. For more information, see "Create rules to process messages" in Chapter 13, "Manage email automatically," of *Microsoft Outlook 2016 Step by Step* by Joan Lambert (Microsoft Press, 2015).

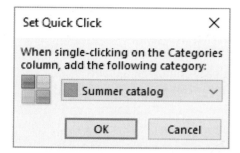

You can apply a category with one click or by using a keyboard shortcut

To quickly view the items that have a specific category assigned to them, you can group items by category or include the category in a search. In a list view of any module, you can sort and filter by category. On the To-Do Bar, you can arrange flagged messages and tasks by category.

To display the Categorize menu

1. Do any of the following:

   - On the **Home** tab of any mail or contact folder, in the **Tags** group, click the **Categorize** button.

   - On the item tool tab (such as **Appointment** or **Meeting**) of any calendar item, in the **Tags** group, click the **Categorize** button.

   - Right-click an item or selection of items, and then click **Categorize**.

The Categorize menu displays recently assigned categories

14

Store information in Outlook notes

You can store miscellaneous information such as reminders, passwords, account numbers, and processes by saving them in electronic notes. Because your notes are available to you from wherever you access Outlook, this can be a very convenient way of retaining information you might need later. And because you're less likely to accidentally delete a note than a message, it is safer than sending information to yourself in an email message.

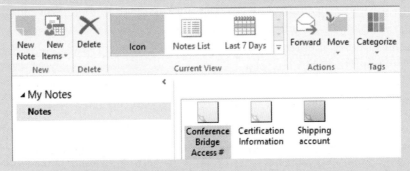

You can categorize notes to easily find them

You can enter only text into a note; you can't format the text or include graphic elements. Notes do support hyperlinks; if you enter a website address and then press Enter, the website address will change to blue underlined text to indicate that it is a hyperlink. You can click the hyperlink to open the website or page in your default web browser.

Although notes are a type of Outlook item, they don't appear in the same type of windows as messages, appointments, contact records, and tasks. Instead, they appear in the form of "sticky notes." By default, note icons and sticky note representations are a pale yellow color, like the color of standard paper sticky notes. When you assign a category to a note, the note color changes to the category color.

You can view, sort, and organize notes in the same way you do other Outlook items. The standard views include Icons, Notes List, and Last 7 Days.

As with other Outlook items, if you're looking for a specific piece of information in a note, you can quickly locate it by entering a search word or phrase in the Search Notes box at the top of the content area.

TIP The first time you access the Notes module, you must do so from the Folder List in the Folder Pane or by clicking Ctrl+5. Thereafter, you can also access it by clicking the ellipsis at the end of the Navigation Bar and then clicking Notes.

To store information in a note:

1. Display the **Notes** module.

2. On the **Home** tab, in the **New** group, click the **New Note** button to display a new note. The current date and time appear at the bottom.

3. Enter the subject or title of the note, press **Enter**, and then enter the information you want to store into the note. The first line of the note becomes its subject.

4. To save and close the note, click the **Close** button in the upper-right corner to display the note in the content area. Only the subject is visible. You can access the stored information by opening the note.

14

To open the Color Categories dialog box

1. Display the **Categorize** menu, and then click **All Categories**.

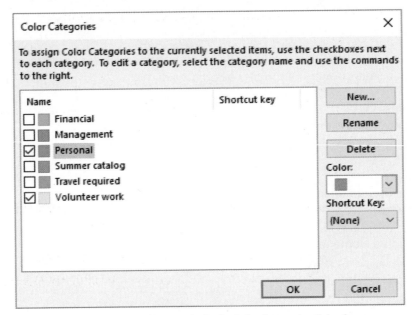

You can manage all aspects of categories in the Color Categories dialog box

To assign a category to a message or other item

1. Select the item or items that you want to categorize.

2. Display the **Categorize** menu, and then do either of the following:

   - If the menu includes the category you want to assign, click the category.

   - If the menu doesn't include the category you want to assign, click **All Categories**. In the **Color Categories** dialog box that opens, select the check box of the category you want to assign, and then click **OK**.

To assign or remove the Quick Click category

1. In any module content list view, click in the **Categories** column for the item.

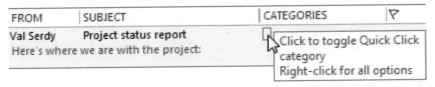

Clicking turns the category on and off

To remove a category from an item

1. Open the item, and then right-click the colored category bar.

2. On the shortcut menu, click **Clear "*Category*"**, **Clear All Categories**, or the name of the category that you want to clear.

Or

1. Select or open the item, and then display the **Categorize** menu.

2. On the **Categorize** menu, click **Clear All Categories**, or click the category that you want to clear.

To create a category

1. Open the **Color Categories** dialog box, and then click **New**.

2. In the **Add New Category** dialog box, do the following, and then click **OK**:

   • In the **Name** box, enter the category name.

   • In the **Color** list, click the color you want to assign to the category.

   • If you want to assign a keyboard shortcut, click it in the **Shortcut Key** list.

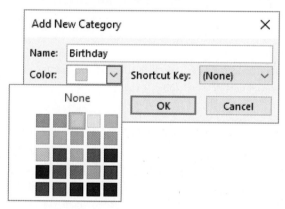

Choose from among 25 colors

14

To rename a category

1. Open the **Color Categories** dialog box.

2. Click the name or select the check box of the category, and then click **Rename** to activate the category name for editing.

3. Change or replace the category name, and then press **Enter** or click away from the active name box.

TIP The category order doesn't immediately change, but the next time you display the categories in a list or dialog box, they will be in alphabetical order.

To delete a category

1. Open the **Color Categories** dialog box.

2. Click the name or select the check box of the category, and then click **Delete** or press **Alt+D**.

3. In the **Microsoft Outlook** message box asking you to confirm the deletion, click **Yes**.

To set or change the Quick Click category

1. Display the **Categorize** menu, and then click **Set Quick Click**.

2. In the **Set Quick Click** dialog box, click the list, click the category that you want to set as the default, and then click **OK**.

Or

1. Open the **Outlook Options** dialog box, and display the **Advanced** page.

2. Scroll down on the Advanced page to display the **Other** section, and then click the **Quick Click** button.

3. In the **Set Quick Click** dialog box, click the list, click the category that you want to set as the default, and then click **OK**.

Organize messages in folders

After you read and respond to messages, you might want to keep some for future reference. You can certainly choose to retain them all in your Inbox if you want, but as the number of messages in your Inbox increases to the thousands and even tens of thousands, it might quickly become overwhelming. (Yes, faithful reader, it happens to the best of us!) To minimize your Inbox contents and avoid an accumulation of unrelated messages, you can organize messages into folders. For example, you can keep messages that require action on your part in your Inbox and move messages that you want to retain for future reference into other folders.

 TIP Because the Outlook search function provides the option of searching within all folders containing items of a particular type, you can easily locate a message that's been moved to a folder without having to remember which folder it's in.

Popular personal-organization experts advocate various folder structures (for paper folders and email message folders) as an important part of an organizational system. You can apply any of these ideas when you create folders in Outlook, or you can use any other structure that works for you. For example, you might create folders that designate the level of action required, create a folder for each project you're working on, or create a folder to store all messages from a specific person, such as your manager, regardless of the message subject.

Subfolders of the Inbox, in the Navigation pane of the Mail module and in the Folders list

When you create a folder, you specify the location of the folder within your existing Outlook folder structure and the type of items you want the folder to contain. You can create folders to contain the following types of items:

- Calendar items
- Contact items
- InfoPath Form items
- Journal items
- Mail and Post items
- Note items
- Task items

The selection you make governs the folder icon that precedes its name in the Folder Pane, the folder window layout, the ribbon tabs and commands available in the folder, and the content of the Folder Pane when displaying the folder.

You can move messages to folders manually, or if your organization is running Exchange, you can have the email system move them for you. You can automatically move messages to another folder by creating a rule—for example, you can automatically move all messages received from your manager to a separate folder. You can also set up different rules that go into effect when you're away from the office.

> **SEE ALSO** For information about automatically moving messages, see "Create rules to process messages" in Chapter 13, "Manage email automatically," of *Microsoft Outlook 2016 Step by Step* by Joan Lambert (Microsoft Press, 2015).

To create a message folder

1. Do either of the following to open the **Create New Folder** dialog box:

   - On the **Folder** tab, in the **New** group, click the **New Folder** button.
   - Press **Ctrl+Shift+E**.

The default settings in the Create New Folder dialog box match the module you open it from

2. In the **Name** box, enter a name for the new folder.

3. In the **Folder contains** list, click **Mail and Post Items**.

4. In the **Select where to place the folder** box, do either of the following:

   - Click your mailbox (at the top of the list) to create the folder at the same level as the Inbox.

   - Click your **Inbox** to create a subfolder of the Inbox.

5. Click **OK**.

To move a message to a folder

1. Drag the message from the message list to the destination folder in the **Folder Pane**.

Or

1. In the message list, select the message you want to move.

2. Do either of the following to display the **Move** menu:

   - On the **Home** tab, in the **Move** group, click the **Move** button.

   - Right-click the message, and then click **Move**.

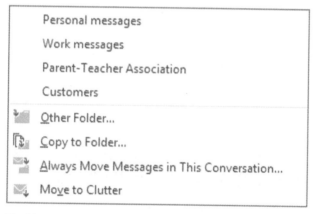

The Move menu automatically includes folders that you create

3. On the **Move** menu, do either of the following:

   - Click the folder you want to move the message to.

   - Click **Other Folder**. In the **Move Items** dialog box displaying the full Folders list, click the folder you want to move the message to, and then click **OK**.

> **TIP** When Conversation view is turned on, moving the last message of a conversation from a folder removes the conversation from that folder.

14

Print messages

Although electronic communications certainly have less of an environmental impact than paper-based communications, you might at times want or need to print an email message—for example, if you want to take a hard copy of it to a meeting for reference, or if you keep a physical file of important messages or complimentary feedback. You can print the message exactly as it appears in your Inbox or embellish it with page headers and footers. Outlook prints messages in Memo style, which prints your name, the message header information, and then the message content as shown on the screen, including font and paragraph formats.

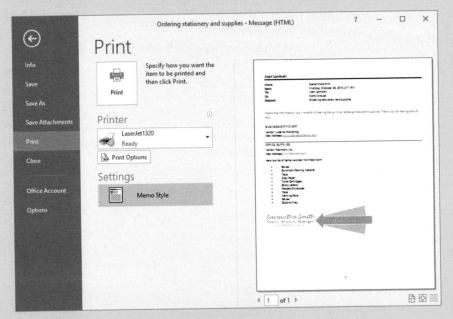

You can preview the message and modify the print settings

To preview and print a message, follow these steps:

1. In an open message window, display the **Print** page of the Backstage view. The right pane displays the message as it will appear when printed. In the **Printer** list, click the printer you want to use. Then do either of the following:

   - To print one copy of the message with the default settings, click the **Print** button.

   - To print only specific pages, print multiple copies, or print attachments, click the **Print Options** button, change the settings in the **Print** dialog box, and then click **Print**.

To print a message with the default settings, right-click the message in the message list, and then click Quick Print.

Skills review

In this chapter, you learned how to:

- Display and manage conversations
- Arrange messages by specific attributes
- Categorize items
- Organize messages in folders

14

Practice tasks

No practice files are necessary to complete the practice tasks in this chapter.

> ⚠ **IMPORTANT** As you work through the practice tasks in this book, you will create Outlook items that might be used as practice files for tasks in later chapters. If you haven't created specific items that are referenced in later chapters, you can substitute items of your own.

Display and manage conversations

Start Outlook, display your Inbox in Compact view, and complete the following tasks:

1. Display the messages in your Inbox as conversations. Notice the changes in the appearance and grouping of the messages in the message list.

2. Change the conversation settings so that the senders are shown below the subject in the message list instead of above it. Consider the benefits of the two options.

3. Select one conversation that has several messages, display the unique messages in the conversation, and then display all the messages in the conversation.

4. Remove redundant messages from the conversation.

5. Select any message in the conversation, and open the **Ignore Conversation** dialog box. Read the message in the dialog box, and then click **Cancel**.

6. Configure the conversation settings to suit your preferences.

Arrange messages by specific attributes

Display your Inbox in Preview view, and then complete the following tasks:

1. Use any method described in this chapter to arrange messages by sender (*From*).

2. Use any method described in this chapter to reverse the default sort order of the message list arrangement.

3. Switch to Compact view. Notice that the messages are no longer arranged by sender; the arrangement is only applied to the view in which you set it.

4. Use any method described in this chapter to group the messages in your Inbox.

5. Collapse a group of messages so that only the group header is displayed, and then expand the group again.

6. Collapse all message groups, and then expand them all.

7. Configure the view and arrangement settings to suit your preferences.

Categorize items

Display your Inbox in Compact view, and then complete the following tasks:

1. Create a new email message addressed to yourself. Enter **Work with categories** as the subject, and send the message.

2. When the message appears in your Inbox, select it.

3. Create a new color category, and do the following:

   - Name the category **StepByStep**.

   - Assign the **Dark Maroon** color to the category.

   - Assign the **Ctrl+F10** keyboard shortcut to the category.

4. Finish creating the category, and close any open dialog boxes. Notice that the selected message now has the StepByStep category assigned to it.

5. Set the **StepByStep** category as the Quick Click category.

6. Switch to Single view. In the message list, point to an unassigned category block in the **Categories** column to display the ScreenTip.

7. Click the block to assign the Quick Click category to the message. Then click again to remove the category.

Organize messages in folders

Display your Inbox, and complete the following tasks:

1. Create a new folder, and do the following:

   - Name the folder **StepByStep**.

   - Configure the folder to contain messages.

   - Save the folder as a subfolder of your Inbox.

2. Finish creating the folder. Then move the **Work with categories** message that you created in an earlier set of practice tasks to the **StepByStep** folder.

3. Retain the folder, message, and category for use in practice tasks in later chapters.

Manage scheduling

15

You can use the Outlook 2016 calendar to organize your daily activities and to remind you of important tasks and events. If you're a busy person and use the Outlook calendar to its fullest potential, it might at times seem as though the calendar runs your life—but that isn't necessarily a bad thing! Using the calendar effectively can help you stay organized, on time, and on task. You can schedule and track appointments, meetings, and events, and block time as a reminder to yourself to take care of tasks. And because you can also set up Outlook on your mobile device, you can be assured of having up-to-date schedule information available wherever and whenever you need it.

If you have a Microsoft Exchange Server account, a calendar is part of that account. Some Internet email accounts also have associated calendars. When you configure Outlook to connect to a different type of account, Outlook also connects to the associated calendar. If you don't have a calendar as part of your account, Outlook creates a blank calendar for you. You can easily schedule appointments, events, and meetings on any Outlook calendar.

This chapter guides you through procedures related to scheduling and changing appointments, events, and meetings; responding to meeting requests; and displaying different views of a calendar.

In this chapter

- Schedule appointments and events
- Convert calendar items
- Configure calendar item options
- Schedule and change meetings
- Respond to meeting requests
- Display different views of a calendar

Practice files

No practice files are necessary to complete the practice tasks in this chapter.

Schedule appointments and events

Appointments are blocks of time you schedule for only yourself (as opposed to meetings, to which you invite other Outlook users). An appointment has a specific start time and end time (as opposed to an event, which occurs for one or more full 24-hour periods).

Events are day-long blocks of time that you schedule on your Outlook calendar, such as birthdays, payroll days, or anything else occurring on a specific day but not at a specific time. In all other respects, creating an event is identical to creating an appointment, in that you can specify a location, indicate recurrence, indicate your availability, and attach additional information to the event item.

You can schedule an appointment by entering, at minimum, a subject and time in an appointment window or directly on the calendar. The basic appointment window also includes a field for the appointment location and a notes area in which you can store general information, including formatted text, website links, and even file attachments so that they are readily available to you at the time of the appointment.

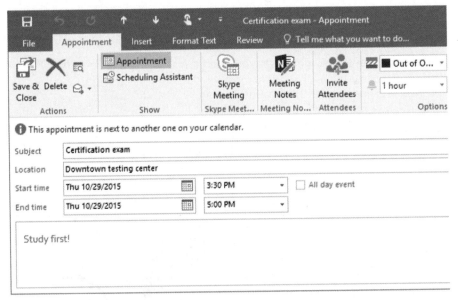

If your organization has Skype For Business, Skype meeting options appear on the Appointment tab

If you create an appointment that immediately follows or precedes another, the Info-Bar at the top of the window indicates that the appointment is adjacent to another on your calendar. If you create an appointment that has a time overlap with an existing appointment, the InfoBar indicates that the appointment conflicts with another.

To schedule an event, you need to provide only the date. You can schedule an event in an appointment window, or directly on the calendar.

 TIP You don't have to create appointments and events from scratch; you can also create them from email messages. For information, see "Convert calendar items" later in this chapter.

When the Calendar view is displayed, events are shown on the calendar in the date area; appointments are displayed in the time slots.

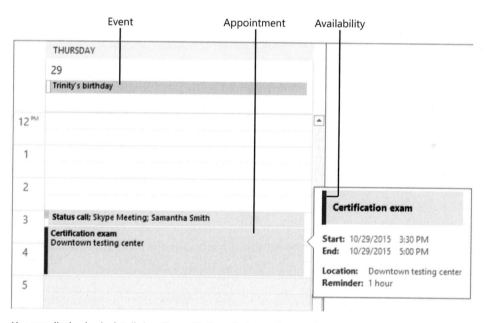

You can display basic details in a ScreenTip by pointing to the appointment or event

 SEE ALSO For information about setting availability, see "Configure calendar item options" later in this chapter.

15

⚠ **IMPORTANT** The procedures in this chapter assume that you're working with an Exchange account. Some functionality might be unavailable if you're working with a calendar that's part of another type of account.

To open a new appointment window

1. In the Calendar module, do either of the following:

    -   On the **Home** tab, in the **New** group, click **New Appointment**.
    -   Press **Ctrl+N**.

Or

1. In any module, do either of the following:

    -   On the **Home** tab, in the **New** group, click **New Items**, and then click **Appointment**.
    -   Press **Ctrl+Shift+A**.

To schedule an appointment

1. Open a new appointment window.
2. In the **Subject** box, enter an identifying name for the appointment.
3. In the **Location** box, enter the appointment location, if it's pertinent, or any other information that you want to have available in the appointment header.
4. In the **Start time** row, enter or select a date and time. Outlook automatically sets the End Time to a half hour after the start time.
5. In the **End time** row, enter or select a date and time. An appointment can span overnight or across multiple days.
6. On the **Appointment** tab, in the **Actions** group, click the **Save & Close** button.

Or

1. Display the calendar in the Day, Work Week, or Week arrangement of the Calendar view.
2. Do either of the following in the calendar pane:

    -   In the calendar, click the time slot at the appointment start time on the day of the appointment.
    -   Drag from the appointment start time through to the appointment end time.

FRIDAY

30

8 AM

9

10

11

Schedule simple appointments directly on the calendar

When you release the mouse button, Outlook displays an editable bar that spans the selected time (or one time slot, as specified by the time scale of the calendar).

> **SEE ALSO** For information about setting the calendar time scale, see "Display different views of a calendar" later in this chapter.

3. In the editable bar, enter an identifying name for the appointment. When you begin typing, Outlook creates an appointment with the default availability and reminder time.

Dentist appointment

When an appointment is being edited on the calendar, it has sizing handles on the top and bottom

15

4. If you want to change the appointment time span, drag the top or bottom sizing handle.

5. Press **Enter** or click away from the bar to create the appointment.

Add holidays to your calendar

Holidays are a type of event, and it can be useful to have them on your calendar so you can plan around days that you might not be working or that businesses might be closed. Instead of creating events on your calendar for individual holidays, you can have Outlook add them for you.

When adding holidays to the calendar, you can choose from 111 countries or regions, and four religions. You can add multiple sets of holidays to your calendar, so if you work with clients or colleagues in another location, you can add those holidays to your calendar so you can anticipate scheduling issues.

To add holidays to your Outlook calendar, follow these steps:

1. Open the **Outlook Options** dialog box and display the **Calendar** page.

2. In the **Calendar options** section, click the **Add Holidays** button to open the **Add Holidays to Calendar** dialog box.

You can add holidays from a specific location or religion to your calendar

3. Select the check boxes of the locations or religions whose holidays you want to add to your calendar, and then click **OK**.

4. After Outlook adds the selected holidays to your calendar, click **OK** to close the **Outlook Options** dialog box.

TIP If you try to install the holidays of the same location or religion twice, Outlook notifies you of this and asks whether you want to import them again. If you inadvertently add the same set of holidays to the calendar twice, the easiest way to rectify the situation is to remove all occurrences of that location's holidays and then add them again.

Outlook adds the holiday occurrences from 2012 through 2022 to your calendar, and assigns a color category named *Holiday* to them.

SEE ALSO For information about categories, see "Categorize items" in Chapter 14, "Organize your Inbox."

To remove a set of holidays from your calendar, follow these steps:

1. Search the calendar for category:holiday. Narrow the search to a specific location or holiday by adding search criteria if necessary, to locate the holidays you want to remove.

		SUBJECT	LOCA...	START	END	CATEGORIES	
		New Year's Day	Italy	Mon 1/1/...	Tue 1/2/2...	■ Holiday	
		Epiphany	Italy	Sat 1/6/20...	Sun 1/7/...	■ Holiday	
		Good Friday	Italy	Fri 3/30/2...	Sat 3/31/...	■ Holiday	
		Easter Sunday	Italy	Sun 4/1/2...	Mon 4/2/...	■ Holiday	
		Easter Monday	Italy	Mon 4/2/...	Tue 4/3/2...	■ Holiday	
		Liberation Day	Italy	Wed 4/25...	Thu 4/26...	■ Holiday	
		Labor Day	Italy	Tue 5/1/2...	Wed 5/2/...	■ Holiday	
		Republic Day	Italy	Sat 6/2/20...	Sun 6/3/...	■ Holiday	
		Assumption	Italy	Wed 8/15...	Thu 8/16...	■ Holiday	

search box: `category:holiday location:italy`

Outlook highlights the search terms in the results

2. Select individual holidays you want to remove; or click any holiday in the list to activate the list, and then press **Ctrl+A** to select all the holidays in the search results. Then press the **Delete** key.

15

To schedule an event

1. Open a new appointment window.

2. In the **Subject** box, enter an identifying name for the event.

3. In the **Location** box, enter the event location, if it's pertinent, or any other information that you want to have available in the event header.

4. In the **Start time** row, enter or select the event date. Then at the right end of the row, select the **All day event** check box.

5. Enter any additional information as you would for an appointment. Then save and close the event.

Or

1. Display the Calendar view of the calendar.

2. Do either of the following:

   - In the Day, Work Week, or Week arrangement of the calendar, on the day that you want to create the event, click the space below the day and date, and above the time slots. This is the event slot.

   - In the Month arrangement of the calendar, click the day that you want to create the event.

3. Enter a title for the event, and then press **Enter**.

Convert calendar items

All Outlook calendar items are built from the same basic template. These two factors define a calendar item as an appointment, event, or meeting:

- Whether the item has specific start and end times or is all day

- Whether you invite other people through Outlook

You can easily convert an appointment into an event or meeting, or convert an event into an appointment or an invited event.

If you want to schedule an appointment, event, or meeting based on the information in an email message that you receive, you can easily do so by dragging the message to the calendar. For example, if a friend or co-worker sends you a message that contains the details of the grand opening for a local art gallery, you can add that information to your calendar. You can retain any or all of the message information as part of the calendar item so that you (or other meeting participants) have the information on hand when you need it. After creating the calendar item, you can delete the actual message from your Inbox.

To create an appointment from an email message

1. Display your Inbox.

2. Drag the message from the message list to the **Calendar** link or button on the **Navigation Bar**.

3. After the cursor changes to a plus sign, release the mouse button to create an appointment based on the message and open the appointment window for editing. The appointment has the subject and content of the original message. The start and end times are set to the next half-hour increment following the current time.

4. Set the date and times for the appointment, and do any of the following:

   - In the **Options** group, change the availability, reminder time, or recurrence.

   - In the **Tags** group, assign a category to the appointment, mark it as private, or change the priority.

   - In the content pane, edit the original message content to suit the requirements of the appointment.

5. In the appointment window, click the **Save & Close** button to save the appointment to your calendar.

> **SEE ALSO** For information about adding message content to your To-Do List, see "Create tasks" in Chapter 11, "Track tasks," of *Microsoft Outlook 2016 Step by Step* by Joan Lambert (Microsoft Press, 2015).

15

To convert an appointment to an event

1. Open the appointment window.

2. At the right end of the **Start time** row, select the **All day event** check box.

3. Change the event date, options, or tags, and then save and close the event window.

To convert an appointment to a meeting

1. Open the appointment window.

2. On the **Appointment** tab in the **Attendees** group, click the **Invite Attendees** button to add a To box to the header and display the meeting window features.

3. Enter contact information for the people you want to invite to the meeting.

4. Add a location if necessary, and then click the **Send Invitation** button.

To convert an event to an invited event

1. Open the event window.

2. On the **Event** tab, in the **Attendees** group, click the **Invite Attendees** button to add a To box to the header and display the meeting window features.

3. Enter contact information for the people you want to invite to the event.

4. Add a location if necessary, and then click the **Send Invitation** button.

To convert an event to an appointment

1. Open the event window.

2. At the right end of the **Start time** row, clear the **All day event** check box.

3. Set the appointment start and end times, and change the options as necessary. Then save and close the appointment window.

Configure calendar item options

Appointments, events, and meetings share many common elements, and you use the same techniques to work with those options in all types of calendar items. The five options that you can configure for all items are:

- **Time zones** You can specify the time zone in which an appointment, event, or meeting occurs. This helps to ensure that the start and end times are clearly defined when you're traveling or inviting people in multiple time zones to an online meeting. You have the option of specifying different time zones for the start time and the finish time. This is useful when your "appointment" is an airplane flight with departure and arrival cities located in different time zones, and you want the flight to show up correctly wherever you're currently located.

- **Availability** When creating an appointment or event, you indicate your availability (referred to as *Free/Busy time*) by marking it as Free, Working Elsewhere, Tentative, Busy, or Out Of Office. The appointment or event is color-coded on your calendar to match the availability you indicate. Your availability is visible to other Outlook users on your network and is also displayed when you share your calendar or send calendar information to other people.

  The default availability for new appointments and meetings is Busy, and for events is Free.

  > **SEE ALSO** For information about sharing your calendar with other Outlook users on your network and about sending your schedule information in an email message, see "Share calendar information" in Chapter 10, "Manage your calendar," of *Microsoft Outlook 2016 Step by Step* by Joan Lambert (Microsoft Press, 2015).

- **Reminder** By default, Outlook displays a reminder message 15 minutes before the start time of an appointment or meeting, or 12 hours before an event (at noon the preceding day). You can change the reminder to occur as far as two weeks in advance, or you can turn it off completely if you want to. If you synchronize your Outlook installation with a mobile device, reminders also appear on your mobile device. This is very convenient when you are away from your computer.

  > **TIP** Reminders can be indicated on the calendar by a bell icon. This option is turned off by default in Outlook 2016. You can turn it on in the Calendar Options section of the Calendar page of the Outlook Options dialog box.

- **Recurrence** If you have the same appointment, event, or meeting on a regular basis—for example, a weekly exercise class, a monthly team meeting, or an anniversary—you can set it up in your Outlook calendar as a recurring item. A recurring calendar item can happen at almost any regular interval, such as every Tuesday and Thursday, every other week, or the last weekday of every month.

15

Configuring a recurrence creates multiple instances of the item on your calendar at the time interval you specify. You can set the item to recur until further notice, to end after a certain number of occurrences, or to end by a certain date. The individual occurrences of the recurring item are linked. When making changes to a recurring item, you can choose to update all occurrences or only an individual occurrence of the appointment.

Recurring items are indicated on the calendar by circling arrows.

- **Privacy** You can tag a calendar item as Private if you want to ensure that the details aren't displayed when you share your calendar or send calendar information to other people.

  Private items are indicated on the calendar by a lock, and identified to other people as Private Appointment rather than by the subject.

You can specify time zones, your availability, the reminder time, and the recurrence, and mark an item as private, when you create the item. Alternatively, you can edit the item later and configure any of these options. The time zone can be specified only in the item window; the other options can be set on the item type–specific tab in the item window or the item type–specific tool tab that appears on the Outlook ribbon when you select an item on the calendar. In single-occurrence items, these tabs are labeled Appointment, Event, Meeting, or Invited Event. In recurring items, the tab names include Occurrence or Series to indicate whether you're editing one or all occurrences of the item.

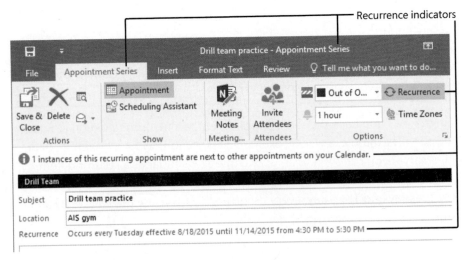

Outlook evaluates recurring items and provides information

You can assign categories and importance to appointments, events, and meetings in the same way that you do to messages and other Outlook items. In some ways, categories are more useful in the Calendar than in other modules.

SUNDAY	MONDAY	TUESDAY	WEDNESDAY	THURSDAY	FRIDAY	SATURDAY
Dec 27	28	29	30	31	**Jan 1, 16**	2
3	4	5	6	7	8	9
10	11	12	13	14	15	16

Color categories provide information at a glance about your schedule.

To specify the time zone of an appointment or meeting

1. Open the item window.

2. On the **Appointment** or **Meeting** tab, in the **Options** group, click the **Time Zones** button to display the time zone controls in the Start Time and End Time rows. The time zone controls display the time zone your computer is currently set to.

3. Click the time zone control that you want to change, and then click the time zone.

Subject	Flight to Seattle		
Location			
Start time	Tue 12/8/2015	9:40 AM	Central Time (US & Canada)
End time	Tue 12/8/2015	11:35 AM	Pacific Time (US & Canada)

Set the time zones to ensure that the time is accurate from any location

To hide the time zone controls

1. Select identical entries in the **Start time** and **End time** time zone controls.

2. On the **Appointment** or **Meeting** tab, in the **Options** group, click the **Time Zones** button to remove the controls.

15

To modify an appointment, event, or meeting

1. Display the calendar in the Day, Work Week, or Week arrangement of the Calendar view, with the appointment visible.

2. In the calendar pane, click the item once to select it. Then do any of the following:

   - On the item type–specific tool tab, make any changes to the options or tags.

   - Drag the item from the current time slot to a new time slot.

   - Drag the top sizing handle to change an appointment start time.

   - Drag the bottom sizing handle to change an appointment end time.

3. To open the item window, in which you can make other changes, do either of the following:

   - Press **Enter**.

   - On the item type–specific tool tab, in the **Actions** group, click **Open**.

To indicate your availability during an appointment, event, or meeting

1. Open the item window, or select the item on the calendar.

2. On the item-specific tab or tool tab, in the **Options** group, click the **Show As** list, and then click the availability.

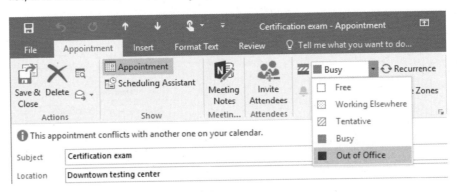

The default availability for appointments is Busy

To change the default reminder for an appointment, event, or meeting

1. Open the item window, or select the item on the calendar.

2. On the item-specific tab or tool tab, in the **Options** group, click the **Reminder** list, and then click the time (or click None to have no reminder).

To create recurrences of an appointment, event, or meeting

1. Open the item window, or select the item on the calendar.

2. On the item-specific tab or tool tab, in the **Options** group, click the **Recurrence** button to open the Recurrence dialog box. The default recurrence is weekly on the currently selected day of the week.

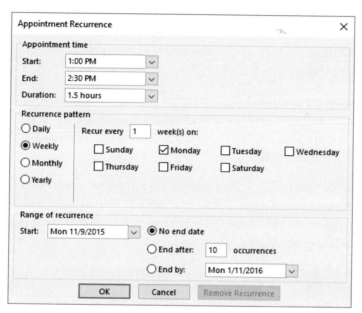

When configuring a recurrence, you can change the times, days, and frequency from the Appointment Recurrence dialog box

3. In the **Recurrence** dialog box, do any of the following:

   - In the **End** list, click the arrow and select an end time for the recurring meeting.

   - In the **Recurrence pattern** section, select how often you want the meeting to recur.

   - In the **Range of recurrence** section, select how many times you want to the meeting to occur, or select the last date you want the meeting to recur.

4. Click **OK** in the **Recurrence** dialog box to replace the Start Time and End Time fields in the appointment window with the recurrence details.

15

Schedule and change meetings

A primary difficulty when scheduling a meeting is finding a time that works for all the people who need to attend it. Scheduling meetings through Outlook is significantly simpler than other methods of scheduling meetings, particularly when you need to accommodate the schedules of several people. Outlook displays the individual and collective schedules of people within your own organization, and of people outside of your organization who have published their calendars to the Internet. You can review attendees' schedules to locate a time when everyone is available, or have Outlook find a convenient time for you.

You can send an Outlook meeting invitation (referred to as a *meeting request*) to anyone who has an email account—even to a person who doesn't use Outlook. You can send a meeting request from any type of email account (such as an Exchange account or an Internet email account).

The meeting window has two pages: the Appointment page and the Scheduling Assistant page. The Appointment page is visible by default. You can enter all the required information directly on the Appointment page, or use the additional features available on the Scheduling Assistant page to find the best time for the meeting.

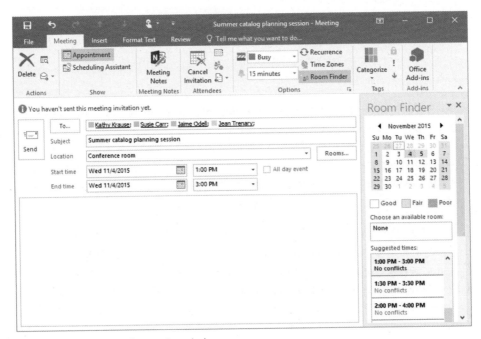

The Appointment page of a meeting window

The Room Finder is open by default on the right side of each page of the meeting window. This handy tool helps you to identify dates and times that work for the greatest number of attendees, in addition to available locations. The monthly calendar at the top of the Room Finder indicates the collective availability of the group on each day, as follows:

- Dates that occur in the past and nonworking days are unavailable (gray).

- Days when all attendees are available are Good (white).

- Days when most attendees are available are Fair (light blue).

- Days when most attendees are not available are Poor (medium blue).

> **TIP** All the capabilities of the Room Finder are available for Exchange accounts, but functionality is limited for other types of accounts. You can display or hide the Room Finder pane by clicking the Room Finder button in the Options group on the Meeting tab.

Managed conference rooms that are available at the indicated meeting time are shown in the center of the Room Finder. At the bottom of the Room Finder pane, the Suggested Times list displays attendee availability for appointments of the length of time you have specified for the meeting.

Selecting a date in the calendar displays the suggested meeting times for just that day. (Scheduling suggestions are not provided for past or nonworking days.) Clicking a meeting time in the Suggested Times list updates the calendar and the meeting request.

People you invite to meetings are referred to as *attendees*. By default, the attendance of each attendee is indicated as Required. You can inform noncritical attendees of the meeting by marking their attendance as Optional. You can invite entire groups of people by using a contact group or distribution list. You can also invite managed resources, such as conference rooms and audio/visual equipment, that have been set up by your organization's Exchange administrator.

A meeting request should have at least one attendee other than you, and it must have a start time and an end time. It should also include a subject and a location, but Outlook will send the meeting request without this information if you specifically allow it. The body of a meeting request can include text and web links, and you can also attach files. This is a convenient way to distribute meeting information to attendees ahead of time.

15

The secondary page of the meeting window is the Scheduling Assistant page, if your email account is part of an Exchange Server network. Otherwise, the secondary page is the Scheduling page, which doesn't include the Room Finder feature.

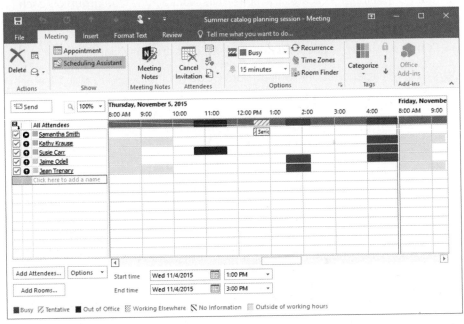

If you're organizing a meeting for a large number of people, you can view collective information about their schedules on the Scheduling or Scheduling Assistant page

The Scheduling and Scheduling Assistant pages include a group schedule that shows the status of each attendee's time throughout your working day. Outlook indicates your suggested meeting time on the group schedule. If free/busy information is available for meeting attendees, the status is indicated by the standard free/busy colors and patterns that match the legend at the bottom of the page. If no information is available (either because Outlook can't connect to an attendee's calendar or because the proposed meeting is further out than the scheduling information stored on the server), Outlook shows the time with gray diagonal stripes. The row at the top of the schedule, to the right of the All Attendees heading, indicates the collective schedule of all the attendees.

> **TIP** You can enter additional attendees in the To box on the Appointment page or in the All Attendees list on the Scheduling or Scheduling Assistant page. You can also add attendees by clicking the To button on the Appointment page or the Add Attendees button on the Scheduling or Scheduling Assistant page, and then selecting attendees from an address box.

You can change the time and duration of the meeting to work with the displayed schedules by selecting a different time in the Start Time and End Time lists, by dragging the vertical start time and end time bars in the group schedule, or by clicking the time you want in the Suggested Times list.

> **SEE ALSO** For information about creating a meeting request from an email message, see "Convert calendar items" earlier in this chapter.

Outlook tracks responses from attendees and those responsible for scheduling the resources you requested, so you always have an up-to-date report of how many people will attend your meeting. The number of attendees who have accepted, tentatively accepted, and declined the meeting request appears in the meeting header section when you open a meeting in its own window.

You might find it necessary to change the date, time, or location of a meeting after you send the meeting request, or to add or remove attendees. As the meeting organizer, you can change any information in a meeting request at any time, including adding or removing attendees, or canceling the meeting. Meeting attendees receive updates. Changes to meeting details are tracked so that attendees can quickly identify them.

To open a new meeting window

1. Do any of the following:

   - On the **Home** tab of the Calendar module, in the **New** group, click **New Meeting**.

   - On the **Home** tab of any module, in the **New** group, click **New Items**, and then click **Meeting**.

   - In any module, press **Ctrl+Shift+Q**.

15

To create a meeting request

1. Open a new meeting window.

2. In the **To** box, enter contact information for the attendees.

3. In the **Subject** box, enter an identifying name for the meeting.

4. In the **Location** box, enter the meeting location. If your organization uses Skype for Business, you can click the Skype Meeting button on the Meeting toolbar to enter Skype meeting information in the Location box and content pane.

5. In the **Start time** row, enter or select a date and time. Outlook automatically sets the End Time to a half hour after the start time.

6. In the **End time** row, enter or select a date and time. A meeting can span overnight or across multiple days.

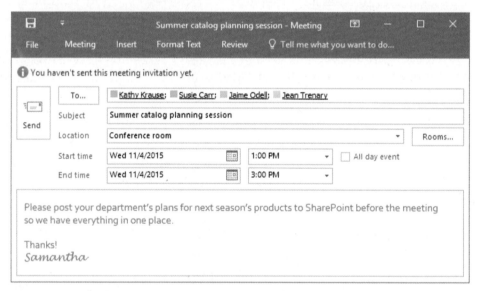

A basic meeting request

7. Verify the meeting details, and then click the **Send** button to add the meeting to your calendar and send the meeting request to the attendees.

To identify times that colleagues are available for meetings

> ⚠️ **IMPORTANT** This procedure is for Outlook users with Exchange email accounts. Free/busy time is available only for attendees in your organization or another connected organization, or attendees that share free/busy information through a web service.

1. On the **Meeting** tab, in the **Show** group, click the **Scheduling Assistant** button. The **All Attendees** list on the **Scheduling Assistant** page includes you and any attendees you entered in the **To** box. The icon next to your name, a magnifying glass in a black circle, indicates that you are the meeting organizer. The icon next to each attendee's name, an upward-pointing arrow in a red circle, indicates that he or she is a required attendee.

   > ✓ **TIP** If you're inviting someone as a courtesy, you can indicate that he or she does not need to attend by clicking the Required Attendee icon to the left of the attendee's name and then, in the list, clicking Optional Attendee.

2. If necessary, scroll to the bottom of the **Room Finder** to display the **Suggested times** list. The times shown are based on your schedule and the schedule information that is available for the attendees.

3. To add attendees, enter their email addresses in the **All Attendees** list, and then press **Tab** to update the Suggested Times list in the Room Finder.

4. If you need to change the meeting time or duration, you can do so by dragging the start time and end time bars on the group schedule or by entering times in the boxes below the group schedule.

5. Click the **Appointment** button in the **Show** group to return to the Appointment page, which reflects the current attendees and meeting times.

6. Verify the meeting details, and then click the **Send** button to add the meeting to your calendar and send the meeting request to the attendees.

15

To edit a meeting request

1. Open the meeting window for editing.

2. If the meeting is one of a series (a recurring meeting), Outlook prompts you to indicate whether you want to edit the meeting series or only the selected instance of the meeting. Click **Just this one** or **The entire series**.

3. Modify the date, time, notes, options, or attendees. Then click the **Send Update** button.

4. If you modified the attendees, Outlook prompts you to specify whether to send updates to all attendees or only to the changed attendees. Click one of the following to send the meeting updates:

   - Send updates only to added or deleted attendees

   - Send updates to all attendees

 TIP You don't need to cancel and reschedule a meeting to change the date or time, or to add or remove an attendee. You can edit the meeting request, remove the attendee, and then send a meeting update to the affected attendees.

To cancel a meeting or a meeting occurrence

1. Select the meeting on your calendar, or open the meeting window.

2. Do either of the following:

   - On the **Meeting** tool tab, in the **Actions** group, click the **Cancel Meeting** button.

   - On the **Meeting Series** tool tab, in the **Actions** group, click the **Cancel Meeting** button, and then click **Cancel Occurrence** or **Cancel Series**.

 TIP The Cancel Meeting button is available only for meetings that you organize, not for meetings you're invited to.

A meeting window containing cancellation information opens.

Cancellation information

Cancelling a meeting removes it from attendees' calendars

3. Do either of the following:

   - In the meeting header, click the **Send Cancellation** button. Outlook sends an updated meeting request to the attendees and removes the meeting from their calendars.

     If you change your mind about cancelling the meeting, click the **Close** button (**X**) at the right end of the message window title bar. Outlook reminds you that you haven't sent the cancellation and provides options. In the message box that appears, click **Don't cancel the meeting and close**, and then click **OK**.

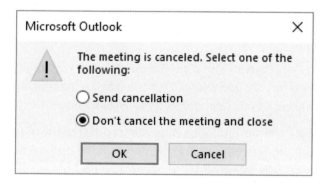

You can't cancel a meeting without notifying the attendees

15

Respond to meeting requests

When you receive a meeting request from another Outlook user, the meeting appears on your calendar with your time scheduled as Tentative. Until you respond to the meeting request, the organizer doesn't know whether you plan to attend.

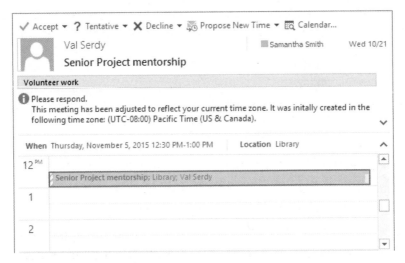

A meeting request in the Reading Pane

The meeting request displays your current calendar information at the time of the meeting, so you are aware of any schedule conflicts at that time. You can respond to a meeting request in one of these four ways:

- **Accept the request** Outlook deletes the meeting request and adds the meeting to your calendar.

- **Tentatively accept the request** This option indicates that you might be able to attend the meeting but are undecided. Outlook deletes the meeting request and shows the meeting on your calendar as tentatively scheduled.

- **Propose a new meeting time** Outlook sends your request to the meeting organizer for confirmation and shows the meeting with the original time on your calendar as tentatively scheduled.

- **Decline the request** Outlook deletes the meeting request and removes the meeting from your calendar.

If you don't respond to a meeting request, the meeting remains on your calendar with your time shown as tentatively scheduled and the meeting details in gray font rather than black.

When accepting or declining a meeting, you can choose whether to send a response to the meeting organizer. If you don't send a response, your acceptance will not be tallied, and the organizer will not know whether you are planning to attend the meeting. If you do send a response, you can add a message to the meeting organizer before sending it.

To respond to a meeting request

1. In the meeting window, in the **Reading Pane**, or on the shortcut menu that appears when you right-click the meeting request, click **Accept**, **Tentative**, or **Decline**.

2. Choose whether to send a standard response, a personalized response, or no response at all.

To propose a new time for a meeting

1. In the meeting window or in the **Reading Pane**, click **Propose New Time**, and then in the list, click **Tentative and Propose New Time** or **Decline and Propose New Time** to open the Propose New Time dialog box.

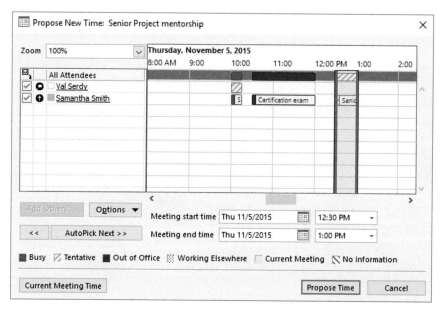

You can respond to a meeting request by proposing a different meeting time

2. In the **Propose New Time** dialog box, change the meeting start and end times to the times you want to propose, either by dragging the start time and end time bars or by changing the date and time in the lists, and then click the **Propose Time** button.

3. In the meeting response window that opens, enter a message to the meeting organizer if you want to, and then click **Send** to send your response and add the meeting to your calendar as tentatively scheduled for the original meeting time. If the meeting organizer approves the meeting time change, you and other attendees will receive updated meeting requests showing the new meeting time.

Display different views of a calendar

Just as you can with other Outlook modules, you can specify the way that Outlook displays calendar information (the view) and the attribute by which that information is arranged (the arrangement).

The Calendar module has these four content views:

- **Calendar** This is the standard view in which you display your Outlook calendar. In the Day, Work Week, or Week arrangement, Calendar view displays the subject, location, and organizer (if space allows) of each appointment, meeting, or event, in addition to the availability bar and any special icons, such as Private or Recurrence.

- **Preview** In the Day, Work Week, or Week arrangement, Preview view displays more information, including information from the notes area of the appointment window, as space allows.

- **List** This list view displays all appointments, meetings, and events on your calendar.

- **Active** This list view displays only future appointments, meetings, and events.

When working in a list view, you can group calendar items by selecting a field from the Arrangement gallery on the View tab.

 IMPORTANT In this book, we assume you are working in Calendar view, and refer to the standard Calendar view arrangements as *Day view*, *Work Week view*, *Week view*, *Month view*, and *Schedule view*.

The available arrangements vary based on the view. In Calendar view and Preview view, the arrangements are based on the time span, and include the following:

- **Day** Displays one day at a time separated into half-hour increments.

- **Work Week** Displays only the days of your work week. The default work week is Monday through Friday from 8:00 A.M. to 5:00 P.M. Time slots that fall within the work week are white on the calendar; time slots outside of the work week are colored.

> **SEE ALSO** For information about modifying the days and hours of the work week shown in Outlook, see "Define your available time" in Chapter 10, "Manage your calendar," of *Microsoft Outlook 2016 Step by Step* by Joan Lambert (Microsoft Press, 2015).

- **Week** Displays one calendar week (Sunday through Saturday) at a time.

- **Month** Displays one calendar month at a time, in addition to any preceding or following days that fall into the displayed weeks.

- **Schedule view** Displays a horizontal view of the calendar for the selected time period. You can add other people's calendars as rows in this view, so that you can easily compare multiple calendars for specific time periods.

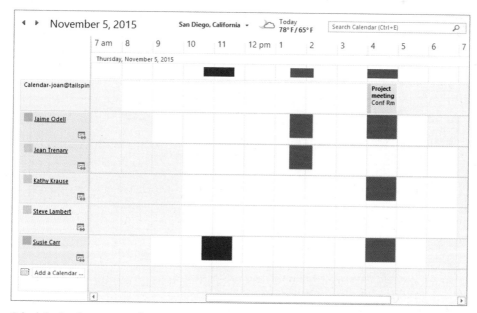

Schedule view for a group of co-workers

This arrangement is very useful for comparing limited time periods for multiple calendars, such as those of the members of a calendar group.

> **SEE ALSO** For information about calendar groups, see "Share calendar information" in Chapter 10, "Manage your calendar," of *Microsoft Outlook 2016 Step by Step* by Joan Lambert (Microsoft Press, 2015).

You switch among arrangements by clicking the buttons in the Arrangement group on the View tab of the Calendar module ribbon.

> **TIP** If you've made changes to any view (such as the order in which information appears) and want to return to the default settings, click the Reset View button in the Current View group on the View tab. If the Reset View button is unavailable, the view already displays the default settings.

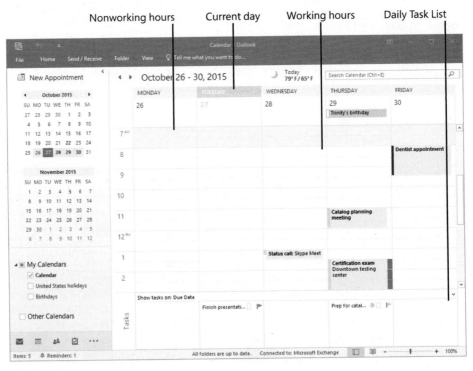

In this view, you can display your entire work week at one time

You can use these additional tools to change the time period shown in the calendar:

- Display the previous or next time period by clicking the Back button or the Forward button next to the date or date range in the calendar header.

- Display the current day by clicking the Today button in the Go To group on the Home tab.

- Display a seven-day period starting with the current day by clicking the Next 7 Days button in the Go To group on the Home tab.

- Display week numbers to the left of each week in Month view and in the Date Navigator. If you implement this option, you can click the week tab to display that week.

> **TIP** Specific weeks are referred to in some locations and industries by number to simplify the communication of dates. (For example, you can say you'll be out of the office "Week 24" rather than "June 7–11.") Week 1 is the calendar week in which January 1 falls, Week 2 is the following week, and so on through to the end of the year. Because of the way the weeks are numbered, a year can end in Week 52 or (more commonly) in Week 53. To display week numbers in the Date Navigator and in the Month view of the calendar, select the Show Week Numbers... check box on the Calendar page of the Outlook Options dialog box.

To display your calendar for a month

1. Do either of the following:

   - On the **Home** tab, in the **Arrange** group, click the **Month** button to display your calendar for the month.

   - Press **Ctrl+Alt+4**.

To navigate in Month view

1. Do either of the following:

   - To the left of the date range in the calendar header, click the **Forward** button to move the calendar forward one month, or the **Back** button to move the calendar back one month.

   - On the **View** tab, in the **Current View** group, click the **Change View** button and then, in the gallery, click **Preview** to display additional details on the monthly calendar.

15

Use the Date Navigator

By default, the Outlook 2016 Calendar module displays the current month and next month in the Date Navigator at the top of the Folder Pane. These compact monthly calendars provide quick indicators of the current date, the time period that is displayed in the content pane, days that you are free, and days that you are busy.

◀		October 2015				▶
SU	MO	TU	WE	TH	FR	SA
27	28	29	30	1	2	3
4	5	6	7	8	9	10
11	12	13	14	15	16	17
18	19	20	21	22	23	24
25	26	27	28	29	30	31

The Date Navigator is a convenient and useful tool

The current date is indicated by a blue square. The date or dates currently displayed in the calendar are indicated by light blue highlighting. Bold dates indicate days with scheduled appointments, meetings, or events. Days of the preceding and following months appear on the two default calendars in gray.

You can display more or fewer months by changing the width or height of the area allocated to the Date Navigator. To change the size of the Date Navigator area, do either of the following:

- Drag the right edge of the Folder Pane to the right to increase the width, or to the left to decrease the width.

- Drag the horizontal border below the Date Navigator calendars down to increase the height, or up to decrease the height.

The Date Navigator displays each month in seven-day weeks. The first day of the week shown in the Date Navigator is controlled by the First Day Of Week setting on the Calendar page of the Outlook Options dialog box. When the Date Navigator displays more than one month, each month shows either five or six weeks at a time—whichever is necessary to show all the days of the currently selected month.

You can display a specific day, week, month or range of days in the calendar by selecting it in the Date Navigator. When you're displaying the Calendar in the Week arrangement, selecting a day displays the week that contains it. Otherwise, the Calendar arrangement changes to show the time period that you select.

Use these techniques to work with the Date Navigator:

- To display a day, click that date.

- To display a week, point to the left edge of the week; when the pointer direction changes from left to right, click to select the week. (You can configure the Calendar Options to display week numbers in the Date Navigator and Calendar. If you do, clicking the week number displays the week.)

- To display a range of days (from two days to a maximum of six weeks), point to the first date you want to display and then drag across the Date Navigator to the last date.

- To change the period of time displayed in the calendar one month at a time, click the Previous or Next arrow on either side of the month name, at the top of the Date Navigator.

- To move multiple months back or forward, press the month name, and then drag up or down on the list that appears.

15

To display a seven-day week in the calendar

1. In the **Date Navigator** at the top of the **Folder Pane**, point to the left edge of a calendar row that contains one or more bold dates.

2. When the cursor changes to point toward the calendar, click once to display the selected seven-day week in the calendar.

To display your work week schedule

1. Do either of the following:

   - On the **Home** tab, in the **Arrange** group, click the **Work Week** button.

   - Press **Ctrl+Alt+2**.

   The first time slot of your defined work day appears at the top of the pane. Time slots within your work day are white; time slots outside of your work day are shaded.

To display your calendar for a day

1. On the **View** tab, in the **Arrangement** group, click the **Day** button to display only the selected day's schedule.

To display today's schedule

1. On the **Home** tab, in the **Go To** group, click the **Today** button. If the calendar wasn't previously displaying the current week, it does so now. The times displayed remain the same. The current day and the current time slot are highlighted.

To display your task list on the Calendar

1. On the **View** tab, in the **Layout** group, click the **Daily Task List** button and then do any of the following:

   - Click **Normal** to display the task list area below the calendar.

   - Click **Minimized** to display a single row below the calendar. The minimized Daily Task List displays a count of your total, active, and completed tasks for the day.

   - Click **Off** to hide the task list.

 TIP The Daily Task List is available in the Day, Work Week, or Week arrangement of the Calendar. It is not available in Month view or Schedule view.

To return the calendar to its default settings

1. In the **Change View** gallery, click **Calendar** to return the calendar to its default settings.

2. Then in the **Current View** group, click **Reset View** to return to the default calendar state.

Skills review

In this chapter, you learned how to:

- Schedule appointments and events
- Convert calendar items
- Configure calendar item options
- Schedule and change meetings
- Respond to meeting requests
- Display different views of a calendar

15

Practice tasks

No practice files are necessary to complete the practice tasks in this chapter.

> ⚠️ **IMPORTANT** As you work through the practice tasks in this book, you will create Outlook items that might be used as practice files for tasks in later chapters. If you haven't created specific items that are referenced in later chapters, you can substitute items of your own.

Schedule appointments and events

Start Outlook, display your Calendar, and then perform the following tasks:

1. Create a new appointment with the subject **SBS Study Session**, and configure it as follows:

   - Set the date to one week from today.
   - Set the time from **11:30 A.M.** to **12:30 P.M.**
   - Specify the location as **Library Meeting Room**.
   - Keep all other default settings, and save and close the appointment.

2. Create a new all-day event named **National Dessert Day**, and configure it as follows:

   - Set the date to the next occurrence of **October 14**.
   - Keep all other default settings, and save and close the event.

Convert calendar items

Display your Inbox, and then perform the following tasks:

1. Locate the **SBS Test** message that you sent to yourself in Chapter 13, "Send and receive email messages."

2. Create an appointment based on the message, and configure it as follows:

   - Change the subject from *SBS Test* to **SBS Rafting Trip**.
   - Set the date to next Saturday, and the time from **11:00 A.M.** to **2:00 P.M.**
   - Specify the location as **To Be Determined**.
   - Keep all other default settings, and save and close the appointment.

3. Display your Calendar.

4. Locate the **SBS Rafting Trip** appointment, and then do the following:

   - Convert the appointment to an all-day event.

   - Keep all other default settings, and save and close the event.

5. Locate the **SBS Rafting Trip** event, and then do the following:

   - Invite a friend to the event.

   - In the content pane, enter **I'm practicing my Outlook scheduling skills. Please accept this invitation.**

   - Send the event invitation.

Configure calendar item options

Display your Calendar, and then perform the following tasks:

1. Locate the **SBS Study Session** appointment that you created in the first set of practice tasks for this chapter.

2. Open the appointment window, and display the time zone controls.

3. Change the **Start time** and **End time** to occur in a time zone that is one hour earlier than your own.

4. Set your availability during the appointment to **Out of Office**.

5. Set a reminder for **1 hour** before the appointment.

6. Configure the appointment to recur **Monthly**, on the **first Monday** of each month, and to end after **3** occurrences.

7. Save and close the appointment series.

Schedule and change meetings

This practice task is designed for Outlook users in Exchange environments.

Display your Calendar, and then perform the following tasks:

1. Create a new meeting with the subject **SBS Project Review**, and configure it as follows:

   - Invite a colleague from your Exchange network.

   - Specify the location as **My Office**.

   - Set the date to next Thursday.

2. In the **Room Finder**, look at the **Date Navigator** and scroll the **Suggested Times** list for information about availability. In the **Suggested times** list, click a half-hour time slot that shows *No conflicts*.

3. Display the **Scheduling Assistant** page of the meeting invitation, and do the following:

   - Wait for the group calendar to display your colleague's availability. Notice the color blocks that identify the working hours and availability of each person and of the group.

   - Verify that the selected time is shown as available for both of you. If it isn't, change the time by dragging the start and end time markers.

4. Return to the **Appointment** page of the meeting invitation and verify the meeting information. In the content pane, enter **I'm practicing scheduling meetings. Please accept this meeting request.** Then send the meeting invitation.

5. On your calendar, locate the **SBS Project Review** meeting, and open the meeting window.

6. Display the **Scheduling Assistant** page of the meeting window, and do the following:

   - Add another colleague to the attendee list, and wait for the group calendar to display his or her availability.

   - Scroll the group calendar backward and forward a few days to identify times that you and your colleagues are busy or out of the office.

   - If necessary, change the meeting time and date by selecting them in the area below the group calendar.

7. Return to the **Appointment** page of the meeting invitation and verify the meeting information. Then send the meeting update to all attendees.

Respond to meeting requests

This practice task is designed for Outlook users in Exchange environments.

Display your Inbox, and then perform the following tasks:

1. Ask a colleague to send you a meeting request.

2. When you receive the meeting request, review the information in the Reading Pane, and then open the meeting request.

3. From the meeting request window, display your calendar. Notice the colors and patterns that represent the unaccepted meeting request and your availability during that time.

4. Return to the meeting request. Respond as **Tentative**, and propose a new time for the meeting.

Display different views of a calendar

Display your Calendar in Calendar view, and then perform the following tasks:

1. Display your calendar for the current month.

2. In the **Date Navigator**, notice the shading that identifies the current day. Click a different day that shows no appointments, to display your calendar for only that day. Then click the **Next Appointment** bar on the right side of the day to display the day of the next appointment on your calendar.

3. Switch to the **Work Week** calendar arrangement, and turn on the display of the **Daily Task List** below the calendar.

4. Change to the **Active** view of your calendar to display only your future appointments, events, and meetings.

5. If you want to, add the holidays from your country or region to the calendar. Notice the change in the calendar content displayed in the Active view.

6. Configure the Calendar to display the view and arrangement that you like best.

Index

Symbols

A

About the authors

Curtis Frye is the author of more than 30 books, including *Microsoft Excel 2013 Step by Step* for Microsoft Press and *Brilliant Excel VBA Programming* for Pearson, UK. He has also created and recorded more than three dozen courses for lynda.com, including *Excel for Mac 2016 Essential Training* and *Excel 2013: PivotTables in Depth*. In addition to his work as a writer, Curt is a popular conference speaker and performer, both as a solo presenter and as part of the Portland, Oregon ComedySportz improvisational comedy troupe. He lives in Portland with his wife and three cats.

Joan Lambert has worked closely with Microsoft technologies since 1986, and in the training and certification industry since 1997. As President and CEO of Online Training Solutions, Inc. (OTSI), Joan guides the translation of technical information and requirements into useful, relevant, and measurable resources for people who are seeking certification of their computer skills or who simply want to get things done efficiently.

Joan is the author or coauthor of more than three dozen books about Windows and Office (for Windows, Mac, and iPad), video-based training courses about SharePoint and OneNote, and three generations of Microsoft Office Specialist certification study guides.

Joan is a Microsoft Certified Professional, Microsoft Certified Trainer, Microsoft Office Specialist Master (for all Office versions since Office 2007), Microsoft Certified Technology Specialist (for Windows and Windows Server), Microsoft Certified Technology Associate (for Windows), and Microsoft Dynamics Specialist.

Joan currently lives in a small town in Texas with her simply divine daughter, Trinity, and an ever-growing menagerie of dogs, cats, and fish.

Acknowledgments

We appreciate the time and efforts of Rosemary Caperton, Carol Dillingham, and the team at Microsoft Press—past and present—who made this and so many other books possible.

The authors would like to thank the editorial and production team members at Online Training Solutions, Inc. (OTSI) for their work on this book and the individual books in the *Step by Step* series that provided content for this compilation. Angela Martin, Ginny Munroe, Jaime Odell, Jean Trenary, Jeanne Craver, Kathy Krause, Meredith Thomas, Steve Lambert, Susie Carr, and Val Serdy all contributed to the creation of these books.

OTSI specializes in the design and creation of Microsoft Office, SharePoint, and Windows training solutions and the production of online and printed training resources. For more information about OTSI, visit *www.otsi.com* or follow us on Facebook at *www.facebook.com/Online.Training.Solutions.Inc* for advance information about upcoming training resources and informative tidbits about technology and publishing.

We hope you enjoy this book and find it useful. While working on this book, we were guided by the feedback submitted by readers of previously published *Step by Step* books. If you'd like to provide feedback about this book, you can use the process outlined in the introduction.

The content in Part 2, "Microsoft Word 2016," was excerpted from *Microsoft Word 2016 Step by Step* by Joan Lambert (978-0-7356-9777-5)

The quick way to learn Microsoft Word 2016!

- Get easy-to-follow guidance from a certified Microsoft Office Specialist Master
- Create visually appealing documents for school, business, community, or personal purposes
- Use built-in tools to capture and edit graphics
- Present data in tables, diagrams, and charts
- Track and compile reference materials
- Manage document collaboration and review
- Fix privacy, accessibility, and compatibility issues
- Create custom styles, themes, and templates

Contents

1 Word 2016 basics
2 Create and manage documents
3 Enter and edit text
4 Modify the structure and appearance of text
5 Organize information in columns and tables
6 Add simple graphic elements
7 Insert and modify diagrams
8 Insert and modify charts
9 Add visual elements
10 Organize and arrange content
11 Collaborate on documents
12 Finalize and distribute documents
13 Reference content and content sources
14 Merge data with documents and labels
15 Work in Word more efficiently

For more information, visit http://aka.ms/word2016sbs/detail

The content in Part 3, "Microsoft Excel 2016," was excerpted from *Microsoft Excel 2016 Step by Step* by Curtis Frye (978-0-7356-9880-2)

The quick way to learn Microsoft Excel 2016!

- Perform calculations and find and correct errors
- Filter, sort, summarize, and combine data
- Analyze data by using PivotTables, PivotCharts, scenarios, data tables, and Solver
- Visualize data with charts and graphs, including new sunbursts, waterfalls, and treemaps
- Build data models and use them in business intelligence analyses
- Create timelines, forecasts, and visualizations, including KPIs and PowerMap data maps

Contents

For more information, visit http://aka.ms/excel2016sbs/detail

The content in Part 4, "Microsoft PowerPoint 2016," was excerpted from
Microsoft PowerPoint 2016 Step by Step by Joan Lambert (978-0-7356-9779-9)

The quick way to learn Microsoft PowerPoint 2016!

- Get easy-to-follow guidance from a certified Microsoft Office Specialist Master
- Learn and practice new skills while working with sample content, or look up specific procedures
- Create attractive electronic presentations and printed publications
- Incorporate professional design elements
- Use built-in tools to capture and edit graphics
- Include audio, video, and animated elements
- Supercharge your efficiency by creating custom slide masters and layouts

Contents

1 PowerPoint 2016 basics
2 Create and manage presentations
3 Create and manage slides
4 Enter and edit text on slides
5 Present text in tables
6 Insert and manage simple graphics
7 Create and manage business graphics
8 Add sound and movement to slides
9 Review presentations
10 Prepare and deliver presentations
11 Work in PowerPoint more efficiently
12 Create custom presentation elements
13 Share and review presentations

For more information, visit http://aka.ms/powerpoint2016sbs/detail

The content in Part 5, "Microsoft Outlook 2016," was excerpted from *Microsoft Outlook 2016 Step by Step* by Joan Lambert (978-0-7356-9778-2)

The quick way to learn Microsoft Outlook 2016!

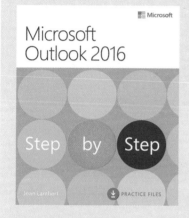

- Organize your Inbox to stay in control of everything that matters
- Schedule appointments, events, and meeting requests
- Track tasks you assign to others and tasks others assign to you
- Keep your contacts up to date and organized
- Send more visually compelling and effective messages
- Work remotely with Outlook items and Microsoft SharePoint site content

Contents

1 Outlook 2016 basics

2 Explore Outlook modules

3 Send and receive email messages

4 Enhance message content

5 Manage email security

6 Organize your Inbox

7 Store and access contact information

8 Manage contact records

9 Manage scheduling

10 Manage your calendar

11 Track tasks

12 Customize Outlook

13 Manage email automatically

14 Work remotely

For more information, visit http://aka.ms/outlook2016sbs/detail

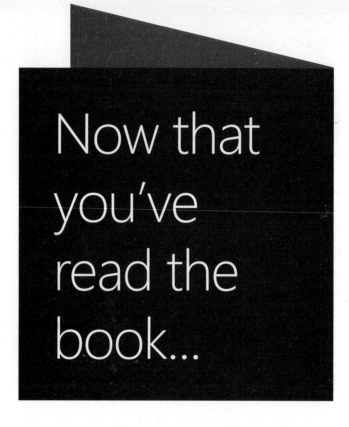

Now that you've read the book...

Tell us what you think!

Was it useful?
Did it teach you what you wanted to learn?
Was there room for improvement?

Let us know at http://aka.ms/tellpress

Your feedback goes directly to the staff at Microsoft Press,
and we read every one of your responses. Thanks in advance!

 Microsoft